# Church Administration and Finance Manual

*Resources for Leading the Local Church*

# Church Administration and Finance Manual

*Resources for Leading the Local Church*

Otto F. Crumroy, Jr.

Stan Kukawka

Frank M. Witman

MOREHOUSE PUBLISHING

**Morehouse Publishing**

P.O. Box 1321

Harrisburg, PA 17105

Morehouse Publishing is a division of the Morehouse Group.

Printed in the United States of America

*Cover design by Corey Kent*

**Library of Congress Cataloging-in-Publication Data**

Crumroy, Otto.
　　Church administration and finance : resources for leading the
　local church / Otto F. Crumroy, Jr., Stanley J. Kukawka, Frank M.
　Witman.
　　　p.　cm.

　Includes bibliographical references and indexes.
　ISBN 0-8192-1747-6　(pbk. )
　1.　Church management　2.　Church finance　I.　Kukawka, Stan.
　II. Witman, Frank.　III　Title
　BV652.C77　1998
　　254--dc21　　　　　　　　　　　　　　　98-27939
　　　　　　　　　　　　　　　　　　　　　　　CIP

To Dr. Robert W. Edgar, president of the Claremont School of Theology, for his vision for theological education.

To Dr. David L. Richardson, who, as the former chair of the Board of Ordained Ministry of the California-Pacific Conference of The United Methodist Church, was initially instrumental in having a course on Church Administration and Finance presented to probationer pastors, and for enabling lay persons to be part of the teaching team.

To Bishop Roy I. Sano, episcopal leader of the Los Angeles Area of The United Methodist Church, and his Cabinet, for their support and assistance in the implementation of a continuing education program in Church Administration and Finance.

To Dr. Marjorie H. Suchocki, dean and vice president for academic affairs of the Claremont School of Theology, for her support and guidance.

To colleagues and students who have opened themselves to the learning process, and from whom we have learned and will continue to learn.

To our wives, Joan Crumroy, Nancy Kukawka, and Elsie Witman, without whose assistance, support, and encouragement this manual would not have come to fruition.

# Contents

CHAPTER 4

# Leading . . . . . . . . . . . . . . . . . . . . . . . . . . . . . . . . . . . . . . . . . . . . . . . . . . . . . . . . . . . . . . 247

CHAPTER 5

# Preface

Have you wondered if there was a more effective and practical way to plan, organize, staff, lead, assess, and report about the administrative and financial functions of your church? "If there was just some way to . . ." "I wonder if someone has a form to . . ."

The ideas and materials presented here about church administration and finance come from the life and career experiences of the authors—each of us with many years of practical administrative leadership in a local church. Virtually all of the procedures, policies, forms, and formats have been or are being used successfully in local churches. While teaching at the Claremont School of Theology, we have been privileged to present this material to more than two hundred pastors, seminary students, and persons in lay leadership positions. The response has been overwhelmingly positive: "Why didn't I have this years ago when I first started my ministry?" "This course should be required of every active pastor." "When are you going to publish this material?"

In response to this positive encouragement, we have assembled this manual. It contains a wealth of practical advice, sample forms, and procedures used effectively by various churches, and it presents a variety of approaches, since churches differ in their individual needs. Thus, the manual can serve as a resource and reference for pastors and church leaders as they face specific and real administrative and financial challenges.

We recognize that individual churches vary in ethnicity, size, location, and gender leadership, and that these differences sometimes affect the management of a church. While we believe the basic principles presented here apply to virtually any church administrative or financial situation, and we have tried to present alternative solutions to some situations, it is beyond the scope of this manual to cover all differences in any depth. A number of books and articles have been written on these specific subjects and we encourage you to seek them out for further study. Some of these are referenced in the bibliography.

You should recognize that reading only this manual will not make you an instant expert on church administration and finance. That takes years of study and practical application of the principles we will present as well as the study of information contained in many other publications. After reading this manual, however, you will have a working knowledge and the tools required to recognize a need or to diagnose a problem; then you will be able to ask the right questions. You will be an effective leader who knows what administrative and financial processes are required and how the church can best benefit from them.

Although we present much of the material in this manual in the context of the pastor's role, remember that all members and participants in Christ's Church will be involved in some way in administrative duties as they worship together and care for each other. While specific responsibilities will differ according to the persons and positions involved, all must participate if a church is to function in an effective, organized way. When we present material that is directed to the administrative tasks of a pastor, we ask that all leadership join in this study so that they understand that pastor's role and how the laity can help. Further, much of the daily detailed church administration and finance work will be in the hands of the laity; thus, much of the material in this manual will apply to the lay leadership. We encourage all people active in the life of a church to study this material and to use it as you find it suitable to your individual situations.

*A word of caution.* After reading this material, you may be tempted to implement the ideas you like rather quickly. As we will discuss in more detail later, people are generally uncomfortable with change, and particularly revolutionary change. Although revolutionary change may be justified in a survival situation, this should be rare in a local church. When you find things in this manual that are directly applicable to your particular church situation, we counsel slow and gradual evolutionary change. In most local church circumstances the operative words are

### Evolution, Not Revolution

We earnestly hope and pray that the materials contained in this manual will make the total ministry of your church easier and more effective, and that you will become better stewards of the substantial resources entrusted to you for the implementation of the mission of your church.

# Acknowledgments

David B. Bates, PE, for his significant contributions to the portions of the manual covering loss prevention and church-related safety issues.

Virginia L. Bihler, for her organizational skills, secretarial expertise, form creation, and other valuable assistance.

Marlaine A. Brown, for data entry, and the creation of some of the forms in this manual.

Dr. Caywood J. Borror, Esquire, for his legal assistance on hiring procedures.

Culver Heaton, FAIA, and Thomas Zartl, AIA, for creation of the document, "Planning Expectations in Anticipation of Purchasing and Developing Property," and the article, "Don't Be a Bungling Building Committee."

Dr. Penelope Mercurio Jennings, Esquire, for her legal assistance in creating the document, "Legal Issues Facing Churches."

Nancy Kukawka, for her untiring attention to detail, and the countless hours devoted to proofreading, collating, assembling, and assuring the quality of early versions of the manual manuscript used during several of our classes.

Diane M. Thomson, for preparation and creation of the major section dealing with Christian education, and for her commitment to helping persons experience the faith.

We are grateful to all of these people, and to many more who contributed to this manual and the course at the Claremont School of Theology, for their dedication, assistance, and support.

## CHAPTER ONE

# Introduction and Overview

## Why a Working Knowledge of Administration Is Important to Pastors and Lay Leadership

Many pastors have, or will have, a stewardship responsibility for people, money, and property that is greater in magnitude than over half the business owners and managers in this country. While these pastors will normally be well trained in worship and congregational care as they enter their ministry, they often seem ill-prepared to participate in church administrative and financial responsibilities. Even though many of the detailed tasks will be delegated to lay leadership, the ultimate responsibility for the effective operation of and positive results in a church will normally rest with the recognized leader of the church—the pastor in charge. If not prepared for this responsibility, how can pastors respond? They struggle and learn the hard way—in the school of hard knocks. Through this manual we hope to ease these hard knocks.

At this point, there are pastors who may be thinking, "Why me? I'm here to minister to my congregation by preaching, teaching, and counseling with those in need. Administrative needs will take care of themselves. And after all, the primary purpose of a church is to be a worshiping community, with the caring for others a natural outgrowth."

While few can argue against this statement as a primary purpose of Christ's Church, one can just as validly argue that there must be an administrative process that supports a church through planning, organizing, staffing, leading, assessing, and reporting on progress if the church is to be viable. Isn't it then natural to argue that the complete ministry of a church is composed of sequential relationships in which caring is an outgrowth of worship, and that this unique caring generates a particular style of administration? As people worship together they will be led to care, and that caring will produce a style of administration that will be seen as participatory and as a means to effect mission. As seen in figure 1 on page 2, there is a strong interrelationship and interdependence that is God-centered. Taking this argument one step further, the responsibilities of the parish pastor naturally are broadened to include this interrelated, important ministry of administration.

What should pastors and persons in lay leadership be concerned about in the administration of their church, and what is involved in the administrative process?

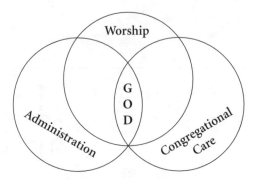

FIGURE 1. Interrelationship of the Three Major Responsibilities of the Parish Pastor

The primary administrative concern should be that vital resources available to the church are used effectively to achieve mission objectives. Those resources commonly include three things: human resources, church money, and church property.

## Human Resources

Much will be said throughout this manual about the importance of human resources in all phases of church administration. People are the greatest resource a church has. Nothing else matters or functions unless dedicated and committed people are involved.

Perhaps it sounds a little strange to say that people must be "managed." But in a positive, humane sense, that is exactly what is required if there is to be an effective, vibrant church. Both staff members and volunteers must be carefully chosen for work that fits them. They must be given adequate guidance about the tasks they are asked to do, through complete and clear position descriptions, policies, and procedures. Then they must be led, using a leadership style that is participatory and one that allows and expects a person to succeed. Finally, we should not forget that progress toward more effective use of people's talents is possible only if we take time to assess, evaluate, and communicate with them about how they have met agreed-upon goals.

## Church Money

The essence of church financial business is, *it is God's business.* Money, as a common denominator in our lives and a basic possession of rich and poor alike, is neither good nor bad. What the church does with money is what is important. It must be used to support the church in a positive way as it strives to serve God's people.

Pastors naturally will be involved in church finances as the church plans for and seeks the funds it needs to accomplish its programs. Pastors need to be aware of members' stewardship potential and habits, and then lead by example in their own stewardship if a realistic church plan and program is to be developed and then financially supported. Of critical importance is the need for a pastor to ensure that the financial health of the church is always completely and clearly communicated to the congregation. Accurate and timely reports showing what has been received for what purpose, and how it was used, are a must.

Equally important is the process for handling and accounting for money as it is received by the church. Members like to know that their contributions are received and used for the purpose they intended. Almost nothing can undermine the mission of the church and its programs faster than questions about the credibility of its financial system. Pastors must be very sensitive to this and have enough knowledge about good financial control and accounting principles to recognize when their church may be in trouble, and then know when and how to seek help and make changes.

Even though pastors need to have a working knowledge of the overall financial management system, the amount of direct, specific involvement in detailed transactions will be minimal. Here it is imperative that qualified lay leadership assume the primary role. We will have much to say about the requirements for good financial management in the church, and how this can be accomplished most effectively, as we move through the manual. The guiding premise will always be: the financial management system must be mission oriented, full of integrity, informative, systematized, and tailored to local church needs.

## *Church Property*

Church property must be carefully and realistically planned for and acquired to fit the mission of the church. Planning should include long-range goals for expansion or other major capital needs, as well as general operating needs in the current year. Financial support for property needs must be carefully considered and made an integral part of the overall plan. The pastor's role in church-property decisions can be a delicate one. Pastors should challenge their congregations toward new heights of stewardship and development, but they must also ensure that decisions are kept in realistic perspective. The whole church will be involved in this planning process.

Once acquired, church property must be properly maintained. The appearance of a church provides newcomers with their first impression, and it conveys how the church feels about itself and others. Maintenance schedules need to be established and responsibilities for maintenance must be clear. Without this organized approach, people do not know who is responsible for what. Also important is an effective insurance program which protects the members and their investment with adequate but realistic coverage, based on an assessment of risk. The role of the pastor in property management will often be as an overall manager and leader, with details handled by the property committee, trustees, custodial staff, or other volunteers.

As pastors consider their role in managing the resources entrusted to them, they naturally want to know where to start and how to go about it. We will continue this overview chapter with an examination of how the pastor's staff, the laity, and the denomination may see the pastor's administrative role, and then present an objective-oriented management approach and the elements of management which comprise that approach. These elements of management—***planning, organizing and staffing, leading, and assessing and reporting***—will be discussed later in separate chapters for ease of presentation. However, they must always be thought of as parts of a continuous, dynamic process of administration leading to one primary goal: mission accomplishment. It is this whole process and the many detailed parts and realistic examples, forms, and checklists that we will share with you as pastors and lay leaders to enhance your own ministry. We want you to recognize and know **what is important, in what environment, and for what purpose.**

## Administrative Responsibilities of a Pastor

It is difficult to define the scope of the administrative responsibilities of a pastor, especially when members of a pastor's staff, members of the congregation, and the denomination with which the church is affiliated each may have a different view of these responsibilities. This makes it even more imperative that the scope of responsibility be defined, or at least that an effective management structure is established, which will guide pastors as they fulfill this important part of their ministry.

Let's first look at some of the varied **expectations a congregation may have of a pastor,** not only as an administrator but in all phases of ministry.

At each of the church administration and finance classes we have taught for the Claremont School of Theology at Claremont, California (where the students are either seminarians taking the class for academic credit, or in-service pastors and lay persons attending the class for continuing education credit), we asked the class to list what they felt were the expectations placed on a pastor by the congregation. The following is a partial list of these expectations:

| | |
|---|---|
| Advocate for local church | Mentor |
| Available | Model of integrity |
| Biblical interpreter | Motivator |
| Budget analyst | Prayer leader |
| Cheerleader | Preacher |
| Chief administrative officer | Program developer |
| Committed to the community | Program manager |
| Committed to the congregation | Property manager |
| Companion | Prophet |
| Conflict resolver | Recruiter |
| Counselor | Role model |
| Enabler | Spiritual leader |
| Encourager | Staff supervisor |
| Example | Teacher |
| Family person | Theologian |
| Friend | Visionary |
| Interpreter | Visitor |
| Manager | Voice for morality |
| Mediator | Worship leader |

You can undoubtedly add to this list from your own experience in the church. Notice that while there are expectations of a spiritual nature there are also many related to administration. There are expectations involving planning, staffing, leading, and literally all the elements of management. It seems that we naturally want our pastors to be administrators as well as preachers and teachers. Obviously, these varied expectations must be channeled into a managerial structure if there is to be any order in the life of a pastor and the congregation.

Now, ***what does a pastor's secretary or administrative assistant expect of the pastor?*** An astute administrative assistant developed the following expectations she and other members of the office staff had of the pastor/employer:

- Keep the local church first in your mind.

- Hold weekly staff meetings. They are imperative. They allow the office staff to be informed about the pastor's schedule and future priorities, and they also allow the staff to keep the pastor up to date on happenings in the church office.

- Don't be afraid to use the office staff. Delegate items to the staff with which they can assist. Routine items can be done by the staff so that the pastor has time for more important matters.

- Let the office staff know your schedule, allowing them to work around deadlines which are important in getting out copy, correspondence, and so forth.

- Allow the staff to assist you in keeping your work area (desk, mail trays, phone message center) clear and functional.

- Give the staff clear instructions about changes to be made on rough draft copy. Don't expect them to read your mind.

- When leaving the office, let a specific person know about how long you will be gone so they can respond to phone inquiries accordingly. The staff is aware that in pastoral calls, time is always flexible and depends on the individual need. If you are delayed extraordinarily, call the office to let them know. It is very important for the staff to be able to contact the pastor at any time in the event of an emergency. [1]

We also would like to share with you a well-thought-out ***portrait of a pastor from a lay person's perspective.*** Especially note both the spiritual and leadership elements that are listed—again demonstrating the importance of integrating an active administration into ministry.

A pastor should have a personal belief in and be a practicing proclaimer that

- This is God's world.

- The Bible is the Word of God.

- Jesus is the Son of God and He is the Answer.

- Each of us is one in the image of God.

- The Church has an awesome responsibility and opportunity.

- Worship is the focal point in the life of the church.

The pastor will

- Be one with us.

- Have the ability and desire to effectively administer the local church, assisted by lay leadership.

- Promote the various church groups, committees, commissions, and so forth to church membership as opportunities for service and personal growth, and as avenues for membership involvement, retention, and local church growth.

- Involve a maximum number of different and differing persons in the life of the church.

- Conduct their personal affairs so that they model a Christian life.

- Know that every individual in the local church does *cherish* the opportunity to *go with and grow with* the pastor in the fruition of *God's kingdom among us.* [2]

Then there are considerations of **what the particular denomination expects of its pastors.** Do these coincide with what the staff and congregation expect? It probably does in most instances, but there may be some additional expectations beyond those of the local church, such as churchwide or local committee membership and participation.

One example of a resource that gives rather specific direction about denominational expectations is *The Book of Discipline of The United Methodist Church.*[3] We have excerpted portions of this book and keyed this example of denominational direction to the four major disciplines of administration (or management) which we will discuss in much more detail throughout this manual:

Planning (**P**)

Organizing/Staffing (**O**)

Leading (**L**)

Assessing/Reporting (**A**)

The pastor shall oversee the total ministry of the local church. . . . administering the temporal affairs of the congregation. [4] [**L**]

The pastor shall give attention to the following specific duties. . . . To be the administrative officer of the local church [**L**] and to assure that the organizational concerns [**O**] of the congregation are adequately provided for.[5]

To offer counsel and theological reflection in the following:

(1) The development of goals for fulfilling the missions of the congregation, the Annual Conference, and the General Church. [**P**]

(2) The development of plans for implementing the goals [**P**] of the congregation and a process for evaluating their effectiveness. [**A**]

(3) The selection, training and deployment of lay leadership within the congregation [**O**] and the development of a process for evaluating lay leadership.[6] [**A**]

It is easy to see, from these lists, that pastors will find themselves involved in administrative tasks. Even if not clearly dictated in written policies of the Church, pastors will still be expected to be responsible for administering their church and participating in the administration of the denomination. There will be reports to be completed, committees to participate in or chair, dialogues to lead, assemblies or conferences to attend, appeals for financial support to be staffed, and so forth.

It should also be obvious, after reviewing these many expectations of a pastor, that Jethro was so right in his advice to Moses: "This job is too big a burden for you to try to handle all by yourself. You're going to wear yourself out—and if you do, what will happen to the people?"[7] Pastors absolutely cannot perform all church functions themselves. They must oversee and administer by delegating to qualified and creative lay persons the myriad of administrative details, while retaining ultimate responsibility for the success of the process and achievement of the mission. They can and should delegate administrative tasks, but not abdicate responsibility for them.

*What pastors and lay persons do in the church must also be in concert with what God tells us to do.* The work of the church becomes a co-mission in which we depend on God's guidance and then figure out how to accomplish God's will using our best efforts. Significant parts of the "how" are to:

- Plan for what we do, in an organized, systematic way

- Be sensitive to the need for and provide timely leadership and direction

- Review progress, always looking toward an end result, with appropriate nurturing during the process

- Constantly communicate the status of the effort with participants

The result should be a clear, effective administration which is systematically applied, identifies needs and the causes of problems, and then moves toward program accomplishment. If effective, it will always support and be interwoven with other parts of the church's mission.

For the remainder of this manual we will consider the **elements of effective management** to be the following, in which objectives are achieved through an effective use of resources.

| | |
|---|---|
| • **P = Planning** | Thinking through ahead of time what needs to be done, how it is to be done, and the resources needed. |
| • **O = Organizing/Staffing** | Dividing and assigning the work of the organization to accomplish common objectives. Assuring that human resources are in place and trained. |
| • **L = Leading** | Encouraging and allowing people to take effective action to complete essential tasks. Providing an example. |
| • **A = Assessing/Reporting** | Measuring progress to objectives, assessing results, and taking appropriate action. Reporting as may be required by the organization or government agencies. |

These basic disciplines are applicable to almost any management situation, whether the situation is a for-profit enterprise or a nonprofit organization such as a church. It is the whole management need and process, viewed in a church context, and referring to actual church experiences, that we discuss in this manual. The ideas and experiences shared will provide guidance in various situations and help ensure necessary tasks are done—by someone, somehow. The material provided will equip you to ask the questions which will cause people to go in the right direction, toward desired goals and objectives.

The following chart lists the many elements and activities which activate each of the four management disciplines of planning, organizing/staffing, leading, and assessing/reporting—POLA. In any effective organization, all, or at least most of the elements and activities listed in this matrix are present and active. Even with the great expectations placed on pastors from many different sources, we propose that a focus on POLA is an effective way for pastors and other church leaders to meet the administrative expectations that are so important in a church.

# Elements of Effective Management

In any effective organization, all, or at least most of the following elements of management are present and active.

**Planning**
Thinking through ahead of time what needs to be done, how it is to be done, and the resources needed.

*Mission Statement*
Determining and documenting the purpose of the organization.

*Forecast*
Looking ahead to estimate opportunities and challenges for the future.

*Goals*
Spelling out in specific terms the goals of the organization.

*Action Plans*
Determining specific actions and objectives required to achieve goals, including time line and specific responsibilities for completion of actions.

*Budgets*
Allocating resources for the needs of the organization.

*Policies*
Documenting decisions applicable to repetitive questions or procedures.

*Procedures*
Documenting methods by which work is done.

**Organizing and Staffing**
Dividing the work of the organization to accomplish common objectives.

*Organization Structure*
Defining the structure of the organization and interrelationships therein. Arranging work in a reasonable, balanced manner.

*Position Descriptions*
Detailing the responsibilities and requirements for a given position in the organization.

*Delegation*
Entrusting responsibility and authority to others and the establishing of accountability for results.

*Working Relationships*
Promoting conditions that result in effective teamwork.

*Selection*
Staffing the organization with competent people.

*Orientation*
Assuring that all members of the team are aware of policies, procedures, goals, and objectives.

**Leading**
Encouraging and allowing people to take effective action to complete essential tasks. Providing an example.

*Initiate*
Starting the required actions of the team.

*Decide*
Making key decisions and resolving conflict.

*Communicate*
Informing team members on all matters that may affect their work. Promoting intrateam dialogue and cooperation. *Listen* for feedback.

*Motivating Environment*
Providing an environment that inspires and encourages proper actions to accomplish desired goals, objectives, and results.

*Develop*
Improving knowledge, skills, and attitude of team members.

*Team Build*
Encouraging and promoting an environment in which a team can produce exceptional results.

**Assessing and Reporting**
Measuring progress to objectives, assessing results, and taking appropriate action.

*Performance Standards*
Establishing measures of satisfactory performance in specific terms such as standards and/or measurable objectives.

*Report*
Measuring and recording results to budgets, objectives, and goals. Reporting results to appropriate people.

*Performance Evaluation*
Evaluating actual individual performance in light of requirements, standards, and objectives.

*Reinforcement*
Recognizing achievement to assure that good work continues and improves.

*Corrective Action*
Correcting variances from standards or objectives promptly to assure results are improved.

## Management Lessons from the Bible

It may surprise you to learn that basic management principles and techniques used today can be found in the Bible, making it one of the oldest textbooks on management in existence. As we begin our study of church administration, perhaps a brief look at what the Bible has to say about management will put our thoughts in perspective.

In Exodus 18:5–27, you will find at least seven management principles articulated or implied by Jethro, the priest of Midian. Take a few minutes to read this story and list the management principles that you find. Then look below to see if you found them all.

[5] Jethro, Moses' father-in-law, came into the wilderness where Moses was encamped at the mountain of God, bringing Moses' sons and wife to him. [6] He sent word to Moses, "I, your father-in-law Jethro, am coming to you, with your wife and her two sons." [7] Moses went out to meet his father-in-law; he bowed down and kissed him; each asked about the other's welfare, and they went into the tent. [8] Then Moses told his father-in-law all that the Lord had done to Pharaoh and to the Egyptians for Israel's sake, all the hardship that had beset them on the way, and how the Lord had delivered them. [9] Jethro rejoiced for all the good that the Lord had done to Israel, in delivering them from the Egyptians.

[10] Jethro said, "Blessed be the Lord, who has delivered you from the Egyptians and from Pharaoh. [11] Now I know that the Lord is greater than all gods, because he delivered the people from the Egyptians, when they dealt arrogantly with them." [12] And Jethro, Moses' father-in-law, brought a burnt offering and sacrifices to God; and Aaron came with all the elders of Israel to eat bread with Moses' father-in-law in the presence of God.

[13] The next day Moses sat as judge for the people, while the people stood around him from morning until evening. [14] When Moses' father-in-law saw all that he was doing for the people, he said, "What is this that you are doing for people! Why do you sit alone, while the people stand around you from morning until evening?" [15] Moses said to his father-in-law, "Because the people come to me to inquire of God. [16] When they have a dispute, they come to me and I decide between one person and another, and I make known to them the statutes and instructions of God." [17] Moses' father-in-law said to him, "What you are doing is not good. [18] You will surely wear yourself out, both you and these people with you. For the task is too heavy for you; you cannot do it alone. [19] Now listen to me. I will give you counsel, and God be with you! You should represent the people before God, and you should bring their cases before God; [20] teach them the statutes and instructions and make known to them the way they are to go and the things they are to do. [21] You should also look for able men among all the people, men who fear God, are trustworthy, and hate dishonest gain; set such men over them as officers over thousands, hundreds, fifties and tens. [22] Let them sit as judges for the people at all times; let them bring every important case to you, but decide every minor case themselves. So it will be easier for you, and they will bear the burden with you. [23] If you do this, and God so commands you, then you will be able to endure, and all these people will go to their home in peace."

[24] So Moses listened to his father-in-law and did all that he had said. [25] Moses chose able men from all Israel and appointed them as heads over the people, as officers over

thousands, hundreds, fifties, and tens. [26]And they judged the people at all times; hard cases they brought to Moses, but any minor case they decided themselves. [27]Then Moses let his father-in-law depart, and he went off to his own country.[8]

Although it has been over three thousand years since this advice was given to Moses, these seven timeless principles are just as applicable today as they were then.

1. Let others help; you can't do it all yourself. In an organization of any reasonable size, some tasks must be done by others.

2. Choose capable people, make them leaders, and *delegate* responsibility and authority to them.

3. Teach and train the leaders. This implies that policies and procedures exist so that actions and decisions are applied consistently to all.

4. Structure the organization so each leader is responsible for only five to ten people. In modern management terminology, supervision of these small groups is called "span of control," and the organizational hierarchy Jethro suggested is called "chain of command."

5. Push responsibility and decision making to the lowest possible and practical organizational level where there is competence to deal with the matter.

6. Deal personally with only the most difficult or the most critical cases and situations, when lower levels are not capable, or when the matters are so significant that they directly impact the survival of the organization.

7. Accept good advice when it is offered. Don't be embarrassed to ask for help.

Watch for how these management principles and techniques are applied in various church situations, as we examine each of the basic elements of management. Begin now to think about how these principles and techniques are or could be applied to your specific church.

## Unique Influences in Church Management

In the remainder of the manual we will discuss specific administrative and financial principles and techniques as they apply to a church. But before doing so we need to consider some of the unique influences that make church management different from business management. Some of these factors may be obvious, but it is well to review them and to put them into perspective.

The Spirit will always be at work, as God works in partnership with us in the church. We, as God's people, join together as believers and organize ourselves as a church for service in the world, with purposes and goals which further identify us as a church and not just as a business. Our spiritual beliefs will direct us and oversee how we develop and implement an administrative style.

The elements of business management that work well in a church include principles and ideas like those in other human organizations. Within every viable organization there must be

• Roles and relationships that are clearly defined and documented

- Management rules and guidelines that need to be carefully followed
- Specific purposes and goals that should be planned, organized, staffed, financed, equipped, led, evaluated, and reported on

There can be times, however, when illogical, sometimes damaging, influences affect how churches are managed, even though these influences may be outside the formal church management system:

- Cultural influences can affect decision making and management in a church. While all are one in Christ, everyone brings their own set of cultural differences: traditions, customs, value systems, lifestyles. All these factors influence convictions and thus strongly influence the direction of a meeting, even the direction of the entire church. This tendency is especially true when culturally diverse groups jointly meet in church facilities, each with their own goals and direction.

- Secular needs can strongly influence how a church works. The secular needs and priorities of the people may replace the priorities and values of the church. Church decisions then are based, not on what is best in God's eyes and for the church, but on how we would do it in our businesses.

- Power in a church must be recognized and channeled toward good. Elected or appointed leaders may attempt to inappropriately control the direction of the church, by using opportunities to review or to veto agendas and plans. Control and supervision over finances or personnel can be misused by official leaders as well as by other individuals, for example, by large donors. Access and control over information needed to deal with problems, and quick, direct access to people with power may all be considered common sources of power.

- Denominational pressures, history, and tradition affect a church, depending on special emphases, problems, politics, and personalities.

What does the realization of these influences at work in the church call us to do?

Certainly, we must learn how to deal with human characteristics. We must learn to clearly enunciate church and committee objectives and to allocate resources with consideration of the church's mission and objectives rather than personal desires. We must work toward spiritually based purposes and goals, and develop an appropriate supporting administrative structure using the best available and most appropriate management techniques. Remember, the complete ministry of the church is composed of sequential relationships in which caring is an outgrowth of worship, and this unique caring generates a particular style of administration.

*The Church is Christ's, not ours.*

## CHAPTER TWO

# Planning

## An Introduction to Church Planning

Any study of a church planning process might begin with a very natural question: "Where do we start?" A flippant answer may be, "At the beginning." But that really is not a bad answer. To begin an effective planning process we must first have a vision of what we are about and why we are doing what we are doing or want to do. This vision may merely be that we wish to "worship God in this place at this time." As simple as this may sound, much effort must go into making this vision reality; however, it does gives us a basic purpose and a place to start as we think about things we want our church to do.

Before we begin our detailed discussion about the planning process, please look at "Management Lessons from the Book of Nehemiah," which immediately follows this introduction to planning. Note the process Nehemiah used to rebuild the destroyed walls and gates of the city of Jerusalem. He had a vision, a mission, a master plan, specific goals, and action plans with specific objectives, and he used effective managerial and supervisory techniques. His methodology was not that different from what we use today for project planning, and can serve as an introduction to our discussion of modern-day management.

With some expansion of a church's basic vision, it can develop a mission statement. Then, to implement the mission statement and to make it an action-oriented document, attainable goals and objectives are developed in the different areas of church life. As we identify specific tasks related to the goals and objectives, action plans will be prepared and assigned to committees and work areas in the church. We now have an active planning process that should produce a desired outcome.

This organized process, and specific elements forming the overall planning structure, will be discussed first in the following pages to set the stage for a later discussion of specific planning areas and methodology.

After we have studied the basics of overall planning, we will present two different models for gathering ideas, needs, and wishes for the church, and demonstrate the process with two examples for each model. Imagine with us how effective these methods might be and the positive results that could occur. Then imagine how you might use these same methods, or variations, in your church to revitalize it to greater mission.

After a mission statement has been generated, goals set, and action plans developed, the financial implications of these plans must be considered and the necessary monetary support planned for and developed. The "Financial Plans" section of this chapter discusses and presents the many facets of this important phase of church planning. You may be especially interested in some of the sample forms covering analytical guidelines, budgeting, and capital management.

This chapter ends with specific examples of local church planning and presents some aids for event planning, property acquisition, construction, computerization, church growth, and other changes in the church which must be planned.

Planning itself, however, never ends. It is a continuous process that allows us to revisit our visions, our mission statements, our goals and objectives, our action plans, and our resource support for these plans on a regular basis. Reassessment of plans, at least annually, gives "drive" to the process; goals will be reached as members stay involved and committed. *Plan your work—then work your plan.*

## Management Lessons from the Book of Nehemiah

Nehemiah had a vision and a mission. That mission was to rebuild the destroyed walls and gates of the city of Jerusalem. His was a classic approach to a huge project, and is as applicable today as it was five hundred years before Christ. Nehemiah's steps can be emulated in any church project that is to be initiated and completed successfully.

| *Project Steps* | *Reference in Nehemiah* |
|---|---|
| 1. *Pray for God's help with the project*<br>Pray not just once, but often, throughout the project. | 1:12, 2:4 |
| 2. *Have a specific long-range plan, with a timetable*<br>Nehemiah's plan was to rebuild the walls and gates of<br>Jerusalem within the time promised the king. | 2:5, 6 |
| 3. *Have short-range action plans to accomplish the project*<br>Nehemiah requested and received permits and<br>requisitions for supplies. | 2:7, 8 |
| 4. *Get personally involved; know the scope and complexity<br>of the project*<br>He inspected the walls and gates, obtained personal<br>knowledge of what needed to be done, and retained the<br>ultimate responsibility and authority. | 2:11–15 |
| 5. *Exhibit leadership, communicate the plan, get people<br>involved, committed, enthused, and motivated*<br>He gave people a reason for rebuilding and told them of<br>God's blessing and the king's support. | 2:17, 18 |
| 6. *Organize, divide the project, assign responsibility*<br>Any large task, is accomplished by dividing it into many<br>smaller tasks, which can be better visualized. | Chapter 3 |

7. *Delegate responsibility*                                      3:1, 2, 23, 30
   Walls and gates were rebuilt by assigning responsibility
   by section, with some sections "in front of their house"!
   (note elements of *involvement, participation, and
   ownership*).

8. *Overcome obstacles with prayer and contingency plans*      4:7–9, 13, 16–19
   Anticipate obstacles; have plans to overcome them.

9. *Before project completion, organize project operation*          6:15, 7:1–3
   The organization to run the project should be planned
   long before project completion.

10. *Celebrate, dedicate, and give thanks*                          12:27, 31
    Completion and closure is important. This is also a time
    for *performance reviews* of participants with an eye to
    similar assignments in the future.

## Basic Planning Principles

### *Elements of Churchwide Planning*

*The whole management process begins with planning,* and with proper planning, optimum results should be attained. Among people experienced in management, it is a generally accepted truism that the most prevalent single reason for the failure of a project, enterprise, or organization is the lack of, or the inadequacy of a plan. Planning is an invaluable focusing process that attempts to detail and prepare for the future. As we saw in the biblical lesson of Nehemiah rebuilding Jerusalem, there must be a vision, a mission, and then an attainable plan before a project can begin.

There are many methods of planning a church or any organization can use. The planning methodology presented here was chosen because we have used it successfully in a number of church situations. The basic elements follow, and we later present examples of how these elements have been developed in specific situations and in differing ways.

**MISSION STATEMENT**

As the genesis of all planning, the mission statement sets the general direction for a given church and serves as a guide for specific programs, projects, and activities. Make it a brief, succinct statement that tells all who read it why the church exists and what it strives to accomplish. A mission statement tends to be broad in scope and articulates a large vision. It generally does not refer to specific goals or objectives. (See example on page 18.)

When the mission statement has been developed, *publish it.* Post it on bulletin boards and print it periodically in the order of worship and the newsletter. Place it in the pew racks for visitors to see and take with them. You might also make it a meaningful part of worship and recite it periodically during the worship service.

## GOALS

Goals are statements of desired outcomes that support and expand upon various parts of the mission statement. Goals are more action oriented and establish the framework for specific actions and measurable objectives. Goals provide a specific direction for work areas in the church. (A completed example is on page 19.)

## ACTION PLANS, WITH SPECIFIC OBJECTIVES

To assure that goals are accomplished in a systematic and timely manner, they are detailed in action plans, which contain data about sequential, specific actions; specific, measurable objectives for those actions; specific responsibility for accomplishing actions and objectives; completion dates; and the financial impact. Action plans are the operative documents of the various committees, commissions, and other work areas in the church. Thus, we need to examine in more detail one method for developing an action plan. The following sequential steps should be taken (A completed example is on page 20.):

1. *Identify the mission-statement item for which the action plan (AP) is being written.* In the example AP, the mission-statement item is: "We will worship God."

2. *Cite the goal or goals which will be accomplished with the AP.* In the example, the goal in support of the mission-statement item reads: "To provide additional worship opportunities, begin a Saturday evening contemporary worship service on September 10 with a specific objective of reaching an average of 75 worshipers in attendance by year end."

3. *Identify the work areas responsible for developing and implementing the AP.* In the example AP, three committees have been designated as responsible for specific portions of planning for and implementing a Saturday evening contemporary worship service. Once these committees know their responsibilities, they decide how they will complete their specific actions.

4. *Divide the large task of achieving the goal into smaller, more manageable specific actions and/or measurable objectives.* Quite often, the specific action may also be a measurable objective. When it is not, a measurable objective should be attached to the action. The first action in the example is to "visit other churches in the area that have established, successful contemporary services" prior to May 30. This is both an action item and a specific objective. "Develop a list of ideas for our service" is more of an objective, but it is also an action item. A clearly specific objective for this AP is to "achieve an attendance of 75 worshipers."

5. *Assign responsibility for specific actions and objectives.* While a committee may be assigned overall responsibility, a specific individual on that committee, perhaps the chairperson, should be designated as the person accountable. The sample AP notes the initials of the accountable person and the assigned committee. There is an axiom in management that says, "If a committee or group is responsible, no one is responsible."

6. *Set a completion date.* In a sequential list of activities, completion dates are very important to keeping the objectives and ultimate goal on schedule. If a com-

pletion date is missed, the first question to ask (with the answer recorded on the AP) is, "What is your new expected completion date?"

7. *Estimate the financial impact of the planned actions.* This is very important for effective financial planning and should involve those persons responsible for the financial affairs of the church.

***Important: Periodically follow up and report on an action plan, to ensure the successful achievement of the goal.***

Following the completed sample pages are blank work sheets with which you can develop a mission statement, goals, and action plans with specific objectives. We urge you to use these in your church, and even for yourself. You might find it interesting to look up Christ's mission statement as stated in Isaiah 61:1–3 and Luke 4:18–19.

## *Mission Statement**

To be Christ's church in this time and place, we will actively

1. Worship God.

2. Study God's Word in the Bible.

3. Grow as Christians and enjoy Christian fellowship through prayer and participation in groups for study, fellowship, and service.

4. Provide congregational care through all the passages of life, from the cradle to life eternal.

5. Use our God-given talents in Christian service to those who are hurting or are in need.

6. Share the Gospel with others, especially seeking out those who are not Christians.

7. Seek to be living examples of Christ's teachings.

* Composite mission statement compiled from those developed by several churches and from input and discussion in the class on church administration and finance at the Claremont School of Theology.

# Sample Goals Development Work Sheet

Goals are statements of desired outcome that support and expand upon various parts of the mission statement. Goals are more action oriented and outline what is to be done to implement mission-statement items without getting into the details of what, who, when, how, and how much. Goals provide specific direction for work areas in the church to develop action plans with specific objectives to "make it happen."

Goals in Support of Mission-Statement Item:  *1. We will worship God.*

1. *To provide additional worship opportunities, begin a Saturday evening contemporary worship service.*

2. *Begin preliminary exploration and planning for a Hispanic worship service to serve the Spanish-speaking local community.*

3. *Involve more lay persons in the worship services, including call to worship, scripture reading, opportunity-for-service announcements, etc.*

4. *Develop an inactive-member visitation program to encourage these members to return to worship and involvement in the life of the church.*

5. *Provide worship and communion opportunities for special needs groups, i.e., shut-ins, those in nursing homes, retirement homes, hospitals, etc.*

6. *Plan to develop a separate choir for the 10:30 worship service.*

*Source of goals:* Weekend planning retreat and/or the congregational survey.

# Sample Action-Plan Development Work Sheet

The action plan details actions that need to be taken to accomplish the goals. Specific sequential actions and objectives are listed along with the responsible person/persons, a completion date for each action item, and the financial impact, if any.

Mission Item: *1. We will worship God.*

Goal: *To provide additional worship opportunities, begin a Saturday evening contemporary worship service on September 10 with a specific objective of reaching an average of 75 worshipers in attendance by year's end.*

Work Areas Responsible: *Worship Committee, Music Committee, Publicity Committee*

| SPECIFIC ACTIONS AND MEASURABLE OBJECTIVES | RESPONSIBILITY | COMPLETION DATE |
|---|---|---|
| 1. *Visit other churches in the area that have established, successful contemporary services. Develop a list of ideas for our service.* | *FW & Worship Committee* | *May 30* |
| Financial Impact | *0* | |
| 2. *Develop worship-service format.* | *FW & Worship Committee* | *June 15* |
| Financial Impact | *0* | |
| 3. *Arrange for musicians and establish rehearsal schedule.* | *PC & Music Committee* | *July 15* |
| Financial Impact | *$300 per week* | |
| 4. *Develop publicity program and schedule including radio spots, newspaper ads, and door hangers in the surrounding area.* | *OC & Publicity Committee* | *June 30* |
| Financial Impact | *$300 per week* | |
| 5. *Rehearsal of worship service.* | *FW & Worship Committee* | *Sept. 9* |
| Financial Impact | *$300 one-time expense* | |

# Mission-Statement Development Work Sheet

As the genesis of all planning, the mission statement sets the general direction for a given church and serves as a guide for specific programs, projects, and activities. Make it a brief, succinct statement that tells all who read it why the church exists and what it strives to accomplish. A mission statement tends to be broad in scope and articulates a large vision.

## Mission Statement

Church Name _____

To be Christ's church in this time and place, we will:

1. _____

_____

_____

2. _____

_____

_____

3. _____

_____

_____

4. _____

_____

_____

5. _____

_____

_____

6. _____

_____

_____

## *Goals Development Work Sheet*

Goals are statements of desired outcome that support and expand upon various parts of the mission statement. Goals are more action oriented and outline what is to be done to implement mission-statement items without getting into the details of what, who, when, how, and how much. Goals provide specific direction for work areas in the church to develop action plans with specific objectives to "make it happen."

Goals in Support of Mission-Statement Item: _____

_____

_____

1. _____

_____

_____

2. _____

_____

_____

3. _____

_____

_____

4. _____

_____

_____

5. _____

_____

_____

6. _____

_____

_____

# Action-Plan Development Work Sheet

The action plan details actions to be taken to accomplish the goals. Specific sequential actions and objectives are listed along with the responsible person/persons, a completion date for each action item, and the financial impact, if any.

Mission Item: _____

Goals to Be Accomplished: _____

_____

_____

Work Areas Responsible: _____

SPECIFIC ACTIONS AND MEASURABLE OBJECTIVES  RESPONSIBILITY  COMPLETION DATE

1. _____ _____ _____

_____ _____

_____

        Financial Impact _____

2. _____ _____ _____

_____ _____

_____

        Financial Impact _____

3. _____ _____ _____

_____ _____

_____

        Financial Impact _____

4. _____ _____ _____

_____ _____

_____

        Financial Impact _____

## Models for Planning

As you begin to contemplate the process of writing a mission statement, implementing goals, and specific action plans, you could logically ask, "But how do I know what types of things we should be planning for our church?" This is a question that invariably comes up when long-range planning is considered, and in fact this question probably will need to be answered before there can be realistic planning. There are a number of different models through which planning can take place and a church can determine its future direction. We will discuss planning examples that fall into one of two different types: church leadership-centered planning, and church membership-centered planning.

### CHURCH LEADERSHIP-CENTERED PLANNING

Sometimes due to membership size, it is difficult, if not impossible, to involve a whole congregation in the type of self-evaluation needed to identify direction. For the process to be manageable, a group of church leaders normally will take the lead in this style of planning. After the study has been completed and suggested directions for the church determined, the congregation must be fully informed and involved in the approval of the new or revised directions and in the planning of resultant actions and activities.

This model begins with church leaders meeting as a planning committee to first study what is needed in the church, and then to develop plans for implementation. It may be that this group will want to study resource material over a period of time, which may guide them toward the needs of their own congregation. Or the group may want to meet with an outside resource leader during a weekend retreat and, together, "brainstorm" the needs of the church.

Some of the basic questions that participants may want to consider as they do their study include:

- Is the church in mission to the extent it should be? Where is the mission emphasis: local and/or beyond the local community? Is there an adequate visitation program, both to members in need and to the community?

- Are worship services dynamic and do they lead the congregation as they should? Is there a need for additional services, perhaps of varying styles?

- Are there enough caring, community-oriented small groups in the church, each led by a trained leader?

- Is the church organization streamlined and is there participatory decision making? Is the staff adequate and working together effectively?

- Do church programs and activities serve people and their needs rather than just involve them?

- Does the church have adequate visibility, and is it accessible to the community?

- Is there adequate parking and other facilities to meet the church's needs?

- Is the financial support for the church solid? [1]

One church we are familiar with completed a *comprehensive self-evaluation* over a twelve-month period, considering the basic questions posed above while using resource material from one of the leading experts on church long-range planning.[2] The step-by-step process this church used to successfully implement this planning method is detailed on page 27. The published "Report to the Congregation on the Long-Range Plan," which documents the mission statement the church developed and the supporting goals, follows on pages 29 and 30.

Another example with which we are familiar involved a *weekend mission planning retreat* at which an outside facilitator led church leaders through a "brainstorming" session, resulting in a viable mission statement and long-range plan readily accepted by the congregation. This process, and the resulting plan and goals, is detailed starting on page 31.

## CHURCH MEMBERSHIP-CENTERED PLANNING

A membership-centered approach to planning differs from the leader-centered approach in that it begins with input from the entire membership, after it is decided that there is need for long-range planning and before church leaders become intimately involved in the process. A congregational survey would be a normal way to begin the process. The results of the survey give the planning group input on what the congregation feels about where church efforts and resources should be directed.

The survey titled "Long-Range Goals for Our Church" included here on page 37 was distributed and completed during the worship service, resulting in the survey form being returned at a higher rate than it would have been had it been part of a mass mailing. In church there can be person-to-person contact and appeal—always more successful than mailings. Although the length of this survey may make it seem foreboding, it is in fact quite easy to complete, because a person merely needs to check choices already presented as possibilities. Some planning by church leaders will be necessary to develop the listing of choices.

The two forms titled "Our Vision . . .," included on page 40, demonstrate a member-centered planning approach that begins with a simple but very important and demanding question about the vision for the future of the church. Of course, there is a basic assumption that this is a healthy church and that it wants to grow both in size and mission. A survey such as this one can be effective in planning for a number of different elements in a church mission or program and emphasizes a most important church need: visioning.[3] At a church in which this approach was used, the results were very gratifying. The forms were completed during the worship service with the membership providing excellent input. The consensus from a summary of the responses served as a basis to establish specific goals and objectives for worship attendance, Sunday school attendance, and new outreach ministries.

## ADVANTAGES AND DISADVANTAGES OF THE TWO APPROACHES

Perhaps the first point to be made is that the approach selected may depend considerably on the size of the church, its cultural traditions, and how eager it is to "move ahead."

A smaller church may always use a membership-centered approach, since it basically gathers as a family and does everything as a committee of the whole. Conversely, if there is a strong patriarch or matriarch, a small church may be leader centered in everything it does. A large church may or may not depend on its leadership to activate planning depending on how active its small groups are. In both circumstances it may be hard to get a consensus unless there is a driving force or goal. Cultural differences almost certainly will influence the planning approach. Some cultures have high respect for leaders while others are family oriented.

Close examination of the two different approaches and the examples presented will show that, in all cases, there was a point at which the leaders of the church became deeply involved. This is probably true of just about any participatory management environment. The members will have their say, however. In either approach, there must be overall congregational acceptance of both the process and the results.

So which approach should you use? That depends on your church situation and need. Whatever approach is selected should have the support of the top leadership of the church as well as the general membership. And as is true with so many worthwhile things, planning is hard work.

## HOW ARE OTHERS PLANNING?

It is always advisable to emulate successful and effective activities of others. In any multichurch community the level of effectiveness will range from dying churches to the church just able to maintain itself to the vital, dynamic, growing church. Successful people and organizations are generally willing to share the programs and processes that led to their success. One needs only to ask. If there is a particularly successful church in the community, contact their leadership and "pick their brains." Although not everything they are doing will fit your environment, there will be usable ideas. After all, gathering facts and ideas is an important part of any planning process.

## A Comprehensive Self-Evaluation Leading to a Long-Range Plan

1. After considerable thought and prayer, the church program committee assumed responsibility for preparing a draft long-range plan for the church.

2. The committee chose resource material from one of the leading experts on church long-range planning, and over a period of twelve months completed a self-evaluation of the church, guided by the resource material.[4]

3. The committee presented the results of this study at an all-church planning retreat, and solicited additional input.

4. A five person subcommittee was appointed to begin drafting the plan.

5. The mission statement was drafted first and approved by the full program committee.

6. Goals which supported and expanded the mission statement were drafted and approved by the program committee. These goals were discussed and approved as they were developed; thus, a continuous dialogue was maintained between the subcommittee and the full program committee.

7. The mission statement draft, as well as the supporting goals, were presented at a meeting of the church governing body and were approved.

8. Action plans were drafted to accomplish the goals. These were presented as suggested action plans to the responsible work areas, who were asked for additions, deletions, modifications, specific objectives, and a completion date for each item.

9. Responses and commitments from the work areas were compiled into an action-plan notebook, and the total plan was presented to a meeting of the congregation for discussion and approval.

10. A brochure, "A Report to the Congregation on the Long-Range Plan," was prepared and mailed to all church members. (See copy on the following pages.) These brochures were also placed in the pew pockets. A copy of the action-plan notebook was placed in the church office and remains available for review by any interested person.

11. The program committee monitors action-plan performance at its regular meetings as the various work areas report on their activities.

Elapsed time:  12 months for the study
12 months for the completion and approval of the plan

This planning process was well accepted by the whole church and particularly by work area committees. A comment heard numerous times from the work areas was, "For the first time we really know what we should be doing."

### *Evolution, not revolution*

A REPORT TO THE CONGREGATION
ON THE LONG-RANGE PLAN
FOR OUR CHURCH

BEGINNING THE 2ND 100 YEARS OF SERVICE
TO OUR GOD
TO OUR COMMUNITY
TO THE WORLD

# MISSION STATEMENT OF OUR CHURCH

To be Christ's Church in this time and place, we will:

I. Worship God.

II. Study God's word in the Bible.

III. Grow as Christians and enjoy Christian fellowship, through prayer and participation in groups for study, fellowship, and service.

IV. Provide congregational care for members, through all the passages of life, from the cradle to life eternal.

V. Use our God-given talents in Christian service.

VI. Reach out to share the gospel and to help transform the world into the Kingdom of God!

## V. USE OF TALENTS FOR CHRISTIAN SERVICE

*"My children, our love should not be just words and talk: it must be true love, which shows itself in action."* I John 3:18

*"So then, as the body without the spirit is dead, also faith without action is dead."* James 2:26

1. Provide training for leaders, chairpersons, and committee members.
2. Generate interest in the Committee and Commission activities of the Church.
3. Encourage membership involvement in service activities.

## VI. OUTREACH

*He said to them, "Go throughout the whole world and preach the gospel to all mankind."* Mark 16:15

*"I tell you, whenever you did this for one of the least important of these, you did it for me!"* Matthew 25:40

1. Provide gospel outreach through personal and corporate evangelizing, and through support of evangelism programs of our denomination.
2. Continue mission outreach to our local community, state, nation, and world, by our support of the Crisis Center, Youth Service Projects, Ministry to the Homeless, our Missionary in Russia, and other worthy needs and mission projects.
3. Through the above, and motivated by our Christian Social Concerns, help transform the world into the Kingdom of God.
4. Provide support to other congregations within our area that have been designated as developing or transitional congregations.
5. Provide concerts, lectures, drama, etc. for the community and our membership.
6. Encourage selected outside group use of our facilities.
7. Maintain a higher profile for our church and members in the community through appropriate publicity.

# GOALS IN SUPPORT OF OUR MISSION STATEMENT

(with Scriptural references for each Mission item)

## I. WORSHIP GOD

*"Sing to the Lord, all the world! Worship the Lord with joy; Come before Him with happy songs!"*  Psalm 100:1–2

*"Come, let us bow down and worship Him; Let us kneel before the Lord, our Maker."*  Psalm 95:1,6

1. Provide additional worship opportunities with the objective of increasing worship attendance and participation.
2. In cooperation with the Worship Commission, work to constantly improve the Worship Services in the areas of liturgy, music, format, and for special occasions.
3. Provide Worship Services for special-needs groups.

## II. STUDY THE BIBLE

*"Your word is a lamp to guide me, and a light for my path."*  Psalm 119:105

*"But these things are written so that you believe Jesus is the promised Savior, God's Son, and by believing have life in His name."*  John 20:31

1. Maintain a vital Church School program for children, youth, and adults.
2. Maintain active Bible study groups.
3. Provide short term Bible study opportunities at special times of the year.
4. Provide opportunities for a personal devotional life.
5. Continually affirm that the Bible is the basic study document for Christian Education.

NOTE: Action Plans and objectives to implement the goals contained herein, are available for review in the church office.

## III. CHRISTIAN GROWTH AND FELLOWSHIP

*"For where two or three come together in my name, I am there with them."*  Matthew 18:20

*"They spent their time in learning from the apostles, taking part in the fellowship, and sharing in the fellowship meals and prayer."*  Acts 2:42

1. Maintain a variety of small groups to promote Christian growth and fellowship.
2. Provide new small groups as needs are identified .
3. Priority for new group development will be:
   a. New member assimilation.
   b. Youth and young adults.
   c. Young parents.
   d. Singles.
   e. Daytime spiritual growth groups.
4. Encourage intergenerational interaction—share, witness, and dialogue.

## IV. CONGREGATIONAL CARE

*So then, as often as we have the chance, we should do good to everyone, and especially to those who belong to our family in the faith.*  Galatians 6:10

1. Maintain an active visitation program involving both the clergy and laity.
2. Continue to provide transportation for elderly and handicapped to worship services as well as to memorial and other special services and events.
3. Assure that the elderly and handicapped have convenient access to our facilities.
4. Assure that addressing the special needs of persons is a missional objective of our church.
5. Maintain a blood bank and publicize the availability appropriately.

# Mission Planning Retreat

## A Weekend

Recognizing that the church was ready to reach out in mission, a small group of church leaders suggested a planning retreat during which we would "brainstorm" the future of the church. An outside facilitator was invited, and the event was advertised to all the church membership, with all invited to attend. On a Saturday afternoon approximately thirty-five members of the church (mostly those holding lay leadership roles) met to begin the process of developing a mission statement that would give the church direction for the future.

Following an opening worship, the participants divided into five groups to reflect on what the congregation is called to do—through scripture, through the history of the Church universal, through the history of the local church, and through dreams, aspirations, and hopes of what the church could be in the future. (Scriptures used as a foundation for discussion included: Luke 4:16–21; Matt. 25:31–40; Matt. 28:16–20; Acts 2:1–47; Eph. 1:3–10; 1:15–23; and 4:11–16.) The lists compiled by the five groups were shared in a plenary setting. At the close of the first session, participants were asked to designate a select number of items they believed to be most important to the mission of the church.

A writing team of five members stayed after the first session to develop a draft mission statement based on the consensus from the lists from session one. That mission statement was presented to the group on Sunday afternoon. The group of thirty-five to forty (essentially the same group which had gathered on Saturday) reviewed the draft mission statement and made a few changes of wording and corrections which resulted in the following finalized mission statement:

> Our church lives to create a Christian community led by the Holy Spirit, that nurtures and supports each individual's efforts to know, love, and serve Jesus Christ. Under the guidance of scripture, we seek to build up the body of Christ through worship, prayer, witness, teaching, fellowship, outreach, and good deeds. We promote the Kingdom of God, both within our congregation and throughout the world.

The participants were then asked to share their dreams, hopes, and visions for the congregation and its ministry, resulting in a list of about seventy ideas. From that compilation, each participant was asked to select the five ideas that seemed most important to their vision of the church. Small groups were formed in which participants shared their five areas of concern, discussed them, and jointly formed five broad areas of concern that best represented the individual concerns.

Each small group then shared its list with the total group. From those lists, seven broad areas of concern surfaced: use of space; children, youth, and young adult ministries; pastoral ministries (programs); member care ministries; stewardship; worship; and outreach. Continuing the conversation, the total group created the goal and priority statements:

- to accommodate a growing church program by analyzing space requirements, maximizing use of space, and providing for space needs accordingly

- to enhance ministries for children, youth, and young adults in the church and community

- to develop strong pastoral programs of clergy and lay ministry which will support a growing church and expanded services to members

- to develop an umbrella of services and member care

- to develop a comprehensive stewardship program

- to provide diverse worship experiences

- to initiate a layered outreach program which recognizes and seeks to meet the needs of our community, nation, and world

Once the goals were determined and defined, the total group was asked to name specific means by which these seven goals could be lived out in the life of the congregation. This was their list:

### to accommodate a growing church program

Evaluate Christian education program

Measure current use

Measure current non-use

Investigate possibility of after-school latchkey program

Investigate possibility of summer program

Increase use of gym

Repair outside basketball court

Make facility-use policy more flexible

Educate membership about needs and use

Study potential expansion of facilities

Prepare cost estimates on options for building use

### to enhance ministries of children, youth, and young adults

Provide more funding for child care—more paid staff

Facilitate a college-age (post-high school) program

Cooperate with local grade school for latchkey program

Encourage more youth participation in worship services

Ensure ongoing pastoral care for youth and children

Increase funding for youth activities

Establish a special youth bulletin board

Communicate youth and children ministries more effectively

Increase biblical education for youth and children

Purchase a new VCR

Involve more high school youth in Christian education

*to develop strong pastoral programs of clergy and lay ministry*

Hire an associate pastor

Strengthen lay visitation, as part of evangelism program

Emphasize pastoral ministry to the laity

Encourage a strong elders' shepherding program

Redefine elders' flocks

Enhance communication of pastoral concerns

Analyze the number of elders and deacons, for possible expansion

Expand prayer ministries

*to develop an umbrella of services and member care*

Study need for midweek social programs and dinners

Consider establishing special study groups

Ensure that there are adequate support groups

Be sensitive to individual member-support needs

Ensure assimilation of each member into church programs

Offer denominational heritage classes

Sponsor parenting workshops

Emphasize singles programs

Hold family retreats

Transport children and elderly in church van

Encourage intergenerational activities

Emphasize a diverse music program

Have an active homebound visitation program

Ensure adequate advertising in telephone yellow pages

Participate in job-help seminars

Provide special services for the elderly and singles

*to develop a comprehensive stewardship program*

Emphasize the spiritual basis for giving

Stress the need for all members to be involved

Present a comprehensive stewardship-education program

Include children in the stewardship program

Develop a year-round stewardship emphasis

Communicate endowment fund opportunities

Follow up on whether new members pledge their support

Emphasize recycling as a part of stewardship

Ensure the stewardship program fits the church master plan

Encourage growth in percentage giving

Use small-group meetings to enhance stewardship communication

### to provide diverse worship experiences

Use peppy songs and singers

Vary communion practices to enhance the meaning

Have the bell choir participate more in worship

Cooperate in interchurch exchanges for worship

Vary worship experiences

Use same song at end of worship, for continuity of feeling

Encourage more youth services and youth participation

Integrate liturgical dance into worship

Use a song leader

### to initiate a layered outreach program

Participate more in service projects

Encourage support for the food basket

Participate in cultural exchanges

Encourage involvement by the youth

Have a sister church

Sponsor mission trips

Take special offerings for outreach needs

Hold special project fund-raisers

Educate regularly during church services

The next step for the congregation was to strategize the "how to's" for the goals and objectives—those that could be done in each of the next three years. Resources that the church might require to meet such objectives needed to be analyzed. Among the people resources of the church, leadership needed to be identified.

One more session of approximately two hours was required to plan strategy to implement the work done. By developing a "game plan" (a strategy), the church would then have the means by which to measure progress in six months, twelve months, two years, and so forth.

The mission statement was presented to the church governing body and congregation soon after the weekend meeting and enthusiastically embraced. It was printed in the church newsletter, posted on bulletin boards, and occasionally recited during worship. The implementing ideas were informally tracked by church leadership and used as a "checklist" of areas for emphasis.

## A Follow-Up

Eighteen months after the initial mission planning retreat, the governing body of the church met to review the mission planning process, to measure progress toward accomplishing the goals and objectives, and to determine the future direction for the church. Approximately thirty-five members participated in this follow-up retreat.

The group was first led through the process used in the initial mission planning retreat, ending with a review of the previously developed mission statement. Participants were asked to affirm that this statement still reflected the life of the church and to determine how the mission statement was being used. The discussion and comments affirmed that the mission statement was still valid and that it was being used to provide information to visitors and occasionally in the order of worship.

As a group, participants reviewed the priorities (goals) and measured progress in the objectives that had been named at the original event. This was a time-consuming process; however, this "measuring" of goals and objectives became a positive and affirming opportunity for participants to see how much had been accomplished at the church during the last eighteen months. This part of the process generated significant discussion and provided an opportunity for the people who had not been a part of the first event to experience and become a part of the energy of the original mission planning work.

Following this review of the goals and objectives, participants were divided into seven small groups, and each was asked to review one of the original goals and objectives with a "what now" framework in mind. Specifically, they were to ask the following questions:

- In light of what has been done in the past eighteen months, are the original objectives still relevant?

- What are the priorities for the coming year?

- Are there some objectives that are missing?

- What group and/or groups would be responsible for these objectives?

The work of each small group was shared in the plenary session. Significant and positive discussion resulted, emphasizing the areas of need and priority, and specific tasks were identified. The whole group then moved to the sanctuary for a closing communion service to celebrate God's guidance in the process.

## The Process—in Perspective

This church leadership-centered planning method was very effective in the church in which it was used, and has proven equally effective in many other churches. The power of this methodology came initially from a united feeling within the church that some long-range planning was needed, now. A long-term study had been tried and had floundered. But a less time-consuming commitment on the part of the leadership and the "brainstorming" approach seemed to give the process an enthusiasm that ensured its success.

As successful as the planning process was, it still might have been better. There should probably not have been an eighteen-month break between the first planning weekend and the second. Church leadership did not receive specific action plans, which would have better organized and documented actions taken during this period. However, the listings of possible tasks existed and were developed as there seemed to be a need. Some people work better in a more structured environment and some do not. But it does seem logical that such a large and important undertaking—the listing of tasks—needs an organizational structure and a means of assigning tasks if it is to be most effective.

How often should the tasks and action plans be reviewed? There is probably no one answer to this question, in that every church situation is different. However, it seems reasonable that the process should be revisited at least every twelve to twenty-four months if the task listings are to stay current. If tasks are assigned to specific committees, then regular reports on progress should be made at least quarterly. A full report about actions taken should be passed on annually to new committee members and financial implications included in the annual budget. It is also important that the congregation stay informed about the tasks and the progress being made if support is to continue and the mission of the church is to grow.

# Long-Range Goals for Our Church

Please help your church planning committee and the various programming committees plan for the next three years by completing this questionnaire.

**GENERAL INFORMATION:**

Age category: ____ youth    ____ under 35    ____ 36 to 50    ____ 51 to 65    ____ over 65

Male ____    Female ____    Married ____    Single ____

Children at home: ____ pre-school    ____ elementary    ____ Jr. High/High School    ____ none

Please check the items which you feel our church should emphasize in its ministry. It is suggested that you check one to three items in each category.

**CHURCH AND SOCIETY**

_____ Support ministries that provide food, shelter, and clothing for the needy in our community.

_____ Match volunteers to special needs of church members; e.g., elderly, shut-ins, handicapped, etc.

_____ Increase our blood bank donations.

_____ Increase awareness of and commitment to peace and justice ministries.

_____ Develop caring ministries for members in major life transitions.

_____ Publicize human services available in our community.

**WORSHIP COMMITTEE**

_____ Increase individual member participation in the worship service through prayer requests, sharing their faith, joys and concerns, lay readers, etc.

_____ More family worship attendance including children and youth.

_____ Increase percentage of members attending worship each week.

_____ More variety in worship service including hymn sings, drama, guest preachers, etc.

_____ Prepare and deliver audio tapes of worship service to shut-ins.

_____ Emphasize preaching of the basic gospel message.

**MUSIC COMMITTEE**

_____ Increase number of persons of all ages in both the singing and bell choirs.

_____ Begin a children's choir.

_____ Begin a youth choir.

_____ Begin a senior-member bell choir.

_____ Have a quarterly Choir and Organ concert on Sunday afternoon.

## EDUCATION COMMITTEE

_____ Improve the facilities and quality of nursery care.

_____ Increase the attendance of church-school-age children in church school.

_____ Provide additional summer programming for all age levels.

_____ Increase attendance at Vacation Bible School.

_____ Increase the pool of church-school teachers.

## ADULT EDUCATION

_____ Increase participation in Sunday morning classes.

_____ Provide adult church school classes in the evening.

_____ Offer a Saturday Seminar at least twice a year.

_____ Increase awareness of adult education opportunities.

## CHRISTIAN UNITY AND INTERRELIGIOUS CONCERNS

_____ Provide opportunities for dialogue with people of other faiths.

_____ Arrange for visits to other churches; e.g., Orthodox, Synagogue, Muslim, etc.

## STEWARDSHIP AND FINANCE COMMITTEE

_____ Increase stewardship of time and talent.

_____ Encourage tithing; i.e., giving of 10 percent of income to the church.

_____ Increase congregational knowledge of church budget and financial needs.

_____ Increase congregational knowledge of where stewardship funds are used in mission.

## YOUTH MINISTRY

_____ Help youth understand themselves, their world, their faith.

_____ Help youth grow in their faith.

_____ Increase active membership and participation in all youth groups.

_____ Involve youth in mission projects.

_____ Integrate our youth ministry with the ministry of the whole church.

## MEMBERSHIP AND EVANGELISM

_____ Improve assimilation of new members into the church family.

_____ Increase church membership by 10 percent per year.

_____ Increase the number of persons involved in small church groups.

_____ Build fellowship through the use of name badges.

_____ Develop a visitation program for visitors and prospective members.

_____ Deepen personal devotional and prayer life of members.

## CHRISTIAN FAMILY

_____ Promote family fellowship.

_____ Plan activities for parenting education.

_____ Plan programming on family communications.

_____ Emphasize the nurturing Christian marriage.

_____ Sponsor Family Camp, All-Church Picnic, Advent Family Workshop, etc.

## MISSIONS COMMITTEE

_____ Better inform the congregation of where mission money is utilized.

_____ More membership involvement in deciding which mission projects to support.

_____ Tour of mission projects and activities in our area.

_____ Increase percentage of church budget going to mission outreach.

_____ Provide opportunities for mission work projects and individual mission service.

## COMMUNICATIONS COMMITTEE

_____ Broadcast Sunday morning worship service.

_____ Produce weekly cable-TV Christian educational program.

_____ Purchase audio-visual camera equipment for use in the church as well as for cable TV.

_____ Increase publicity about church programs and activities in our service area.

## CARING CONGREGATION COMMITTEE

_____ Purchase church van to provide transportation to Sunday worship, senior member events, youth group events, etc.

_____ Provide close-in special parking for elderly and handicapped.

_____ Provide large-print Order of Worship and music for Sunday worship.

## LIBRARY COMMITTEE

_____ Recruit a librarian to supervise and organize the library.

_____ Provide resource books for Bible and other Christian-related studies.

_____ Develop a reading program for children, youth, and adults.

## OTHER SUGGESTIONS FOR MINISTRY

_____

_____

_____

_____

Please go back over the survey quickly and circle the 3 or 4 items you feel are the most important for our church to become involved in at this time.

## OUR VISION
## CHURCH AND SUNDAY SCHOOL ATTENDANCE

As a member of this church, I am happy to vision
about how many people we can be serving in Worship and
Sunday School by the year _____.

**I believe we can have** _____ **in worship each Sunday.**

(Current Worship attendance averages _____ .)

**I believe we can have** _____ **in Sunday School each Sunday.**

(Current Sunday School attendance averages _____.)

## OUR VISION
## SPIRITUAL GROWTH & MISSION

As a member of this church, I am happy to vision about how we can
deepen and expand the "Spiritual Growth" of those we serve and what
we should be doing additionally in mission outreach.

Idea 1. _____

_____

Idea 2. _____

_____

Who should we be serving that we may not be serving at present?

_____

## Staying the Course With Organized Plans Assessment

*Plan your work—then work your plan*

Once an accepted plan is in place, the real work has just begun. Each committee is organized to enact the plan. In so doing, they not only keep objectives in mind, coordinate with others, and keep track of what happens, but just as importantly track and periodically assess results.

If the plan is well conceived, objectives and tasks will be specific enough to be quantitatively tracked and assessed. If the organization is effective, actions taken will be documented in a notebook, which is passed each year from one committee chair to the next. With this documentation, the church can assess where it is on the plan continuum. Without this discipline, the church may stumble along, essentially doing "what comes naturally," just maintaining the status quo.

During the year, each committee should track its own progress and evaluate where adjustments might be needed in the portion of the plan for which they are responsible. Coordination with other groups certainly will be required. At budget time each year committees should ensure the financial implications of their plans are reviewed and expenses included in their budget requests.

Formally, every twelve to twenty-four months, the long-range planning committee should assess progress and plan for adjustments in both the plan and support organization.

- This might be done during a planning retreat in which all plan participants come together for a day of reassessment and coordination.

- The congregation might be resurveyed to determine changing ideas.

- Demographic and other related changes might be considered.

Such a reassessment gives organizational form and "drive" to the process. Goals will be reached as members stay involved and committed.

*When a plan is worked, it will be successful.*

*Evaluation is constant and organized, and must be dynamic.*


# Financial Plans

## Planning for Financial Support

After establishing a mission, setting goals, and developing action plans, financial implications of the church's plans must be considered and financial support planned and developed. This is true for not only the annual budget but for long-term requirements as well.

How much funding will be needed and how much will be available? These may be significantly different amounts. Are there methodologies and tools available that will help in these decisions?

A good place to start is the analytical guidelines for planning discussed on page 42. There are a number of ratios, formulas, and other guidelines for church life, just as there are in business. Many of these can be useful in basic church planning, and can form a bridge or transition to the important subject of how and where financial support is to be obtained.

Beginning on page 43 specific ideas and examples are presented with which to begin an analysis of financial resources. A key to success is to know as closely as possible what potential financial resources can be counted on to support the life and mission of the church, and then to develop the necessary plans to tap these resources effectively. Most churches probably underestimate the potential financial resources present in their church and community. Normally, *financial support follows mission planning,* not the reverse; people respond best to personal appeals that are tied directly to purposes and causes.

The great challenge to all church financial life—the annual budget—is discussed on pages 50–55, where it is emphasized that to be successful the same people who make the plans must be involved in creating the budget, and the same people who create the budget must be ready to support it. Thus, all church members should be involved directly or indirectly. If the program of the church is articulated clearly the dollars needed should come.

Capital-management planning is equally important and includes cash and savings management, borrowing, and developing reserves through wills and endowments. A sample permanent fund policy is included on pages 61–63. The elements of an effective capital funds program are discussed on pages 74–75.

*An effective plan includes financial implications and a design to attain the financial support necessary to implement the plan adequately.*

## Analytical Guidelines for Planning

For effective planning in any environment, be it in business or the church, analytical tools are necessary. These tools are most useful when employed to assist in defining parameters, identifying trends, or otherwise setting the structure of the plan. Analytical tools must be used to assist, not to guide planning; they are to aid, not to limit. We will mention and discuss here just a few of the myriad tools available. Each planner is encouraged to seek out these aids and to use them as appropriate.

In his book *Twelve Keys to an Effective Church,* Dr. Kennon Callahan discusses a number of different analytical aids which can be used in a diagnostic approach—all to make the reader think empirically. He challenges local congregations to determine the outer limits of their future using mission-related formulas. He contends congregations should define visitation and outreach goals, determine the level of a maximum "comfortably filled" worship area, establish the number of relational groups they should have, recognize the level of operating budget needed to support salaries and benefits of the pastor and staff, and even suggests a ratio of parking spaces needed to accommodate the number of worshipers.

Comparing descriptive data about a church with data from similar churches is obviously an excellent source of analytical guidelines for planning. With the computer age, most denominations can or should be able to make available data comparing, as a minimum:

- Worship-attendance trends and the relationship to membership
- Sunday school participation, by age grouping

- The number of small groups and level of active participation

- The amount of evangelistic and visitation efforts

- Financial support per worshiper, by type of gift

Significant differences in results when a church's data is compared to data from another church should prompt analysis about possible environmental differences or other changes taking place, and changes in programming that might be needed.

## Financial Resources Analysis

Every church faces a number of important financial questions as it plans for future years and makes rational decisions about the availability of financial resources. Where will the funds come from to support programs that have been planned? Can members extend themselves further at this time? How much more (or less) can be expected from members who join or leave?

There are generally four factors which should be considered *and kept in balance* in any analysis of whether or not a given local church has solid financial resources.

*Current support income:* A church needs to think of income as more than the money received to support the general budget. The level of total gifts for all purposes gives a better indication of the financial health of a church. A good analysis will also relate the total income of the church to average worship attendance, as well as to membership. Dollars given per worshiper can be used to estimate financial resources available or lacking.

*Development income:* A projected increase in worship attendance can be translated directly into new net income. Although the amount may differ by denomination and financial support expected of its members, normally an average amount of new support can be expected with each new worship attendee.

*Endowments and other assets of the church:* Endowments can be a large source of income, if managed properly. (This area will be discussed in depth later in this manual.) Other assets such as property, facilities, stocks, bonds, and other liquid and capital assets should also be considered as potential sources of support for church plans.

*Debt:* The amount of debt, the interest rate, and the payment schedule all must be considered in the context of current and projected economic conditions and with regard to the continuing ability and commitment of the membership to shoulder debt.

It may also be important to develop potential financial resources through analysis of the occupational groups that make up the life and mission of the church. Data should be available about the average income in that region for occupational categories present in the congregation. Information about how the community may be changing economically should be available and may directly affect a church plan.

Sources of demographic or economic development data include:

- The public library's research department, where census reports, referenced to business data, are available by zip code or census tract

- A local Chamber of Commerce, where economic development information should be available

- City planning department

- Advertising firms, where geographic and demographic information should be readily available in various commercial formats

- A church's denominational headquarters, which may have data comparing individual churches with each other

It is probably true that most churches underestimate the potential financial resources present in their church and community. Remember that to develop these resources the most effective churches emphasize their mission, plan their programs well, communicate their plan and programs, and then ask directly and personally for the funding required. They emphasize their goal of helping people and their effectiveness, illustrated by a wise use of donations and the highest integrity in accounting for contributions. They don't forget to thank contributors for the support and for what it accomplishes.

Two demonstrations follow of material that can be developed to assist in financial resources planning:

- The first item on page 45 outlines the results of data gathered about a local church from census sources at the public library. Note the type of important information which can directly affect the long-range plans of the church.

- The next item on page 46 is a data statement about the same church and how it compares with like-sized churches in worship attendance, in its geographical area, and in the denominationally defined region. This information was available from the regional headquarters. Note the relatively high giving per worshiper but low worship attendance at the local church.

## Census Source Data: An Example

The following conclusions can be drawn from census research done at a public library about demographic, economic, and other changes that may take place in a community:

- Most growth will take place south of our city and in other communities south of our city.

- The population of our city proper will age slightly as people already in their homes retire and stay put.

- New housing starts will concentrate to the south. They will be above median cost and will be built for young families. At least one adult, probably both, in the household will be college educated.

- The ethnic mix of the area will not change significantly; however, there may be some change in the northern part our city, and there may be a higher percentage of African American professionals in the adjacent area.

- There will be a growing segment of single-parent households along with an attendant drop in household income, as well as a need for support groups and services such as childcare.

- There will be bipolar growth: aging people already living in our city versus young, affluent families moving into the southern part of the area; affluent people buying new housing versus single parent households with shrinking discretionary income.

*Conclusion:* The primary service needs will be for:

- Aging people
- Young families
- Single-parent households
- Children from young families
- Children and youth from single-family households

## Comparative Data Statement for A Church for Year Ending _____

| | Denominational Region | Geographical Area | Worship Attendance 150–349 | Local Church |
|---|---|---|---|---|
| Total number of churches | 432 | 73 | 71 | — |
| Total participating members | 77,419 | 17,257 | 28,808 | 484 |
| Total average worship attendance | 41,270 | 8,518 | 14,624 | 195 |
| Average participating members | 179 | 236 | 406 | 484 |
| Average total worship attendance | 96 | 117 | 206 | 195 |
| % members attending worship | 53% | 49% | 51% | 40% |
| Total all type receipts | $51,726,521 | $11,602,058 | $19,927,593 | $449,732 |
| Total operating receipts | 38,717,739 | 8,455,202 | 14,276,781 | 187,964 |
| Total capital receipts | 7,229,561 | 2,011,799 | 3,219,919 | 234,004 |
| Total outreach | 5,779,221 | 1,135,057 | 2,430,893 | 27,764 |
| Average gift per participating member | 668 | 672 | 692 | 929 |
| Average total receipts per worshiper | 1,253 | 1,362 | 1,363 | 2,306 |
| Average operating receipts per worshiper | 938 | 993 | 976 | 964 |
| Average capital receipts per worshiper | 175 | 236 | 220 | 1,200 |
| Average total outreach per worshiper | 140 | 133 | 166 | 142 |
| Total outreach (% of total receipts) | 11% | 10% | 12% | 6% |
| Total outreach (% of operating receipts) | 15% | 13% | 17% | 15% |

When studying the data on page 46, notice trends or variations that can affect data and how these statistics might be used as indicators of needed changes in church direction and programs:

*Worship attendance data may mean more than participating members data.* With rare, but sometimes significant exceptions, worship attendance defines the health of a church program, including the health of its stewardship, and marks a church's direction. The most active, committed members come to worship regularly. Some of the cases in which attendance may not be as important can include churches with dedicated homebound members and seasonal attendance by, for example, retirees or students.

*Percentage of members attending worship and what this could mean.* Generally, smaller churches have a higher percentage of members attending worship since this is a "gathering of the family." As a church grows in size, it may see a drop in the percentage of participating members who attend regularly, possibly due to a loss of identity as a family grouping. Thus, creation of this small-group family feeling becomes a challenge to churches as they grow in size; statistical data can help to identify this need. Another significant need that can be identified is whether members feel "crowded" at worship, or wish to come at a different time. Perhaps there is a need for an additional service if worship attendance is to grow. The local church in the comparative data statement may very well be in this position, since its percentage of members attending is about 10 percent less than other churches of like size.

*Relationship between operating receipts and worship attendance.* One of the better indicators of stewardship potential and the health of a church is the average gift per worshiper to operational needs when compared to other churches of like size. It can be more challenging to encourage support for church salaries, utilities, and so forth than for special programs. Knowing this relationship can help define a viable stewardship program.

*Influence of capital campaigns on receipt averages.* Note the possible effect of a capital campaign on the local church when compared to other churches. The average gift per participating member is high, as are the capital receipts and total receipts per worshiper; however, average operating receipts per worshiper are lower. This could indicate the influence of the capital campaign, unless there are large, individual gifts affecting the data.

*Outreach support when there is a capital campaign or other special need.* Notice particularly the difference in the percentage of outreach support when compared to total receipts and operating receipts. One can readily see how special capital or program needs in a church can affect members' desires to support outreach programs. For the health of the church, these are indicators to watch carefully.

## The Budget—Program, Then Dollars

Church budgets are often created by, or at least influenced by, the same members who

- Make long-range plans
- Develop programs
- Determine monetary needs to support programs
- Develop individual parts of the overall budgets
- Give, to support program needs

Thus, *all* members of the church are involved either directly or indirectly in the financial plan—the receiving and spending plan—for the church. The greater the involvement by members who do the planning and programming, the greater the acceptance by members. The greater the acceptance, the greater the support. When members know, accept, and understand the need, and trust the people doing the asking, the money will come. This is true of any size church.

The budget process can be summarized as follows. First, *both* receipts and expenses should be planned for. There may be unique opportunities for gaining receipts other than regular contributions (e.g., use of facilities). Expenses must follow mission and program plans, and changes in these plans, and must be adjusted accordingly. This planning needs to be done each year and include long-term needs as well as current operating needs. The treasurer may normally take the lead in developing financial information to aid the budget committee.

Several months before the beginning of the financial period, written requests should be sent to committee and program heads and others who need to review their needs. (An example of such a letter is on page 50.) The communication necessary between the budget committee and program committees of the church includes the following:

- Financial data from previous years, current committee budget, and current variance from budget (including percentage changes through the years)
- Inflationary changes to show real growth need
- Explanation of significant changes
- Mission changes and capital items over two to three years
- A specific due date
- Follow-up, for procrastinators

All input is put together and compared to previous periods and anticipated programs. Adjustments are inevitable and probably will need to be negotiated. The figure for receipts, representing the amount needed from members as contributions, should be calculated and will be the amount the stewardship committee uses as its goal.

The budget committee presents its figures to the governing body, which reviews, discusses, maybe makes changes, and presents the final budget to the congregation for its approval. This gives another opportunity to inform the congregation and to gain its acceptance, a time when the mission of the church and how this mission is to be carried out is emphasized. The dollar figures only represent the means to accomplish the mission of the church.

The congregation considers, approves, and embraces the budget as its own. This leads right into the stewardship campaign. (If it is the practice of the church to hold the stewardship campaign before preparing a balanced budget, then the budget approved by the congregation becomes a "goal" program-oriented budget; the "expenditure" budget is prepared later.)

As the financial year begins, the treasurer prepares a flexible, month-by-month budget, incorporating information about receipt and expenditure changes during different periods. This becomes the cash-flow needs document with which the treasurer and finance committee work.

Adjustments during the year are always necessary, due to unanticipated costs, changes in income, and new programs that may be developed. Budget shifts within departments usually can be readily allowed. For larger needs, approval of the governing body should be sought.

On pages 51–54 is an example of how a medium-sized church budget might look and move through the governing body toward congregational approval. This example shows a detailed line-item budget. There are as many ways of presenting the budget as there are churches. Another successful way is to present to the congregation a pictorial booklet that emphasizes the programs of the church and only presents the dollar figures in summary. *The best way is the way that is most acceptable to the local church and one that emphasizes church programs.* Whatever method is used, the budget proposal is not a place for misunderstanding, factional disputes, or other disruptions. The church must be behind the budget to support it!

When members understand and are committed, emotionally and intellectually, they will give.

**Budget support comes from faith and facts.**

# Sample Budget Letter to Committee Chairpersons

The following is a draft letter containing five elements, keyed by number. A successful budget letter:

1. Asks for *involvement.*
2. Tells the reader *why* they should be involved.
3. Suggests *what to do.*
4. Sets a *time limit* for response, three to four weeks after the letter is sent.
5. Adds a word of *encouragement.*

[ Date ]

All Committee Chairpersons:

*Budget time for next year is upon us!!* We would like you to be a specific part of this process. (1)

How can you help? First, we ask you to look on the budget as a financial-need statement of what you see as the *program* needs and direction of the church in your area. We will assess our action plans for next year to further God's work in our community, and then put a dollar figure to them. (2)

Specifically, please consider the following: (3)

- What program changes might be expected?
- Did we have too much or too little monetary support this year, related to what we need next year?
- Don't forget what changes the new building may make on your programs.

So we can react to your recommendations in time, please send your comments and monetary data in to Joe Smith, Budget Chairperson, by [date]. (4)

This is an exciting time—a time when we all commit ourselves to a strong program for our church and the funds to support it. *We all must help!* (5)

In God's Service,

Brenda R. Jones
Board Chair

# Sample Budget Letter to a Governing Body

This letter goes to all board members at least a week before their meeting and should introduce the proposed budget in a positive, factual way, emphasizing the programs of the church and the ability of the members to financially support the budget.

[ Date ]

All Board Members:

*Budget time for next year is here again!* Our budget committee has prepared the attached General Fund operating budget for next year for your consideration. It will be presented and reviewed at our next meeting on [ date ].

The budget committee carefully reviewed all data from previous periods, input from other committee chairpersons, and projections from our long-range planning group. An open meeting composed of all interested committee chairpersons and other members of our church was held on [ date ] to draft the proposed budget, and we believe a strong consensus for the budget was attained.

A summary of the proposed budget appears on the first page, and a more detailed breakdown follows the summary. We find ourselves in a generally strong financial position as we end this year and trust this will carry over into next year. Because our members have been so faithful with their stewardship this year, we feel we can project about the same need in giving this coming year, even though we project an increase in expenses of almost 11 percent.

Proposed increases for next year respond to the need for (1) a cost-of-living increase for the staff; (2) a full year's salary for the associate minister; (3) expansion of the nursery and Children's Church program; (4) greater emphasis on evangelism and Christian witness; (5) financial record-keeping assistance, as our church grows; and (6) some small increases in property maintenance needs.

These truly are exciting times as we continue to move forward in Christ's work in our community. Please review the attached budget and give it prayerful consideration. Come to the board meeting with your questions and your support.

In God's Service,

Brenda R. Jones
Board Chair

# Proposed Budget Summary

## General Fund Proposed Budget: Summary

| Item | 3 Yrs Ago Actual | 2 Yrs Ago Actual | Last Year Budget | Request |
|---|---|---|---|---|
| BUDGETED OUTREACH | $ 22,788 | $ 24,009 | $ 29,842 | $ 29,810 |
| WORSHIP & PASTORING | 98,977 | 106,494 | 122,612 | 138,451 |

Includes ministerial salaries and allowances, pensions, hospitalization, disability insurance, continuing education, and other worship and music-related salaries and program costs.

| | | | | |
|---|---|---|---|---|
| CHRISTIAN EDUCATION | 10,195 | 10,088 | 11,700 | 13,550 |

Includes Sunday School, library, youth, camp scholarships, nursery costs, and vacation bible school.

| | | | | |
|---|---|---|---|---|
| WITNESS & FELLOWSHIP | 2,674 | 1,769 | 4,185 | 5,375 |

Includes evangelism, new member costs, lay programs, flowers, stewardship, video and audio supplies and equipment, kitchen supplies, and fellowship programs.

| | | | | |
|---|---|---|---|---|
| Total Program Expenses | $134,634 | $142,360 | $168,339 | $187,186 |
| ADMINISTRATION | $ 39,322 | $ 34,496 | $ 35,896 | $ 42,070 |

Includes office salaries, supplies, and equipment costs; denominational meeting expenses, employer's social security and worker's compensation; and the financial management service contract.

| | | | | |
|---|---|---|---|---|
| CHURCH PROPERTY | 42,511 | 44,223 | 49,925 | 52,275 |

Includes custodial salary, utilities, maintenance and equipment, yards and grounds, and church insurance. (Does not include rental property costs.)

| | | | | |
|---|---|---|---|---|
| Total Admin & Property | $ 81,833 | $ 78,719 | $ 85,821 | $ 94,345 |
| Total General Fund Exp | $216,467 | $221,079 | $254,160 | $281,531 |
| TITHES, OFFERINGS, GIFTS, OTHER INCOME | | | | |
| General Fund Giving | $207,237 | $218,261 | $271,295 | $271,000 |
| Net Rental Income* | 4,098 | 2,046 | 570 | 2,032 |
| Interest Income | 1,069 | 936 | 1,000 | 1,000 |
| Other Income | 5,029 | 11,147 | 9,000 | 7,499 |
| Total Income | $217,433 | $232,390 | $281,865 | $281,531 |
| INCOME, LESS EXPENSES | $ 966 | $ 11,311 | $ 27,705 | $ 0 |

*Includes the net of rental property income and related expenses.

# Proposed Budget in Detail

## General Fund Proposed Budget

| Account | 3 Yrs Ago Actual | 2 Yrs Ago Actual | Last Year Budget | Request |
|---|---|---|---|---|
| 860 BUDGETED OUTREACH | $ 22,788 | $ 24,009 | $ 29,842 | $ 29,810 |
| **WORSHIP & PASTORING** | | | | |
| 800 Minister Salary & Allowances | 59,964 | 61,764 | 61,764 | 63,764 |
| 802 Minister Pension & Annuity | 10,856 | 10,831 | 10,856 | 10,856 |
| 801 Minister Hospitalization | 5,434 | 5,544 | 6,193 | 5,544 |
| 812 Special Ed Senior Minister | 759 | 757 | 750 | 750 |
| 804 Assoc Min Salary & Allowances | 4,912 | 8,720 | 19,162 | 29,604 |
| 805 Assoc Min Pension | 559 | 932 | 2,391 | 3,850 |
| 837 Assoc Min Reimb Expenses | | | 1,660 | 3,000 |
| 810 Guest Ministers | 50 | 150 | 200 | 200 |
| 807 Music Director Salary | 7,449 | 8,925 | 9,200 | 9,522 |
| 808 Organist Salary | 6,586 | 6,386 | 7,136 | 7,386 |
| 811 Guest Musicians | 65 | 315 | 250 | 600 |
| 813 Special Ed Music Dept | 68 | 89 | 100 | 300 |
| 870 Worship Supplies | 375 | 236 | 400 | 525 |
| 871 Communion Supplies | 390 | 482 | 400 | 400 |
| 872 Bulletins | 763 | 486 | 800 | 800 |
| 874 Music Dept Supplies | 747 | 877 | 1,050 | 1,050 |
| 875 Robe Maintenance | | | 300 | 300 |
| Subtotal | $ 98,977 | $106,494 | $122,612 | $138,451 |
| **CHRISTIAN EDUCATION** | | | | |
| 830 Sunday School Supplies | $ 2,115 | $ 1,765 | $ 2,750 | $ 2,750 |
| 832 Library Books/Supplies | 117 | 108 | 150 | 150 |
| 833 Youth Activities | 942 | 1,002 | 1,500 | 1,700 |
| 834 Camp Scholarships | 1,548 | 1,733 | 1,500 | 1,750 |
| 835 Nursery/Children's Church | 3,936 | 4,623 | 4,800 | 6,200 |
| 836 Vacation Bible School | 1,536 | 857 | 1,000 | 1,000 |
| Subtotal | $ 10,195 | $ 10,088 | $ 11,700 | $ 13,550 |
| **CHRISTIAN WITNESS & FELLOWSHIP** | | | | |
| 840 Evangelism Publicity | $ 150 | $ 150 | $ 200 | $ 700 |
| 841 Evangelism Lit & Supplies | | 196 | 300 | 300 |
| 850 New Member Supplies | 572 | 367 | 500 | 500 |
| 852 Flowers & Cards | 94 | (81) | 100 | 100 |
| 831 Lay Programs | 900 | 1,173 | 1,500 | 1,800 |
| 838 Lay Delegates | | | 535 | 750 |
| 851 Kitchen Supplies | 337 | 230 | 300 | 300 |
| 853 Fellowship Programs | (58) | (260) | 100 | 100 |
| 858 Singles Ministry | 45 | 66 | 50 | 250 |
| 854 Stewardship Material | 522 | 165 | 300 | 275 |
| 859 Wellway | 100 | 89 | 200 | 200 |
| 880 Video Supplies | 360 | 306 | 400 | 400 |
| 881 Video Equip & Maintenance | 167 | 19 | 200 | 200 |
| 857 Drink Machine | (514) | (652) | (500) | (500) |
| Subtotal | $ 2,674 | $ 1,769 | $ 4,185 | $ 5,375 |
| TOTAL PROGRAM EXPENSES | $134,634 | $142,360 | $168,339 | $187,186 |

| Account | 3 Yrs Ago Actual | 2 Yrs Ago Actual | Last Year Budget | Request |
|---|---|---|---|---|
| CHURCH ADMINISTRATION | | | | |
| 806 Admin Assistant Salary | $ 19,457 | $ 16,866 | $ 17,372 | $ 17,980 |
| 824 Financial Assistant Salary | | | | 3,300 |
| 809 Financial Management Service | 1,800 | 1,800 | 1,800 | 1,800 |
| 803 Denominational Meetings | 864 | 1,439 | 1,500 | 2,700 |
| 814 Social Security Taxes | 4,347 | 3,891 | 4,124 | 4,560 |
| 815 Worker's Compensation Insurance | 2,703 | 2,848 | 2,900 | 2,900 |
| 820 Postage | 2,537 | 2,508 | 2,750 | 2,750 |
| 821 Office Supplies | 3,460 | 1,774 | 2,100 | 2,500 |
| 822 Newsletter | 1,078 | 705 | 750 | 380 |
| 823 Office Equip & Maintenance | 2,999 | 2,627 | 2,500 | 3,200 |
| 824 Office Miscellaneous | 75 | 38 | 100 | |
| Subtotal | $ 39,322 | $ 34,496 | $ 35,896 | $ 42,070 |
| | | | | |
| CHURCH PROPERTY | | | | |
| 816 Custodian Salary | $ 15,238 | $ 14,609 | $ 16,000 | $ 16,500 |
| 890 Water & Garbage | 2,229 | 2,787 | 3,500 | 3,500 |
| 891 Gas (Heating) | 1,907 | 1,756 | 2,000 | 2,000 |
| 892 Electricity | 12,973 | 15,096 | 16,500 | 16,500 |
| 893 Telephone | 1,042 | 1,120 | 1,100 | 1,650 |
| 894 Custodial Supplies | 588 | 661 | 750 | 750 |
| 895 Building Maintenance & Equip | 2,851 | 1,920 | 4,075 | 4,500 |
| 896 Yards & Grounds | 758 | 1,053 | 500 | 1,000 |
| 897 Church Insurance | 4,927 | 5,222 | 5,500 | 5,875 |
| Subtotal | $ 42,511 | $ 44,223 | $ 49,925 | $ 52,275 |
| TOTAL ADMIN & PROPERTY | $ 81,833 | $ 78,719 | $ 85,821 | $ 94,345 |
| TOTAL GENERAL FUND EXPENSES | $216,467 | $221,079 | $254,160 | $281,531 |
| | | | | |
| TITHES, OFFERINGS, GIFTS, OTHER INCOME | | | | |
| 600 General Fund Giving | $207,237 | $218,261 | $271,295 | $271,000 |
| 611 Interest Income | 1,069 | 936 | 1,000 | 1,000 |
| 612 Other Income | 5,029 | 11,147 | 9,000 | 7,499 |
| Subtotal | $213,335 | $230,345 | $281,295 | $279,499 |
| | | | | |
| RENTAL PROPERTY | | | | |
| 610 Rental Income | $ 11,700 | $ 11,050 | $ 11,700 | $ 11,700 |
| (Less Expenses:) | | | | |
| 900 Jordon Property Mortgage | (4,318) | (4,318) | (4,318) | (4,318) |
| 901 Rental Repairs | (124) | (1,415) | (3,500) | (2,000) |
| 902 Property Tax on Rentals | (2,636) | (2,659) | (2,700) | (2,700) |
| 903 Insurance on Rentals | (524) | (612) | (612) | (650) |
| Net Rental Income | $ 4,098 | $ 2,046 | $ 570 | $ 2,032 |
| TOTAL INCOME | $217,433 | $232,390 | $281,865 | $281,531 |
| TOTAL INCOME, LESS EXPENSES | $ 966 | $ 11,311 | $ 27,705 | $ 0 |
| | | | | (1) |

(1) Anticipated overage due to support for new associate minister for which salary was required only half of last year; thus request for this year can be slightly less.

## Sample Budget Letter to Congregation Members

This letter has one purpose: to set the stage for a positive acceptance of the budget and stewardship campaign. The material attached could be detailed financial data similar to that reviewed by the board; however, an excellent approach would be a pamphlet which emphasizes the various parts of the church program, and includes only summary financial data by program. The most important part of the meeting will be the positive comments made. Remember: *People respond to people!* Ask, with faith and facts!

[ Date ]

Dear Friends in Christ:

We have said it many times: *We are a church family*. That has been so evident recently in all our services, activities, and fellowship we've shared. So our family can continue to share together, planning has already begun for the new program and financial year.

A significant piece of this planning is the budget process. Enclosed is information about the proposed budget for this coming year. This proposal was developed by committee chairpersons, compiled by the budget committee, and accepted by the board. We will present it to you for congregational acceptance this coming Sunday [state where and when]. All members of the congregation are encouraged to attend. This will be an informal presentation with ample time for discussion and questions. Most of all, we want you to have a budget plan which you feel you can support with all your heart.

Our church family can rejoice over so many things: the loving spirit we give to one another; the way we give beyond ourselves through local, national, and worldwide outreach; the activities our young people share; worship services that glorify God and uplift us; the fellowship of one another.

This proposed budget will allow us to share these and many more activities and programs and help us serve God and one another throughout the coming year. Please give it your prayerful consideration and join us at the congregational meeting. Your participation is important and needed! We hope to see you Sunday as together we look forward to the future.

Brenda R. Jones
Board Chair

Joe Smith
Budget Chair

## Capital Management Planning

**CASH MANAGEMENT**

Effective financial support planning will include careful cash management of available resources. There may be opportunities for earnings on cash reserves and possibly even checking accounts. Trust or endowment funds may be available to the church. Effective borrowing of needed funds is an art to be carefully developed.

A church with all its operating or reserve funds in regular non-interest-bearing accounts may be wasting an opportunity for earnings. Although it seems more difficult for nonprofit organizations to receive special banking privileges at reduced rates, a church can still shop around and usually find a stable local bank willing to offer interest on checking as well as savings accounts at reasonable rates, and free checking to small accounts.

For cash reserves of a less immediate need, certificates of deposit will pay better interest than checking or savings accounts. A denominationally supported financial group also may offer excellent earnings opportunities. Savings and loans and credit unions may pay higher rates; however, one should always ensure all accounts are federally insured. Also remember that deposits in one institution cannot exceed $100,000 if they are to be federally insured.

There may be opportunities to centralize women's, youth, Sunday school, and other miscellaneous accounts into one so that interest can be earned on these small accounts. This depends on how independent the groups are about their funds.

If a church receives stocks and bonds as gifts, probably the best conservative policy is to quickly convert them into cash. That makes the donation available for current ministry, or available later for a special project, and eliminates the implication that the church is an investment group rather than a church. This policy also eliminates a possible criticism if the securities markets should turn down and the gift is reduced in value, perhaps at a time when it is needed for a project or program.

For trust or endowment funds there should be a carefully prepared written investment policy, with the funds under the management of a capable committee of people with financial and legal expertise. This special subject is discussed in greater detail on pages 57–60.

Although gifts from members usually must be considered the primary source of financial support of a church's mission, there are times where borrowed funds are necessary—and even smart:

- For special projects, such as emergency repair work. However, members will usually make special gifts for such events, if they clearly know the need.

- For new facilities or major programs. These are more long-term needs and can be well planned, using funds from denominational sources at good rates (and their advice is invaluable), local banks—if credit rating is good—and bonds (although these can be expensive).

The procedure for borrowing by a church is similar to the procedure individual borrowers follow. A clear plan of need is developed, considering all factors—especially how the loan will be repaid. A detailed application precedes preparation of a formal mortgage and includes such information as:

- Identification of the borrower

- Signatures of responsible officers, and whether they are to be held liable

- Complete financial information, including a statement of assets, liabilities, net value, and current operating results

- Number of contributing members and their giving over recent years

- Growth trends of membership, and projection for the future

- Church credit history, including bill-payment history

The amount to be borrowed and length of time for the loan is a major decision. The shorter the period, the better, unless there is rising inflation, when interest on funds saved can be greater than interest on loans. Of course, there are no tax advantages to long-term mortgages. Probably most important, members can lose enthusiasm for paying back a loan. *People respond best to causes, not debt repayment.*

General guidelines about how much to borrow usually specify that when three or four of the following guidelines result in about the same total, that figure can be borrowed with reasonable confidence:[5]

- Keep total debt within two-and-one-half times current total annual receipts.

- Borrow no more than the current property value, not including the new project.

- Borrow no more than $1,000 multiplied by the number of active members.

- Keep payments on building debts within one-fourth to one-third of total monthly current expenditures.

- Borrow no more than two or three times the amount raised in cash and three-year pledges before the building project begins.

- Borrow no more than today's members feel they can repay; do not expect membership growth to carry the debt burden.

A monitored amortization plan must be an essential part of any amount borrowed so that changes can be made if there is a financial advantage. Tell members how much the mortgage is costing them daily in interest; they will be astounded and may respond by paying off the debt sooner than scheduled.

In summary, effective cash management in a church setting is just as important as it is in any business setting. *Members want to know their gifts are used in a professional and ethical way for a well-planned program!*

### DEVELOPING RESERVES THROUGH WILLS, ENDOWMENTS, AND INSURANCE

Reserves through wills, endowments, or insurance proceeds can do much for a congregation in expanding the witness and mission of Jesus Christ, through its ability to serve human needs in the community and around the world. This is certainly an important aspect of stewardship—a stewardship of accumulated resources.

Reserves must not be thought of as an augmentation to regular annual giving of members or diminish the opportunities for responsible stewardship by present or future members. If reserves do affect annual giving, the mission health of the church will probably suffer.

The first step, and absolutely the most important, is to establish a policy for handling gifts from wills, endowments, or insurance proceeds. It is imperative for the health of the church that such a policy be established to avoid unnecessary and sometimes nasty controversies. *DO NOT ACCEPT A GIFT UNTIL A POLICY IS IN PLACE!!*

A discussion about basic issues in writing such a policy begins below. Following on pages 61–63 is a sample policy suggested by the Christian Church Foundation, an organizational body of the Christian Church (Disciples of Christ).[6] Other denominations provide such policy examples, covering many of the same points.

The committee responsible for administering this program should be carefully chosen to ensure absolute integrity as to designated funds and to guarantee a use of proceeds that will be in the interest of the entire congregation, its mission, and programs. Committee members can have strong opinions about these funds that could cause something very positive to become very negative to the life of the church. If the basic policy is developed with adequate checks and balances, negative influences can be avoided or at least minimized.

The responsible committee must also be involved in developing a program of education, information sharing, and practical programs related to this area of Christian stewardship. Newsletter reminders can be a starting point. Sponsoring wills and estate-planning seminars on a regular basis might be feasible and offer a word of encouragement to procrastinators; resource persons are available from most general church levels and seminaries.

Always remember to recognize the donor of all memorial gifts and bequests. A personal thank-you or note is essential. Recognition in a newsletter may also be appropriate. A special worship service could be celebrated each year to recognize all individuals who have remembered the church in their wills or who have established endowment funds in the name of the congregation. Memorial Day and All Saints' Day are good times for this recognition. Remember to celebrate not only the lives of the givers but the kinds of mission and ministry their gifts make possible.

Remember the income tax benefits of such gifts. A significant example is "deferred giving." After selling property, a home, or a business at a profit and facing large tax indebtedness, one can set up an irrevocable trust in the name of a church. The church receives the gift when the donor dies. The donor can deduct the present value of the gift now (based on Internal Revenue Service charts) to avoid capital gains taxes and to receive income from the trust until the donor dies.

Possibly the best final advice is to contact the foundations department of the denomination, which may offer free help, in handling this important area the right way.

## BASIC ISSUES ABOUT WRITING CONGREGATIONAL POLICIES
## FOR WILLS, BEQUESTS, AND MEMORIALS

In just about any church there are three primary divisions of gifts:

- Regular gifts for ongoing operational support

- Special-project gifts for any special designated purpose, such as new facilities, special outreach efforts, other capital improvements, and so forth

- Accumulated resource gifts for special financial reserves, originating from wills, bequests, annuities, memorials, and so forth.

It is the area of accumulated resource gifts that many churches need to emphasize as a special opportunity for members to continue their support after their death. Ensuring proper and positive handling of these gifts, however, can prove especially challenging. With an effective educational process people will learn that it is possible for mature Christians to leave from 10 to 100 percent of their estate residual to the church—at considerable tax savings during their lifetime.

To build a successful program congregations need to make and document a clear and complete policy prior to receiving any funds. This clarifies for prospective donors how their gifts will be used and handled.

Several major concerns need to be addressed in writing a policy. First, the mission of Jesus and the church must be primary to any policy: the love of Christ for us and others must be paramount. *A church cannot hurt from too much money, but it can die from lack of mission.*

Second, the policy should contain clear lines of accountability and authority. Integrity and accountability, as well as openness about the program, gives people confidence that their funds are being used as intended. The policy should assign responsible persons who must perform their duties in a positive way, with no one person given too much responsibility or liability. The policy must mandate an open and full fiscal reporting to the congregation, to be made on a periodic basis.

Third, the policy needs to answer the congregation's questions so thoroughly that there will be little need for amendments. It is important that a policy for holding long-term gifts be as stable as possible to instill confidence and credibility. Changes should be allowed only after approval of at least a two-thirds or three-fourths majority in the governing body and congregation.

Next, the policy should address suggested uses of designated gifts. The use of those gifts must conform to church goals and values. Generally, congregations will want to encourage undesignated gifts for greater flexibility. This option can be effectively presented with a well-written policy that carefully specifies how the funds will be used.

Lastly, policies governing the investment of funds are crucial. The investment policy should be pre-determined to avoid later congregational concerns and the personal liability of fund administrators. Because it is rare that every church will have professionally qualified investment managers as members, an outside group should be given this responsibility. Probably every denomination has experts on its general church staff who can help with investments; by using church-related investment experts, the special concerns of the church can be accommodated. Generally, the resources of a foundation will be available through your denomination, and this foundation will use a leading investment firm and return to the investor regular income plus growth of the principal.

There can be many different combinations of fund-earnings distribution; however, a policy should address this important issue carefully and completely. Again, this is an area where prior decisions are important, to avoid confusion or controversy later. Overall, the church mission ought to be the primary consideration in deciding how funds are designated for use. The church exists not to accumulate funds but to use them to further the witness and work of Christ.

A policy written for a healthy, active congregation might specify that proceeds from undesignated funds be used for local expenses, local outreach causes, in support of denominational concerns, and to retire capital improvement debt. The percentage designated for each purpose will vary with almost every congregation. But if the church is to reach out in its mission, the amount designated for local operating expenses will be minimal—maybe not more than 10–20 percent. The active membership needs to feel ownership of current operating needs and to respond to their own stewardship needs. They should not rely on endowment-fund proceeds. They then can rejoice in the opportunity to use endowment-fund earnings for extended mission needs, and if appropriate, for the retirement of capital improvement debt.

Many resources are available to assist a church in writing a good policy. The best place to start is with denominational staff experts. One can also effectively use the experience of other churches by asking them to share their policy statements. On the following page is a sample policy proposed by the Christian Church Foundation, a part of the Christian Church (Disciples of Christ).

# A Congregation's Permanent Fund Policy: A Sample

## I. Purpose:

The primary purpose of the Permanent Fund of [name of congregation] is to expand the witness and mission of Jesus Christ in the world, serving human needs in our community and around the world. It is not intended to compete with the regular annual giving of members or to diminish the opportunities for responsible stewardship by present or future members.

All assets received by the Permanent Fund shall be considered permanent. "Income" from the Permanent Fund will be spent for ministry. For purposes of this document, "income" shall refer to:

1. Dividends and interest earned on investment of Permanent Funds.

*or*

2. An annual withdrawal of _____ percent of the market value of the Permanent Fund's investment portfolio. This percentage amount shall be reviewed periodically to ascertain that the buying power of the original gift is not being deflated.

## II. Types of Gifts:

Permanent Funds are usually not memorial funds or reserve funds or building funds. A separate policy should govern these gifts.

Gifts to a congregation's Permanent Fund come in a variety of forms, including stocks, bonds, real estate, tangible property, and cash. All bequests and gifts received in any form other than cash will be converted to cash at its fair market value as soon as is practical. On some rare occasions, a church may want to refuse a gift or bequest to its Permanent Fund. This should be done by the Church Board upon the recommendation of the Permanent Fund Trustees.

All gifts designated for the Permanent Fund shall be considered permanent and therefore cannot be spent. "Income" from the Permanent Fund will be spent for ministry. Undesignated gifts in the form of bequests, the residual value of charitable trusts and charitable gift annuities, and life insurance shall be the property of the Permanent Fund.

## III. Permanent Fund Trustees:

The Permanent Fund of [name of congregation] shall be managed by at least five (5), and no more than seven (7) trustees, elected by the congregation.

Terms of office shall be for three years. They may be reelected one time, but cannot serve for more than six (6) consecutive years. The senior minister and Chair of the Board of the congregation will be ex-officio members without vote.

**THE RESPONSIBILITIES OF PERMANENT FUND TRUSTEES WILL BE TO:**

A. Meet quarterly (e.g., on the second Monday of the months of February, May, August, and November). They shall elect their officers each year (President, Vice President, Secretary/Treasurer) from the trustees as needed.

B. Publicize the fund to the congregation, sponsor "planned giving seminars," contact prospective donors, and promote other activities which will bring growth in the Permanent Fund.

C. Provide a written annual report to the Church Board and Congregation which shall include a list of new gifts received, income received, and total value of the Permanent Fund.

D. Trustees shall not have responsibility for the expenditure of income from the Permanent Fund. Trustees will provide the income from the fund to the Stewardship and Finance Department of the congregation for expenditure according to item IV (income distribution).

E. Trustees shall have responsibility for investing the corpus of the Permanent Fund, subject to the confirmation of the Church Board. It is recommended that an agency of the Christian Church (Disciples of Christ), such as the Christian Church Foundation, Inc., or the Board of Church Extension, be considered to manage all or part of the Permanent Fund.

F. Although it is not required, trustees are encouraged to make provisions in their own financial planning to provide a gift to the Permanent Fund of [name of congregation].

## IV. Income Distribution:

A. "Income" from designated gifts will be distributed according to the donor's instructions.

B. Unrestricted "income" will be distributed as follows:*

1. 10 percent will be spent according to the recommendation of the Stewardship Committee with the confirmation of the Church Board. However, support to the operational budget may never represent an amount greater than 20 percent of the total operational budget.

2. 50 percent will be designated for outreach causes and transferred to the Outreach Committee for expenditure. These funds will not be considered as part of the regular budget expenditure for outreach causes. The Outreach Committee will report to the Church Board within six months concerning these expenditures.

3. 30 percent will be designated for retirement of outstanding debt(s) on congregational properties. If the congregation has no debt, then this 30 percent will be distributed according to items 1 and 2 above, or directed to a "reserve fund" to meet future capital needs.

4. 10 percent will be given to regional programs and causes, including a direct donation to the regional office.

* The percentages in each category are only examples and they may be changed to fit the needs and goals of any local congregation. We advise that a local congregation spend no more than 10–20 percent of permanent fund "income" to meet local expenses; the example in item IV is a way for a local congregation to do this.

## V. Amending Procedures:

The policy may be amended by a three-fourths majority vote of the Church Board at two successive meetings upon published written notice of proposed changes to the Board Members at least two weeks prior to the first meeting. Reasons to amend may be catastrophic events such as earthquakes, fires, or floods.

## VI. Termination:

In the event that [name of congregation] should terminate its ministry, the assets of the Permanent Fund shall be transferred to the Christian Church Foundation, Inc., of the Christian Church (Disciples of Christ) with instructions concerning distribution of future "income."

This sample policy was developed for use by congregations of the Christian Church (Disciples of Christ) by the Christian Church Foundation, Inc.[7]

Special project gifts and memorials are essential sources of additional income for a church, especially as it plans for capital improvement. As is true in so many other areas of church administration, it is equally important that a systematic program for special gifts and memorials be established and administered if members are to respond positively. Whether a church uses the following or similar forms to account for special gifts or memorials, it is imperative that they use something. Again, the church's financial integrity is at stake. Members want and have a right to know their funds are being used as they designate.

*Brochure: Gifts and memorials.* Pages 65–70 present a sample brochure that does an outstanding job of communicating to prospective givers how gifts or memorials may be given in support of items needed for a new church. Notice how well organized and professional the brochure is, how items are numbered, how an amount is associated with the item, and how other needed information is included to help donors toward a positive decision.

*Acknowledgment letters.* On page 71 is an example of a letter used to acknowledge gifts. Note how the letter carefully specifies how the gift is being used and confirms the wishes of the donor. Letters such as these are important not only to the donor but also to the church as a way of documenting that the correct action has been taken on each gift.

*Memorial fund recap form.* On page 72 is a document which formally records the gift in church records. Of course, the same basic information could be maintained in a computer database for longer-term retention. Note that this form serves also as a "checklist" to ensure all administrative functions related to the gift are performed.

*Designated memorial gifts form.* A form used to list individual gifts designated for specific items in the brochure is shown on page 73. This list can serve as a record of gifts pledged as well as actual gifts made. Again, this form easily could be computerized.

*Sample Brochure*

# GIFTS AND MEMORIALS

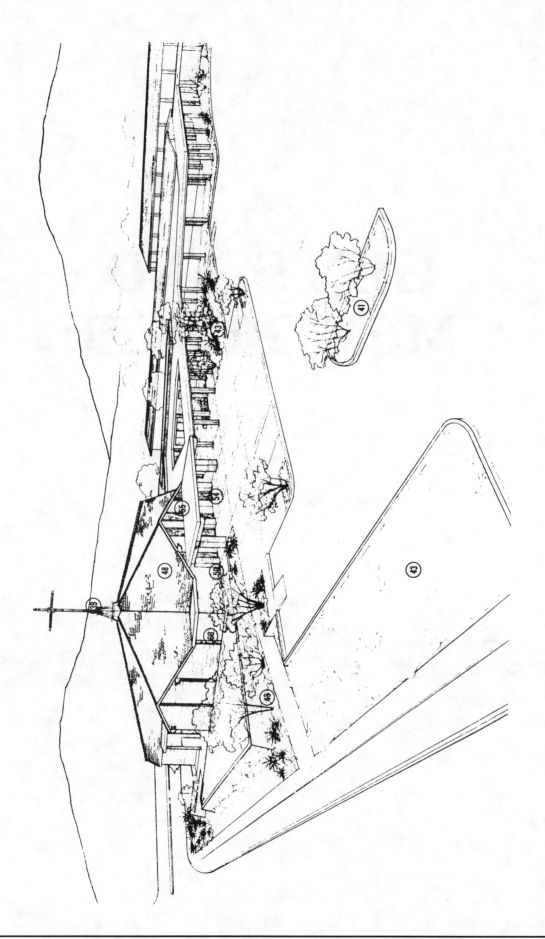

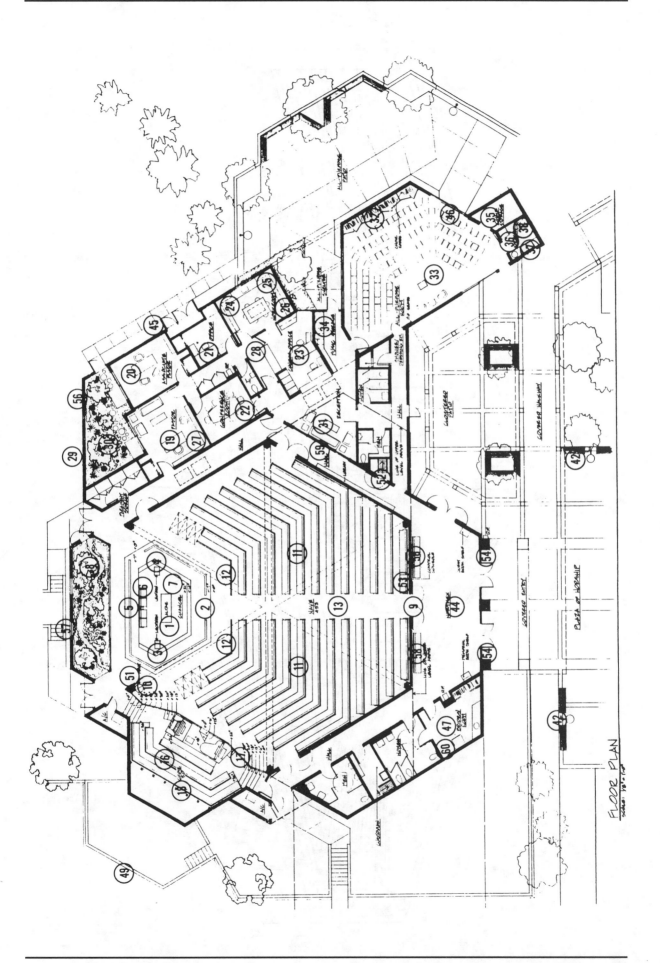

FLOOR PLAN

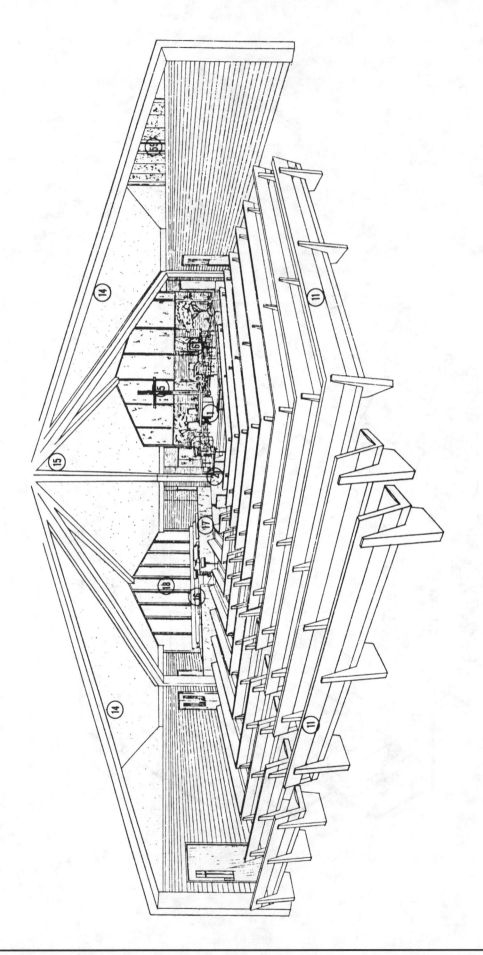

This brochure has been prepared to explain how gifts and memorials may be given. The items available, and their costs, are listed below. Each item is numbered, and its corresponding number on the drawings indicates its location. In the case of multiple items (windows, pews, etc.), one or more may be given. The cost listed for most items attempts to include a portion of the cost necessary to that item's installation.

# SUGGESTED MEMORIAL LIST

## CHANCEL AND WORSHIP

| | | |
|---|---|---:|
| 1. | Altar (to be custom carved) .......... $ | 3,000 |
| 2. | Communion Rail .................... | 2,500 |
| 3. | Pulpit ............................ | 700 |
| 4. | Lectern ........................... | 500 |
| 5. | Chancel Cross ..................... | 1,500 |
| 6. | Clergy Seats (4 required) each ....... | 500 |
| 7. | Chancel Carpet .................... | 9,500 |
| 8. | Chancel Garden .................... | 8,000 |

## NAVE

| | | |
|---|---|---:|
| 9. | Nave Doors (to be custom carved) ... $ | 5,000 |
| 10. | Baptismal Font .................... | 800 |
| 11. | Nave Pews (24 required) each ....... | 1,200 |
| 12. | Pew Screens (2 required) each ....... | 1,200 |
| 13. | Nave Carpet ....................... | 9,000 |
| 14. | Recessed Lights (58 required) each ... | 250 |
| 15. | Spot Lights (14 required) each ....... | 300 |

## CHOIR

| | | |
|---|---|---:|
| 16. | Choir Pews (3 required) each ........ $ | 900 |
| 17. | Choir Screen ...................... | 2,300 |
| 18. | Organ Grille ...................... | 2,000 |

## ADMINISTRATION FURNISHINGS

| | | |
|---|---|---:|
| 19. | Pastor's Office .................... $ | 3,000 |
| 20. | Associate Pastor's Office ............ | 2,000 |
| 21. | Office ............................ | 1,000 |
| 22. | Conference Room .................. | 2,400 |
| 23. | Church Office ..................... | 1,700 |

## ADMINISTRATION UNIT

| | | |
|---|---|---:|
| 24. | Countertops ...................... $ | 1,200 |
| 25. | Base Cabinets ..................... | 3,000 |
| 26. | Wall Cabinets ..................... | 2,000 |
| 27. | Book Shelves ...................... | 1,300 |
| 28. | Carpeting ......................... | 2,500 |
| 29. | Garden Grille ..................... | 1,800 |
| 30. | Garden Landscaping ............... | 1,500 |

## RECEPTION ROOM

| | | |
|---|---|---:|
| 31. | Furnishings ....................... $ | 1,500 |

## ALL-PURPOSE BUILDING FURNISHINGS

| | | |
|---|---|---:|
| 32. | Choir Robe Cabinets (4 required) each $ | 250 |
| 33. | Carpeting ......................... | 1,900 |
| 34. | Music Storage Cabinet ............. | 700 |
| 35. | Chair and Table Storage Room ...... | 3,000 |
| 36. | Kitchen Base Cabinets ............. | 700 |
| 37. | Kitchen Wall Cabinets ............. | 550 |
| 38. | Kitchen Equipment ................ | 1,500 |

## EXTERIOR

| | | |
|---|---|---:|
| 39. | Spire Cross and Crown ............ $ | 5,000 |
| 40. | Item Omitted ...................... | 0 |
| 41. | Parking Light Standards (14 req.) each | 1,000 |
| 42. | Plaza Benches (2 required) each ....... | 600 |
| 43. | Landscaping ...................... | 27,000 |

## ADDITIONAL ITEMS

| | | |
|---|---|---:|
| 44. | Church Narthex ................... $ | 65,000 |
| 45. | Administration Wing ............... | 125,000 |
| 46. | Chapel and All-Purpose Room ....... | 75,000 |
| 47. | Bride's Room ..................... | 10,000 |
| 48. | Tile Roof ......................... | 10,000 |
| 49. | Corner Sign and Wall .............. | 7,500 |
| 50. | Dedication Stone and Box .......... | 400 |
| 51. | Eternal Light and Counterweight ..... | 965 |
| 52. | Sound System ..................... | 6,000 |
| 53. | Control Console .................. | 500 |

## FACETED GLASS WINDOWS

| | | |
|---|---|---:|
| 54. | Narthex (Lower Window) (4 req.) each $ | 3,000 |
| 55. | Narthex (Upper Window) (2 req.) each | 2,000 |
| 56. | Pastor's Garden Wall .............. | 2,000 |
| 57. | Chancel Garden Wall (2 req.) each ... | 2,000 |
| 58. | Nave South Clerestory (2 req.) each | 3,800 |
| 59. | Nave East Clerestory (2 req.) each ... | 3,800 |
| 60. | Bride's Room ..................... | 800 |

**FOR FURTHER INFORMATION,** or to arrange a conference with a member of the Building Committee, call the Chairperson at her home. A meeting may also be arranged through a call to the church office.

To assure that all items will blend with the design and architecture of the new buildings, and to avoid duplication, all designated gifts and memorials must be arranged through this committee.

Memorials and designated gifts may be made now in cash, or paid over a period of the next few months. The memorial gifts program should be concluded by the end of the calendar year, or sooner, as commitments are completed. All gifts are tax deductible.

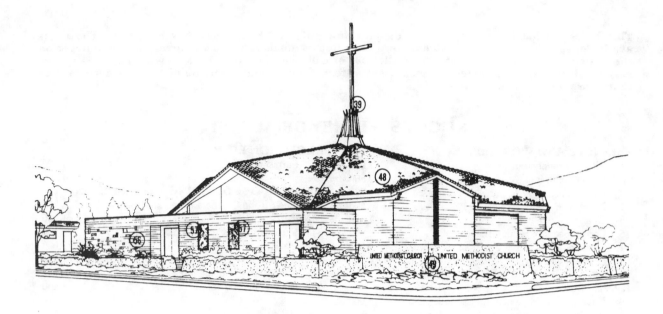

Memorials and gifts to the facilities of the family church have long been a most thoughtful and lasting way for Christians to cherish the memory of their loved ones, and to honor friends or relatives. Such an opportunity is now ours at the church.

The spiritual beauty of a sanctuary is enhanced by its material furnishings. Each item of church furniture, each window, each thing used or observed through the order of worship, adds its voice to a hymn of praise to God. Each item and building used for worship, for administration and for Christian education, helps meet the spiritual needs of today and tomorrow.

Every member, or other church friend - every family - in our church, has the opportunity to share in this program of beautification. The need for a memorial and living gifts program is a real one for both the church and its people. For just as we would exalt God by the living of our spiritual lives, so we would praise God through the material furnishings and fixtures which beautify our new sanctuary, our chapel and our administration unit.

Those who wish to make designated gifts in the memory of loved ones, or living gifts in honor of loved ones still in our midst, will have a part in our worship, Christian education and administration for years to come. A Book of Remembrance will be placed on permanent display in the narthex of the sanctuary. In it will be displayed the names of donors, the item given, and the names of those memorialized or honored.

When persons are unable to purchase complete items, because of their cost, several persons could combine their resources to provide a memorial item.

Checks should be made payable to the Gifts and Memorials Building Committee.

## *Sample Acknowledgment Letter*

[Date]


Jim and Laura Smith
5678 Any Street
Any City, ST 55555


Dear Jim and Laura,

Thank you for designating the use of the Cindy Smith Memorial Fund for a video player to be used in our Sunday school.

Your willingness to do this is greatly appreciated and will be a great help to the Christian education program at our church.

The memory of Cindy is very precious to all of us. The use of the fund in this way provides a continuing reminder to us of her presence when she was teaching Sunday school at our church.


Sincerely,


Pastor Brown

## MEMORIAL FUND RECAPITULATION AND DISTRIBUTION

1. Date_____

2. Memorial/Honor Fund Name_____

3. In Memory/Honor of_____

4. Memorial Item(s) chosen _____

5. Donor (If not item #2)_____

6. Amount $_____

7. Source(s)_____

8. Received $_____

9. Balance Due On Item (if any) $_____

10. Acknowledged Total Gift Designation In Letter - Date/Copy of Letter _____

11. Cash Added (In addition to above Memorial/Honor Fund(s)_____

12. Memorial/Honor Fund Amount_____

13. Letter Asking For Permission To Designate Fund and Reply_____

## Designated Memorial Gifts

| No. | Item | Date | Name | Price | Rec'd to date | Balance | Letter |
|-----|------|------|------|-------|---------------|---------|--------|
|     |      |      |      |       |               |         |        |
|     |      |      |      |       |               |         |        |
|     |      |      |      |       |               |         |        |
|     |      |      |      |       |               |         |        |
|     |      |      |      |       |               |         |        |
|     |      |      |      |       |               |         |        |
|     |      |      |      |       |               |         |        |
|     |      |      |      |       |               |         |        |
|     |      |      |      |       |               |         |        |
|     |      |      |      |       |               |         |        |
|     |      |      |      |       |               |         |        |
|     |      |      |      |       |               |         |        |
|     |      |      |      |       |               |         |        |
|     |      |      |      |       |               |         |        |
|     |      |      |      |       |               |         |        |
|     |      |      |      |       |               |         |        |
|     |      |      |      |       |               |         |        |
|     |      |      |      |       |               |         |        |
|     |      |      |      |       |               |         |        |

## CAPITAL FUNDS PROGRAM PLANNING

One of the most important planning efforts in which any church can be involved is for new capital to build and/or improve facilities. Of course, a highly significant part of this planning will be answering, *"Where will the money come from?"*

Any capital funds program must be aimed toward a visible, worthy need which motivates member support. Experience shows that members support capital campaigns most readily if they are for a sanctuary; they see the sanctuary as the central facility for worship and thus essential to church life. Next, members will support education facilities or a fellowship hall as places for family activities. They may be less interested in supporting ministerial housing, a parking lot, or an organ because these needs do not seem as necessary. ("We've been doing fine with what we have.") The area which receives the least support is debt retirement. Many churches insist that members "invest up front" for capital needs. Members find it difficult to get excited about paying voluntarily for something they already have.

A capital funds program goal must be carefully set if it is to be attained. Congregations vary considerably in how they perceive themselves; that is, one church may be very active and alive while another one may be dying on the vine. To gauge the commitment of the congregation, compare the total actual giving of individuals to the following:

- If the congregation sees itself as highly mission-oriented and active—a real mover and shaker and a "superb" church—then in three years it should raise in capital funds three times what was given the year before for operational support.

- If the congregation believes it is doing well and it is basically a "happy" church— one which can fight, hug, make up, and so forth—then in three years it should raise in capital funds two times what was given the year before for operational support.

- If the congregation is "unhappy" and there is frequent conflict or only tolerable acceptance, then in three years it may raise an equivalent amount in capital funds to what was given the year before for operational support.

For most any building or major improvement project, a church usually will need to have one-third of the total cost in cash, one-third in pledges, and one-third in borrowed money. As a broad general guide to planning, in most programs *20 percent of the people will give 80 percent of the money.* This will certainly be true of a church's first capital program.

Some additional general planning guidelines: about 66 percent of the congregation will commit to a capital program. Thus, *34 percent of the congregation gives nothing.* Of the 66 percent who give:

- 3 percent give the first 25 percent

- 10 percent give the second 25 percent

- 20 percent give the third 25 percent

- 67 percent give the fourth 25 percent

Knowing these background generalizations, church leaders can plan the capital campaign around how the congregation perceives itself in light of the planning guidelines noted above. A later section of this manual presents more details on capital funds programs and stewardship in general.

## Project and Event Planning in the Local Church

### Introduction

As we again reflect on the Nehemiah story and consider the implications of our mission objectives, action plans, and financial support, one readily realizes that successful projects and events normally occur in the local church only after careful planning.

Here we will look at some examples of project- and event-tracking aids and see how they facilitate planning and satisfactory completion of work (see pages 77–79). Next we present some specific aids to help in church property acquisition and construction, beginning on page 80. A property acquisition checklist and advice to a building committee, both prepared by an architectural firm which specializes in church building, will be of special interest. The sample building loan proposal will demonstrate the type of documentation expected by lending institutions. The sample form for a volunteer-talent search demonstrates the type of activities which may be done by volunteers, saving considerable amounts in construction costs.

Church administrative processes benefit from computerization as long as the transition from manual records to computer records is well planned. Does the basic manual system work well, and what parts of it will benefit from computerization? Is equipment being considered suitable for long-term uses? Will it meet future needs? Are software programs being considered those that best fit the church's needs? All these questions and many more should be considered when planning for computerization (see pages 95–97).

Growth is a desirable goal of many churches. However, careful planning must take place if a church is to grow in a viable way. Lessons learned by one such church are presented beginning on page 99, followed by a brochure on page 103 that outlines the results of a study about why some churches have succeeded in growing in an environment of membership decline in mainline churches.

A congregation can ease the effects of a pastoral change for both itself and the pastor if it is prepared with data about the church and its activities. Beginning on page 110 is a guide, in checklist form, of considerations and concerns which should be addressed.

Other examples of project and event planning could be presented, but we believe the examples here will demonstrate the need for careful planning, and direct attention to areas in your own church that can be enhanced through an organized planning process.

### Aids for Planning

*Action plans in chart format.* On page 77 is one example of an action plan in chart form. The advantage of this type of presentation is that all actions and their relationship to other actions are seen at a glance.

In this example, the start-up of a preschool is planned and charted. This chart can serve as the top sheet to the total plan and detail what needs to be done and at what time. A more detailed action plan, similar to the example on page 20, is also necessary, not only to expand on the actions required, but to indicate the person or persons responsible, to establish objectives if applicable, and to estimate financial impact.

Any action plan, whether presented as a chart, narrative, or in any other form, needs periodic review to track progress. In the preschool project example, a monthly formal review might be appropriate. There are always ongoing informal reviews as the people responsible discuss the project on a daily basis, but these should be a supplement to and not a substitute for a periodic formal review. In the preschool project example, the formal review is scheduled for February. An *X* is placed on the continuum line for each appropriate action item. If the *X* appears shown in February, the item is on schedule. If the *X* appears in March or later, as in items 3 and 11, these are ahead of schedule. When the *X* appears in January or earlier, as in items 6 and 7, major discussion is necessary to determine how these items can be brought back on schedule. Action items marked with a *C*, as in items 5 and 17, are complete. A new chart, with new *X*s and *C*s, is prepared for each monthly formal review.

*Event planning.* The event planning sheet on page 78 aids in the planning of activities, programs, projects, special day events, and so forth. The primary purpose of this type of planning aid is to prompt the planner to consider various needs that will help make the event run smoothly and be successful. Quite often, critical needs are overlooked until the last minute, causing panic, stress, and often conflict. This sheet assures that the essential tasks are not overlooked.

*Event evaluation.* It is important to have a post-event evaluation so that future events can be improved and better planned. The evaluation sheet on page 79 contains the types of questions that might be asked of participants.

# Time-line for Organizing a Preschool

**Progress Report for February**

| | Sept. | Oct. | Nov. | Dec. | Jan. | Feb. | March | April | May | June | July |
|---|---|---|---|---|---|---|---|---|---|---|---|
| 1. Licensing | | | | | | X | | | | | |
| 2. Bylaws and Operating Guide Policies and Procedures | | | | | | X | | | | | |
| 3. Job Descriptions | | | | | | X | | | | | |
| 4. Personnel Policies | | | | | | X | | X | | | |
| 5. Selection of Director | | | | C | | | | | | | |
| 6. Develop Program | | | | | X | | | | | | |
| 7. Prepare Annual Budget and Set of Books | | | | | X | X | | | | | |
| 8. Establish Bank Account | | | | | | | | | | | |
| 9. Insurance | | | | | | | | | | | |
| 10. Major Purchases (equipment and supplies)/Inventory | | | | | | X | | | | | |
| 11. Staff Handbook | | | | | | | X | | | | |
| 12. Advertise and Screen Applicants for Staff | | | | | | X | | | | | |
| 13. Orientation and In-service Training for Employees | | | | | | | | | | | |
| 14. Develop Publicity Campaign (Brochure-advertisement) | | | | | | X | | | | | |
| 15. Enrollment Forms and Children's Records | | | | | | X | | | | | |
| 16. Parent Handbook | | | | | | X | | | | | |
| 17. Hiring or Use of Outside Professional Services | | | C | | | X | | | | | |
| 18. General Maintenance/Color Scheme | | | | | | | | | | | |
| 19. File for Fictitous Business Name | | | | | | | | | | | |

## EVENT PLANNING SHEET

EVENT: _____  DATE(s) _____

PLACE/ROOM(s) _____  TIME(s) _____

Goals and objectives: _____

_____

_____

PERSON RESPONSIBLE: _____

Other Workers: _____

_____

OTHER GROUPS INVOLVED _____

PROGRAM OF (circle)   LOCAL CHURCH   DISTRICT   CONFERENCE   GENERAL CHURCH   ECUMENICAL

### PUBLICITY

Person in charge: _____   Date needed: _____

IN CHURCH (circle)
 HERALD   ORDER OF WORSHIP   POSTERS   ANNOUNCEMENTS

PUBLIC MEDIA (circle)
 ENTERPRISE   DAILY NEWS   CIRCUIT WEST   POSTERS   OTHER

| MATERIALS/EQUIPMENT Needed | RESPONSIBLE PERSON(s) | DATES | |
| --- | --- | --- | --- |
| (Films, Speakers, Books, Supplies, Tools, Mailings, Handouts, A.V. Equip.) | | Begin | Complete |
| | | | |
| | | | |
| | | | |
| | | | |
| | | | |
| | | | |

### PLANNING MEETINGS

| PURPOSE OF MEETING | Date | Who Should Attend |
| --- | --- | --- |
| | | |
| | | |
| | | |
| | | |

CLEANUP AND RESTORATION TO BE COMPLETED BY   Date _____ Time _____
RESPONSIBLE PERSON(s) _____

BUDGET INFORMATION: Estimated Cost _____  Estimated Income _____

COMMENTS: _____

_____

_____

## Evaluation Sheet

1. Name of Event: _____ Date: _____

2. What was your general impression of this event?

   _____

   _____

3. Do you think the goals for this event were achieved? Why or why not?

   _____

   _____

4. What did you find most helpful or enjoyable?

   _____

   _____

5. What was not very helpful or enjoyable?

   _____

   _____

6. What changes would you suggest be made in the future?

   _____

   _____

7. Do you recommend this event be continued?   ❏ Yes   ❏ No

8. Other comments?

   _____

   _____

   _____

   _____

   _____

Name (if you wish): _____

## Property Acquisition and Construction

Perhaps some of the most important and often most extensive projects undertaken by a church are property acquisition and construction. Here, almost more than anywhere else, extremely careful planning is needed.

A property acquisition checklist that should be used when a church contemplates a purchase of land appears on pages 81–83. Investigation into and planning for the various factors noted can save money and headaches. This checklist was prepared by an architectural firm[8] and is based on its experience in the construction of more than three hundred churches in Southern California. While some of the items on the checklist may be unique to Southern California, most of these factors should apply anywhere in the United States. However, before making a purchase, it would be well to determine if there may be additional factors unique to your area.

Beginning on page 84 is a paper prepared by the same architectural firm mentioned above, offering some sage, if not "tongue-in-cheek," advice about how building committees can be most effective.

The report presented on pages 89–93 contains the type of information that will be required by a financial institution or denominational financing source before it considers providing funds for land acquisition and/or construction. This same or a similar document can also be used as an information piece for a congregation trying to generate support for the project. While this document provides basic background information, which can have multiple uses, one must realize that financial institutions may have their own forms and requirements that will need to be completed.

Churches can often save considerably on construction costs by using the talents in a congregation. The form on page 94 provides an opportunity for volunteers to present their skills and willingness to participate in the building project. During the construction of a sanctuary at the church served by one of the authors, $300,000 was saved in labor costs on a building project that totaled $1,500,000, a 20 percent cost reduction. Perhaps even more important than this substantial saving was the congregational involvement, support, and ownership in the building project. This latter benefit will last for years as people enter the sanctuary and are pleasantly reminded that they were involved in a portion of the construction.

# PROPERTY ACQUISITION CHECK LIST

| Undev. Land | Developed Land | |
|:---:|:---:|---|
| ✱ | ✱ | Consult an Architect. |
| ✱ | ✱ | EXISTING BUILDING / LAND - Will the building and/or land accommodate the current needs and anticipated future growth?  Would the building and/or land that is being purchased be attractive to a another buyer in the future? |
| ✱ | | ENVIRONMENTAL IMPACT REPORT (EIR) - If there is any possibility that the site would present a problem  from an environmental point of view, a large scale project, habitat of protected species, etc., then one of the conditions of purchasing the property should be a favorable EIR. |
| ✱ | ✱ | ENVIRONMENTAL SITE ASSESSMENT - One of the conditions of purchasing the property should be a favorable Environmental Site Assessment.  This is to assess the potential for existing soil or ground water contamination resulting from human activities.  If the assessment indicates potential contamination, then actual borings can be made to establish the type and extent of the contamination.<br><br>Some lending institutions are requiring this type of assessment prior to finalizing a loan.<br><br>(A hospital bought a building and land on which another hospital had been built.  Diesel fuel soil contamination was discovered several years after the purchase was made.  Contamination resulted from a leaking pipe.  State mandates that the soil be brought to a particular level of lack of contamination.  In the this case, the decontamination process has cost nearly $3 million, is not complete and could go to about $5 million.  If the hospital is not able to negotiate a lesser standard of contamination, the cost could run to $10 million or more.  Current cash outlay is in excess of $100,000 per month.) |
| ✱<br>(2)<br>(3) | ✱<br>(2)<br>(3) | SOILS REPORT - This will be required to obtain a Building Permit if new buildings are to be constructed.  The Architect will provide the locations of proposed buildings and anticipated loads of the building to the soils engineering firm. |
| ✱<br>(2)<br>(3) | ✱<br>(2)<br>(3) | GEOLOGY REPORT - Normally not required except by some governmental agencies where extensive earthwork has been performed or where the soil is historically unstable. |

| Undev. Land | Developed Land | |
|---|---|---|
| ✱ (3) | ✱ (3) | SURVEY - This will be required if new buildings are to be constructed. It should include site boundaries, land contours, buildings, easements, rights-of-way, utilities, etc. |
| ✱ | ✱ | EASEMENTS - Utility companies and others may have recorded easements through a site. These should be determined prior to finalizing the purchase because it may severely restrict the portion of the site that can be developed. |
| ✱ | ✱ | RIGHTS-OF-WAY   Public agencies may have rights-of-way for future improvements adjacent to or through the site. These should be determined prior to finalizing the purchase because the right-of-way may result in a piece of property that is too small, cut up, and/or irregularly shaped that cannot be properly developed. |
| ✱ | ✱ | DEDICATIONS OF LAND - Local governmental agencies may require that land for future improvements be dedicated to the City, County, etc. These should be determined prior to finalizing the purchase because the dedicated land will reduce the property size and may result in property that is too small to be properly developed. |
| ✱ | ✱ | ZONING - Very few localities will allow a church to be built without a Conditional Use Permit (CUP), Special Use Permit (SUP), etc. Check with the local Zoning Department to determine the zoning, and if a CUP/SUP will be required. |
| ✱ | | DEVELOPMENT COSTS - Local Governmental agencies may require that the first developer in a new area pay for all of the public development (streets, underground utilities, fire hydrants, etc.). As adjacent property is developed, the original developer is reimbursed proportionately by subsequent developers. This work would be very costly. The reimbursement would occur at the time of subsequent developments, immediately or years later. |
| ✱ | ✱ | FIRE SERVICE - Is there adequate water pressure to meet the minimum requirements of the Fire Department? In newer areas and urban areas, this is generally not a problem. In old areas and rural areas without water lines or undersized and deteriorated water lines, this could be a problem. |
| ✱ | ✱ | DESIGN RESTRICTIONS - Some communities and in certain areas of some communities the architectural style is dictated by local ordinances. Is the required architectural style acceptable? Will the required architectural style add considerable cost to the building? |
| | ✱ | BUILDING DEMOLITION - Many older buildings are either historically and/or architecturally significant. Is it possible to demolish the building simply by obtaining a demolition permit? Is a lengthy and costly review process going to be required? |

| Undev. Land | Developed Land | |
|---|---|---|
| * | | **BUILDING REMODELING** Many older buildings are either historically and/or architecturally significant. Is it possible to remodel the building, interior, and/or exterior, to fit the proposed use by simply obtaining a building permit? Is a lengthy and costly review process going to be required? |
| * | | **BUILDING REUSE** An existing building that will be reused should be inspected to determine the condition of all of the building elements. What elements of the building are approaching their useful life? What will it cost to maintain or replace these elements in the near future |
| * | | **ASBESTOS** - Asbestos removal and/or encapsulation can be very expensive and buildings built before 1975 will certainly have asbestos containing materials (ACM), unless they have previously been removed. This would include vinyl asbestos tile in the floor.<br><br>If ACM's have been encapsulated or not removed, any remodeling and/or additions will have to deal with the ACM's and the associated additional costs.<br><br>If the building is to be demolished, the materials in the building will first have to be tested and any ACM's removed and properly disposed of prior to a demolition permit being issued. |
| * | | **EXISTING MASONRY BUILDING** - Since 1933. the Building Code has had several major revisions regarding structural design of masonry buildings. When purchasing developed land with a masonry building that will be reused, it would be wise to have a structural review done. The review will determine the extent of structural upgrading required and the potential cost involved. |
| *<br>(3) | *<br>(3) | **CHEAP LAND AND/OR BUILDING** - Be suspicious. What were the previous uses: uncontrolled dump, pottery manufacturing, service station, plating factory, etc.? Are many of the building materials asbestos containing materials?<br><br>All of these items would result in very expensive site work, removal of contamination, and removal/encapsulation of ACM'S. |

Footnotes:

(1)   An EIR may be required even on a site that is already developed. This requirement would be based on local regulations and/or the size of the project.

(2)   If the soil, geological formations, or those in the surrounding area do not appear normal, it would be wise to have some testing done prior to purchasing the site.

(3)   If the land is being offered at a bargain basement price - be suspicious. It may be necessary to have soils testing, geological testing, and a survey performed to determine if there are problems with the site. This should be done prior to purchasing the site.

Prepared by: CULVER HEATON, FAIA, THOMAS ZARTL, AIA & ASSOC., ARCHITECTS
Pasadena, CA

## "DON'T BE A BUNGLING BUILDING COMMITTEE"

Church building programs face a dilemma in the form of a constantly rising cost of construction and a constantly growing need for church facilities.

On each new project the architect faces a committee which has requirements twice those that can be met by the budget available. The committee doesn't need an architect. What it needs is a genie. The better solution seems to be a businesslike approach to the problem. Both parties must understand their duties and obligations. Beautiful, worshipful, economical structures can be built by talented architects working with sensible committees.

The Mephistopheles who tempts all building committees is "cost per square foot." Committees use this phrase rather freely, but to each person it means a different thing. Let us consider what this measure of cost includes. Starting from the site preparation and excavation, the measure is used to price the foundations, floors, structure of walls, roof, ceiling, wall finishes, ceiling finishes, electrical system, heating system, air conditioning, painting, ornamentation, masonry work, and sculpture—all the way to the final washing of the windows.

Each one of these items is highly variable in cost. For instance, what finish do we mean when we say concrete floor? For 60 cents a square foot, we can cover it with chemical stain and wax. For 75 cents a square foot, we can dust on a color hardener and apply wax, or over the concrete slab we can apply vinyl composition floor covering at $1.65 a square foot. If we wish to provide glue-down carpet over the slab, this could be done for $2.50 a square foot. If we wish to include a colored admix in the concrete when it is poured and then apply a colored wax surface, it will cost $3.25 per square foot. Oak parquet floor panels can be applied over the concrete at $4.60 a square foot; a resilient maple gymnasium floor with a steel suspension system applied over the concrete slab is $7.60 a square foot. Or if we would like to have marble terrazzo, it can be applied over the slab at $10.00 a square foot. Note how the cost has increased from 60 cents to $10.00 per square foot on the flooring alone! This is an increase 16 times greater than the original flooring.

When one says that a building costs a certain amount per square foot, each person on the committee has a different idea of what is involved. Proceeding in such a manner can result only in misunderstanding.

I heard recently of a project that had an ample budget of $600,000. When the bids were opened, the low bid was over $1,000,000. How can this state of affairs be prevented? The answer is: know what you are talking about; know what everyone is talking about; finally, get them all to agree and then proceed in a businesslike manner.

It is my belief that an architect does not design a building. The architect and the owner, through teamwork, produce a successful building, and the preliminary design is a good place to start. If you ask the average owners what they want in a building, the response will be, "As much as our funds will buy." In other words, they are not prepared with a well-thought-out answer. Ask contractors how much a building is going to cost and they will tell you to decide what you want. Show them working drawings and they will tell you accurately. This is much too late, however. The committee and the architect need this information in the first design phase to avoid disaster. In my experience I have found it satisfactory to proceed as follows:

1. Prepare a site analysis before the preliminary drawings are undertaken. The purpose of this is to create a master plan of the entire site in general terms.

2. Establish on a superficial basis a unit cost for each of the elements, explaining carefully to the committee that this is not the detailed cost estimate; the only purpose of this step is to make the committee realize that the three buildings they were talking about are going to cost $600,000 instead of the $300,000 they actually have to spend. This is the proper time to start to be realistic and to concentrate on those elements that are actually within your budget. With this resolved, the committee is ready to get down to business.

3. Following the site analysis, preparation of the preliminary drawings should start on the adjusted program. During this stage of the work, every element of the design is carefully considered and reconsidered until all the teaching, recreational, and worship elements of the program are incorporated into the plans.

   During the preliminary drawing stage, the architectural design of the exterior and interior of the building is carefully worked out, and the materials for the walls, floors, and ceilings are determined. Problems of heating, ventilation, and lighting are also resolved. Upon completion of preliminary drawings, we have all the information regarding structure and the materials, but lack, of course, the working drawings with which to build.

4. At this point, it is imperative that a detailed cost estimate of the entire project be prepared. To undertake such a breakdown of materials and equipment will require an early decision on their type and quality, and will take the committee from the area of generalities to specifics.

5. The resulting estimate, in all probability, will be too high, but is not this the proper time to find it out? No expensive working drawings have been prepared, no embarrassing announcement has been made to the congregation, and all the elements in the estimate are in writing, so that the committee can analyze each of the parts that make up the total estimated price.

6. Now the committee is in a position to participate as a member of the designing team. Each element of the cost estimate can be scrutinized in relation to the cost of the whole project. The member who previously insisted on an improbable request now understands. Experience has taught me that nothing will make realists out of a building committee faster than showing them the total cost estimate! From that point on, there is total cooperation, and the materials and details that were indispensable a short time before suddenly take on a new look.

   The completed preliminary cost estimate has two main parts:

   a. In addition to the building shell itself, the following items must be carefully itemized:

      (1) Specific items of roofing, such as tile, shakes, or metal.

      (2) Unusual wall materials such as face brick or stone.

      (3) The extent of carpeting or other custom flooring material.

(4) The amount of air conditioning involved.

(5) Special artwork or decorative treatment.

(6) Special teaching equipment, such as chalkboards and tackboards, or visual aids.

(7) Church furniture: altars, pulpits, church seating, and pews.

(8) Classroom seating and tables.

(9) Office furniture and cabinets.

(10) Kitchen equipment and cabinets.

(11) Space dividers and moving walls for teaching and fellowship areas.

(12) The type of flooring to be used in the gymnasium.

(13) The type of athletic equipment to be included.

All of the above are very individual and should be resolved to the satisfaction of the particular committees' needs. These costs, as well as those listed below, can never be covered by a simple square foot-cost.

b. A building committee often overlooks the cost of the necessary off-site and on-site improvements required with a project, including the following:

(1) Fire hydrants that may be required by the building department.

(2) Public sidewalks, curbs, and driveway approaches.

(3) Utility services for the added load.

(4) Added parking and curbs that may be required for the added seating.

(5) Plaza and walks, walls and benches.

(6) Yard and parking lighting.

(7) Landscaping and irrigation.

(8) Church signs.

Itemized budgets must be established by the building committee on the items that are appropriate to its needs. Since all of the building and site costs are estimates, it is important that contingency plans be established in the event of cost overruns.

7. At this point, a wise architect will require written authorization from the building committee, which will state the building(s) authorized for working drawings, the estimated cost, and the date of final approval of the preliminary drawings. This businesslike precaution is a final check to avoid misunderstanding, since, if the authorization is wrong, the committee chairperson will not sign it or the architect will not accept it.

8. The architect now begins to prepare the working drawings, with the cost estimate constantly under examination by the drafting people and engineers involved to see that the work they are doing conforms to the committee's approval. The building committee continues as part of the design team by

checking the working drawings during their preparation and finally approving them for bidding purposes. It is only fair that the reader realize the problem that faces estimators. Actually, they are trying to outguess scores of subcontractors several months before the working drawings and final bids are prepared. The high and low bids turned in by the contractors will probably vary as much as 25 percent, even though they are prepared from working drawings that were studied carefully over a three-week period and after consultation with scores of subcontractors. Each of the contractors is convinced before opening of bids that its bid is lowest. Naturally, they did not undertake three weeks of work for fun. Yet there is often a large percentage of people who expect the architect, working months in advance, to outguess all the contractors, who, in the end, cannot outguess each other.

Naturally, some variance must be allowed in the committee's figures. In all probability, 15 percent is realistic. Often, building committees are apt to insist that the architect's estimate be identical with the successful contractor's bid. The architect's answer to this suggestion is to design to 85 percent of the budget. Both the architect and the committee will be ahead if they design as a team to hit the budget on the head, and then, if the low bid is slightly in excess of the budget, negotiate with the low contractor to arrive at a revised contract that equals the budget.

9. During construction, the committee can avoid costly extras by proceeding in a businesslike manner. All members should agree in advance that direct discussions with the contractor shall be limited to passing the time of day. Any complaints or criticisms regarding the contractor should be directed to the architect. Since half of the complaints on both sides are due to misunderstandings, many hurt feelings will thus be avoided; fair resolution of the remaining questions can be accomplished in a spirit of mutual respect.

10. Mutual respect can be accomplished best by fair architectural supervision. All must learn that when contractors are right, they are right, and when the owners are right, they, too, are right. Contractors who believe the myth that architects believe the owner to be right—right or wrong—and owners who believe that all contractors are villains are both outdated. Fair treatment of the contractor will gain a valuable ally on the owner-architect-contractor team.

11. Since the design process never stops, it is wise for the committee to allow itself a nominal contingency factor in excess of the contract price for changes and improvements that may become apparent as the work advances. It is imperative that any such changes be negotiated by the architect, and a change order prepared. This document should be signed by both the owner and the contractor before the work commences. Thus the committee will always know its total obligation.

12. The building committee must keep in mind its stewardship of the church's money and strive to be businesslike at all times. Even if the committee conducts its personal business affairs in an informal manner, it must be accountable for its decisions.

Each meeting should have carefully kept minutes, and each decision should result from a vote. Informal relationships with the contractor and architect should be avoided. I do not wish to imply that a building project is an unhappy experience—quite the contrary. But it is wise to remember that from preliminary drawings to completion of construction is a long period of time, and memory can be faulty.

There are two other points that will make the whole operation run more smoothly. First, a congregation cannot assimilate in a thirty-minute presentation what has taken the architect and the committee three months of painstaking effort to conceive. A congregation can best be brought up-to-date by the presentation of a series of color slides which develop, step-by-step, the problems that have faced the committee.

On one project, although a seven-acre site was available, a large group in the congregation was convinced that the church should be built on the corner. In the presentation of the preliminary drawings, it appeared that the architect agreed, but as the slides unfolded, showing the future use of the adjoining land, it was clear that the traffic and congestion would make the corner an undesirable location. In succeeding slides, each of the problems was resolved so that, in the end, when the actual committee recommendation was presented, preconceived opinions were forgotten, and the congregation was ready to give fair consideration to the committee's proposals.

Second, before any committee invests a substantial sum in securities, a careful investigation should be made of the resources and the future of the security under consideration. Proper counsel and competent financial advice should be sought, and the decision should not be based on prejudiced opinions. Likewise, in the design of your church, plan for the next century, since our hope is in the future. Respect the counsel of your architect, who is aware of the evolution that takes place in the construction industry and in the science of education.

The architect seeks, as you do, a worshipful, effective, and economical church plant, and has the ability to visualize the final result. When this is achieved, you, too, can see the success of the project and appreciate the architectural and construction talents that were brought to the project. [9]

# Sample Loan Proposal

*Purpose.* To provide external financing to supplement cash on hand for the construction of a sanctuary, administrative offices, and multipurpose room/chapel on our present site.

*History.* The congregation has been meeting continuously since 1889. After approximately forty years at another facility, the church moved to its present location in 1968.

The existing facilities are located on five acres of land donated to the church by a pioneer family in this valley. The two educational wings were moved to this property from the former property while the fellowship hall was constructed on the current site. The cost of these improvements, $252,000, was financed by The Bank of the City on a fifteen-year loan which was paid in full, and on time. The pioneer family house, located on the northwestern corner of the property, has served as church offices and as housing for the associate pastor. This structure will be removed and replaced by our new sanctuary and accompanying facilities. The house has been sold for $15,000 with the cost of removal the responsibility of the new owner.

In 1979 the previous property was sold for $155,000, and the funds were invested in certificates of deposit. These funds, now totaling over $250,000, are the financial basis for undertaking the proposed new construction.

Recently, a property-use feasibility committee presented to the membership three plans of development for the church. The resulting congregational decision was to undertake development of a plan allowing for the construction of a sanctuary, office facilities, and multipurpose room. A Special Church Conference decided to proceed with this development, incorporating an owner/builder approach, instituting a three-year building fund campaign, and establishing a building committee to initiate and coordinate these proceedings.

*Fulfillment.* The Foundation in Faith Building Fund Crusade has been completed, receiving pledges in excess of $451,000 to be paid over a period of three years. Over $200,000 of these pledges have already been received. These funds, combined with the proceeds from the sale of the previous property, as well as interest income, project the cash raised within the congregation of approximately $750,000 by the time construction is started.

During the last year, preliminary plans and working drawings have been developed with the architect. These plans indicate an estimated construction cost of $1,454,123. Based on the experience of local churches who have used an owner/builder approach in construction, we anticipate that this cost can be reduced by about 20 percent through the use of volunteer labor, donated materials, and through eliminating the need for a contractor.

The following is a breakdown of this financial information:

| | |
|---|---|
| Architect's estimate | $ 1,454,000 |
| Cost reduction—volunteer help | −300,000 |
| Foundations in Faith Crusade—received | −200,000 |
| Proceeds from previous property sale | −374,000 |
| Interest income | −25,000 |
| Other anticipated income | −80,000 |
| Contingencies | 20,000 |
| Construction loan required | $ 495,000 |
| Line of credit requested | $ 500,000 |

A line of credit in the amount of $500,000 will allow construction to start in September, with completion expected in September of the following year.

Our church has a continuing commitment to our congregation, future congregations, and to the community. It is a commitment in faith grounded in our heritage. For these reasons, we are undertaking this building project.

## Income Statement

### Current Year

| Income: | | |
|---|---:|---:|
| Giving/Donations | $353,421.72 | |
| Lease of Facility | | |
|     Child Development, Inc. | 28,612.97 | |
|     Be Free | 1,844.00 | |
|     Miscellaneous | 84.00 | |
| Interest Income | 37,441.66 | |
| Gross Income | | $421,404.35 |
| | | |
| **Expenses:** | | |
| Current Budget | | |
|     Salaries & Compensation | $ 84,350.36 | |
|     Worship Expense | 3,123.20 | |
|     Education | 5,983.01 | |
|     Church Administration | 41,887.84 | |
|     Board of Trustees | 6,959.53 | |
|     Missions | 13,554.92 | |
|     Evangelism | 263.79 | |
|     Finance | 1,502.34 | |
|     Membership | 389.90 | |
|     Parish Life | 16.79 | |
| Mortgage Retirement | 22,927.67 | |
| Building Expense | 73,190.69 | |
| Taxes | 585.28 | |
| Miscellaneous | 21,311.53 | |
| TOTAL EXPENSES | | $276,046.85 |
| **NET INCOME** | | $145,357.50 |

## STATEMENT OF CONDITION

### As of Year End

| ASSETS: | |
|---|---:|
| Cash on hand | $ 526,760.25 |
| Vehicles | 2,500.00 |
| Real Estate | 2,573,500.00 |
| Office Equipment | 60,000.00 |
| Music/Sound Equipment | 80,000.00 |
| Church Furnishings | 75,000.00 |
| Furniture (Parsonages) | 35,000.00 |
| Organ | 10,000.00 |
| Note held | 3,000.00 |
| TOTAL ASSETS | $3,365,760.25 |
| LIABILITIES | NIL |
| NET WORTH | $3,365,760.25 |
| TOTAL LIABILITIES AND NET WORTH | $3,365,760.25 |

## SCHEDULE I

Cash on hand

| | |
|---|---:|
| Bank A | $ 29,818.77 |
| Bank B account # | 21,256.46 |
| Bank B account # | 72,438.95 |
| Bank B account # | 100,000.00 |
| S&L A | 100,000.00 |
| S&L B | 100,000.00 |
| Credit Union | 103,246.07 |
| **TOTAL** | $ 526,760.25 |

## SCHEDULE II

Vehicles:

| | |
|---|---:|
| Ford Bus—24 Passenger | $ 2,500.00 |

## SCHEDULE III

Real Estate:

Church Property:
- Five Acres and Church Facility
- Built and Acquired in 1968
- Cost $252,000 (cost of construction only)
- Value $2,433,500
- Mortgage—None
- Net Value        $2,433,500.00

Pastor's Residence:
- Built and Acquired 1961
- Cost $18,500
- Value $140,000.
- Mortgage—None
- Net Value        140,000.00

Total Value Real Estate    $2,573,500.00

### *Other Appropriate Attachments:*

1. Architectural renderings of the proposed construction—floor plans, elevations, landscaping, decorating schemes, etc.

2. Architect's construction estimate.

3. Contractor quotations, if available.

4. Inventory of volunteer talent that will reduce the cost of construction by $300,000.

5. Growth history of the congregation—at least the past ten years or so.

6. Projected growth of the congregation—next ten years.

7. Financial history of giving—past ten years.

8. Projected giving—next ten years.

9. Any special uses planned for the property—day care, preschool, rental to school district, etc.

10. Projected income from these special uses.

11. Any other material that will substantiate to the lending institution the stability and financial strength of the congregation.

12. Any special forms, paperwork, or requirements of the particular financial institutions to which this proposal is being made.

# VOLUNTEER TALENT SEARCH

Name _____

Address _____

Phone No. _____

Please check "yes" or "no".  If "yes", also check correct "Degree of Skill" column.

| HERE IS WHAT I CAN DO: | YES | NO | DEGREE OF SKILL Good Fair Poor | | | WILLING TO LEARN? | CONDITION OF EQUIPMENT |
|---|---|---|---|---|---|---|---|
| Tractor Work - Grading | | | | | | | |
| Do you own a tractor? | | | | | | | |
| Foundation Form Building | | | | | | | |
| Concrete Finishing | | | | | | | |
| Framing - Walls, etc. | | | | | | | |
| Cutting Rafters | | | | | | | |
| Electrical Work - Wiring | | | | | | | |
| Rough Plumbing | | | | | | | |
| Finish Plumbing | | | | | | | |
| Finish Wiring (install fixtures) | | | | | | | |
| Lathing (paper & wire) | | | | | | | |
| Sheetrock Installation | | | | | | | |
| Drywall Taping | | | | | | | |
| Painting | | | | | | | |
| Roofing   - Shakes | | | | | | | |
| - Composition | | | | | | | |
| - Hot Mop | | | | | | | |
| Wheel Barrow Work | | | | | | | |
| Landscaping  - Trees | | | | | | | |
| - Lawns | | | | | | | |
| Sprinkler Systems | | | | | | | |
| Clean Up | | | | | | | |
| Do you have the tools for the categories you have checked? | | | | | | | |
| Food Service | | | | | | | |
| Laborer | | | | | | | |
| Other Skills _____ | | | | | | | |

AVERAGE AMOUNT OF TIME AVAILABLE TO GIVE PER WEEK _____

## Computerization

There are few events in local church administration that need to be planned for more carefully than computerization. Computers are a part of practically every church and affect all parts of a church's administrative process as well as other parts of its ministry.

The church has been a natural for computerization from the very beginning of the computer era. To name only a few, uses for computers include:

- Membership lists and profiles of members

- Lists and addresses of organization leaders

- Financial budgeting, record keeping, and reporting

- Official documentation and records

- Word processing of all types

- Church library catalog

- Any function that requires mass storage and filing/processing, calculating, typing, mailing

- Teaching opportunities of all types, using multimedia computer technology

Membership and attendance records are enhanced greatly through computerization. Member participation can be tracked more completely by activity. Pastors and the lay leadership now have access to vast amounts of information about members and their families: their talents and interests; their attendance at not only church services, but participation in other church activities; groups with which they are involved; and as many other uses as can be imagined.

Churches also are finding invaluable help from computers in financial record keeping. Estimates of giving and contributions can be easily maintained with either specially designed software or programs uniquely designed on a database. Reports to contributors are easily compiled as often as desired; many times they can be uniquely designed. Gifts made in various designated funds are easily tracked. Historical data on a contributor's giving habits can be tracked, giving stewardship committees invaluable information about future potential. Pastors can be made aware of individual giving patterns that change, for pastoral concern. *Caution:* Security systems must be planned so that this highly confidential data can be accessed only by authorized persons.

Accounting records are now maintained in a much more timely way, can be more accurate, and can provide more complete reporting data. A "fund" accounting system must be used, different from most businesses, but there are a number of specially designed church accounting computer programs which will handle this need. Historical records which can be easily compared from one year to the next provide a great source of financial data. Budgeting becomes much more accurate with more complete background data, allowing for variable budgeting according to how funds are expended. Bank reconciliations and other control features are made very complete and easy by computers. A greater integrity in the system is ensured if the computer system is properly used.

*Another important word of caution:* Especially in areas of membership and financial records, your manual system must work well before putting it on a computer.

Good manual controls translate into good computer controls; computers do not necessarily put controls in place without adequate manual intervention. Records can be handled as well or as poorly on a computer as they can be manually.

Remember the educational opportunities of computers when planning for Sunday school or Vacation Bible School. Computer Bible stories, maps, games, and so forth abound. Church libraries can offer a multitude of Bible-study programs as well as computerized catalogs.

How does a church choose a computer system that will be compatible with its needs, and, when the time comes, know what upgrade is needed?

Church size may be one significant factor which will dictate the extent of computerization. Small churches in which the pastor has no administrative help can benefit greatly in time saved by the pastor, as well as in the quality of orders of worship, newsletters, letters, and records. Most other churches can benefit from computerization in just about all ministerial, educational, and administrative functions. *However, you need to evaluate each individual function in terms of the type of computerization that might be needed before any system is purchased.*

Equipment and software used can be as varied in church settings as they are in secular settings. Whatever is used must fit the specific needs of the church. An integrated church management system might be considered, and there are many choices. Ask yourself if you need each of the elements of the system under consideration, and whether the system capability will fit your need. Each church must plan carefully for computerization and develop its needs first rather than respond to what the computer software offers. Factors to consider include:

- Church size and volume of transactions
- Who will be doing the input and where
- Location of the computer
- Need for networking; that is, linking several computers together
- Where and how financial receipt and expenditure transactions are recorded
- By whom and where reports will be prepared

In addition to identifying as clearly as possible what you need, find a knowledgeable person in the congregation or elsewhere who can help you match your needs to the hardware and software available. Try to find someone who has had some experience in church systems; they tend to be somewhat different than commercial systems. Also try to find someone whose experience matches the size of your church or administrative need.

When purchasing hardware and a software system remember to keep long-term needs in mind. The optimum system is one which meets your needs now but which can be easily expanded. Once church administrators realize what they can get from computerizing their records, their recognized needs will grow. Much of the church-management software is modular, and thus it can be purchased to fit your specific needs. The primary consideration will be whether the software you are considering is simple enough to operate in your present environment and still comprehensive enough to be useful when needs expand. When considering hardware, beware of the old equipment available from members who wish to help. Computer obsolescence is so great that even when you purchase new equipment and software it will grow old very quickly. So don't forget to budget for long-term computer needs.

A word about networking may be helpful. As your church computer needs grow, you will quickly find that the computer that the church administrative assistant uses will be busy when the financial people, the minister, the evangelism committee, the librarians, or the educational department wants to use it. Then it is time for networking—joining two or more computers together to work from the same church management programs, using the same database. Repetitive data, such as names and addresses, can be changed once within the system, and all users will have access to this change immediately. A pastor's input to the Sunday order of worship can be used by the secretary without reentry. Financial giving data can be merged with membership data for records of giving, without data reentry or correction. A standard church network of computers for a small-to-medium-sized church may be the master computer for the secretary, a networked computer for the pastor, and another for the financial/educational/library personnel.

What can computers do for your local church? Just about anything you need or want them to do. They have become as indispensable as the copy machine.

## *Planning for Church Growth*

Our mission as Christians is clearly stated in the Great Commission in Matthew 28:19. Thus, we must accept that church growth is one of our primary objectives. What should our action plans be to implement this objective of spiritual and numerical growth?

We can probably successfully support a hypothesis that growth in numbers will follow growth in Christian spirituality. As people who are the church become excited about things that are happening at the church, others will be interested in becoming a part of that Spirit-filled group. They will want to experience for themselves why members of the church feel good about themselves and their lives, and are so friendly and helpful to each other; why they want to participate in Bible and related study groups; why they want worship to be uplifting through varied and meaningful services; why they want their children to spend time at the church in Christian-led activities and programs which appeal to youth; and why they are always looking for ways to reach out and help others in the community and the world who are in need. In short, people will join a group if asked, and if they sense that they will experience a spiritual "something" that is life-changing and that will help them live their lives to the fullest.

To attain this Spirit-filled atmosphere there must be intentional effort. After careful study of needs, there should be specific and attainable growth goals and action plans established. The church must recognize the community demographic, the economic, ethnic, and racial environment surrounding it, and determine how best to respond. It should challenge members to evangelize through visitation: people respond first when personally asked. Worship services should be studied for possible change. Facilities need to be evaluated for adequacy and attractiveness. Educational and study programs should be reviewed to ensure they are keeping up with changing expectations. Fellowship opportunities should be many and varied to meet changing needs.

Possibly most important to an intentional effort toward church growth is to study how others have accomplished their goals. This area is one in which church leaders need to attend classes or seminars and to review the writings of others on church growth to take advantage of their study and experiences. A local church can benefit greatly just from a fresh look at new ideas. For example, a vibrant, Spirit-filled, fellowship-oriented church had leveled off in its worship attendance and could not determine why it was not growing, considering other community growth activity. Through research and willingness to consider new possibilities, it learned that, when compared to similar churches, a lower percentage of its membership attended worship, its one worship service was almost always "comfortably full," and it had only a part-time student associate pastor in addition to the senior pastor, while other churches had employed full-time associates. Was it time for a second service? Would a full-time associate help? During the following two years, after an early-morning worship service was initiated and a full-time associate was brought on staff, worship attendance steadily grew, and the church developed even more creative and positive activities in response to its mission. Out of a denominational grouping of seventy, it became a member of a select group of seven churches which had grown.

We offer two resources which suggest some specific ideas when considering planning for church growth. You might note that both of these resources emphasize the need for a defined mission for the church (a mission statement) and that evangelical and growth goals must be established.

*Fourteen lessons learned in becoming a growing church.*[10] This excerpted article beginning on page 99, describes the experiences of a Midwestern, suburban church which, after years of low or no growth, sought help, studied and visited other growing churches, and formulated specific goals toward church growth. The church began to grow dynamically as defined by worship attendance, Sunday school attendance, small groups, volunteers, musical groups, and so forth. A number of the lessons learned may surprise some people and perhaps be contrary to usual thinking. Nevertheless, there was growth success and we can learn from how it was accomplished.

*A Guide to Church Growth.*[11] The brochure beginning on page 103 summarizes a study of growing United Methodist churches in Southern California. This study, performed by four Doctor of Ministry students at the Claremont School of Theology, contains a wealth of information on how some churches have succeeded in growing in an environment of membership decline in many mainline denominations.

The common thread found in these growing churches was that they apply the "Three Rs" as part of their strategies and practices:

*Reach Out—Receive—Retain*

# Fourteen Lessons Learned in Becoming a Growing Church

After a decade of declining worship attendance, membership, and Sunday school enrollment, the United Methodist Church of Whitefish Bay, Wisconsin, showed a remarkable turnaround. Here are the symbols of that growth and the lessons from that experience.

| Symbols of Growth over 13 Years | From | To |
|---|---|---|
| Worship Attendance | 400 | 618 |
| Church School Attendance— | | |
| Children/Youth | 300 | 650 |
| Adult Education | 60 | 260 |
| Number of Small Groups | 28 | 96 |
| Number of Volunteers | 400 | 675 |
| Number of Singles Active | 20 | 175 |
| Number of Music Groups | 3 | 13 |
| Persons in Hands-On Mission Work | 15 | 150 |

1. *The United Methodist denomination has neither helped nor hindered growth.* Our particular help came from the American Institute for Church Growth workshops led by Lyle Shaller, and by studying and visiting other growing churches of various denominations. Ninety percent of the persons choosing a local church do not consider denominational affiliation to be important; it is the program and ministries offered by the local church that make the difference.

2. *Most brainstorming is a pooling of ignorance.* To stop the pooling of ignorance, church leaders, members of the long-range planning committee, and church staff were encouraged to go to regional and national training sessions that were based on current research and successful practices of other churches.

3. *The staff of the church must be freed to lead and to create but not substitute gimmicks for careful planning.* The staff needs to be free to dream and create. The job of policy-making committees is to find ways to support dreams and creativity, not to discover reasons why they might not work. On the other hand, new ideas and programs must pass a twofold test. First, ask if the idea is consistent with the priorities and mission of the church. Second, ask if there are sufficient numbers of lay people who will support the idea with time, talent, and treasure.

4. *Lay support is critical.* Lay support comes as people attend training sessions to capture a vision of what the church can be. New directions for the church are seldom approved the first time they are brought up. New ideas require a lot of discussion and revision, sometimes over many months, before they are perfected and accepted.

5. *Risk failure.* Many new programs or staff positions must be started without any guarantee of success. Sometimes a new staff person needed to start a new program may be funded outside of the budget with a special fund appeal. When that staff person met a true need that position paid for itself through increased giving and participation, whereupon that position can be included in the budget. Over the last several years, a youth worker, volunteer coordinator, and singles ministry worker were funded in this manner.

6. *Small groups don't just happen; they may die as quickly as they are formed.* New small groups must meet two criteria; first, they must meet real needs; and second, leaders must be recruited before the group begins.

7. *A certain amount of disorder is really creativity and openness.* Quality programming is vital. But it is a mistake to assume that everything has to be perfectly organized and approved by every committee in the church. Individual communities as well as staff persons need the freedom to try new ideas without organizing the idea to death.

8. *Gracefully, let some people attend another church.* Although it is painful to realize that you can't serve the needs of everyone, one of the gracious things that a church can do is to let some members move on to a church that will meet their needs. However, exit conversations can reveal problem situations.

9. *Adult education is best done in long-term groups.* The largest jump in adults in Christian education came in this church by seeking long-term commitments to Christian education and by spending time building friendships in class—not by finding a more dramatic or charismatic teacher of a better subject.

10. *As the church grows, expect decisions to get larger and easier.* Adding the first part-time staff person was a major decision for the church, particularly with a tight budget. Each additional staff person was easier to accept. It was difficult to find support for a first-ever volunteer in mission. By the second or third time, the idea of giving extra money for missions became an expectation.

11. *Pray, study the Bible, and hold hands at every possible moment.* The Christian supportive fellowship should be experienced in every church group or activity. Every committee and group meeting in the church begins and ends with prayer. When praying, we join hands. We also hold that Bible study is assumed to be the fundamental basis for Christian education for children, youth, and adults.

12. *Lay people prefer doing ministry rather than deciding about ministry.* Those who engage in ministry prefer that to talking about ministry. Any individual or group that becomes excited about an area of ministry that is consistent with the mission and policies of the church should have the freedom to pursue that work.

13. *The heart of ministry is friendship, fellowship, and food.* It is not unusual for our church to have meals or luncheons served from four to eight times each week. The fellowship hall has become the center for building friendships. There is no better way to create fellowship than to do as Jesus did in Zaccheus's

house: share conversation and food. Sinks and counters have been placed in three additional meeting rooms so several small groups can include refreshments or meals at the same time.

14. ***Outreach is more than marketing principles.*** We have discovered that the principles of marketing and research are important in developing ministry. However, over 50 percent of all the first-time visitors to our church still come through personal invitation. There is absolutely no substitute for people inviting friends and relatives to worship with them. For many years our denomination has subtly preached that persons should respect the privacy of others. The people in the pews have welcomed this as an excuse to leave the outreach of the church to someone else. The best marketing tool around is a personal invitation to hear about Christ and His Church.

---

### The Real Reasons People Join a Church

Why do people join a church? Six percent join on their own; 10 percent join for the youth program; 6 percent join because of the pastor's sermon; 3 percent join because of a special need; 2 percent join because of a pastor's visit, 7 percent join because of a good church school; 1 percent join because of a revival; and 65 percent join because they were invited by a friend or family member.

---

***Characteristics of a growing church:*** A research committee in the Central Illinois Conference of The United Methodist Church found the following commonalities in twenty-five growing congregations:

- A contagious sense of expectancy, including (a) a sense of the power of the gospel to change lives and confidence in their ability to be agents of that change, and (b) a good self-image.

- An effective lay/pastor partnership, including (a) a pastor with strong initiative, and (b) the willingness of the pastor and lay people to work hard.

- Disciplined planning, including (a) a definite goal-setting process with wide participation, (b) constant searching for new ideas, and (c) a willingness to learn from past experience.

- A program including: (a) an emphasis on spiritual aspects, (b) interesting worship and music, (c) well-prepared and relevant preaching, and (d) varied activities that relate to people's needs.

- Effective use of the church's own advantages and opportunities, including: (a) a willingness to serve those who live in the community, and (b) an ability to use the advantages of its size, leadership, abilities, heritage, style, and theological stance.

Excerpted from an article written by Dr. Richard Jones, pastor of The United Methodist Church of Whitefish Bay, Wisconsin, and presented here with his permission.

# A Guide to Church Growth

*Summary of a Study of*
*Growing United Methodist Churches in the*
*California-Pacific Annual Conference*

Commissioned by the

Y. S. Mae Foundation

Conducted by the

Claremont School of Theology

**A WORD OF APPRECIATION**

The leadership and guidance of the Claremont School of Theology and the dedicated and diligent work of the Project Team in developing the information in this brochure is gratefully acknowledged.

### CHURCH GROWTH PROJECT TEAM

Dr. Chan Hie Kim—Project Supervisor
Bethellen Balikian—D. Min. Candidate, CSC
James Fredette—D. Min. Candidate, CSC
Mike Walters—D. Min. Candidate, CSC
Jae Yoo Yoo—D. Min. Candidate, CSC

### CHURCH GROWTH PROJECT COMMITTEE

John Chang—Chair
Rev. Don Bommarito
Rev. Lothair Green
Dr. Chan Hie Kim
Dr. Allen Moore
Dr. Marjorie Suchocki

Stan Kukawka—Vice Chair
Dr. Robert Edgar
Rev. Dan Kennedy
Dr. Jim Mahin
Rev. Joon Shoung Park

**PREFACE**

Within the California-Pacific Annual Conference are churches that are growing, others that are stable, and still others that are declining. While there are many books and writings on church growth, they tend to be rather general in scope. It was felt that a detailed study of and determination of factors common to growing churches in our own Annual Conference would be of more specific use to other churches in our Conference that would like to grow also.

Accordingly, the Y. S. Mae Foundation commissioned a study of growing United Methodist churches with the objective being the development of a Guide to Church Growth that would be based on factors, actions, or activities that might be found to be common to churches experiencing growth.

A summary of this study is contained within this pamphlet. All of these ideas and suggestions presented have been successful in promoting growth in churches within the California-Pacific Annual Conference. It is our hope and prayer that this information will serve as a guide to those churches that are serious about acting on the Great Commission given to all Christians—to bring people to our Lord, Jesus the Christ.

*Go therefore, and make disciples of all the people, baptizing them*
*in the name of the Father, the Son, and the Holy Spirit,*
*teaching them to observe all things whatever I have commanded you;*
*and behold, I am with you always, even to the end of the age.*
*(Matthew 28:19)*

# BACK TO THE "3 Rs"

## of

# CHURCH GROWTH AND EVANGELISM

**THE "3 Rs" FOR GROWING UNITED METHODISTS**

**REACH OUT !**

**RECEIVE !**

**RETAIN !**

## I. REACH OUT

A. *Develop a mission statement* that is responsive to the biblical mandate and is reflective of the inclusiveness of the United Methodist tradition.

B. *Establish evangelism and church growth goals,* preferably for growth in worship attendance.

1. Goals should consider factors beyond the control of the local church, such as:
   - Demographic changes
   - Economic climate

2. Goals should reflect what we can do together:
   - We have little control over the number of people who may join us, but we can visit as many people as we choose.
   - We have no control over who moves into our parish, but we can indicate our commitment to growth by devoting 5 percent of our parish budget for church growth.

3. Goals have fringe benefits:
   - Attainable, measurable, specific, and challenging goals can become the means to motivate United Methodists to action.
   - Goals can strengthen and raise parish morale.
   - Goals + faith = hope for the future.

C. *Reach out—the ways and means*

1. Identify the uniqueness of your church, let your light shine through creative advertising: yellow pages, newspaper ads outside of the "tombstone" section, advertising of other churches, cross-street or zip direct mail, radio and television spots, press releases.

2. Prospect list including: Sunday visitors, persons who have turned to the church sacramentally (marriage, baptisms, and burial), fringe friends of the church; and consider a "bring-a-friend Sunday," door-to-door visitation, and garnering the names of those who attend groups meeting at the church. One might also garner a list by visiting parishioners at their place of work and meeting their coworkers.

3. Make every Sunday special: variety in liturgy, well-paced worship, mini-series in sermons and/or Christian education, expand worship-service times, expand the quality or quantity of music.

4. Facilities—provide parking and directional signs (both inside and outside), sound systems, exterior and interior lighting, clean-up days with special emphasis on restrooms, narthex, nursery, and grounds.

5. Evaluate the possibility of church renovation or even relocation.

6. Respond rather than react to changing ethnic, racial, and religious diversity (for example: three of four Roman Catholics marrying Protestants join Protestant churches.)

7. Become sensitive to the multiplicity of newcomer needs: transportation to events (especially senior citizens and children), weeknight church school, after-school programs for latchkey kids, neighborhood "get acquainted" events, neighborhood Bible studies, seminars for those "recovering," enrichment programs focusing on the arts, etc., and Sunday evening worship and educational experiences during vacation times.

8. Train lay visitors to call on new residents, Sunday morning attendees, inactives, and for door-to-door visitation.

## II. RECEIVE

A. *Intentional hospitality*

- Select, train, and assign hosts/hostesses for worship services and other events.
- Select hosts/hostesses who relate easily to strangers and perceive intentional friendliness as good manners.
- Train hosts/hostesses to be familiar with the church's programs, history, and beliefs.
- Assign hosts/hostesses to the sanctuary portals both prior to and following worship. One host/hostess should be standing nearby the pastor as visitors leave and note their names and/or needs, and should circulate during fellowship hour to introduce newcomers to others.
- Greeters are not hosts/hostesses. They are a necessity but are probably not trained, nor do they have the time to answer questions. They are, however, necessary to convey friendliness.
- Train church school teachers to act as hosts/hostesses in adult and children's programs.
- Train ushers to greet with a welcoming smile, seat newcomers in appropriate areas, and ascertain any special needs that may require attention.

B. *Newcomer and faith-at-work classes*

1. Traditional newcomers classes:
   - As required, to create a sense of community and to develop friendship bonds between new members and their sponsors.
   - Sessions should be inspirational and informational.

2. Nontraditional newcomers classes:

   Faith at Work with sessions on:
   - Our Christian Faith and Daily Work
   - Our Christian Faith and Marriage
   - Our Christian Faith and Contemporary Issues
   - Our Christian Faith at Work through the Church

3. Seasonal courses:
   - Advent, Lent, Pentecost, focusing on faith issues.
   - Real-Life courses such as "Making It as a Blended Family," "Life after Divorce," "Single, Again?"

C. *An "ask me" table in a highly visible and accessible area*

1. Staffed by trained, friendly, knowledgeable volunteers.

2. Lay volunteers who can provide answers to questions or who provide reliable follow-up on questions.

D. *Photo gallery displaying members*—new members' pictures are displayed separately (for a time) then added to main photo gallery.

E. *Fellowship events*—Picnics, coffee hours, evening fellowship dinners, topical retreats (marriage encounters; newly divorced; single again?), all of which include trained volunteers to invite, welcome, and include newcomers in activities.

F. *Couples and singles groups* designed to be both invitational and accepting of newcomers.

G. *Develop a "data bank" on members* which includes talents, areas of interest and potential service, birthdays and anniversaries, significant life events, and any other categories which may facilitate involvement.

## III. RETAIN

A. *Visit, write, telephone* all parishioners who have missed three weeks of worship or whose worship pattern changes abruptly. This presumes keeping excellent attendance records—an absolute necessity!

B. *Develop a pastoral calling system* for visiting every church member at least once a year.

C. *Minimize the summer slump*

1. 60 percent of families who change residences do so between May and September. A high priority among newcomers is for their children to make friends before school starts in the fall.

2. People are creatures of habit. Summer cutbacks in church activities encourage people to "drop out"; Summer "dropouts" can easily turn into fall and winter "stayouts."

D. *Worship*

1. The well-prepared and delivered sermon is vital to growth in worship attendance.

2. Increase worship pace—television viewing has impacted congregants with an expectation of movement.

3. Orders of Worship should be devoid of "church lingo" that may not be familiar to visitors, but should include the words to the Lord's Prayer and hymnal references to the Gloria Patri and Doxology.

4. Expand the Ministry of Music—include familiar hymns.

5. Include children and youth music.

6. *Do not* scold the congregation—newcomers hide in the pews when the pastor scolds the congregation for their shortcomings and failures.

7. Use trained lay liturgists and preachers.

8. Increase the role of Intercessory Prayer.

9. Offer the Lord's Supper at least once a month.

E. *Develop off-campus and on-campus sub-congregations.* For example:

1. An apartment ministry for singles, seniors, etc.

2. Commuter's luncheon group at a convenient restaurant located within walking distance of many working members and friends.

3. Singles ministry (unless leadership is 50 percent male, singles groups almost always drift into 100 percent female groups).

4. Sub-congregations around needs or interests: ethnic, family relationships, work schedules, etc.

5. A new face-to-face group is needed for every 25 new members added to the congregation.

6. Neighborhood Bible studies.

7. Holiday meals and activities that are inclusive of all family types.

F. *Develop an "abundant life" center*

 1. Include an educational component addressing issues pertinent in contemporary culture—"Making It on a Single Parent's Pay," "Financial Planning for the Newly Single," etc.

 2. Foster ongoing support groups for "newly single," etc.

 3. Provide on-or off-site counseling resources.

G. *Planning retreats* for newly elected church leaders, and re-entry retreats for those going out of leadership.

H. *Church camp/retreats for all ages*

 I. *Recognize and respond to life passages*

 1. Identify church members who are going through significant life changes and passages that may affect continuing church involvement: death or divorce, empty nest, unemployment, bankruptcy (either personal or corporate), etc.

 2. Select, train, and meet regularly with lay persons who can help mentor, care, support, and encourage people in transition; the pastor should be involved, but lay persons are also crucial.

## A Congregation Prepares for a Pastoral Change

Inevitably, there will be pastoral change in every church. It is a natural, expected occurrence often brought on by sudden illness or death, as well as by planned retirements, voluntary moves, and so forth. A church which plans for this event will remain strong through a phenomenon that most members dislike: change. This change can be a positive event for the congregation if it knows its mission and ministry and has its administrative house in order.

The following is a list of questions that the various committees of the church might consider when there is a pastoral change. A simple booklet could be prepared, by area of emphasis. Serious candidates for the position would be especially interested in the answers to these questions, which help give a foundation for a joint understanding about the church and its programs. Different denominations may have somewhat different names for these bodies or may combine these functions. Nevertheless, the information that comes from this list of questions is the minimum that a pastor needs to have to properly discharge pastoral as well as administrative responsibilities.

### WORSHIP

1. What is the format of the present worship service(s)? How many services are there?

2. What is the average worship attendance? Has it been going up or down?

3. What are the feelings regarding the present order of worship?

4. Do lay people lead parts of worship? How are they selected?

5. How often is communion shared? How is it served?

6. Is there a music director and what are the responsibilities of this person?

7. What are the number, size, and types of choirs? What are the age groupings? When do various choirs sing?

8. What is the primary instrument used in worship? Is there a bell choir?

9. Is there a liturgical art and dance ministry?

10. Has a "contemporary" service been considered? Reaction?

11. What are the special, seasonal worship services?

12. Is there an acolyte program? Who administers it?

13. Who is responsible for securing greeters? How often are they rotated?

14. What are the wedding policies, procedures, and administration? Is there an informative brochure?

15. What are the funeral/memorial service procedures and policies? Is there an informative brochure?

16. How often does the worship committee meet? Are minutes kept?

**EDUCATION**

1. What is the current average attendance in church school? Average attendance history?

2. What is the status of staffing? Is there team teaching?

3. What training and guidance is provided teachers?

4. How does the church school help families fulfill their Christian education potential?

5. How do youth relate to and participate in worship, church decision making, and the total church life?

6. What is included in the adult education program? Is there Bible study?

7. Are there community youth groups using the church (e.g., Scouts)?

8. Are children and youth involved in summer camping? Are adults involved as campers and/or leaders?

9. What enrollment and attendance records are kept? Who is responsible for them? How are they kept up-to-date?

10. Is there a church library? What is in it? Is computer-assisted learning available?

11. How often does the education committee meet? Are minutes kept?

**EVANGELISM**

1. What attempt is there to communicate the church to the community using print and electronic media? Is the church on the World Wide Web?

2. Is there a brochure of regular church events?

3. What is the strategy for reaching new areas/older areas of the community?

4. Is there an active calling program in the church and community?

5. Is there an active communications committee?

6. How effective is the advertising? What is presently being done? What is planned to be done? Where do the ads appear? When?

7. Is there a regular church newsletter? Who is responsible for it?

8. How are new members assimilated into the church?

9. What small groups (prayer, Bible study, discussion) exist, or are planned?

10. How recently have membership records been brought up-to-date?

11. How often does the evangelism committee meet? Are minutes kept?

**MISSIONS**

1. Does the church support its own missionary? If so, to what extent?

2. Are youth and/or adults involved in short- or long-term mission services?

3. Are mission benevolence gift commitments paid?

4. What special offerings are taken? How are they promoted? Are special envelopes used?

5. Is there a local community outreach program? How is it administered?

6. How often does the missions committee meet? Are minutes kept?

## SOCIAL CONCERNS

1. How is the congregation alerted to Christian social concerns?

2. What projects are underway? What projects are anticipated?

3. What work-fellowship opportunities exist with people for whom the church should have concern?

4. How often does the social concerns committee meet? Are minutes kept?

## PERSONNEL RELATIONS

1. Who are the employees of the church?

2. Are there active, written personnel policies?

3. Have position descriptions been prepared for each of the employees? Have these been reviewed in the past twelve months?

4. Is there a personnel file for each employee? Is it kept up-to-date?

5. Is there an annual, documented performance review and evaluation?

6. Are there unfilled staff positions?

7. Are there written personnel policies and position descriptions for lay leadership?

8. Who fills the lay leadership positions in the church? Is there an active nominations committee to ensure continued leadership?

9. Are there outstanding personnel issues that need to be resolved?

10. How often does the personnel committee meet? Are minutes kept?

## STEWARDSHIP

1. What are the long-range goals for stewardship?

2. What plans are there to implement these goals on a short-range basis?

3. What plans are in process to involve persons in the life of the church?

4. How are the financial and service needs of the church kept before the congregation?

5. When will the next stewardship enlistment program take place? Who will lead it?

6. How often does the stewardship committee meet? Are minutes kept?

## FINANCE

1. How and when is the offering counted? What is the step-by-step procedure for handling all types of receipts?

2. How often are reports of giving sent to the membership? Does a letter go with them? What is the format of the record of giving?

3. What is the step-by-step procedure for paying bills? Is a check request used?

4. What are the outstanding unpaid obligations? Are any denominational support obligations unpaid?

5. Where are the bank accounts, what are the account numbers, and who has access? What savings accounts are there? Who is authorized to sign on the various accounts?

6. How is the accounting system handled? Is it automated and integrated with the church management system?

7. Is there a budget? Do financial reports compare actual results with the budget?

8. Are financial reports prepared monthly and financial results communicated to the governing body and congregation?

9. Is there an endowment or "planned giving" program? Who is responsible and how is it communicated to the congregation? Is there a written policy?

10. When was the last independent financial review or audit done? Is there an active audit committee?

11. How often does the finance committee meet? Are meeting minutes kept?

**TRUSTEES OR PROPERTY**

1. Is the church incorporated? If not, why not?

2. Does the church have a safe-deposit box? Who has access? What is in it?

3. What long-term financial notes are there? What are the details of the church obligation?

4. How recently has insurance been reviewed? Is coverage in a package policy to cover all needs? Is it part of a denominational or group plan? Who is the agent?

5. Is there a reserve fund for property repairs, etc.?

6. Are equipment purchases planned, or a reserve fund set up, for church office equipment?

7. Is there "other income" (rent, etc.)?

8. Is there a building committee? Who is responsible?

9. Is there a memorials committee? Who is responsible?

10. Is there a pastor's residence committee? Who is responsible?

11. Are there special landscape and irrigation plans? Who is responsible?

12. How often do the trustees or property committees meet? Are minutes kept?

**OFFICIAL BOARD (GOVERNING BODY)**

1. Is there an adopted mission statement? Has it been recently reviewed?

2. Is there a strategic plan in place with overall goals and objectives?

3. When was the last planning retreat? Is another one planned?

4. Do committees report regularly about their progress on their action plans?

5. Is this body concerned about the spiritual and relational lives of its members as well as the status of programs and activities?

6. Is there a formal church organization chart?

7. Who is on this board?

8. How often does the governing body meet? Are minutes kept?

## CHAPTER THREE

# Organizing and Staffing

## Christ's Church in Action

To accomplish its mission and plans in a vibrant way, Christ's Church must be organized and staffed so that it can move easily within itself and within the community in a positive direction toward positive results. It must know where it is going and how it is to get there, and how it is to do this in an organized and effective way. Having said this, we must quickly add that the organization and staffing structure that is required will vary with almost every church.

Small churches may function quite informally and successfully because they act as a family. As churches grow in size and organizational complexity, more formal structure is needed to guide the direction of activities.

In this chapter we will consider various characteristics of both small and large congregations and how the local church organization needs to relate to these characteristics. Some possible organizational structure and accountability charts will be reviewed with regard to how these might be typical of a local church. This section ends with a review of unique challenges that face churches with multiple pastors.

Various personnel management considerations form the basis for all meaningful relationships. Within this context we examine why position descriptions are important and how they can enhance a positive relationship within the church. Other personnel concerns such as interviewing and record keeping also will be presented from a practical viewpoint.

How any local church actually functions within both its formal and informal organization leads us to consider how committees interpret, enact, and coordinate. The church staff must function together as a unit, and there are certain ways this is possible with a positive interaction by each staff member. The legal issues facing churches will be presented to assist you in this important area.

Finally, we will present examples of personnel documentation required of any church organization, no matter how small or large. These examples include typical staff and volunteer position descriptions, personnel policies, sexual harassment policies, injury and illness prevention ideas, employment records of many types, and a set of sample personnel documentation forms.

We caution you always to remember that your organization and staffing must serve you and fit your individual needs. It must not be allowed to control you. Don't forget your needs may change over time. As long as you change your organization and staffing for valid reasons and not just to create an illusion of progress while producing confusion, inefficiency, and demoralization, you will progress smoothly toward your goals. Your organizational structure and personnel staffing policies and procedures should be designed so "that all of the ministry gifts of members can be both individually offered and collectively harmonized for the upbuilding of the body of Christ."[1]

## Local Church Organization

### Effects of Congregational Characteristics on Organization

To organize is to facilitate the interrelationships of people toward joint synergistic effort, with organization enabling a natural grouping of people or functions. Local churches, regardless of denomination, can vary greatly in operational organization structure depending on size, composition, and characteristics. Optimally, a church should be organized to respond effectively to its mission as it sees it, in the place and time in which the church operates. A church must strive to fine-tune its organizational structure, to consider size, established church polity, desires, needs, and makeup, and what it can do to fulfill its mission.

*Size.* Although churches vary considerably in size, the small church is the normative institutional expression of worshiping congregations on the North American continent. More than a quarter of all Protestant congregations on this continent have fewer than thirty-five in worship attendance on an average Sunday. More than half average less than seventy-five in worship. By contrast, there seems to be a natural assumption that the larger church is the norm, and thus much of the organizational discussion about structure and operations is large-church directed, leaving the majority of our churches without adequate recognition of organizational concerns or structural advice.

There are and will always be certain natural operational differences between large and small churches. The seeming lack of orderliness of a small church many times is part of why it works well. Conversely, the larger church may of necessity function under a more detailed organization, while at the same time encourage unique small-group dynamics in its activities.

The small church is able to allow for business to be conducted informally; have decisions made simply and directly by consensus; and work as a group, giving everyone a voice. Within this small group there seems to be a natural order which encourages persons to work together even when there are differences. Perhaps it is the group's basic spirituality that allows this to happen. It also may just be human nature that small groups work together well in that there is less inhibition in a small group and leadership emerges more readily. But the flip side is that such a group may not readily see the need to reach beyond itself. It is this need to "reach out" in an organized way that the pastor and lay leadership of a small church must understand and respond to if the group is to be as active in service to Christ as it potentially can be.

A larger church will naturally use a more organized structure and approach, with related subgroups developing programs and reporting to an administrative body for coordination, consensus, and support. Although decisions may sometimes be delayed by such a structure, they will usually be made with deliberate study and consideration of alternatives while the necessary consensus is gained. Often it is true that a larger church will function best if it recognizes and uses small groups in a positive way. The natural order which encourages persons to work together in a small group can be used just as effectively in a larger church, if small groups are allowed to function in their natural way. Thus, there is a direct tie between how a small and large church will ultimately function, regardless of the organizational structure they work within. The "community of believers" is the important element, and there is a wealth of talent, wisdom, and resources within the community, regardless of size.

*Composition and characteristics.* While church polity may create organizational structures that are effective in larger churches, this may be a cumbersome requirement in a small church. In our opinion, whether dictated or not, churches should be allowed to seek an organizational structure that works for them, within the general guidelines of denominational polity. Many times large and small churches have different priorities, requiring different structures. A small congregation may average 70 to 120 percent of reported membership in worship while a large church may average only 40 to 50 percent. A small congregation places a higher priority on relationships, calls each other by name, respects the rights and privileges of each member, and makes sure bills are paid—out of personal interest and concern. A large congregation may place a higher priority on functional aspects of ministry, with a carefully administered organizational structure, and look for smooth operations with a systematic approach to fund-raising and stewardship.

A listing of the characteristics of congregations of varying sizes is presented on pages 118–124. Although these are generalizations and may not always apply to every church in a particular size category, we believe a careful study of these characteristics should assist the pastor and lay leadership in considering an operational structure that fits the specific church being served. Certainly, recognition that these characteristics may exist will assist church leadership in recognizing the dynamics of their own congregation and in designing responses to it.

Of significant importance are the changes that take place in churches as they mirror changes in society—changes that can dramatically affect how a church's operations are structured. Churches must adapt to accommodate ethnic and cultural changes as members bring their own traditions. It is not uncommon to find large church facilities being used by multiple groups, often of differing cultures. Questions of organizational authority and responsibility quickly surface as they seek to work together. There may be one or several pastors serving a church's several congregations. The best advice we can give to meet these challenges is that churches with these situations and concerns should seek others who have solved similar problems satisfactorily, and learn from their successes and mistakes. An understanding of and sensitivity to all involved is an excellent place to start.

*A positive response.* To respond positively to size, composition, or characteristic issues, what approach should church leadership take in organizing and pastoring a congregation?

There are a number of concerns to consider. If a pastor enters a new pastorate (many times a small church), the congregation may want to maintain the status quo for a period of time. The astute pastor will recognize this need, be patient, control frustration and feelings of isolation, and work toward understanding the church culture and environment. The pastor can use this time as a learning period, working within the established organization. As the pastor and congregation begin to know and respect each other, the pastor can begin to guide the church toward development of a vision, mission, plans of action, and an organization to accomplish these tasks. However, this must be done as a group. There will be various mind-sets to overcome: frustrations about where to start; congregations with poor self-esteem and those in a survival mode; conservatism; and maybe even suspicion of "What is the pastor up to?"

If an established pastor sees the need for the congregation to move in a new direction, some of the same status quo deterrents may exist. The organizational structure may be in place, but it may not be functioning effectively enough to allow the church to move ahead in mission. In fact, in an established pastorate, the pastor may be perceived as part of the status quo problem. A pastor trying to maintain a cooperative feeling within the church, for instance, may be seen as being too conciliatory. An astute pastor and key lay leaders will seek ways to challenge the congregation to change. A joint awakening may result in a strong corporate body eager to reach out. An outside facilitator frequently can help this to happen. Any time a pastor and congregation develop, together, they can only become strong, together.

There will always be opportunities for greater ministry in any situation. Pastors should approach any ministry as if it were to be an entire life's work. They will need to

- Start from the known

- Promote self-esteem

- Stress the higher value which we all place on persons

- Look for and record manifestations of pride

- See how caring is reflected, and how this may be used and publicized

- See how organization and administration may evolve from congregational care and worship

- Learn how to recruit, train, and work with volunteers

- Develop a growing vision for the congregation, and help them envelop it

Regardless of organizational structure, size, or composition, a pastor must focus primarily on what is most important to any church: *worship*. As worship brings members together in Christ, it will facilitate congregational care so that the church can consciously identify needs, spoken and felt, and plan and act on these needs, using a supporting organization and administration.

## *Characteristics of Congregations of Varying Sizes*

Every church is different: attitudes, composition, location, ethnicity, spirituality, and so forth all influence the direction and focus of churches. But perhaps the most significant factor is the size of the worshiping congregation. Just a realization of the characteristics of congregations of different sizes may define for a church where it is presently and perhaps what it may want to do to move to a new level of mission. This goal may not always be a growth in numbers, although that may be a prime mission element. More important, such a process will involve how a certain church sees itself in relationship to the community it serves and the opportunities for service, regardless of size. The following generally accepted characteristics for congregations of different sizes are presented to assist in this realization. We also comment briefly after each grouping about the organizational alignment which might be expected to be most effective.

### "Fellowship" (up to 34 in worship)

- An overgrown small group.

- Special emphasis on relationships.

- Tough, self-sufficient, independent.

- Controlled by the laity rather than the pastor.

- A patriarch or matriarch controls norms and changes.

- Pastor's role is one of a temporary "family chaplain."

- Pastor may be part-time with perhaps a multicharge responsibility.

- Visitors find it hard to break into the close-knit circle.

- A "gatekeeper" welcomes worship attendees.

- New members are "adopted" into the family only after a long period.

- The group seldom plans. It does whatever is necessary as it comes up.

As many as 28 percent of all Protestant churches are of this size.

The "fellowship" church, as the name implies, will be a close-knit grouping which functions organizationally as a committee of the whole. It may have specific members with position titles, with some members holding several titles. However, the decisions are made as a group with leadership either emerging naturally or forced on the group, depending on whether there is a strong patriarch or matriarch. This church probably would have little use for denominational polity or formal organizational structure. The grouping can function in a positive way when it works together to accomplish something it believes is needed.

### "Small church" (35 to 99 in worship)

- Maybe three small groups exist, such as for Bible study, social purposes, work projects, and so forth.

- There is an inner fellowship circle, with some members in and some out.

- The matriarch or patriarch is influential, but uses power to veto rather than as a dominating influence.

- Pastor may be part-time or perhaps full-time at upper end of this size range.

- The pastor has a more prominent place and must be strong in relationships; is looked to for loving reassurance, counseling, and teaching.

- Only a small proportion of members are inactive.

- The maximum planning time frame is about twelve months.
- The pastor's salary package is about 60 to 70 percent of total expenditures.

Up to 42 percent of all Protestant churches and one-fifth of all church attendees worship in a church of this size.

The "small church" will have an established formal organizational structure, with position titles and a small number of committees. The committees will normally function independently but also come together for coordination and consensus. It will be during the joint meetings where the real decisions are made. Thus, the entire structure, although formally established, will usually operate somewhat informally and even may be influenced by strong leaders or an inner "fellowship" circle. The danger with such a "formal" structure in a small church is burnout, as leaders with too many jobs for too long just get tired. The challenge is to keep the formal organization as simple as possible while still structured well enough to accomplish its purposes effectively.

### "Middle-sized" (100 to 174 in worship)

- Has about five small groups.

- Church work involves more committees with the governing body making policies and granting permission. These tend to be program-oriented churches.

- Patriarchs or matriarchs are more in the background of decision making, quietly sizing up the will of the congregation and vetoing matters that do not have sufficient consensus.

- The pastor's workload is heavy, considering the variety of activities in the church, as well as the need to be in personal touch with the members. There may be need for additional help with pastoral work as the process of administration takes more time.

- Usually one pastor, although the church may need added part-time staff with specific skills to grow and keep up with church activities and programs.

- Planning needs to be done at least a season ahead and may be tolerated by the congregation for up to eighteen to twenty-four months.

- Greater problems of communication, with people potentially going in different directions.

- Various groups become entry points for new members who find their church identity mostly in the small group.

- This size is sometimes thought of as being the "optimum size," because:

  a. A variety of ministries is possible.

  b. There are enough leaders with a variety of skills to carry out programs.

  c. The church can afford and justify having a pastor.

  d. A church of this size has the lowest per-member cost for paid staff: 24 to 45 percent of annual church expenditures.

  e. Property can be maintained without becoming a dominant concern.

f.  The church is small enough for most members to know one another and to initiate ministry and local outreach spontaneously.

Fourteen percent of all Protestant churches are of this size.

This "optimum size" church will definitely be formally organized with committees assigned specific program areas and responsibilities. Coordination is needed among committees and staff to assure all are going in the same direction. The governing body becomes a place where reports are heard, goals and policies are set, and the direction of the church is affirmed. Committee responsibilities are designed to support the mission of the church and generally to address basic functions of worship, evangelism, outreach, education, finance and stewardship, and property; other ad hoc groups are formed as needed. The lay leadership must show strength and give direction, as well as the pastor. All work together.

### "Awkward size" (175 to 224 in worship)

- "Awkward" because they are too big to be adequately served by one pastor, but often they feel they cannot justify or afford additional program staff.

- Often have large number of inactive members.

- Fluctuate in attendance like a thermometer; up when things go well, drop quickly when there are rough times.

- Hit a plateau and find it difficult to become larger in membership.

- Continues to have "family feeling" like a middle-sized church, but people may drift into inactivity with little notice.

- Discussion about need for additional staff relates to specialized skills.

- Pastor takes on prominence as symbol of congregational unity and stability.

- Has ten to twelve small groups; members get their sense of belonging in these groups.

- Long-range planning for up to five years is needed, but may be resisted as being too structured and constricting.

Maybe five percent of all Protestant churches could be in this category.

The organizational structure for a church of this size will resemble that of the medium-size church, except that there may be more program-related groups to take on specific responsibilities. Coordination may become more difficult as more groups are involved. There becomes even a greater need for solid lay leadership as the pastor becomes busier. Insistence on use of the formal organizational structure may be needed to ensure a united direction.

The pastor and congregation must be intentional in planning, or drifting may result with potentially disastrous consequences. If a church of this size wishes to break through this plateau and to grow in numbers and mission, it will take

- More staff, more meeting rooms and programs, higher per-person operational costs, more parking, and a determination to pay the price for expansion.

- A meaningful worship service for everyone, which usually means more than one service.

- Giving up the comfortable, cozy feeling of this size and acceptance that a larger congregation will be different—a congregation of congregations.

### *"Large" (225 to 449 in worship)*

- A congregation of congregations with some large groupings and at least twenty-eight to thirty smaller groups.

- Two or three pastors will be required to serve this congregation adequately, in addition to other church staff.

- Pastors must be well organized, skilled in building relationships with strangers, competent at remembering names, good leaders and administrators, and effective in working with a staff with multiple pastors.

- Most members will not be able to recall more than a few names of other members.

- There may be two or perhaps three worship experiences each Sunday morning.

- Communication is always a problem, with a redundant system needed.

- Securing volunteers a problem; needs a person to recruit and nurture volunteers.

- More conflict among staff and members about church direction.

- Large enough to operate three or more specialized ministries, such as weekday nursery school, drama group, day care center, multiple choirs, and so forth.

- Hits a plateau of 350 to 450 at worship and finds it difficult to break the barrier. To do so, the church must take different approaches to growth and expanded mission.

Interestingly, congregations which average 225 or more in worship attendance account for only 11 percent of all Protestant congregations, but include about one-half of all church attendees on Sunday. The "large-church" category accounts for about 8 percent of all Protestant congregations and 23 percent of the worshipers.

Organizationally, these churches must emphasize a highly formal structure both for the church staff as well as for the lay volunteers. Persons serving as coordinators will be needed to ensure the orderliness that will be desperately needed, but which could disintegrate so easily. Formal planning and coordinating sessions may be the most productive organizational groupings. The church will probably need to recognize that there really is more than one congregation and that programs can successfully move in several directions simultaneously.

### *"Huge" (450 to 699 in worship)*

- Marked by great diversity with many activities occurring at the same time in different places.

- Several worship services, each with its own distinctive attendance.

- A diversity of sizes in groups with which members will identify.

- Usually three or more pastors; at least a senior pastor, pastor of education, and a pastor of membership and congregational care.

- There will be a well-organized administrative operation, usually consuming a large proportion of the senior pastor's time and energy.

- Specialization is a way of life for both pastors and lay leadership.

- The staff may tend to dominate policy-making decisions, unless there is strong lay leadership.

- Need to make long-range plans up to three to five years ahead.

- Much harder to obtain volunteers, with staff taking over positions that lay persons might assume in a smaller church.

- The total cost of the church staff may take from 50 to 70 percent of the budget; probably not less than 40 percent.

- There will need to be seventy to eighty small groups to adequately serve the membership.

Only about 2 percent of all Protestant churches are of this size, but they account for maybe 20 percent of all worshipers.

The organization becomes quite complex, with several program coordinators and a business administrator on staff. There must be strong leadership, both pastoral and lay. Planning, setting of goals, and action plans are absolutely necessary and will consume much of the formal organization's time. Since there is more reliance on the paid staff, there becomes an even greater need for staff coordination. A single lay oversight group becomes difficult to administer as the number of committees and program groups becomes greater.

### *"Minidenomination" (700 and more in worship)*

- Independence is a significant characteristic.

- Frequently disregards denominational channels for selecting a pastor or staff.

- May have four or more pastors, depending on membership numbers; pastorates are generally long-term.

- May develop its own curriculum and training programs.

- May operate its own camp or retreat center.

- The needed number of small groups is so large that it takes a great deal of effort to organize and keep them going.

- Full representation and participation by all groups proves unwieldy in the church's overall operation. Therefore, the emphasis is on smaller, highly skilled groups to design what works and then to go with it.

- Dropout rate among members may be as high as 5 percent.

- Extremely difficult to get volunteers; a coordinator is essential.

- The senior pastor is the chief executive and has little time for one-on-one relationships unless a business or church administrator is added to the staff.

- A church this size fluctuates between a representative democracy and a benevolent dictatorship.

- Staff costs amount to 50 to 70 percent of total church expenditures.

Approximately 1 percent of all Protestant churches are in this category, accounting for about 7 percent of all worshipers.

The church organization for a "minidenomination" may resemble that of a holding company responsible for several major firms. The church's several congregations and program departments resemble smaller churches, with each having its own operating organization. The "holding company" organization functions as an umbrella with functions of planning, organizing, and administrating.

## *Organizational Structure*

In his book *Human Behavior at Work: Organizational Behavior*, Keith Davis notes, "Organization sets relationships among people, work, and resources. Whenever people join in common effort, organization must be employed to get productive results."[2] This statement is as true for a church as it is for any secular organization.

While organizational charts that define lines of accountability and responsibility are typical in business organizations, they are much less commonly seen, but no less important, in church settings. Some typical lines of accountability for the church staff, and organizational structures and relationships among various committees— for both small and large churches—are presented on the following pages. It is quite likely that position titles shown on these charts will vary from one denomination to another; however, the nature and purpose of the functions are likely to be very similar. It is also possible that there may be less relational accountability to denominational officials; if so, your chart would exclude these relationships.

It has been our experience that a graphical presentation of organization, such as shown on pages 125–128, often brings the interrelationships of people in a church into focus, fosters greater understanding of responsibilities, and promotes cooperation. For these reasons, you are encouraged to develop depictions of organizational structure for your particular situation. Whether you use a typical hierarchical line chart as illustrated, or whether you prefer to model your organization in some other way, the point is that defining your organizational structure will facilitate your administrative ministry.

# Small-Church Organization Structure

**TYPICAL LINES OF ACCOUNTABILITY**

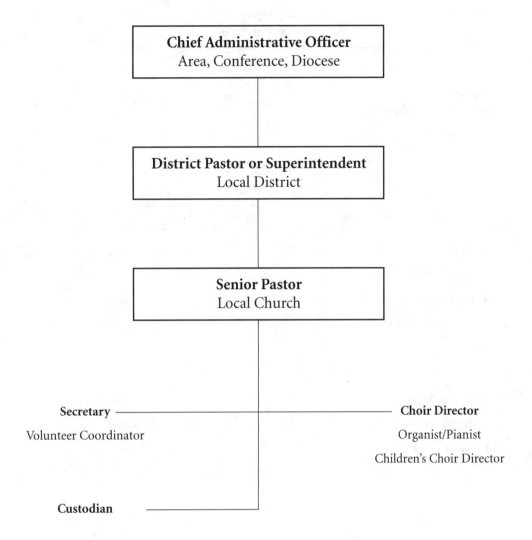

The titles for some of these positions may be somewhat different depending on the particular denomination; however, the functions will be similar in nature and purpose.

## *Small-Church Committee Structure*

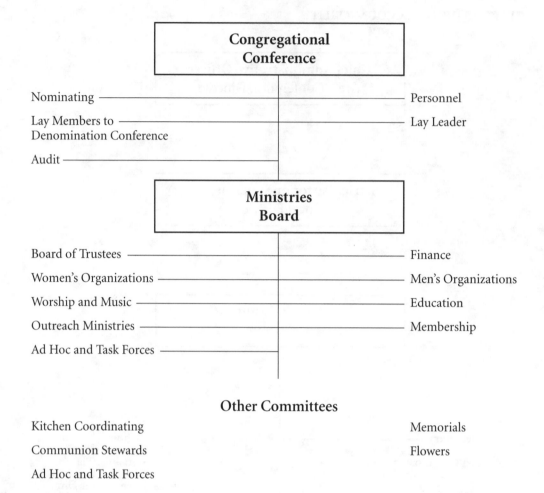

**Congregational Conference**

Nominating —————————————————————— Personnel

Lay Members to —————————————————————— Lay Leader
Denomination Conference

Audit ——————————————

**Ministries Board**

Board of Trustees —————————————————————— Finance

Women's Organizations —————————————————————— Men's Organizations

Worship and Music —————————————————————— Education

Outreach Ministries —————————————————————— Membership

Ad Hoc and Task Forces ——————————————

### Other Committees

Kitchen Coordinating                                    Memorials

Communion Stewards                                     Flowers

Ad Hoc and Task Forces

The titles for some of these committees may be somewhat different depending on the particular denomination; however, the functions will be similar in nature and purpose.

# Large-Church Organization Structure

**TYPICAL LINES OF ACCOUNTABILITY**

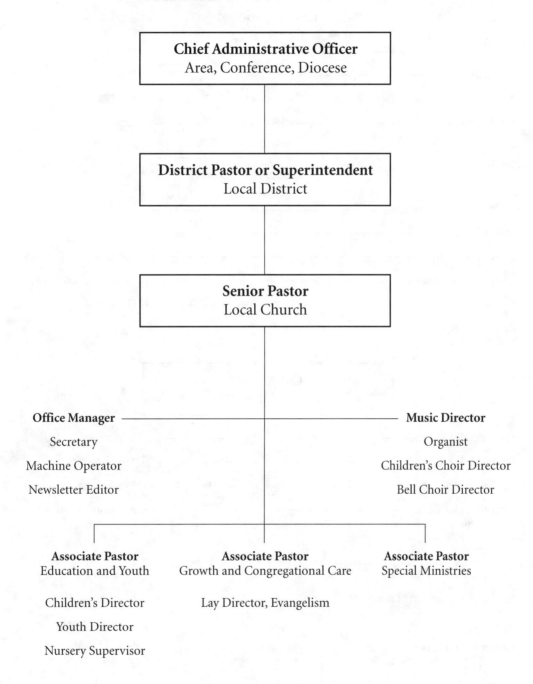

The titles for some of these positions may be somewhat different depending on the particular denomination; however, the functions will be similar in nature and purpose.

## Large-Church Committee Structure

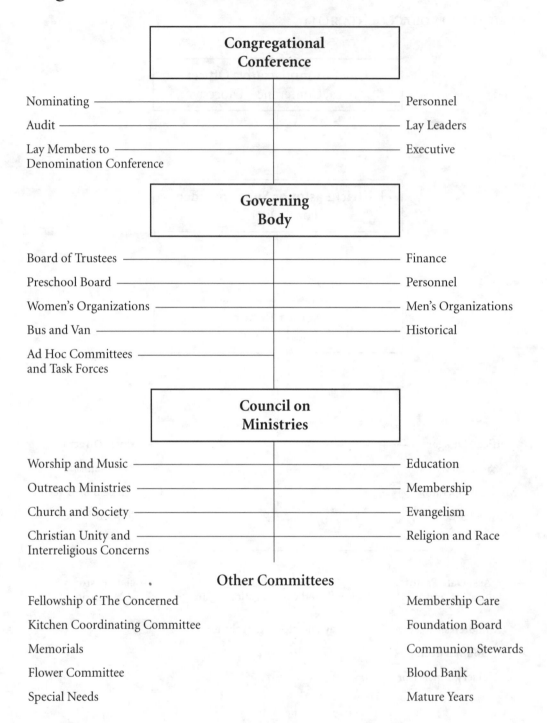

**Congregational Conference**

Nominating ——————————— Personnel

Audit ——————————————— Lay Leaders

Lay Members to ——————————— Executive
Denomination Conference

**Governing Body**

Board of Trustees ——————————— Finance

Preschool Board ——————————— Personnel

Women's Organizations ——————— Men's Organizations

Bus and Van ——————————————— Historical

Ad Hoc Committees ————————
and Task Forces

**Council on Ministries**

Worship and Music ——————————— Education

Outreach Ministries ——————————— Membership

Church and Society ——————————— Evangelism

Christian Unity and ——————————— Religion and Race
Interreligious Concerns

### Other Committees

| | |
|---|---|
| Fellowship of The Concerned | Membership Care |
| Kitchen Coordinating Committee | Foundation Board |
| Memorials | Communion Stewards |
| Flower Committee | Blood Bank |
| Special Needs | Mature Years |

The titles for some of these committees may be somewhat different depending on the particular denomination; however, the functions will be similar in nature and purpose.

## Staff Organization and Relationships with Multiple Pastors

Thus far we have discussed the characteristics of churches of various sizes, and how their size affects how they organize to accomplish their mission. We have looked at unique organizational concerns of both small and large churches and presented some typical organizational structures and accountability charts. The major area we have yet to discuss in detail is the church with more than one pastor.

Unique organizational and relational challenges face large churches as they move from a single pastor to multiple pastors. These challenges, as well as gender and cultural differences among staff members, must be recognized and carefully dealt with if the large church is to function in an effective, organized manner.

Often pastors are unprepared for the challenges of a multipastorate:

- Senior pastors may move into or grow into a multipastorate with little or no experience with the organization and relationships that are required.

- Associate pastors often may come from seminary into a multipastorate church having been trained in the skills needed for a single pastorate—the norm.

- Second-career pastors who may have had experience as staff members or supervisors of groups of employees may come to a multipastorate with expectations that do not match those of the senior pastor or other staff members.

Obviously, a multipastorate church must develop an organization and network of relationships that allow the roles of each member of the staff to be defined and developed, and then that allow these roles to meld together. The goal is to form a working environment that serves the church through an enlightened leadership in relationship with the laity.

The senior pastor would normally be expected to take the lead in role definition, but the senior pastor may have come to or evolved into the multipastorate with little or no training in how to assume the lead. The experience of many churches has been that it is the associate pastor who pushes for role definition. Unless done carefully and unless the senior pastor is receptive, conflict can result.

There must be early and complete communication between the senior pastor and associate pastors about their respective roles and relationships. Who will be primarily responsible for the various functions in worship, congregational care, and administration? Clearly defined roles, a supporting organizational structure, and specific, well-defined position descriptions should be developed along with a listing of specific, measurable objectives for each major responsibility listed on the position description. This information helps each pastoral staff member know who is responsible for which task and what duties staff members have committed to perform. How each member of the pastoral staff relates to the other, as well as how other staff members and the laity relate to each pastoral staff member, also must be examined and taken into consideration.

How does a multipastorate church reach this utopian-sounding organization and relationship? All involved must recognize the need for role definition and be willing to participate in the process. An outside facilitator may be helpful. A careful analysis of present roles and listing of desired changes should be done first, based on a clear understanding of the mission of the church. Specific, well-defined position descriptions should follow.

Agreement must be reached about the roles each pastoral staff member is to fill. This may take some time as the staff experiments with various working relationships. Questions will surface. Will the senior pastor continue to be involved deeply in all areas of worship, congregational care, and administration, or will some parts of these functions be delegated to associate pastors? Will associates be expected to "find their own niche" or will they be assigned specific functions and responsibilities? Ultimately, will a well-organized, functional relationship fit best, or will a looser, more relational mix be appropriate, where the senior pastor is the "teacher" and the associate pastors the "apprentices"?

Associate pastors need to be recognized for and evaluated against the role that they are given and that they accept. The laity needs to understand, accept, and support the role of each. Meetings of the church's governing body should include a report from each associate, as well as the senior pastor. Other visible means of recognition should be sought to ensure a clearly understood relationship.

Whatever working relationship is used, it seems imperative that staff members meet regularly, not only to coordinate their activities but to support each other in their tasks. This is especially true when lay persons become active volunteer members of the staff, often assuming important "pastoral" duties. Staff meetings should be a time to plan, coordinate, relate, and support. The frequency of such meetings will probably be dictated by need, as perceived by members of the staff; weekly meetings are certainly preferred so each member can stay in touch.

The goal is a smooth-working staff that supports all the needs of the church as it worships and reaches out to others. Such a goal is worth striving for.

## Personnel Management in the Local Church

Since people make an organization function effectively, selecting staff for an organization may well be the most important single function of church management. With the right mix of personnel and leadership, all things are possible. All churches will experience a significant managerial challenge as they mix paid staff with dedicated volunteers.

In this portion of our comments on organizing and staffing we will look first at the basis for meaningful personal relations and how this affects all relationships in the church. We will discuss expectations, evaluations, and growth and personal development. Some reasons why position descriptions are so important and why they should be developed will be presented. We then offer specific guidelines for writing position descriptions, emphasizing that this is a guiding document for the employee or volunteer that needs to be clear, detailed, and complete. Two suggested position description work sheets are included: one for a pastor and one in generic format.

Since the hiring of personnel is an important event in church life, we offer some guidance, first concerning the interview. It is perhaps the most important time spent with a job applicant. How the interviewer needs to be properly prepared to conduct an interview, what one should look for in a résumé, and some tips on effective interviewing are discussed. Only certain questions should be asked during an interview, and, in fact, some questions an interviewer might consider important are actually inappropriate and illegal. These questions are discussed so you will be properly prepared for this important event. One must never forget to request and verify references, and we give you guidance concerning this important part of the selection and hiring process.

The section on personnel management in the local church ends with thoughts on what should be included in personnel records and the legal concerns facing churches regarding personnel. We all may want to believe that "no one would ever sue the church." However, this is not true, and churches must be aware of the risks they face and prepare for them.

## *The Basis for All Meaningful Relationships*

All meaningful human relationships are based on mutual respect. The normal daily relationships that exist, to be meaningful, must be based on a trust that we are who we say we are and will act accordingly, and on the value that we place on each other as we interact. In a work environment, each staff member deserves an opportunity to ask:

- What do you expect of me?

- How am I doing? Am I meeting your expectations?

- If I am to grow and develop, what part must we *both* play?

*What do you expect of me?* Whether consciously or unconsciously, we all place expectations on the people with whom we have a meaningful relationship. They, in turn, have expectations of us. This is certainly true of spouses and children, and, in the church, of coworkers, those who are supervised, the pastor, as well as staff and volunteers. Expectations can be articulated verbally or in writing, and may be explicit or implied. Quite often, verbal and implied expectations lead to misunderstandings and disagreements. It follows, therefore, that written and explicit expectations, such as those found in agreements or contracts, are the most effective. This is especially true in formal organizational settings, whether religious or secular. In the most effective organizations, *a position description* is commonly used to detail work-related expectations.

The popular use of position descriptions is generally attributed to Dr. George Odiorne, a professor at the University of Michigan at the time, and a management consultant. Dr. Odiorne was retained to study an organization that was having serious performance, turnover, and morale problems. His approach to this situation was to ask many different employees, "What, specifically, does your supervisor expect of you on this job?" Next, he asked the supervisors of these people, "What, in specific detail, do you expect of this employee?"

The match between the two lists averaged about 40 percent. Is there any wonder that this organization had a performance and morale problem? About 60 percent of the time, people were doing things the supervisor didn't expect of them, and perhaps didn't even want them to do. Conversely, 60 percent of the time the employees were doing things for which they would never receive acknowledgment or recognition.

From this study, Odiorne developed the process known as Management by Objectives (MBO) and wrote a popular management book by that title.[3] In brief, the MBO process follows these steps:

1. A *position description* is developed for each staff member, including management, which details the duties, responsibilities, and expectations of the position quite explicitly.

2. *Specific objectives* are developed *jointly* with the staff member for as many of the responsibility statements as practical. This makes the position description operative and acceptable to both parties. A good specific objective must incorporate all of the following elements:

   - Objectives must be specific.

   - Objectives must be measurable.

   - Objectives must be time related.

   - The responsible person or persons must be identified.

3. A *performance evaluation* is given periodically.

*How am I doing? Am I meeting your expectations?* Performance appraisals, formal and informal, are absolutely essential if there is to be adequate communication between a supervisor and employee (or pastor and staff member). Few people are so self-reliant or secure that they can go for very long without some reinforcement, recognition, or evaluation of their contributions. Unacceptable behavior often can be traced to a lack of recognition or attention and may actually be an indirect and counterproductive way to get the desired attention.

Performance is compared to objectives or expectations and is articulated and conveyed, in either a secular or church setting, through

1. Periodic formal performance reviews or appraisals in which the supervisor and staff member jointly review expectations and performance in a positive, reinforcing way.

2. Periodic team meetings to report on how objectives are being met.

3. A self-appraisal with relation to agreed-upon objectives.

4. Verbal or written recognition of performance, which can be spontaneous or formal.

*If I am to grow and develop, what part must we both play?* Growth and personal development are very important to maintaining continued motivation. Although people generally do not like change, especially unexpected change, they can get bored, frustrated, and complacent with their work when they see no opportunity to grow. Productivity and morale suffers. The *opportunity* for change and growth must be present as a motivating factor. It is important to recognize, however, that growth and development of a staff member is a joint responsibility of the employer/pastor and the staff member.

1. In cases where the church provides the opportunity and the staff member is motivated, that person must accept the challenge if there is to be growth and development.

2. Supervisors should watch for signs that a person has plateaued or is "coasting" and be alert to ways of encouraging growth and development of staff members

who wish to do so. Opportunities for growth and development should be available to any person who wishes to take advantage of the opportunity.

3. Counseling and mentoring is a key factor in growth and development as part of practical, hands-on training and growth opportunities.

## The Importance of Position Descriptions

Position descriptions outline what an individual is to do as a part of the church organization. They define a particular piece of the church's mission, objectives, and action plans in which an individual will participate, and how one is to perform. The position description is the practical link between a church's planning process and the implementation of those plans, and it is the most effective means of communicating specific expectations and responsibilities from the church to the individual. It is a guiding document for that individual, whether clergy, lay employee, or volunteer, and therefore it must be clear, detailed, and complete.

Although there may be natural resistance to the perceived restrictions that position descriptions appear to present, it is this very setting of boundaries for an employee's work that organizes the work so assigned tasks can be accomplished in an effective and efficient way. Position descriptions are people-oriented and serve to structure a person's daily tasks—something most people welcome.

Position descriptions will aid in many ways in any church setting. They can:

- *Define the responsibilities of a position.* This definition sets the boundaries and structure of a specific position as it relates to all other jobs in the organization. Position responsibilities serve as a basis for establishing specific performance objectives on which the church and staff member can agree.

- *Provide a criterion for recruiting, interviewing, and selection.* Details about a job and its responsibilities will help define what a position entails and thus this will naturally make recruiting, interviewing, and selection of a new employee easier.

- *Maximize understanding about the duties and responsibilities of a position.* With a set listing of duties, an individual and supervisor can better communicate about what is required.

- *Help an organization know if there is proper delegation of duties.* By comparing the listed duties of various positions work can be delegated to the level where it can best be performed. This review will also help an organization determine if all essential functions are assigned or if duplication of effort exists.

- *Serve as a basis for meaningful performance evaluations.* Both the supervisor and staff member have a better opportunity for an evaluation oriented to objectives when specific responsibilities are outlined and understood. A periodic self-evaluation is also possible with established goals, so there are no surprises when the formal evaluation is received.

- *Act as a training aid.* Position descriptions can help identify areas where training is needed, if individuals are not able to perform certain work requirements. Training can then be directed toward these areas.

- *Provide objective criteria for corrective action, reprimand, or termination.* With written duties and requirements, there should be fewer questions about whether disciplinary action is justified when the work is not performed up to standards (after training has been provided).

- *Show compliance with equal employment opportunity requirements.* Statements in position descriptions that clearly define job requirements may serve as evidence against possible charges of discrimination under equal employment opportunity rules.

- *Serve as a basis for setting wage and salary grades.* Especially in a large organization, position descriptions are essential when setting wage and salary levels, in that comparisons of duties and responsibilities can be made objectively.

## *Guidelines for Writing Position Descriptions*

A position description arises from a need to define what people are to do and how they are to perform effectively in an organization, within the context of the entire organization's objectives. With this broad goal in mind, a position description must be prepared carefully, and the necessary time taken to make it a document that will not only define what is to be done, but also motivate an individual effectively.

What should a position description contain?

- A short statement describing the position and general responsibilities, followed by a listing of more specific responsibilities. These should be clear and as detailed as possible, generally in descending order of importance. However, remember that these are "responsibility" statements, not detailed procedural statements. For example, the responsibility of an administrative assistant may be to "order supplies as needed." How supplies are to be ordered would appear in an office-procedure guide.

- An individual's line of accountability should be included. This section also may include important points of coordination with other positions.

- The skills required for the position should be listed, some in detail if they pertain to technical abilities. For example, there can be a big difference between "know how to use a computer," and "be proficient in the following computer programs: WordPerfect . . ."

- Required education and experience should be shown, including the type of education and amount and type of experience required.

- Special requirements or working conditions should be discussed if these are pertinent to the job needs. There may be special licenses required or unusual duty hours that need to be listed.

- The final responsibility statement should be quite general to allow inclusion of "other responsibilities and tasks that may be requested from time to time."

Remember that a position description names the factors and requirements of the work to be done, not a person who may fill the position. Also remember that, to be a positive, motivating document, the position description should be carefully reviewed with new staff members or volunteers, who should be provided a copy. The date the position description was prepared or last revised should be recorded on the document.

How, when, and by whom are position descriptions developed?

- *Always* write a position description for a new position before recruiting and interviewing begins. The position description should serve as the major criterion by which candidates are judged during the interviewing and selection process.

- *Always* review and rewrite a position description for an existing position that has been vacated and for which a replacement is planned. This is the best time to make changes in position responsibilities, if needed.

- In situations in which position descriptions do not currently exist, introduce the development process carefully. People may construe the change as a restriction on their freedom or perhaps even as a way to define them out of a job, rather than as a means to set positive parameters for performance.

- Involve the staff in defining work performance requirements. Try to make it a team effort, something in which all are involved and have ownership, rather than a directive from management. Incumbents can participate by describing their own work requirements, being careful not to describe themselves. For open positions, supervisors may want to draft the initial description and have staff members with whom the person filling the open position will interact review and comment on the draft.

- Use a standard format so different positions can be seen in relation to each other.

- Be sure to build in occasions for periodic review and updates. Position descriptions can easily become outdated as requirements change and should be reviewed at least every two years.

- Finally, management should review all position descriptions to ensure that, as a group, they adequately describe what needs to be done to meet organizational goals and objectives.

The position description becomes the guide to develop specific, measurable, time-related goals and objectives for each individual. Generally, one or more specific objectives can be developed for most of the responsibility statements in a position description.

*Position description work sheets.* The following pages contain work sheets for developing position descriptions for clergy and for other positions in your church, both staff and volunteer. We urge you to use these work sheets and to refer to the sample position descriptions, starting on page 159, for guidance on suggested content. *Do not*, however, just copy the sample position description from the manual. Each position description must be customized to the circumstances and uniqueness of each position.

# *Clergy Position Description Work Sheet*

Position: _____

**General Responsibility Statement:** The basic functions of a pastor are contained within the following general categories:

*WORSHIP*
*CONGREGATIONAL CARE*
*ADMINISTRATION*

While some degree of the actual work performed in these areas may be delegated to others, staff or volunteers, the ultimate accountability for assuring that the following responsibilities are implemented rests with the pastor. The responsibilities described cover the total ministry of the church.

## *Specific Responsibilities:*

**WORSHIP**

1. _____

   _____

2. _____

   _____

3. _____

   _____

**CONGREGATIONAL CARE**

*Nurture*

1. _____

   _____

2. _____

   _____

3. _____

   _____

*Evangelism and Membership*

1. _____

   _____

2. _____

_____

3. _____

_____

4. _____

_____

*Christian Education*

1. _____

_____

2. _____

_____

3. _____

_____

*Parish Life*

1. _____

_____

2. _____

_____

3. _____

_____

**ADMINISTRATION**—In cooperation with Personnel Committee, Governing Bodies, Finance Committee, and other involved work areas, assures that:

1. _____

_____

2. _____

_____

3. _____

_____

4. _____

_____

5. _____

_____

6. _____

_____

7. _____

_____

8. _____

_____

9. _____

_____

10. _____

_____

12. _____

_____

*Requirements for this position:*

Qualifications: _____

_____

_____

_____

_____

Education: _____

_____

_____

_____

_____

Experience: _____

_____

_____

_____

_____

## General Position Description Work Sheet

Position: _____

General Responsibility Statement: _____

_____

_____

Specific Responsibilities:

1. _____

_____

2. _____

_____

3. _____

_____

4. _____

_____

5. _____

_____

6. _____

_____

7. _____

_____

8. _____

_____

9. _____

_____

Qualifications, Education, Experience required for this position:

_____

_____

_____

_____

## Interviewing to Fill a Position

The interview is perhaps the most important time you will spend with an applicant. The decision to hire can lead to a long-term, productive, and mutually satisfying relationship—or just the opposite.

An interview is your opportunity to get to know a candidate and to determine whether they can meet the requirements of the open position. The candidate will have questions, although you should expect they will have done their homework and be somewhat familiar with the organization and the position for which they are applying. Together, you will each be trying to determine whether there will be a proper "fit" of the candidate with the existing organization and the supporting environment. A positive interview should be one in which both the organization and the interviewee find out as much as possible about each other and know at the end of the interview whether the candidate is right for the open position.

The following are some guidelines for a competent, positive interview.

*What the interviewer needs:*

1. A comprehensive position description. (The candidate being interviewed should have been provided a copy beforehand.)

2. A candidate's résumé and/or application for employment. Look for:

   a. How well the résumé fits the position to be filled.

   b. Organization and presentation of the résumé. Spelling or grammatical errors are an indication of sloppy work and a lack of attention to detail.

   c. Specific accomplishments applicable to the position to be filled.

   d. Gaps in employment. These need to be explained.

   e. Job hopping—less than two years per job or four jobs in ten years. Are there good reasons for the changes in employment or is this an indication of instability?

   f. Possible "common ground" to open the interview and to put the candidate at ease.

3. A list of questions or discussion items, prepared before the interview.

4. A relatively open-ended time period.

5. No interruptions or distractions.

6. A quiet and comfortable environment.

*How to conduct the interview and what is important:*

1. Take a few minutes to get acquainted and to make the candidate comfortable. Perhaps there are some items on the résumé that provide common ground.

2. Ask the candidate for permission to take notes during the interview.

3. Talk as little as necessary and listen carefully to not only what is being said, but to what is not being said. Many interviewers dominate the conversation, talking over 50 percent of the time, when they should take about 10 to 20 percent of the interview time.

4. Don't be reluctant to ask the tough questions, if necessary.

5. Ask follow-up questions when the situation needs to be clarified, more information is needed, or the candidate seems to be avoiding an issue or seems reluctant to go into detail.

6. Use short periods of silence to draw out more complete responses. Let the candidate be a little anxious about whether he or she responded to the question adequately, rather than moving on to another subject too quickly. You may cut off some pertinent input. Prompting, like "please go on" or "and . . ." will also elicit additional information.

7. Try to use one-on-one interviewing, and not more than two-on-one. You want to create as little stress as possible to facilitate a positive interview. More than two interviewers can add stress for the candidate and should not be used unless the reaction to stress needs to be determined.

8. Three or more different people, preferably persons working at different levels of the organization, should interview each candidate. This gives both the employer and the candidate an opportunity to discuss the position differently and allows for a broader base of information with which to evaluate how the candidate will meet the needs of the organization and fit into the position. The higher the responsibility level of a position, the more important multiple interviews become for providing a broader base of evaluation.

9. Interviewers should get together and share their impressions of the candidate on the day of the interview. Time tends to blur important first impressions.

### GENERAL OBSERVATIONS ABOUT INTERVIEWING

The primary focus of the interview should be on the candidate and their qualifications. Sometimes an experienced interviewee will try to dominate the interview with questions that take attention away from themselves and therefore minimize the essential information that needs to be gathered about them during the interview. To be a positive experience, an interview must allow time for all persons to learn all they need to know to make a correct decision.

Making the right choice in filling a position is extremely important. It is generally accepted that supervisors know within a few months if a mistake was made in hiring, but it takes up to two years to correct that mistake. Given current labor laws, terminating an employee for cause is a time-consuming process, even without incurring the possibility of a lawsuit.

A good general rule when selecting a candidate is *never settle for second-best*. Do everything within your power to hire the best candidate for the position, even if it means a delay in hiring and going through the search and interviewing process again. Too many times people feel pressure to fill an open position, hire a less-than-ideal candidate, and are often sorry soon thereafter.

### INTERVIEWING FOR A CHURCH POSITION

Although the guidance presented above will apply to most churches, some adjustments in interviewing procedure will take place in churches of differing sizes and requirements.

Those churches which "call" their clergy will go through a detailed, sometimes quite time-consuming process of finding a new pastor or associate pastor. When it comes time for the formal interview, there may be multiple interviews. Members may feel it their right to be involved in an interview, which could become a "mass" of people firing questions at a candidate. Obviously, this scene should be avoided. A church should follow a strict process of selection that basically follows the interview guidelines discussed earlier.

Even small churches should follow the basic guidelines for interviewing. There may be a greater temptation for members of the "church family" all to be involved in interviewing and selecting an employee. Conversely, if a single person is responsible for hiring and firing, the advantages of using the opinions of several qualified interviewers will be lost.

## Interview Questions

The following is a partial list of questions that might be asked of a candidate to learn more about them, their work experience, how they think about work-related matters, and how they might fit into the existing organization. Not all these questions need be asked during any one interview. Indeed, some may be inappropriate for a specific position or individual. This list is intended to stimulate an interviewer's thinking in preparing a unique written list of appropriate questions. Detailed notes should be taken on the responses as well as on other pertinent information revealed during the interview. As a courtesy, it is a good practice to ask the candidate if they have any objection to notes being made.

Note that most of these questions are open-ended and require thought and articulation to form a reasonable response. Questions that can be answered in a word or two, or with a "Yes" or "No," should be avoided, since they generally elicit little in-depth information.

*General interview questions:*

1. Describe the work situation you find most stimulating or motivating.
2. Describe the work situation you find least motivating or most upsetting.
3. What do you see as your major strengths or talents?
4. What do you feel are your major weaknesses?
5. How does your previous experience relate to this position?
6. Tell me about your greatest job-related achievement or success.
7. Describe your greatest job-related failure.
8. What do you know about this position and/or our organization?
9. Why do you want to work for our organization?
10. What do you think you can contribute to our organization?
11. What are your goals for the next five, ten, twenty years?
12. How much do you expect to earn in five, ten, twenty years?

13. What do you think determines a person's progress in a good organization?

14. What type of supervisor do you prefer?

15. Define "cooperation." Define "teamwork."

16. Of the jobs you have held, which did you like the most and why?

17. Of the jobs you have held, which did you like the least and why?

18. Why did you leave your last job (and any job you have held)?

19. Have you ever been convicted of a crime, other than minor traffic violations?

20. Can you be bonded?

21. Describe the ideal job for you.

22. What have you done to show initiative and willingness to work hard?

23. What salary range will you consider?

24. What would you like me to know about you that we haven't discussed.

*Additional questions possibly appropriate for a supervisory position:*

1. How would you acknowledge a significant work-related contribution of an employee?

2. One of our current challenges is _____. How would you go about resolving this issue?

3. What would you do about an employee who is chronically tardy or absent?

4. You have confirmed that an employee is telling lies about another employee. What would you do?

5. It has come to your attention that an employee has been stealing. What would you do?

6. How do you feel about performance evaluations?

*Inappropriate and illegal interview questions.* Only questions that are related in some way to the work situation for which the candidate is being considered are appropriate. Any questions related to race, religion, sex, age, family situation, dependents, national origin, or to highly personal matters are not only inappropriate but may not be legal, on the basis that the answer may lead to possible discrimination.

## Reference Checks

### Never, ever hire a person without a thorough and multiple reference check!!!

The only way to ascertain how a candidate will perform in a work situation is by doing a thorough reference check. Some people you may interview are excellent actors and can make a very good impression even though they may not be qualified for the position. The sample employment application form (page 232) contains a place for the applicant to release the employer from liability, which allows a reference to provide information about the applicant. This release should be used, perhaps sending it by fax, if a reference is reluctant to answer questions. Typical questions that might be asked of a reference are listed on the telephone reference check form on page 234. Completed reference checks should be filed in the personnel folder if the person is hired.

The candidate should be prepared to supply a list of references from previous work experiences. These references should have been contacted by the candidate and thus should expect to be called. This prior contact tends to reduce the reluctance of a reference to answer your questions.

The suggested minimum number of references to be interviewed:

- Two or more people for whom the candidate worked.

- Two or more people with whom the candidate worked—peers.

- Two or more people who worked for the candidate, if this is a supervisory position.

If references cannot be contacted or are uncooperative, the candidate should be asked to supply additional references until the suggested minimum number of references are interviewed.

Letters of recommendation are generally meaningless unless the person who wrote the letter can be contacted directly and will verify what was said in the letter. After all, have you ever seen an uncomplimentary letter of reference?

Personal references need to be contacted only if the candidate is just out of school and has a sparse work history. Personal references usually supply very little information on the candidate's qualifications to fill a given position. They may, however, supply worthwhile information on the candidate's character, values, habits, interests, and so forth.

**The most telling question** that can be asked of a reference, particularly if a reference is reluctant to answer questions, is: **Would you hire this person (again) if you had an open position that this person was qualified to fill?** Few people will hedge on this seemingly innocuous question, and an answer of "No," or a hesitation to respond, speaks volumes in terms of an unacceptable reference.

Another good wrap-up question, for both a reference and a candidate, is: *Is there anything that I should have asked that I didn't ask?* It is sometimes surprising how much information an open-ended question of this type will elicit.

## Personnel Records

It is *extremely* important that complete personnel records be maintained. First, it is in the staff member's interest that there be a complete record because memories fade, supervisors change, or other things happen to make the documentation in a personnel file invaluable. Second, these records are important in any legal or arbitration proceedings in which the church may become involved. The outcome of these proceedings is often highly dependent on the content and completeness of the personnel records.

The following properly completed and dated materials should be in the personnel folder of each person on the payroll, full-time or part-time:

- Application for employment

- Interview notes and reference-check information

- Correspondence with the employee or prospective employee
- Hiring records, including tax, medical, and other pertinent material
- Position description with an indication that it was discussed with the staff member, that is, signed or initialed
- Orientation and training records
- Signed forms acknowledging receipt of personnel policies, sexual harassment policy, keys, credit cards, and so forth
- Record of attendance, tardiness, illness, vacations, time off, leaves, and so forth
- Signed performance reviews
- Specific objectives, signed
- Commendations
- Promotions
- Wage and benefit adjustments
- Warnings, reprimands, suspensions, and so forth
- Separation reports, voluntary or involuntary
- Exit interview

*Be fully aware that personnel records are no longer "confidential."* They must be opened to the employee and others with a "need to know." Keep in mind that: ***The only items that should be in the personnel folder are those that the employee has provided, has seen or is aware of, or of which they have been given a copy.***

## Legal Concerns Regarding Personnel

Legal concerns regarding personnel are extensive and complex, with many statutes and regulations relating to various aspects of employment. Moreover, these laws and regulations change continually. Therefore, it is well beyond the scope of this manual to cover this subject in any depth or detail, but three general concerns should be kept in mind.

***Discrimination.*** Churches need to ensure that hirings, promotions, wage and benefit actions, reprimands, terminations, and all other personnel actions are administered fairly, justly and, *above all,* uniformly. The EEOC (Equal Employment Opportunity Commission) administers these laws and regulations. Sexual harassment is a form of discrimination and is thus covered by EEOC regulations. The Americans with Disabilities Act deals with potential discrimination against employees with disabilities and the reasonable accommodations that must be made.

***Safety in the Workplace.*** The health and welfare of all employees must be safeguarded in the work environment. If hazardous materials or conditions are present, measures must be taken to ensure that no harm comes to the employee who follows prescribed procedures. Standards and regulations have been developed and are administered by OSHA (Occupational Safety and Health Act).

***Collection of Taxes and Deductions.*** The various deductions required by law—income tax, social security, Medicare, and so forth—must be properly deducted, accounted for, and promptly remitted to the appropriate government agencies. State and Federal IRS (Internal Revenue Service) offices, as well as other government agencies, administer these laws.

Starting on page 241 is a paper titled "Legal Issues Facing Churches," written by an attorney who is also a lay person in the church of one of the authors. [4] This paper delves in more depth into potential legal issues in which a church may get involved.

Churches are not immune to legal action and potentially large settlements, and judgments can have a major impact on church finances. Prior to 1985, lawsuits against churches were rather rare. But in the current litigious climate, more and more churches are being sued over issues ranging from employee disputes to personal injury. Pastors and staff should consult lawyers and accountants to assure that the church complies with all federal and state regulations.

## The Local Church in Action

### *The Functioning Church Organization*

As a church plans its mission and organizes to accomplish its plan, it must work to ensure that both the paid staff and lay volunteer staff function together cohesively toward common goals.

Local church organization has previously been discussed as being necessary, even in the smallest congregation. As a church changes in size and mission, the organization must be flexible enough to bring positive change in the life of the church. Every church, even though formally organized under denominational rules or guidelines, will differ from every other church in the way it functions with Christian love.

Thoughts about official and unofficial organizations within churches, and how the formal organization must consider and integrate the informal groups, are presented on page 147. The pastor is the one individual in a position to influence the melding of the formal and informal organizations in a positive way.

Committees are integral to any church organization. How they must interpret, enact, and coordinate the direction of the church is discussed on pages 148–149. Also stressed are the roles of these committees, the records they should maintain, and the need for full coordination and communication.

Pages 149–155 contain several discussions about how various elements of the church staff (both paid and volunteer) must function together. The office administrative assistant is examined as the "keystone" to the church staff; financial staff members (quite often lay volunteers), such as the treasurer and financial secretary, are discussed in light of their important support roles; the jobs of program staff, such as choir director, organist, education director, custodian, are presented and their intertwining roles emphasized; and lastly there is recognition that part-time employees or volunteers may fill several positions very well.

For organization to be effective, a church must first recognize what organization is needed, fully document and implement the needed structure, and then use this organization to accomplish the mission and enhance its programs in a synergistic way.

## The Official and Unofficial Organization

Although different denominations may encourage different levels and forms of church organization, some organization must exist if the mission and plans of the church are to be accomplished.

Organization that is formal helps everyone know what to expect, with whom to coordinate, and what each person should do. However, a church is replete with opportunities for informal organization that can either complement the formal organization or conflict with it. Real church life takes place where people are in mission: in Sunday school classes, in the choir, within youth groups, in men's and women's groups, in covenant groups, and so forth. One might even say the "church" becomes a group of "small churches" gathered together for worship.

This grass-roots level of performance is of the utmost importance and can exist within or outside the formal organization. One can easily find this performance level among informal teams of people cooperating within each church group. The goal is to bring these activities inside the total organization—or at least within knowledge of the total organization, so that everyone is contributing to the overall church mission and its objectives.

The organizational structure should provide a formal connection with each of these informal groups. This is most easily done through the department or group supervisor, who, when carefully chosen, can effectively represent the group to the total organization. A day-care program may be a good example in that, although it might exist outside the formal organization, the program can affect other church activities such as the Sunday school, especially when facilities and classrooms are shared. An effective way to coordinate such informal groups can be a "luncheon" including the department or group supervisors, pastor, and lay leadership, during which informal group activities and concerns are discussed.

Not all informal groups will always want to cooperate fully with the formal structure. Opportunities for channeling dissident informal groups need to be recognized. The pastor is the one person in a position to deal with such groups and to bring them into the overall structure. The pastor must be aware of factions and find ways to use them for the total good. Some strategies include:

- Find something informal groups would *want* to do and give them the job. Praise them for the accomplishment.

- Watch for opportunities to integrate pastoral leadership into their activities. Attend their meetings and show involvement in their activities, as you examine, together, how their activities can be integrated into church objectives—*slowly!!*

- Find ways to show Christian love to someone who has been a problem.

As pastors work with dissident groups, they must balance the needs of these groups with those of the rest of the church, showing how the dissident groups can become assets. Tough? Sure! But, so are many human relationships.

Together, Christ's work is accomplished in an organized and energized way as official and unofficial organizations meld their goals and activities.

### The Task of Committees: Interpret, Enact, and Coordinate

One of the most common elements of formal structure is the committee, which involves various staff and lay people, working together, to interpret, enact, and coordinate all effort.

To use an analogy, and assuming the reader has had some experience fishing, using worms for bait, one might consider a local church very much like a "can of worms," in a positive sense.

- The church, as the "can," may be large or small, plain or fancy; it may be well planned or have no direction. The "can" surrounds the worms and gives a foundation, parameters, and boundaries for what the worms can do.

- The "worms" might be thought of as the people in every department, committee, or program in the church.

- All "worms" are clustered together in the can, usually in a ball under some covering. Each is doing its own thing, within limits. Yet, they are always entwined, overlapping, unable to move very far in one direction or to accomplish much without similar, complimentary movement by all the other "worms."

- When someone (maybe the pastor) tries to pull on the end of one worm, that person may break off the end if they pull too hard—havoc results. Even if they pull slowly, evenly, and the worm comes out whole, all the other worms in the cluster will move in reaction to the removal of one worm, because the group as a whole has been affected.

The points of this analogy may be obvious. Every group in the church must consider itself entwined with every other group. Although they may be separate entities and work independently, they must in the end work together. As the direction of the church changes, their efforts must change in concert with the whole.

What does this mean in a specific church? What must committees do to ensure they are part of the whole?

- Each committee must recognize its role, examine its role in light of what has already been done, and integrate this knowledge with specific tasks identified during the planning cycle and the development of action plans. If changes in direction take place, each committee will want to react in a positive way.

- To ensure continuity, a standard set of records for each committee should be kept current and should be passed on upon a change in committee leadership. These records should include:

  1. A statement of purpose as well as a responsibility statement

  2. Minutes of previous meetings

  3. Schedule of specific, regular events, for example, special worship days

  4. Checklists related to specific events

  5. Committee plans and actions related to its part in long-range plans

  6. List of other groups with which coordination is usually necessary and what this coordination entails

7. Budget requests and actions taken

- The committee should hold an organizational meeting at least annually, during which it determines what is to be done during the year and how action plans and other tasks are to be accomplished.

Individual officers and board and committee chairpersons should get together and develop outlines of specific programs for the church year, including schedules and calendars. This can be accomplished at a new officers retreat. Coordination and teamwork should be of paramount importance if the church is to avoid being a place of conflict and strife.

Throughout the year, all programs must be coordinated and enacted as a team; the pastor and lay leadership will be instrumental in this coordination. Although there are a number of good ways to assure coordination, one means is through informal leadership lunch meetings once a month. Members of lunch groups then go to respective committees or "homerooms" and communicate plans and test ideas with other members. Each month, feedback returns to the leadership group, resulting in the development of new thoughts or ideas. When decisions are based on considerable discussion and testing, the church moves ahead in a positive, coordinated direction.

*Communication: the essence of group interaction*

## The Church Staff Functioning Together

Each church, regardless of size, will have a regular staff for daily operations. At a small church this may include only a pastor and part-time volunteer secretarial and program staff. A larger church will normally employ one or more pastors, an administrative assistant, music director, organist, possibly a financial assistant or business administrator, custodian, and program specialists as needed. Whatever the size of the church staff, the operating structure and environment must allow all to work together. Staff functions are all interrelated, and therefore the staff must be considered an integrated unit. We will now review some of the key considerations necessary to ensure that the staff functions as an integrated unit, and identify how each part functions as a part of the whole.

### ADMINISTRATIVE ASSISTANT—KEYSTONE TO THE STAFF

The church "secretary" (better named administrative assistant) plays a key role in all church interrelationships. This person is, in the true sense of the term, the "keystone" to effective staff functioning. Primarily, this person serves as

- An information center—a receptionist and telephone communicator, and one who causes information to flow to and from the pastor and church leaders

- One who processes written communication of all types—reports, memos, letters, documents, mail, bulletins and newsletters

- An assistant to the pastor, church officers, and total organization

- A scheduling center

- An archivist
- Perhaps even a financial clerk—keeping petty cash, receiving payments and making disbursements, maybe maintaining financial records for the treasurer and financial secretary (especially at small churches), and acting as purchasing agent

The administrative assistant must demonstrate a high level of confidence and be operationally stable to function effectively. In many instances this person speaks for the pastor and thus *is* the pastor when the pastoral staff is not available. The position is challenging since church administrative assistants are often underpaid and overworked and expected to be almost perfect—a master of all subjects and detail. Needless to say, the person filling this position must be knowledgeable, well-organized, and an expert in working with people.

A pastor has a number of expectations of a church administrative assistant, most of which relate to intangible talents critical to a church setting. A church administrative assistant must

- Learn how the pastor thinks and anticipate how tasks need to be done; have an open attitude toward the pastor
- Be organized, and in turn help the pastor to be better organized
- Recognize that people come first, and that other tasks may have to wait
- Be willing and able to learn new approaches, and to learn to use new office equipment
- Ask for or set priorities, especially when there is more to do than can possibly get done
- Develop an ability to look ahead and anticipate needs
- Have pride in the work being done
- Be accurate and use good judgment
- Be flexible and open to changes in their responsibilities
- Be willing to assume responsibility in the pastor's absence, without going beyond the "bounds" set by the pastor
- Recognize that there is great variety in the job; this may call for adaptability in a given work period, particularly when emergencies arise
- Be respectful of the confidentiality needed in the office
- ***Be impeccably trustworthy and have the highest integrity***

The laity also see the administrative assistant as available to help with their tasks, and may expect the church administrative assistant to

- Relay messages accurately
- Return calls as soon as possible
- Accomplish a given task in a professional manner
- Be as knowledgeable as possible about a subject

- Be friendly, personable, and willing to listen to concerns without being overly chatty

- Maintain a filing system in which items can be found easily

- Be able to reach the pastor in case of emergencies

- Have supplies of all shapes and sizes available

- Maintain a room-use schedule for organized use of the facilities

- Arrange for childcare for last-minute meetings

If the church does not have an administrative assistant, the pastor fits the bill just fine in the eyes of many. It is human nature for people to expect others to help with administrative detail. If an administrative person is not available, the next person in line—either up or down—must fill the need.

The message may be obvious: even if you can't afford it, *get an administrative assistant.* A part-time schedule may be possible and will prove effective if the job is well defined, scheduled carefully, and all are made to understand the time and work parameters of the position. The laity will respond to that arrangement; they, too, can schedule their activities. A talented, interested volunteer is a must if payment is not possible.

Some of the same thoughts and criteria apply to relationships with staff members, both paid and volunteer, if the administrative assistant is to be the effective "keystone." Staff members must recognize that this position is truly the center of all church activity and respond with adequate information about all their activities.

It is imperative also that the same importance be given the office space and location. After all, *the office is the church, during the week.* An organized office in a good location will add much to the image of the church.

### *Is your keystone in place?*

### THE TREASURER AS FINANCIAL MANAGER

Among the most important support functions in a church are the roles of treasurer and financial secretary. We first look at the role of the treasurer as financial manager of the church.

Although large churches likely will have a business administrator on staff to coordinate all financial needs, most churches will have a treasurer who usually can be considered the chief financial officer. This member safeguards the congregation's funds, spends according to the budget, and gives financial guidance to officers and leaders of the church.

More specifically, a church treasurer performs a number of extremely important functions for the life of the church which must be coordinated with all other committees and groups.

*First and foremost, **treasurers must instill integrity and credibility** into the finan-* cial management system for which they are responsible. There is no room for compromise. If the treasurer succeeds in this critical objective, members will have little or no concern about what happens to their contributions.

The treasurer is responsible not only for safekeeping of funds and for maintaining financial documents in an orderly and efficient way, but also for spending within budgetary limits, paying bills on time, and communicating complete information about the financial health of the church. The treasurer:

- Tracks variances from the budget—both receipts and expenditures
- Alerts department/committee chairpersons about their budgets and spending patterns and encourages their participation at budget preparation time, so the dollars can fit the program of the church, not the reverse
- Keeps funds given for a specific purpose separate—not necessarily always in separate cash accounts—but through proper accounting
- At budget time, prepares analyses which show receipt and spending patterns over time
- Advises the congregation (through a weekly newsletter, or some other means) about the church's financial posture—always in a positive way

The treasurer serves as financial advisor to all other groups in the church which have their own funds (such as Sunday school classes), and may even, in small churches, maintain these accounts. There can be financial advantages if funds from various groups are combined; for example, interest income. However, care must always be taken that accounting records are carefully established and maintained to ensure a clear division of funds among groups.

Staff members with whom the treasurer must work closely include:

- The church administrative assistant, who might usually handle mail, match receiving reports with billings, handle petty cash, encourage members to use check request forms, and be available to explain unusual events or circumstances
- The financial secretary, to ensure that all gifts and offerings are credited according to a donor's desires, that proper accounting codes are used, and that appropriate trend analyses of giving patterns are prepared
- Everyone else in the church, for there is little activity in which money is not involved

Qualities sought in a treasurer might include:

- An active, devoted Christian who is willing to give a good deal of time to detailed work
- One who can instill confidence and absolute integrity in the position
- One with basic accounting knowledge, but more important, one who is sensitive to overall financial management needs
- One who has excellent human relations skills (complete, effective communication is important)
- Depending on the size of the church, the job might be held by a long-term volunteer, or by a part-time paid individual

*One word of caution:* the treasurer must not be allowed to control, and must communicate. This job entails a great deal of responsibility, but only specific, limited authority. In other words, it is the treasurer's job to support the program of the church and decisions made by the congregation and its representatives. If the congregation's stewardship is not sufficient to finance programs, then the treasurer reports this fact to the congregation and lay leadership. The treasurer does not determine which bills to pay and where the money is to come from in times of shortage without full knowledge of congregational officials. Treasurers do not usually enjoy being the bearers of bad tidings, but sometimes that is their job.

## ROLE OF THE FINANCIAL SECRETARY

The financial secretary receives and records member gifts. The work of the financial secretary is essential to the administration of the congregation's entire program. Money is a tool to help accomplish goals and objectives, and thus an important and necessary part of the church.

*Receiving and recording of income must be impeccably accurate* if the integrity and credibility of the entire financial management system is to be maintained. People get suspicious and cautious when errors are made in recording their contributions—and rightfully so.

This position requires an extremely capable person, willing to serve, who is accurate beyond question and handles errors, when they do occur, in such a way that the confidence of contributors is not shaken. Usually the financial secretary will be a lay volunteer, but in larger churches this position is often filled by a paid staff member, or financial assistant.

Primarily, the financial secretary:

- Ensures the receipt of gifts is smooth, well-organized, well-supervised, and has required internal controls. The financial secretary is responsible for and trains volunteer money counters.

- Maintains a record of income and communicates this in total to the treasurer, and in detail to individual contributors. The financial secretary may make a summary report to the congregation, depending on the division of duties with the treasurer.

- May participate in the stewardship campaign by providing information. In some small churches the financial secretary may be in charge of the campaign.

Interaction with other church staff members may include regular communication with the stewardship committee for feedback on giving trends; with those in charge of special projects in which gifts are received; with the pastoral staff whenever giving trends need to be brought to their attention; and, of course, with the treasurer to ensure integrity of the accounting system.

A typical position description for a financial secretary is included on page 171. Details about these duties, as well as related forms and procedures that may be useful, are presented in chapter 5.

## THE INTEGRATED ACTIVITIES OF PROGRAM STAFF MEMBERS

Program staff members, such as the choir director, organist, education director, and custodian, must all integrate their various activities with each other and lay committees if there is to be cohesion. Each has their own managerial responsibilities and program tasks; but as they plan, organize, staff, finance, motivate, direct, and evaluate their programs, they must do so considering the needs of the congregation, its worship, outreach and educational programs, and recreational activities. The interweaving of these various activities is what makes the church a viable, active, single entity with a specific purpose.

*Choir director and organist.* Music, as one of the primary influences in our lives, can enhance worship a great deal if presented properly (as can related programs in dance, drama, and art). In addition to meeting the need for ample facilities and equipment, the performing arts department must manage its resources—instruments and equipment—in an organized, effective way. This includes tuning and cleaning instruments on a regular basis; cleaning robes while they still can be cleaned; repairing straps and pitching and polishing bells to enhance the sound; filing and repairing music; storing costumes properly; and so forth. Additionally, the department needs to work with finance personnel to decide on budgetary needs.

Scheduling of activities is critical. The department's work must be fully coordinated and integrated with worship programs, special worship services such as funerals and weddings, and with educational and recreational activities.

The formal church organization may place the personnel of the performing arts department under the supervision of the worship committee. However, if there are paid staff members, as is frequently the case, the organization must allow for formal position descriptions and performance evaluations by an assigned supervisor. This may be the responsibility of the pastor or a designated representative. In any case, the intertwined activities of this department call for innovative organizational alignments which can best serve the church in achieving its goals and in gaining full church support for the program.

*Education director.* Education, in some form, is part of almost every church activity, and the church probably will be formally organized to carry out an education ministry. Personnel responsible for this area will want to ensure that they follow the mission and guidelines of the church as a whole.

Although, organizationally, the education department may appear as a separate entity, it must be integrated with all other activities. The education director will want to look for ways to cooperate with other church programs, including worship opportunities, youth activities, formal Sunday school events, Vacation Bible School, and so forth. Integrated activities with the church library may prove advantageous as computer-enhanced learning programs become available.

The education director may report directly to one of the pastors if that person's specialty is education. Again, a complete job description and evaluation system will be needed.

*Custodian.* Although usually considered a member of the support staff, the custodian should be an integral part of all program planning to ensure adequate preparation for space and equipment, as well as cleanup.

The custodian may report directly to a pastor or be responsible to the church trustees or property committee. A clear understanding of the custodian's organizational responsibility is important if this person is to be effective and not be at the whim of various individuals or committees. Beyond the normal position description and evaluation requirements, specific descriptions about who resolves conflicts in duties and sets priorities should be in place. An active lay assistance program for seasonal maintenance requirements can help the custodian during extra-busy times.

As discussed later, the custodian will perform most effectively with checklists, schedules, and other job-enhancing aids.

***The effectiveness of integrated teamwork.*** Whether a small church, where the "family" gets together and gets the job done whenever some need is identified, or a large church with a large, paid staff, each needs organization that allows for its parts to be fully integrated and intertwined. Opportunities for integration should be actively sought in every church. How better to go about God's work than in an organized, cooperative way?

## PART-TIME EMPLOYEES OR VOLUNTEERS

An average-size church normally functions with one, two, or maybe three full-time personnel and a number of volunteers. Additionally, there may be several part-time paid employees, such as a choir director, organist, nursery attendants, and maybe a custodian.

Churches usually rely on volunteers for other functions, but there may be viable reasons why additional personnel should receive a small salary. Human nature being what it is, there may be a rationale for encouraging a person to greater work with compensation. Examples of positions in which a small compensation may be appropriate and beneficial include:

- A retired pastor may be helpful with counseling or calling.

- A trained teacher could effectively assist church school activities.

- A retired accountant or auditor may serve as a financial assistant.

- Someone trained in procurement may serve as a central purchasing agent.

The primary idea is to bring other professionals into the church in cases where this would add to the program and be cost-effective. The return from part-time paid personnel may be greater than from volunteers in that:

- They may feel more responsible for their work.

- They do the job and don't put it off.

- They are concerned about "earning their pay."

- They tend to avoid burnout since they work part-time. If replacement becomes necessary, termination is easier than with volunteers.

Although not appropriate for each organizational setting, the use of part-time paid staff duties to complement the pastor can prove a viable solution to the need for quality assistance. However, qualified volunteers often can be found in congregations, and one must never create an organizational structure in which volunteers cannot be used effectively. Members need opportunities to serve God, as they are able. The key is to shape the organization and staff in the way that best fits the unique needs of the individual church.

# Organizational Documentation
## *Essential Organizational Documentation*

Every organization, secular or religious, must keep certain essential documents. Proper documentation promotes understanding of the functioning of that organization and ensures that people are treated fairly. The most important pieces of this documentation are listed and described below. The samples contained in this manual provide an example of the type of documentation that allows an organization to function properly and effectively. However, we caution that we cannot include a complete list since different organizations have different requirements. Likewise, the sample documents are not purported to be complete, or to apply in all cases, and will need to be customized.

***Position descriptions.*** Once an organizational structure is set, the next step is to define the responsibilities of each person in that structure. This is usually done with a position description. Typical descriptions for most jobs in a church are presented beginning on page 158 and represent samples from which you can develop position descriptions unique to your church.

A sample form acknowledging receipt of the position description is included on page 208. This form should be signed by the employee (staff member) and a copy filed in their personnel folder so there will be no future misunderstanding about whether the employee either received a copy of the description or that it was discussed.

***Personnel policies.*** Any organization with two or more employees should have a set of personnel policies that define specific benefits, requirements, and procedures. The primary purpose of these policies is to ensure that employees are treated fairly and consistently. Employers, whether religious or secular, have the most difficulty with charges of discrimination when personnel policies are not applied uniformly or are nonexistent. Any exception to documented policies establishes a precedent and can permanently modify the policy; thus, it is important that set policies be followed carefully.

Each employee should be given a copy of the personnel policies and should be asked to sign a form acknowledging receipt, understanding, and a willingness to abide by these policies. This signed copy should be put in the employee's personnel folder. A sample copy of an acknowledgment form is included on page 219.

***Sexual harassment policy.*** Lawsuits involving sexual harassment have become frequent. To minimize this threat and to sensitize employees to this important issue, a sexual harassment policy and training program should be carefully developed. The sample policy beginning on page 220 can serve as a model. Perhaps your denomination has suggested a policy which can be used as well. Any policy developed should be consistent with state, federal, and denominational policies. Again, each employee should be given a copy of this policy and asked to sign an acknowledgment that they have received, reviewed, and agreed to comply with the policy (sample form on page 224). This signed acknowledgment should be placed in their personnel folder.

***Injury/illness prevention program.*** In any workplace safety should be a primary concern—for the benefit of both the employee and employer. Everyone loses if an employee is injured. The employee may lose work, or, at a minimum, suffer pain. The employer loses productivity and may have to endure a worker's compensation claim or other costly expense. A safe workplace will enhance the operating environment and credibility of the church as one which cares about its employees. The Injury/Illness Prevention Program on pages 225–227 presents a model of the type of safety program which can be effective.

*Memo of employment.* When a person is hired, the conditions of employment should be detailed in writing to avoid future misunderstandings. Benefits promised orally at the time of employment can easily be forgotten or misunderstood as the years go by. The requirement for a written agreement also demonstrates a desire for an environment of clear communications and recognizes the importance of church policies. Examples of Memos of Employment for full-time and part-time positions are included on pages 228–229. The employee should be given a copy of this memo and a copy placed in their personnel folder.

*Forms required by governmental agencies.* In the employment process, many of the forms that need to be completed are required by government agencies. In addition to the various tax forms with which most people are familiar and which are described in IRS Circular E and Publication 15A, there is the Immigration and Naturalization Service Form I-9 which requires employment eligibility verification. This form is to be completed as part of the hiring process and maintained in the employee's personnel file in the event the Immigration and Naturalization Service wishes to see it. Failure to comply, even for a part-time position, may result in a substantial fine. Additionally, the Occupational Safety and Health Administration (OSHA) requires that you post a permanent notice to employees regarding job safety.

It would be convenient if there were a single place to go to find out about all the required forms and employment rules. However, that does not seem to be the case. Our best advice is to check with your local state employment office and small business bureau, as well as to ask your denominational experts for help. Also, one can usually find a commercially prepared booklet or manual on starting and operating a business in your state.

*Entitlement records.* As established by your personnel policies, employees are generally entitled to time off from work for vacations, sick leave, personal time, and so forth. Meticulous records of these entitlements and their use should be kept to ensure fairness and to avoid misunderstandings. The following sample forms are included starting on page 230 and suggest a means to accomplish this record keeping:

- Entitlement record sheet

- Time-off application

- Request for sick leave

*Personnel records.* We have previously stressed the importance of keeping complete personnel records. To aid in this task, the following sample forms may be found beginning on page 232:

- Application for employment

- Telephone reference check

- Employee reprimand

- Employee warning notice

- Employee separation report

- Exit interview

## Typical Staff Position Descriptions and Index

The following pages contain typical church staff position descriptions (PDs). The format and content may vary somewhat since these PDs were collected from a variety of church sources. There is no single correct format for a PD. Some contain position requirements or skills required; some do not. Others list specific responsibilities while still others list examples of duties. The format and titles are not important as long as the PD contains a listing of duties and responsibilities that are accepted and understood by those using them. The "typical staff position descriptions" that follow provide guidance for the development of PDs for the unique organizations, sizes, and requirements of virtually every church.

It cannot be emphasized enough that these PDs are merely guidelines. Please *do not* simply copy them and adopt them as is for a given position in your church. *Do* take the time to develop new, specific, customized PDs for the unique positions found in your church. If there is an incumbent in the position for which a PD is being developed, as is quite often the case, it is wise to get them involved. One method is to draft a list of responsibilities for a given position, clearly mark it "Rough Draft," and then give it to the incumbent for review and comment. Work together to finalize it. This procedure usually results in a more ready acceptance of a document that may affect the individual in a significant way.

# Position Description

**POSITION:** SENIOR PASTOR (WITH AN ASSOCIATE PASTOR)

**GENERAL RESPONSIBILITIES:** The basic functions of the Senior Pastor are contained within the following general categories:

**Worship     Congregational Care     Administration**

While some degree of the actual work performed in these areas may be delegated to others, staff or volunteers, the ultimate accountability for assuring that the following responsibilities are implemented rests with the Senior Pastor. The responsibilities described cover the total ministry of the church. (Note: Responsibilities may vary somewhat with overall church or denominational polity.)

**SPECIFIC RESPONSIBILITIES:**

## Worship

1. Plans and executes the orderly progression of worship so that the experience becomes meaningful and inspiring for all involved.
2. Preaches or arranges for others to preach.
3. Plans for the major seasons of the liturgical year.
4. Works with the worship committee to implement a mutually acceptable philosophy of worship.
5. Involves laity in the worship services.

## Congregational Care

*Nurture*

1. Implements a program of calling on those with needs brought on by illness, hospitalization, bereavement, family difficulties, etc.
2. Implements a program of regular calling on members, constituents, and potential members.
3. Counsels those in need.
4. Officiates at weddings, funerals, and other significant celebrations.
5. Assists congregation to become effective and caring for the sake of the Kingdom of God.

*Evangelism and Membership*

In cooperation with the evangelism and membership committees, assures that:

1. Plans and procedures are developed by which new persons can become committed to Christ and received into the church.
2. Effective public relations programs for the church are developed and implemented.
3. Newcomers to the church and community are contacted and visited in a timely manner.
4. Procedures are developed and implemented whereby new members are quickly integrated into the life of the church.
5. People who have become inactive are quickly identified and means are developed by which these persons are reactivated in the church.

*Christian Education*

1. Implements a broad-based Christian education program in the church.
2. Teaches a class on a regular basis, such as Confirmation, Disciple, Adult Education, Advent Series, etc.
3. Participates in leading camping and/or adult retreats beyond the local church.

*Parish Life*
1. Assures that plans are developed and implemented to include more persons in all-church fellowship activities.
2. Assures that plans are developed and implemented to maintain and expand small-group involvement in the church.

**Administration**

In cooperation with the governing board of the church:
1. Activates effective administration by causing the key management functions of planning, organizing/staffing, leading, and assessing/reporting to be implemented.
2. Oversees the fiscal program of the church.
3. Organizes, leads, coordinates, and evaluates the church staff.
4. Works with the nominating committee and assures that key lay positions are filled with competent, committed persons.
5. Has regular involvement with the following groups in the church:

| | |
|---|---|
| Personnel Committee | Governing Body |
| Worship Committee | Finance Committee |
| Board of Trustees | Evangelism & Membership |

6. Maintains contact with all other work areas of the church, directly or indirectly through staff or lay leaders.
7. Assures that an annual budget is developed for the church and that means for funding that budget are implemented.
8. Assures that an annual and long-range plan is developed for the church, including specific objectives for both self and the church. Causes the plan and objectives to be updated at least annually.
9. Assures that proper fiscal controls are in place, periodic audits are performed, and that appropriate reports are prepared as required.
10. Assures that proper and complete personnel records are maintained.
11. Assures implementation of the communications and public relations activities of the church, including the newsletter, press releases, publicity articles, etc.

**BASIC POSITION REQUIREMENTS:**
1. Strong Christian commitment.
2. High standards in morals, attitude, and outlook, with awareness of the importance of example.
3. Ability to organize and activate own responsibility.

**SKILLS REQUIRED:**
1. Understanding of, and commitment to, a sound theology of discipleship and a willingness to share that philosophy to assist others in making a commitment to Christ and His church.
2. Basic strengths in worship leadership, preaching, pastoral care, evangelism, and administration, with ability to develop and effect those ministries. Knowledge of the educational process is also helpful.
3. Demonstrated ability to facilitate the full ministry of the church through lay leadership.
4. Demonstrated ability to work with and get along with all age groups.

**ACCOUNTABILITY:** To the Personnel Committee.

Revision date:

# *Position Description*

**POSITION:** SENIOR PASTOR

**SPECIFIC RESPONSIBILITIES:** The Senior Pastor is the primary leader of the church and is responsible for the total ministry of the church. (Note: Responsibility may vary somewhat with the polity of the church or denomination.)

A. WORSHIP
1. Plans for the orderly progression of a meaningful worship experience.
2. Leads worship and preaches or arranges for others to preach.
3. Plans for the major seasons of the liturgical year.
4. Works with the worship committee to implement a mutually acceptable philosophy of worship.

B. EVANGELISM
1. Assures that newcomers to the church and community are visited.
2. Works with the evangelism committee to identify people who have become inactive, and develops plans to reactivate these persons.
3. With the help of the committee, develops an effective public relations program for the church.
4. Encourages committee members to develop procedures by which new persons can become committed to Christ and received into the church.

C. PASTORAL MINISTRY
1. Calls on those in hospitals, nursing homes, homebound, constituents, and members as required.
2. Counsels as may be required.
3. Conducts weddings and funerals as required.
4. Assists in making the congregation an effective, caring one.

D. ADMINISTRATION
1. Has full responsibility for the administrative and fiscal matters of the church.
2. Provides leadership and coordination for the staff.
3. Assures that long-range plans for the church are developed and implemented.
4. Establishes annual goals for self in cooperation with the personnel committee.
5. Meets on a regular basis with the following groups and committees in the church: governing board, worship, evangelism, finance, trustees, personnel, nominating, parsonage, audit, planned giving, preschool board, and youth council.
6. Assures that a complete internal control system is in effect for the proper approval of all bills prior to payment.
7. Edits the church newsletter.

E. PARISH LIFE
1. Develops means to relate new people more fully to the church through new member fellowships.
2. Develops means to include more persons in all-church camping and weekend camping events.
3. Assists in developing means to bring persons in small geographical areas into fellowship opportunities.

F. EDUCATION
1. Teaches in the Sunday school ministry, primarily in adult education.
2. Participates in leadership of summer camping and in adult retreats on an Area/District/Synod level.

**BASIC POSITION REQUIREMENTS:**

1. Strong Christian commitment.
2. High standards in attitude, outlook, and morals, with awareness of the importance of example.
3. Ability to organize and activate own responsibilities.

**SKILLS REQUIRED:**

1. Demonstrate ability to work with, and get along with, persons of all ages.
2. Basic strengths in preaching, administration, pastoral care, and worship leadership, with ability to develop and effect these ministries. Knowledge of education process and techniques.
3. Ability to facilitate the full ministry of the church through lay leadership.
4. Understanding of, and commitment to, a sound theology of discipleship, and a willingness to share that philosophy to assist others to reach that commitment.
5. Ability to work with lay volunteer ministry groups.

**ACCOUNTABILITY:** To the Personnel Committee.

Revision date:

# Position Description

**POSITION:** ASSOCIATE PASTOR OF CHRISTIAN EDUCATION AND YOUTH

**GENERAL RESPONSIBILITIES:** The Pastor of Christian Education and Youth shares in all the basic functions of pastoral ministry with special emphasis in areas related to Christian education and youth ministry.

**SPECIFIC RESPONSIBILITIES:**

## Worship

1. Participates in the leadership of worship in the congregation on a regularly scheduled basis.

2. Plans and executes and/or supervises meaningful worship experiences for:

   | | |
   |---|---|
   | Camps | Youth Ministry events |
   | Confirmation Sunday | Christian Education Sunday |
   | Youth Sunday(s) | Other times as requested by the Senior Pastor |

3. Meets with staff, education, and worship leaders to promote positive worship experiences for children, youth, and their families.

4. Plans and promotes worship education and leadership skill development for children and youth.

5. Coordinates the schedules of Sunday programming between worship and educational activities to enhance the worship experience of families.

## Congregational Care and Nurture

1. Participates in contacting those in need, particularly those related to the areas of education, children, and youth.

2. Participates in staff consultation regarding youth in crisis and is available for counseling with those in need.

3. Maintains office hours for youth and young adults wanting unscheduled consultation.

4. Participates in weddings, baptisms, funerals, memorials, and other transitional times of life.

5. Counsels with youth and their families in preparation for confirmation.

6. Works actively to engage persons in ministry.

## Christian Education

1. Provides general direction, guidance, and vision for all areas of Christian education.

   Church and Sunday school for all ages     Preschool

   Curriculum scope, sequence, and evaluation     Confirmation

   Volunteer recruitment, training, and evaluation     Camping

   Youth Fellowships

2. Participates in development of seasonal emphases as related to education.

3. Supervises education staff development.

4. Provides motivation, guidance, and resources for the education steering committee and volunteers.

5. Actively seeks and supports young persons and others who may be experiencing a call to service and ministry.

6. Develops, supervises, and evaluates internship programs.

7. Periodically teaches courses to enhance education leadership development.

8. Maintains an awareness of curriculum and educational technology to ensure that present and future needs can be appropriately addressed.

9. Maintains community contact and awareness to enhance opportunities for education, mission, and outreach.

## Administration

1. Supervises the following education professional staff and volunteers, directly or indirectly. Prepares annual performance appraisals as appropriate.

   Director of Youth Ministry     Youth Group Counselors

   Director of Children's Ministry     Childcare Providers

   Church and Sunday School Teachers     Aides

   Director of Early Childhood Ministry     Summer Interns

2. Develops and administers the Christian education area budget.

3. Works in cooperation with the trustees to ensure a safe, clean, and adequate physical plant for all purposes of education, including projection of future needs.

4. Maintains appropriate personnel records and Christian education statistics.

5. Coordinates education needs, calendar, space, staffing, and financial resources with other staff, work areas, and church leaders to enhance the total life and ministry of the church.

**ACCOUNTABILITY:** To the Senior Pastor.

Revision date:

# *Position Description*

**POSITION:** ASSOCIATE PASTOR OF CONGREGATIONAL CARE AND GROWTH

**GENERAL RESPONSIBILITIES:** The Associate Pastor of Congregational Care and Growth shares in all the basic functions of pastoral ministry with special emphasis in areas related to congregational care, such as visitation, counseling, and special needs, as well as growth of participation in worship and other church activities.

**SPECIFIC RESPONSIBILITIES:**

## Worship

1. Conducts and oversees the early Sunday morning service of Holy Communion at least 35 Sundays of the year.

2. Plans and conducts the Saturday evening contemporary worship service.

3. Participates in the leadership of worship at other times as scheduled.

4. Plans, conducts, and/or supervises worship experiences for retreats and other special occasions.

5. Plans and implements worship education and skill development for acolytes.

6. Coordinate monthly worship services at an area retirement home.

7. Coordinates Communion for members who are convalescent or homebound.

## Congregational Care

*Nurture*

1. Develops and offers avenues for spiritual direction, support, and growth.

2. Participates in contacting those in need, particularly those who are going through life transitions such as illness, loss, and grief.

3. Offers pastoral supervision of the lay counseling and mentoring program.

4. Offers pastoral supervision for lay ministers in the fellowship of the concerned, Communion callers, and transportation ministry.

5. Is available for counseling with people in need or crisis.

6. Participates in weddings, baptisms, funerals, memorials, and other rituals of transition in the life of the congregation.

7. Works actively to engage persons in ministry.

*Congregational Growth*

1. Develops programs to promote growth in worship attendance and other outreach activities of the church.

2. Works with the evangelism committee and assists them in developing their programs and activities.

3 Encourages the entire congregation toward being visitor-sensitive and friendly in their Christian outreach.

## Christian Education

1. Teaches as often as possible.

2. Conducts yearly training course for lay counselors and mentors.

3. Conducts continuing education for lay counselors and mentors.

4. Coordinates the yearly men's retreat.

## Outreach

1. Has regular involvement with the following committees:

   Outreach and Mission

   Church and Society

   Christian Unity and Interreligious Concerns

2. Maintains congregational involvement and support of the Interfaith Crisis Center and serves as the clergy representative on the board of directors.

3. Oversees the shelter ministry at our church.

4. Provides a liaison between mission and outreach programs of our church and community-based groups with which the church networks.

## Administration

1. Supervises the Lay Director of Evangelism.

2. Assists in annual budget preparation.

3. Works with staff and membership to develop short-and long-term plans for congregational care, outreach ministries, and growth in worship attendance.

ACCOUNTABILITY: To the Senior Pastor.

Revision date:

# Position Description

**POSITION:** PASTOR FOR HISPANIC MINISTRIES

**GENERAL RESPONSIBILITIES:** Responsible for maintaining and expanding the Spanish-language ministry. Serves as an advocate for the Spanish-speaking with community agencies.

**SPECIFIC RESPONSIBILITIES:**

1. Maintains, expands, and promotes a faith community among Spanish-speaking people in the community served by our church.
2. Initiates new outreach ministries with Spanish-speaking people within the local community.
3. Trains leaders to support Spanish-speaking programs.
4. Shares Christ in a multiplicity of places and in a variety of cultural settings.
5. Conducts door-to-door evangelism as part of advocacy for the Spanish-speaking.
6. Educates the Anglo congregation about the need and opportunities for Spanish-speaking ministries.
7. Provides a cross-cultural education to bridge the gap between English-speaking and Spanish-speaking members of the congregation.
8. Coordinates and leads a Wednesday evening fellowship group and Bible study.
9. Serves as a Sunday morning adult teacher and worship leader.
10. Coordinates the emergency food fund for help to all families in the congregation.
11. Teaches English class as may be required.
12. Acts as liaison to community agencies on behalf of the Spanish-speaking in the congregation.

Desirable: Driver's-license class that allows the utilization of church vehicles to provide transportation for parishioners and youth as may be required.

**ACCOUNTABILITY:** To the Senior Pastor.

Revision date:

# Position Description

**POSITION:** SECRETARY OR ADMINISTRATIVE ASSISTANT

**SPECIFIC RESPONSIBILITIES:**

1. Performs skilled secretarial work for the pastors.
2. Supervises other office personnel.
3. Coordinates internal administrative function of the pastors.
4. Secures, trains, schedules, assigns, and supervises activities of volunteer office assistants.
5. Makes appointments for pastors as required.
6. Schedules room reservations in the office and other areas of the church complex.
7. Establishes and maintains master calendar for the church.
8. Composes correspondence as required.
9. Maintains confidentiality of relationships and records.
10. Participates in staff meetings.
11. Transcribes dictation and types rough drafts; reproduces a variety of materials.
12. Types and reproduces orders of worship, the newsletter, and monthly church calendar.
13. Maintains complete records of weekly worship attendance.
14. Maintains a current church directory.
15. Processes bills for approval by pastor or other officials of the church.
16. Orders supplies as needed.
17. Performs any other normal office procedures as required.

**ACCOUNTABILITY:**

1. Administratively responsible to the Senior Pastor.
2. Does work only for the Senior Pastor, Associate Pastor, Pastoral Intern, and Director of Christian Education or Youth Work and refers any other requests for secretarial work to the Senior Pastor for consideration.

**SKILLS REQUIRED:**

1. Knowledge of:

   a. Modern office procedures.

   b. Business English, including vocabulary, correct grammatical usage, and punctuation.

   c. Modern filing methods.

    d. Operation of standard office equipment, including a computer.

    e. Thorough knowledge of the following computer programs: Microsoft Word, Pagemaker, Microsoft Excel, Calendar Maker, SuperPaint, etc.

2. Ability to:

    a. Meet the public tactfully and courteously, to answer questions in person or by telephone, and to route calls effectively.

    b. Establish and maintain cooperative and effective working relationships.

    c. Type with accuracy at a speed of not less than 60 words per minute.

    d. Understand and carry out oral and written directions.

    e. Formulate written communications with accuracy of facts and meaning.

    f. Handle urgent and emergency situations as they arise.

    g. Compile and maintain accurate and complete records and reports.

    h. Make arithmetic calculations with speed and accuracy.

    i. Be flexible and able to plan, organize, and complete assignments with a minimum of direction.

**EXPERIENCE REQUIRED:**

A minimum of five years of increasingly responsible secretarial and administrative experience.


Revision date:

# Position Description

**POSITION:** TREASURER

**GENERAL RESPONSIBILITIES:** As the chief financial officer of the church, the treasurer safeguards the congregation's funds, disburses funds within budgetary guidelines, accounts for all receipts and disbursements according to fund designation, and gives financial guidance to officers and leaders of the church.

**SPECIFIC RESPONSIBILITIES:**

1. Ensures an adequate financial internal control system with detailed procedures in place that will safeguard the handling of all funds.

2. Coordinates with the financial secretary to ensure all receipts are recorded properly, according to fund designation.

3. Writes, secures signatures, and disburses checks from each fund for which the treasurer has responsibility.

4. Ensures that all disbursements are proper according to budgetary limitations, are supported by detailed documentation, and are recorded in accounting records which are segmented by fund.

5. Makes all disbursements on a timely basis. If cash flow problems occur, the treasurer will bring this to the attention of the finance committee immediately.

6. Tracks variances with the budget (both receipts and expenditures) and alerts department or committee chairpersons about their budgets and spending patterns.

7. Prepares analyses which show receipt and spending patterns over time, for use during budget preparation.

8. Makes a formal monthly report of receipts and expenditures, and how they relate to the budget, to the finance committee. Prepares less-detailed reports for the governing body and congregation to ensure full communication of financial status.

9. Serves as a member of the finance committee and governing body.

**ACCOUNTABILITY:** To the governing body, through the finance committee.

Revision date:

# *Position Description*

**POSITION:** FINANCIAL SECRETARY

**GENERAL RESPONSIBILITIES:** The financial secretary receives and records member gifts and supervises the counting of all offerings.

**SPECIFIC RESPONSIBILITIES:**

1. Ensures that detailed procedures are in place for counting all offerings, making the bank deposit, recording member gifts, and reporting receipts to the treasurer and individual giving members.

2. Organizes and supervises the teller committee; secures and trains tellers for each week of the year.

3. Ensures that tellers prepare a weekly report of receipts and that all accompanying documentation is retained (including copies of checks received).

4. Ensures that deposits of weekly receipts are made safely and as soon after receipt as practical.

5. Oversees the posting of member records of giving to ensure absolute accuracy. Makes reports to members at least quarterly and as required by the IRS.

6. Advises the pastor when there are significant giving changes by individual members, so the pastor can be sensitive to pastoral care needs.

7. Assists with the stewardship campaign by providing giving history.

8. Coordinates with the treasurer, office clerical staff, etc., as required to ensure a smooth and accurate accounting of receipts.

9. Serves as a member of the finance committee.

**ACCOUNTABILITY:** To the finance committee.

Revision date:

## *Position Description*

**POSITION:** RECEPTIONIST/OFFICE CLERK

**SKILLS REQUIRED:**

1. Knowledge of:
   a. Modern office procedures.
   b. Business English, including vocabulary, correct grammatical usage, and punctuation.
   c. Modern filing methods.
   d. Operation of standard office equipment.
   e. Computer proficiency in word processing and spreadsheets.

2. Ability to:
   a. Meet the public tactfully and courteously, answer questions in person and by telephone, and route calls effectively.
   b. Establish and maintain cooperative and effective working relationships.
   c. Type with accuracy at a speed of not less than 55 words per minute.
   d. Understand and carry out oral and written directions.
   e. Formulate written communications with accuracy of facts and meaning.
   f. Handle emergency situations as they arise.
   g. Maintain confidentiality on sensitive matters.

**EXAMPLES OF DUTIES:**

1. Receives visitors, answers inquiries, and provides information courteously and efficiently.

2. Makes appointments as required.

3. Schedules room reservations.

4. Establishes and maintains master calendar.

5. Composes correspondence as may be requested.

6. Maintains confidentiality of relationships and records.

7. Participates in staff meetings.

8. Inventories existing supplies and maintains sufficient inventory of office supplies.

9. Maintains filing system, and retrieves information on request in a timely fashion.

10. Types the weekly newsletter and order of worship on the word processor.

11. Places wedding services on calendar and maintains wedding notebook.

12. Opens "general" office mail; routes designated mail.

13. Keeps computer records of weekly attendance.

14. Performs any other normal office procedures as required.

15. Performs other tasks as may be requested from time to time.

**ACCOUNTABILITY:** Administratively responsible to the church secretary.

Revision date:

# Position Description

**POSITION:** DIRECTOR OF YOUTH MINISTRIES

**GENERAL RESPONSIBILITIES:** Plans, organizes, and implements a wide range of activities for youth, from junior high through young adults. Recruits and trains adult volunteers. Recruits and trains youth leadership. Maintains regular office hours and availability to youth. Works with church staff and work areas to help implement the church mission.

**SPECIFIC RESPONSIBILITIES:**

1. On an ongoing basis, plans for, organizes, and implements a youth activities program for junior high, senior high, and young adults.
2. Plans, organizes, and implements special youth worship services, retreats, camps, trips, etc.
3. Plans, organizes, and implements the annual youth service project.
4. Develops youth leadership to assist in ongoing and special youth programs.
5. Recruits, orients, and trains adult volunteers to assist in youth activities and special events.
6. Visits with youth on school campuses and other places where youth gather.
7. Visits with families of youth involved in youth programs to recruit adult volunteers for the youth programs of the church.
8. Maintains regular contact with youth as may be required. Available on a limited basis for crisis intervention and counseling. Serves as a resource for individual youth for the development of their own faith journey and to assist in coping with challenges of daily life.
9. Maintains regular and announced office hours for purposes of record keeping and general maintenance of correspondence, contacts, and availability.
10. Works cooperatively with the youth council, education committee, church staff, and other work areas of the church, as appropriate, to coordinate youth activities with those of the whole church and to help achieve the church's mission goals.
11. Advocates youth issues to the congregation with the objective of making the youth more visible to and involved with the congregation.
12. Performs other duties as may be requested or required from time to time.

**POSITION REQUIREMENTS:**

1. Demonstrated Christian character and commitment in daily life and the ability to articulate a personal faith journey.
2. A minimum of 3 years experience in leading youth activities, preferably church youth activities.
3. A college degree in a related field such as teaching, counseling, social work, etc. is desirable.
4. Ability to organize programs and activities and to activate responsibilities with a minimum of supervision and follow-up.

**PERSONAL REQUIREMENTS:** High standards in attitude, outlook, and morals, with an awareness of the importance of example. ENTHUSIASM!!

**ACCOUNTABILITY:** Administratively responsible to the pastor.

Revision date:

## Position Description

**POSITION:** DIRECTOR OF MUSIC

**GENERAL RESPONSIBILITIES:** Coordinates the total music program of the church in a manner that enhances the spirit of worship and assists the congregation in praising and serving God.

**SPECIFIC RESPONSIBILITIES:**

1. Coordinates the total music program of the church, including the chancel and adult handbell choirs, as well as the youth and children's choirs.

2. Directs the chancel choir and adult handbell choir.

3. Selects music for the worship service appropriate to the worship themes and seasons. Assists the pastor in the selection of music for the worship services.

4. Develops an annual budget for the music programs of the church and administers the budget when approved.

5. Establishes objectives annually for self and the various music groups for which responsible. Reports periodically on progress toward attaining objectives.

6. Promotes growth and stability of all choirs.

7. Develops musical skills of choirs, through rehearsals, coaching, workshops, etc.

8. Supervises the activities of the music director for youth and children's choirs. Formally evaluates the performance of these individuals at least annually.

9. Plans, organizes, and promotes the quarterly community concert series sponsored by the church.

10. Purchases music and related supplies within budget allocations. Administers and cares for the music library, instruments, and other materials related to the music programs of the church.

11. Coordinates and cooperates with the pastoral staff as well as the office staff.

12. Participates as a member of the worship committee and is responsible to this committee for the music program of the church.

13. Coordinates activities with the pastor.

14. Performs other related tasks as may be requested from time to time.

**ACCOUNTABILITY:** Administratively responsible to the pastor.

Revision date:

## *Position Description*

**POSITION:** MUSIC DIRECTOR—CHILDREN'S AND YOUTH CHOIRS

**GENERAL RESPONSIBILITIES:** Encourages children and youth to become interested and involved in the music program of the church. Provides music for worship services.

**SPECIFIC RESPONSIBILITIES:**

1. Encourages and involves the young people in music programs of the church through organized children's and youth activities.

2. Periodically involves children and youth in providing music for the worship services.

3. Establishes a worshipful, positive feeling and movement in the worship service through selection of music appropriate to worship themes.

4. Provides music for other occasions, as requested.

5. Promotes growth, stability, and develops musical skills of choir members.

6. Coordinates/cooperates with the director of music and other music program personnel.

7. Coordinates/cooperates with the pastors and office staff.

8. Establishes objectives annually and periodically reports progress toward attaining objectives.

9. Administers and cares for the physical properties and materials related to the children's and youth music programs.

10. Performs other related duties as may be requested or required.

**SKILLS REQUIRED:**

1. Knowledge of music with an emphasis on church music.

2. Ability to teach music to young people.

3. Ability to work cooperatively with others—parents, youth, and children.

4. Ability to work cooperatively with the church staff.

5. High standards in attitude, outlook, and morals, with awareness of the importance of example. ENTHUSIASM.

**ACCOUNTABILITY:** Administratively responsible to the Director of Music.

Revision date:

## Position Description

**POSITION:** ORGANIST

**GENERAL RESPONSIBILITIES:** Provides organ/piano music for all worship services and other occasional gatherings. Enhances the service of worship with appropriate music which assists the congregation in praising and serving God.

**SPECIFIC RESPONSIBILITIES:**

1. Provides organ/piano music for all worship services.
2. Establishes a worshipful, positive feeling and movement in the worship service through selection of music appropriate to worship themes.
3. Provides music for other occasions, as requested, such as weddings, funerals, celebrations, etc.
4. Provides accompaniment for rehearsals of the choir and other musical groups.
5. Coordinates/cooperates with the director of music and other music program personnel.
6. Coordinates/cooperates with the pastors and office staff.
7. Establishes objectives annually and periodically reports progress toward attaining objectives.
8. Continues to grow in musicianship.
9. Performs other related duties as may be requested or required.

**SKILLS REQUIRED:**

1. Knowledge of church music and organ repertoire for church services.

2. Choir rehearsal techniques.

3. Ability to:

   a. Play pipe organ and piano proficiently.

   b. Sight-read music.

   c. Play a wide variety of hymns and transpose hymns as required.

   d. Improvise.

   e. Accompany both soloists and choirs in rehearsals and services.

   f. Prepare and play prelude, offertory, and postlude.

   g. Work cooperatively with others—adults, youth, and children and staff.

**ACCOUNTABILITY:** Administratively responsible to the Director of Music.

Revision date:

## Position Description

**POSITION:** ACCOMPANIST/ASSISTANT CHOIR DIRECTOR

**RESPONSIBILITIES:**

1. Provide organ, piano, and/or keyboard music for all worship services and other occasional gatherings.

2. Provide accompaniment for rehearsal of the adult choir and other choral groups as requested.

3. In absence of choir director, direct choir and play organ for worship service.

**SKILLS REQUIRED:**

1. Knowledge of:

   a. Music—especially church music for worship services.

   b. Choral rehearsal technique.

2. Ability to:

   a. Sight-read music.

   b. Play wide variety of hymns.

   c. Transpose hymns.

   d. Improvise.

   e. Accompany both soloists and choirs in services and rehearsals.

   f. Rehearse vocal and instrumental soloist, and ensembles.

   g. Play four-part choral parts in rehearsal.

   h. Prepare and play prelude, offertory, and postlude.

   i. Play two manual pipe organ.

   k. Direct choir on occasion as may be required.

   l. Work cooperatively with a variety of people and ages.

**ACCOUNTABILITY:** Administratively responsible to the Director of Music.

Revision date:

# Position Description

**POSITION:** CUSTODIAN

**GENERAL RESPONSIBILITIES:** Provides cleaning and minor maintenance for the total church facility. Maintains an inventory of custodial supplies.

**SPECIFIC RESPONSIBILITIES:**

1. Provides cleaning for the total church facility such that the interior of the church has a clean and pleasing appearance. Resupplies rest rooms.

2. Performs minor maintenance such as changing burned-out light bulbs, fluorescent tubes, etc.

3. Reports other than minor maintenance to the church office.

4. Maintains an adequate supply of cleaning, paper products, and minor maintenance supplies.

5. Orders the supplies noted in item 4 through the church office.

6. Assures that equipment needed for custodial duties is maintained in good repair.

7. Arranges rooms for special events as may be requested from time to time.

8. Performs the following cleaning and maintenance activities weekly:

    a. Checks the office master calendar for use of facilities that may affect custodial care.

    b. Reports immediately any damage to equipment and/or buildings.

    c. Deep-cleans one room each week.

    d. Dusts and damp-mops all floors.

    e. Vacuums all carpets and rugs.

    f. Dusts flat surfaces (tables, counters, windowsills, tops of pews, altar, etc.).

    g. Empties trash in each container, and as needed, cleans container.

    h. Returns rooms to normal prescribed settings.

    i. Restrooms: Cleans inside/outside of all toilets and disinfects; cleans all washbowls, sink counters, and mirrors; fills all paper-product dispensers.

9. Strips and waxes floors every six months.

10. Performs other related duties that may be requested or required.

**ACCOUNTABILITY:** Administratively responsible to the pastor.

Revision date:

## Position Description

**POSITION:** WEDDING HOSTESS

**FUNCTION:**

1. Assists families with wedding preparations.
2. Coordinates the arrangements for all staff involved in the wedding.
3. Where there is to be a reception, contacts the reception hostess of the women's organization who will be responsible for reception arrangements.

**SKILLS REQUIRED:**

1. Knowledge of:
   a. Current church wedding practices.
   b. Acceptable commercial resources for wedding party to utilize.

2. Ability to:
   a. Adapt to specific needs of wedding party, where appropriate.
   b. Work with persons of all ages.
   c. Supervise work of wedding custodian.

**EXAMPLES OF DUTIES:**

1. Contacts the wedding couple to make detailed arrangements for the wedding as they relate to the church.
2. Arranges for the necessary staff.
3. Confirms date and time with the church's room-use calendar.
4. Quotes and collects fees as they are scheduled, and remits them to the church office.
5. Conducts the wedding rehearsal as may be requested by the pastor.
6. Clarifies with all persons involved the regulations for conduct on the church grounds, as well as rules relating to the florist, photographer, and videographer.
7. Directs the wedding custodian in their responsibilities.
8. Arranges to have church facilities open one hour in advance of the wedding service.
9. After the service is concluded, assures all wedding equipment is returned to storage, and facilities are ready for normal use.

**ACCOUNTABILITY:** Administratively responsible to the pastor.

Revision date:

## Position Description

POSITION: WEDDING CUSTODIAN

FUNCTION: Under the direction of the wedding hostess, provides custodial services before and after wedding services.

SKILLS REQUIRED:

1. Knowledge of:
    a. Modern cleaning methods of floors.
    b. Cleaning materials, disinfectants, and equipment in custodial work.

2. Ability to:
    a. Understand and carry out oral and written instructions.
    b. Willingness to cooperate with staff and other persons in the church.
    c. Do manual labor.
    d. Work well with those contacted in the course of the work.
    e. Perform general custodial work.
    f. Use electrical cleaning equipment.

EXAMPLES OF DUTIES:

1. Cleans all rooms involved, before and/or after a wedding, depending on requirement as established by the wedding hostess.

2. Before a wedding:
    a. Is on hand one hour before service, or as the wedding hostess requests.
    b. Assists wedding hostess in setup of rooms and other arrangements.
    c. Puts in place the kneeling bench and candelabra, etc.
    d. Restocks restrooms with supplies and empties wastebaskets.
    e. Opens narthex doors and other rooms that may be used for the wedding.

3. After a wedding
    a. Puts wedding items away.
    b. Cleans floors—sweeps and vacuums.
    c. Checks and cleans restrooms.
    d. Empties wastebaskets.
    e. Turns off lights, heat, and cooling/ventilating system.
    f. Takes all items that may have been left by bridal party or guests to church office and notifies wedding hostess.
    g. When there has been a reception, assists in putting necessary equipment away, and cleans the social hall.
    h. Locks and checks for security all sliding glass doors in the social hall and other rooms which might have been used for the wedding.

ACCOUNTABILITY: Administratively responsible to the pastor. Functional direction from the wedding hostess.

Revision date:

## Typical Volunteer Position Descriptions and Index

There are many volunteer positions in a church that lay members are asked to assume. One of the first questions that a person might ask when approached about filling a position is, "What is involved?" or "What will be my responsibilities?" A position description is an excellent way to answer these questions, and also serves as a reference and reminder of the responsibilities assumed.

The following pages contain typical position descriptions (PDs) for positions in the church that are usually filled by noncompensated volunteers. Note that the format and content vary somewhat since these PDs were collected from a variety of church sources. There is no single correct or preferred format for a position description. Actually, the format is of minor importance as long as the PD contains a complete list of duties and responsibilities that are understood and accepted. It cannot be emphasized enough that these PDs are merely guidelines. Please *do not* simply copy them and adopt them as is for a given volunteer church position. *Do* develop new, specific, customized PDs for the unique positions in your church that are filled by volunteers.

Worship:

*While these PDs are written for the chairperson, they also give guidance about the specific responsibilities of committee members.

# Position Description

**POSITION:** LAY LEADER

**GENERAL RESPONSIBILITIES:** Serves in coordination with pastor/s to implement the local church mission and programs effectively. Serves as liaison between the congregation and the pastor/s.

**SPECIFIC RESPONSIBILITIES:**

1. Meets regularly with the pastor/s to discuss the state of the church and ministry needs.

2. Serves as liaison from the congregation to the pastor/s, inputting congregational concerns as may be required.

3. Serves as a member of governing body of the church and the all-church conference.

4. Serves as interpreter to the congregation of actions and programs of the pastor/s and local church leadership.

5. Serves as interpreter to the congregation of actions and programs of the denomination.

6. Plans and implements the Laity Sunday worship service.

7. Participates and makes presentations on study and training opportunities.

8. Promotes the lay speaker program in the local church.

9. Performs other tasks and projects as may be requested by the pastor/s.

Revised:

## Position Description

**POSITION:** CHAIRPERSON OF THE GOVERNING BODY

**GENERAL RESPONSIBILITIES:** The governing body of the church provides for the planning and implementation of church programs for worship, nurture, education, administration, and outreach. The governing body also reviews and approves all major new programs and/or expenditures for the church. The chairperson shall assure that these responsibilities are accomplished and that the administrative tasks of the governing body are completed.

**SPECIFIC RESPONSIBILITIES:**

1. Plans and implements a governing body and/or all-church planning retreat annually, or as needed, the results of which will be a long-range plan for the church.

2. Assures that the various work areas in the church are implementing their part of the long-range plan in an effective manner.

3. Considers and approves major new programs or expenditures proposed for the church.

4. Convenes regular meetings for the purpose of receiving activity reports from the various work areas of the church and to conduct other business that may come before the governing body.

5. Assures that a written record of the proceedings of these meetings is maintained.

6. Compiles a year-end composite report for the all-church annual meeting.

Revised:

# Position Description

**POSITION:** CHAIRPERSON OF THE BOARD OF TRUSTEES

**GENERAL RESPONSIBILITIES:** The board of trustees holds legal title to all church properties and is responsible for the maintenance of property. The chairperson shall assure that these responsibilities are accomplished and that the administrative tasks of the board are completed.

**SPECIFIC RESPONSIBILITIES:**

1. As chairperson, acts as the spokesperson and agent of the board of trustees in any matters involving church property, including purchase, sale, mortgage, encumbrance, construction, repairing, and remodeling of any and all property.

2. Assures proper and timely maintenance and upkeep of all church property.

3. Assures that proper insurance is obtained and maintained on church property.

4. Assures that periodic inspections are performed on church property and that discrepancies are corrected.

5. Consults with church groups regarding use of church facilities by groups from outside of the church and approves all policies related to such use.

6. Convenes required meetings and assures that a written record is maintained of proceedings.

7. Compiles regular reports and a year-end report to the governing body as well as to the all-church conference.

The chairperson shall be elected by the board of trustees from among its members.

Note: Different churches or denominations may have different names, responsibilities, and/or procedures for the group or groups that own and maintain church property.

Revision date:

# Position Description

**POSITION:** CHAIRPERSON OF AUDIT COMMITTEE

**GENERAL RESPONSIBILITIES:** The audit committee assures that financial records of all groups in the church are examined yearly for sound financial practices and accuracy. This committee also assures that proper procedures are being used to maintain financial records. The chairperson shall assure that these responsibilities are accomplished and that the administrative tasks of the audit committee are completed.

**SPECIFIC RESPONSIBILITIES:**

1. Arranges for a churchwide annual financial review in coordination with the pastor/s and finance committee.

2. Informs the governing body about the financial situation of the church and the condition of the financial records.

3. Recommends to the governing body throughout the year such adjustments in the financial review procedure as may be required by the financial situation of the church.

4. Interprets financial review procedures to members or groups with budgets and anyone else in the church with an interest and need to know.

5. Acts as a resource to groups in the church that wish to examine or change their financial procedures.

6. Convenes required meetings and assures that a written record of proceedings is maintained.

7. Compiles a year-end report for the all-church conference.

Revision date:

## Position Description

**POSITION:** CHAIRPERSON OF FINANCE COMMITTEE

**GENERAL RESPONSIBILITIES:** The finance committee shall assure that adequate financial resources are available to enable the church to fulfill its mission and approved programs. In addition, this committee administers the financial resources of the church and reports on the financial status and interprets financial procedures to committees that have budgets as well as to members of the church. The chairperson shall assure that these responsibilities are accomplished and that the administrative tasks of the finance committee are completed.

**SPECIFIC RESPONSIBILITIES:**

1. Assures that adequate financial resources are available to enable the church to fulfill its mission by organizing and implementing a stewardship program.

2. Develops a churchwide annual budget in coordination with committees and all other work areas in the church.

3. Administers the financial resources of the church.

4. Keeps the committees and the congregation informed as to the financial situation of the church.

5. Interprets financial procedures to committees and members of the church.

6. Guides the treasury functions.

7. Recommends to the governing body throughout the year such adjustments in the budget as may be required by the changing financial situation of the church.

8. Makes provision for an annual review of all church financial records in coordination with the audit committee.

9. The chairperson of the finance committee shall:

   a. Be an authorized check cosigner.

   b. Convene regular meetings and assure that a record is kept of all proceedings.

   c. Participate as a full voting member of the governing body.

   d. Compile a year-end financial report for the all-church conference.

Revised:

# Position Description

**POSITION:** CHAIRPERSON OF THE NOMINATING COMMITTEE

**GENERAL RESPONSIBILITIES:** The nominating committee is responsible for recommending to the governing body a slate of candidates to fill all of the elective offices in the church. The chairperson is responsible for assuring that this task is accomplished in a timely and orderly manner and that all administrative matters of the committee are completed.

**SPECIFIC RESPONSIBILITIES:**

1. Be familiar with descriptions and responsibilities of various church elective positions.

2. Be familiar with church members, their experiences, and abilities.

3. Assure that as close a match as possible is made between elective position responsibilities and members' abilities when they are placed in nomination for a given position.

4. Assure that a representative cross section of age, sex, race, etc., is nominated to serve on all committees and especially as chairpersons.

5. Assure that new members are considered for appropriate positions commensurate with their experience and capabilities.

6. Maintain written records of proceedings of the nominating committee.

7. Prepare a nominating committee report for the meeting of the governing body and/or the all-church conference.

Revision date:

# *Position Description*

**POSITION:** CHAIRPERSON OF THE PERSONNEL COMMITTEE

**GENERAL RESPONSIBILITIES:** Responsible for all personnel matters for both the professional and lay staff of the church. Assures that position descriptions are current, objectives are established, and performance is evaluated. The chairperson shall assure that these responsibilities are accomplished and that the administrative tasks of the committee are completed.

**SPECIFIC RESPONSIBILITIES:**

1. Assures that position descriptions are reviewed at least biannually and are current with the requirements of each position in the church.

2. Recommends to the finance committee and governing body compensation recommendations for the pastors and other church staff.

3. Prepares an annual budget for the personnel expenses of the church.

4. Assures that mutually agreeable specific performance goals and objectives are established by the pastors and church staff.

5. Coordinates these goals with established church goals and negotiates as may be necessary.

6. Interprets the work of the pastoral and lay staff to the congregation.

7. Evaluates performance of pastors and church staff against established goals and objectives.

8. Assures that personnel policies, including a sexual harassment policy, are established and maintained.

9. Recommends ministerial candidates to the governing body.

10. Assures that personnel files are maintained current and complete.

11. Assures that new staff members receive a proper orientation and copies of their position descriptions as well as personnel policies.

12. Assures that compensation changes are communicated to appropriate personnel.

13. Convenes required meetings and assures that written records of the meetings are maintained.

14. Compiles a year-end report for the all-church conference.


Revision date:

## Position Description

**POSITION:** CHAIRPERSON OF THE COMMUNICATIONS COMMITTEE

**GENERAL RESPONSIBILITIES:** The communications committee shall serve as a resource body for advice and guidance in all aspects of communication and publicity for the church—audio, video, photographic, written, graphic display, etc. This committee will assist any group within the church with a need and/or desire to publicize programs or activities. The chairperson shall assure that these responsibilities are accomplished and that the administrative tasks of the committee are completed.

**SPECIFIC RESPONSIBILITIES:**

1. Convenes communications committee meetings and assures that a written record of the proceedings is maintained.

2. Serves as liaison to other committees and group leaders regarding resources and services available through the communications committee.

3. Keeps groups and individuals aware of publicity deadlines of various media, both internal and external to the church.

4. Prepares the communications committee's annual budget request and administers the approved budget.

5. Assures that requested and approved projects are carried out to satisfactory completion, on budget, and on time.

6. Reviews current avenues of internal and external publicity to:

   a. Determine current effectiveness and audience impact.

   b. Recommend modifications for improvements.

   c. Report recommendations to the governing body for approval and implementation of any modifications or improvements.

7. Oversees a regular review and updating of communication and publicity equipment and resources within the church.

8. Oversees the planning and presentation of a yearly communication and publicity workshop.

9. Assures that the church's Internet site is kept up-to-date.

Revision date:

## *Position Description*

**POSITION:** CHAIRPERSON OF THE EDUCATION COMMITTEE

**GENERAL RESPONSIBILITIES:**

The purpose of the education committee is:

1. To help develop and administer the local church's overall plan for Christian education.

2. To be aware of the Christian education needs of all age groups in the church.

3. To coordinate a comprehensive plan for Christian education.

The chairperson shall assure that these responsibilities are accomplished and that the administrative tasks of the committee are completed.

**SPECIFIC RESPONSIBILITIES:**

1. To work closely with the superintendent of the church school, pastors, and the governing body in developing plans and strategies for the educational ministry.

2. To guide in developing policies and procedures to help ensure quality Christian education.

3. To help identify, recruit, and train teachers and leaders.

4. To develop and oversee the Christian education budget.

5. To interpret the educational program to the congregation and the community.

6. To promote Christian Education Sunday and other special events related to education.

7. To nurture a churchwide atmosphere of developing Christian education.

8. To convene regular meetings, set agendas, and maintain written records of meeting actions.

**ABILITIES NEEDED:**

1. A growing knowledge and profession of the Christian faith.

2. Awareness of educational needs for Christian development in a broad age range.

3. Active participation in worship in the local church.

4. Willingness to work with others.

5. Time to carry out responsibilities.

6. Organizational skills.

7. Openness to learn.

Revision date:

## Position Description

**POSITION:** CHAIRPERSON OF THE EVANGELISM COMMITTEE

**GENERAL RESPONSIBILITIES:** The evangelism committee shall promote the evangelistic outreach for the church and provide opportunities for members to increase their own desire and ability to be evangelistic about their faith. The chairperson shall assure that these responsibilities are carried out and that the administrative tasks of the committee are completed.

**SPECIFIC RESPONSIBILITIES:**

1. Create activities and structure to respond to the evangelistic needs of our church.

2. Create a means for our church to provide opportunities for the unchurched community to become acquainted with and committed to Jesus Christ.

3. Publicize events to the larger community which may attract them to Jesus Christ and the church.

4. Prepare an annual budget and administer the budget when approved.

5. Meet as required and assure that minutes of the proceedings are maintained.

6. Participate in the all-church planning activities.

7. Compile a year-end report for the all-church conference.

Revised:

# Position Description

**POSITION:** CHAIRPERSON OF THE MEMBERSHIP COMMITTEE

**GENERAL RESPONSIBILITIES:** The purpose of the membership committee is to plan and implement membership classes, promote visitation programs for visitors, constituents, and members, and sustain and support responsible church membership. The chairperson shall assure that these responsibilities are accomplished and that the administrative tasks of the committee are completed.

**SPECIFIC RESPONSIBILITIES:**

1. Plans and implements programs to encourage persons to become associated with the church.

2. Assists the pastor and membership to be involved in membership development programs.

3. Establishes growth goals for church membership and especially worship attendance, in coordination with the pastor and governing body.

4. Secures leadership and coordinates the ongoing program of new member assimilation and involvement in the activities and responsibilities of the church.

5. Designs and implements an ongoing program of visitation and calling on members who have become inactive.

6. Implements an ongoing program of visitation with visitors and constituents.

7. Convenes required meetings and assures that a written record of proceedings is maintained.

Revision date:

# Position Description

**POSITION:** CHAIRPERSON OF THE OUTREACH COMMITTEE

**GENERAL RESPONSIBILITIES:** The purpose of the outreach committee is to relate social concerns of the community as well as the larger mission-oriented needs and goals of the church to the congregation so that they can be kept informed of these needs and encouraged to address them both individually and collectively. The chairperson shall assure that these responsibilities are accomplished and that the administrative tasks of the committee are completed.

**SPECIFIC RESPONSIBILITIES:**

1. Know needs of the local community for social-action projects and develop programs to meet these needs where possible and/or assist other helping agencies.

2. Keep the congregation aware of the outreach mission of the church through:

    a. Occasional articles in the newsletter and/or order of worship.

    b. Fliers and handouts, order of worship inserts, etc.

3. Develop mission studies in which the congregation may participate, such as:

    a. Missionary correspondence.

    b. Mission films and/or missionary speakers.

4. Develop mission projects in which the congregation may participate, such as:

    a. Work projects.

    b. Missionary support.

    c. Aid to homeless and hungry.

5. Be aware of and coordinate with mission-oriented and social-action programs covered by other groups within the church.

6. Hold regular meetings and record actions and decisions in written minutes.

7. Compile year-end report for the all-church conference.

Revision date:

# Position Description

**POSITION:** CHAIRPERSON OF THE PARISH LIFE COMMITTEE

**GENERAL RESPONSIBILITIES:** The purpose of the parish life committee is to provide opportunities for developing social as well as spiritual relationships among members. This committee also promotes the formation of small groups within the church membership. The chairperson shall assure that these responsibilities are accomplished and that the administrative tasks of the committee are completed.

**SPECIFIC RESPONSIBILITIES:**

1. Provide opportunities for fellowship activities such as:
   a. Church potluck dinners.
   b. Family camp.
   c. Trim-a-Tree Christmas program.
   d. Other theme activities (i.e., tennis tournament, talent show, ice cream social, ski trip, etc.).

2. Provide opportunities for enrichment groups:
   a. Covenant/spiritual growth groups.
   b. Adult fellowship groups.

3. Identify needs for small groups within the church and take action to organize them.

4. Convene regular meetings and assure that a written record is maintained of the proceedings.

5. Compile a year-end report for the all-church conference.

Revision date:

# *Position Description*

**POSITION:** CHAIRPERSON OF THE WORSHIP COMMITTEE

**GENERAL RESPONSIBILITIES:** The purpose of the worship committee is to help the congregation become aware of the meaning and practice of worship and to assist the pastor in planning and conducting the worship service, including music and the other arts that may be conducive to worship. The chairperson shall assure that these responsibilities are accomplished and that the administrative tasks of the committee are completed.

**SPECIFIC RESPONSIBILITIES:**

1. Maintains awareness of the needs and concerns of the congregation for meaningful worship and communicates these needs and concerns to the pastor.

2. Assists the pastor in planning of worship services throughout the seasons of the Christian year.

3. Provides for ushering, furnishings, appointments, and sacramental elements for worship.

4. Promotes adequate musical leadership and musical programming.

5. Recruits greeters, ushers, and other essential worship participants.

6. Recruits lay readers as may be required for scripture reading during the service of worship.

7. Establishes standards for altar paraments, banners, etc.

8. Convenes regular meetings and assures that a written record of actions and decisions is prepared.

9. Compiles an annual report for the all-church conference.

Revision date:

## Position Description

POSITION: CHURCH SCHOOL SUPERINTENDENT

GENERAL RESPONSIBILITIES:

1. To accept general administrative and supervisory responsibility for the church school and other educational programs.

2. To relate the educational ministry of the church school to the total ministry of the church.

SPECIFIC RESPONSIBILITIES:

1. To provide oversight to the church school program:
   a. Staffing—Assures that all classes are covered, arranges for substitute teachers, assists supply coordinator(s).
   b. Church School Office—Supervises work of attendance workers, prepares quarterly student lists, prepares yearly master list.
   c. Classrooms—Ensures clearly marked, identifiable classroom locations; encourages their maintenance and cleanliness.

2. To help identify, recruit, orient, train, and support volunteer teachers and leaders.

3. To work with teachers and education committee members in selecting appropriate curriculum.

4. To coordinate quarterly teacher meetings.

5. To work with age-level coordinators to provide appropriate classes and groups for all ages.

6. To work with chairpersons and age-level coordinators to ensure promotion of Christian education throughout the congregation; aid in publicity for Christian education opportunities.

7. To plan special worship times and other observances for the total church school.

ABILITIES NEEDED:

1. A growing knowledge and profession of the Christian faith.

2. Interest in and awareness of educational needs for Christian development in a broad age range.

3. Active participation in worship in the local church.

4. Willingness to work with others.

5. Time to carry out responsibilities.

6. Organizational skills.

7. Openness to learn.

ACCOUNTABILITY: Education committee.

Revision date:

# Position Description

**POSITION:** CHILDCARE COORDINATOR

**GENERAL RESPONSIBILITIES:**

1. To help develop the church's plan for childcare.

2. To coordinate a comprehensive church plan for childcare.

**SPECIFIC RESPONSIBILITIES:**

1. Periodically reviews the church's existing childcare plan and makes changes as needs arise.

2. Coordinates paid and volunteer childcare for worship services.

3. Coordinates childcare for other church activities if requested, using either paid or volunteer workers.

4. Assists in interviewing and hiring paid childcare provider(s).

5. Keeps records of hours worked and submits monthly time sheets for paid providers.

6. Supervises childcare providers (paid and volunteer). Assures all policies are being followed.

7. Arranges for substitute childcare providers when necessary.

8. Assures supplies are adequate and orders supplies when necessary.

9. Arranges for laundry to be done.

10. Assures toys are for proper ages and in good repair. Arranges for toy cleaning.

11. Establishes goals, evaluates performance, and makes progress reports to the education committee.

12. Attends meetings of the education committee.

**ABILITIES NEEDED:**

1. A growing knowledge and profession of the Christian faith.

2. Interest in and love for children.

3. Active participation in worship in the local church.

4. Willingness to work with others.

5. Time to carry out responsibilities.

6. Organizational skills.

7. Openness to learn.

**ACCOUNTABILITY:** Education committee.

Revision date:

# *Position Description*

**POSITION:** CHILDREN'S COORDINATOR

**GENERAL RESPONSIBILITIES:**

1. To help in developing the church's plan for children's ministries.
2. To know the needs of children in the church and community.
3. To coordinate a comprehensive plan for children's ministries.

**SPECIFIC RESPONSIBILITIES:**

1. To review the local church's present ministry with children.
2. To assess the needs of children.
3. To learn from church and community leaders and parents the hopes for future children's ministries.
4. To suggest and implement new ideas for children's ministry.
5. To work with others involved in children's ministries to provide an inclusive and well-coordinated program (e.g., childcare, junior church, children's choir, etc.).
6. To attend meetings of the education committee.
7. To set goals, evaluate performance, and make progress reports to the education committee.

**ABILITIES NEEDED:**

1. A growing knowledge and profession of the Christian faith.
2. Interest in and love for children.
3. Active participation in worship in the local church.
4. Willingness to work with others.
5. Time to carry out responsibilities.
6. Organizational skills.
7. Openness to learn.

**ACCOUNTABILITY:** Education committee.

Revision date:

# Position Description

POSITION: YOUTH COORDINATOR

**GENERAL RESPONSIBILITIES:**

1. To help develop the local church's plan for youth ministries.

2. To know the needs of youth in the church and community.

3. To coordinate a comprehensive plan for youth ministries.

**SPECIFIC RESPONSIBILITIES:**

1. To review the church's present ministry with youth, on a regular basis.

2. To determine the needs of youth in the church and community.

3. To learn from church and community leaders, parents, and youth about the hopes and needs for future youth ministries.

4. To suggest and implement new ideas for youth ministry with the education committee.

5. To work with others involved in youth ministries to provide an inclusive and well-coordinated program (i.e., youth director, pastor, counselors, Sunday school teachers, etc.).

6. To attend meetings of the education committee.

7. To set goals for youth ministries, evaluate performance against those goals, and make progress reports to the education committee.

8. To be responsible for designated finances in relation to youth ministries.

**ABILITIES NEEDED:**

1. A growing knowledge and profession of the Christian faith.

2. Interest in and love for youth.

3. Active participation in worship in the local church.

4. Willingness to work with others.

5. Time to carry out responsibilities.

6. Organizational skills.

7. Openness to learn.

**ACCOUNTABILITY:** Youth director and education committee.

Revision date:

# Position Description

**POSITION:** ADULT COORDINATOR

**GENERAL RESPONSIBILITIES:**

1. To help in the local church's plan for adult ministries.
2. To know the needs of adults in the church and community.
3. To coordinate a comprehensive plan for adult ministries.

**SPECIFIC RESPONSIBILITIES:**

1. To review the church's present ministry with adults.
2. To assess the current needs of adults in the church.
3. To learn from church and community leaders and other adults their hopes for future adult ministries.
4. To suggest and implement new ideas for adult ministry.
5. To work to provide an inclusive and well-coordinated adult program.
6. To attend meetings of the education committee.
7. To set goals, evaluate, and make progress reports to the education committee.

**ABILITIES NEEDED:**

1. A growing knowledge and profession of the Christian faith.
2. Active participation in worship in the local church.
3. Willingness to work with others.
4. Time to carry out responsibilities.
5. Organizational skills.
6. Openness to learn.

**ACCOUNTABILITY:** Education committee.

Revision date:

## Position Description

**POSITION:** ACOLYTE COORDINATOR

**SPECIFIC RESPONSIBILITIES:**

1. Oversees the acolyte program of assistance to pastors in the service of worship.

2. Schedules acolytes for each service of worship. Supervises and assists, as required, during the performance of their duties.

3. Publicizes to the whole congregation the need for acolytes and recruits frequently, especially from new families in the life of the church.

4. Serves as a member of the worship committee. Attends monthly meetings and is willing to accept tasks and responsibilities for programs and activities of the committee as related to the acolyte program.

**ACCOUNTABILITY:** To the worship committee.

Revision date:

# Position Description

**POSITION:** COMMUNION COORDINATOR

**GENERAL RESPONSIBILITIES:** Assures that appropriate elements are available at each Communion service.

**SPECIFIC RESPONSIBILITIES:**

1. Obtains a calendar of Sunday morning worship services and other special occasions when Communion will be served.

2. Understands the different ways of serving Communion and the type of preparation required for each.

3. Checks with pastors prior to each Communion service, prepares elements in advance of the service, and places them in accordance with instructions.

4. Properly disposes of elements that are left over after the Communion service.

5. Prepares elements as may be required for Communion to be taken to those who are homebound, in hospitals, in nursing homes, etc.

6. Serves as a member of the worship committee.

**ACCOUNTABILITY:** To the worship committee.

Revision date:

## Position Description

**POSITION:** FLOWER COORDINATOR

**GENERAL RESPONSIBILITIES:** Assures that appropriate floral displays are present at each worship service and other special occasions.

**SPECIFIC RESPONSIBILITIES:**

1. Obtains or develops a calendar of worship services and other special occasions which require floral displays.

2. Promotes congregational involvement in contributing flowers for each Sunday and for special events (e.g., Christmas poinsettias, Easter lilies, etc.).

3. Assures that donors are properly recognized in the order of worship and are given the opportunity to express a subject of honor for the floral display.

4. Coordinates with the florist for timely delivery and appropriateness of displays.

5. Serves as a member of the worship committee.

**ACCOUNTABILITY:** To the worship committee.


Revision date:

# Position Description

**POSITION:** GREETER COORDINATOR

**GENERAL RESPONSIBILITIES:** Assures that greeters are present at all services of worship so worshipers are warmly welcomed.

**SPECIFIC RESPONSIBILITIES:**

1. Obtains or prepares a calendar of worship services and other special occasions which require greeters.

2. Assures that greeters are present at all of the required occasions, scheduling greeters at least four weeks in advance.

3. Recruits new members to be greeters as appropriate.

4. Trains greeters in the preferred methods of making worshipers welcome.

5. Assures that greeters know how to direct newcomers to Sunday school, child-care, and other frequently asked for locations.

6. Serves as a member of the worship committee.

**ACCOUNTABILITY:** To the worship committee.


Revision date:

## Position Description

**POSITION:** HEAD USHER

**GENERAL RESPONSIBILITIES:** Assures that seating of worshipers as well as other tasks such as serving of Communion and the collection of the offering is accomplished in an orderly and competent manner.

**SPECIFIC RESPONSIBILITIES:**

1. Secures calendar of regular Sunday morning worship services as well as other special occasions which require ushers.

2. Schedules ushers for each of the occasions noted in item 1.

3. Oversees orientation and training of ushers, involving new members as appropriate.

4. Assures ushers' knowledge of room setup, special seating needs, order of worship availability, and offering collection.

5. Gathers offerings in accordance with procedures arranged with pastor.

6. Arranges for a worship attendance count to be taken at each service.

7. Serves as a member of the worship committee.

**ACCOUNTABILITY:** To the worship committee.


Revision date:

# Position Description

**POSITION:** TELLER COORDINATOR

**SPECIFIC RESPONSIBILITIES:**

1. Oversees the process for recording and depositing all receipts from offerings and other sources.

2. Secures and trains tellers for each week of the year.

3. Assures that tellers prepare a weekly report of receipts.

4. Assures safe, regular deposit of weekly receipts.

5. Assures that established procedures for counting, recording, and depositing of money are followed precisely.

6. Serves as a member of the finance committee.

**ACCOUNTABILITY:** To the finance committee.

Revision date:

## *Position Description Acknowledgment*

I have received and read the _____
position description, understand the requirements of the position, and accept the
responsibilities and duties described. I have been given an opportunity to ask for
clarification on any matters regarding this position about which I had questions or
about which I may have been unclear.

     Date: _____

     Employee Signature: _____

     Print Name: _____

# Lay Employees Personnel Policies

*(NOTE: These sample personnel policies are intended as guidance only and will not apply directly to any church or organization. Personnel policies must be customized to each and every church organization.)*

## I. General

The following policies apply to all full-time and part-time lay employees of the church. Full-time employees are considered those who work 40 hours per week. Part-time employees work less than 40 hours per week. Specific instances that may arise and that are not covered by these personnel policies will be referred to the Personnel Committee (PC). Exceptions to these policies can only be made by the PC and must be documented in writing along with complete reasons for making the exception.

## II. Administration of Personnel Policies

The administration of personnel policies is delegated by the PC to the senior pastor or their specifically designated representative. In all subsequent sections of these policy statements, the term "senior pastor" shall mean the senior pastor or their specifically designated representative.

## III. Authority to Employ

The senior pastor is delegated the authority to conduct employment interviews and negotiations to fill vacancies in established positions and to hire qualified individuals, with the advice of the chairperson of the PC, after consultation with the PC.

## IV. Terminations

Termination of employment will be by the senior pastor, with the advice of the chairperson of the PC, after consultation with the PC.

### A. VOLUNTARY RESIGNATION BY THE EMPLOYEE

Written notice shall be given to the senior pastor at least two weeks in advance of the desired termination date.

### B. INVOLUNTARY TERMINATION

1. *Termination because of excess in current work force:* Notice of release shall be in writing, and only after full counseling between the employee and the senior pastor. Two weeks notice, or salary in lieu of notice, shall be given to the released employee.

2. *Termination for unsatisfactory work performance:* Notice of release shall be in writing, and only after full counseling between the employee and the senior pastor. Two weeks notice, or salary in lieu of notice, shall be given to the released employee.

3. *Termination for cause:* An employee guilty of misconduct, or conduct inconsistent with the welfare of the church, may be dismissed without prior notice or severance pay. An employee so discharged shall be given specific reason(s) for dismissal and complete details for the termination shall be documented for inclusion in the employee's personnel folder.

### C. RETURN OF CHURCH PROPERTY

All church property, including keys, must be returned to the church prior to the terminated employee receiving final compensation. If the employee is responsible in any way for handling funds, keys will be returned, and combinations to safes and signature authorizations will be changed immediately upon notification of employee termination.

## V. *Procedures Relating to New Employees*

### A. PROBATIONARY PERIOD

All new employees shall be in a probationary status for a period of up to six months. The new employee's work performance shall be evaluated by the senior pastor or immediate supervisor prior to the expiration of the six-month probationary period. Based on this evaluation a recommendation shall be made as to either permanent employment status or termination.

### B. REQUIRED FORMS

1. Upon accepting employment, *employees must prepare a Form W-4* Withholding Exemption Certificate. It is the responsibility of the employee to report any change of dependency status, and to submit a new W-4 form accordingly. Each employee must also complete a Department of Justice Immigration and Naturalization Service I-9 Employment Eligibility Verification form.

2. Each employee must file with the senior pastor a *statement of next of kin,* with compete address and telephone number, for the purpose of notification in case of illness or accident.

3. Each employee will receive a *Memo of Employment* which defines the term and conditions of employment.

### C. PERSONNEL FILES

A file will be kept for each employee and will contain all documents obtained at the time of employment, references, performance evaluations, letters of commendation, reprimands, and records of entitlement such as vacation, sick leave, leaves of absence, etc. It shall be the responsibility of each employee to report any circumstances concerning health or domestic situations or problems that may have a direct bearing on their future availability to perform assigned duties. All documents placed in the personnel file of the employee, subsequent to their employment, shall be done with the full knowledge of the employee.

## VI. Salaries and Wages

### A. SALARY AND WAGE SCHEDULE

The salary and wage schedule for full- or part-time employees is recommended by the PC, with final approval by the governing body of the church.

### B. REVIEW OF SALARY AND WAGES

The salary and wage schedule is normally reviewed annually, just prior to preparation of the annual budget, but may be reviewed more often at the discretion of the PC.

### C. SALARY AND WAGE PAYMENTS

Salaries and wages are paid twice each month, on the 15th and the last day of the month. When either of these dates falls on a Saturday, Sunday, or holiday, payment will be on the last working day prior to the weekend or holiday.

## VII. Working Hours

### A. CHURCH OFFICE CLERICAL STAFF

Working hours are from 8:00 A.M. to 5:00 P.M., Monday through Friday, with an hour for lunch. The church office is closed on Saturdays, Sundays, and holidays designated in Part VIII.A.1. of this policy.

### B. MUSIC STAFF

Hours of work will be those required by the nature of the work, as determined by the individual in consultation with the senior pastor or direct supervisor.

### C. YOUTH DIRECTOR

Hours of work will be those required by the nature of the work, as determined by the individual in consultation with the senior pastor or direct supervisor.

### D. CUSTODIAN

The work required normally approximates 15–20 hours per week. The work schedule may be arranged to suit the available time of the employee, with approval of the senior pastor or direct supervisor. Once the schedule is arranged and agreed to, however, deviations will not be permitted without prior approval. Duties performed for church-related, but independent functions such as weddings are not a part of the regularly assigned work schedule and are in addition to the normal workweek. The custodian will be paid for such services in accordance with established rates specified in special event policies.

### E. WORK BREAKS

A 15-minute midmorning and a 15-minute midafternoon rest period, or work break, will be allowed for full-time employees. The break is to be taken at a time which prevents undue interference with work. Unused rest periods are not to be taken in conjunction with lunch hours or quitting time, or to be accumulated for compensatory time off. The lunch hour is to be taken midway through the work day, and not to be worked through in order to end the work day early.

### F. OVERTIME

The church does not participate in pay for overtime and, as a general rule, overtime work is to be avoided. Overtime may be allowed with prior written approval of the senior pastor. Compensatory time off will be one hour off for one hour overtime worked, and it is to be taken within 30 calendar days, at a time approved by the senior pastor. Time not taken within the 30-day period is forfeited, unless the compensatory time off was requested by the employee and not allowed by the church within the 30-day period, in which case it will be taken as soon as possible.

### G. ABSENCES DURING WORKING HOURS

1. *Personal errands,* such as shopping and routine appointments, shall be at a time other than during church working hours.

2. *Requests for time off for personal reasons,* such as family events, legal, or civic duties (other than jury duty), shall be cleared and approved in advance by the senior pastor, and will be charged to annual leave (see Part VIII. B).

3. *Any emergency absence* shall be brought to the attention of the senior pastor as soon as possible. Any injury or illness while at work, or affecting work of the employee, shall be reported immediately.

4. *For a death in the immediate family,* two days of compensated bereavement time will be allowed. For deaths beyond the immediate family, time may be taken but must be charged to annual leave.

## VIII. *Employee Benefits*

### A. HOLIDAYS

1. *The following holidays will be observed:* New Year's Day, Martin Luther King Day, President's Day, from noon of Good Friday, Memorial Day, Independence Day, Labor Day, Thanksgiving Day, the day after Thanksgiving, Christmas Day, and two floating holidays. The floating holidays must be taken in the calendar year in which they are granted, and must have the prior approval of the senior pastor.

2. When a holiday falls on Saturday, the preceding Friday will be observed. Holidays falling on Sunday will be observed the following Monday.

3. *Religious holidays:* Employees may be excused by the senior pastor for up to three hours during the day to attend established, special religious services. If an employee wishes a full day for such observance, this must be taken as a portion of annual leave.

### B. ANNUAL LEAVE

All persons employed on a regular basis will be granted annual leave (vacation) with full pay as specified below:

1. *Vacation Period:* Every effort will be made to grant annual leave at the times requested. However, because of the limited staff, the needs of the church, as determined by the senior pastor, will be given first consideration.

2. *Annual leave allowance* is based on length of continuous service as follows:

   a. *Full-time employees:* From the beginning of the first year of employment until the end of the sixth year, annual leave allowance shall accrue at the rate of 5/6 day for each full month worked. (For a full calendar year worked, this equals 10 days.)

      From the beginning of the seventh year of employment until the end of the eleventh year, annual leave allowance shall accrue at the rate of 1.25 days for each full month worked. (For a full calendar year worked, this equals 15 days.)

      From the beginning of the twelfth year, annual leave allowance shall accrue at the rate of 1.66 days for each full month worked. (For a full calendar year worked, this equals twenty days.)

   b. *Part-time employees:* The director of music, organist, youth director, custodian, pastoral intern, and director of education, when employed on a 12-month basis, shall receive vacation with pay equaling two of their normal work weeks per year. Beginning with the seventh year of employment, they will earn paid vacation at the rate of three of their normal work weeks per year. Beginning with the twelfth year of employment, they would earn at the rate of four normal work weeks per year.

3. Annual leave shall not be allowed until six months of continuous service has been completed, and shall not be allowed in excess of the earned leave accrued.

4. No more annual leave than the employee earns in a year may be taken in one continuous period, unless approved by the senior pastor at least 60 days in advance.

5. Maximum accrued leave may not exceed 20 working days. Under normal conditions, employees are encouraged to use the regular allowance of annual leave each year.

6. All annual leave shall be requested in writing, and approved subject to the needs of the church. For full-time employees, annual leave of more than two working days' duration will normally be requested in writing, at least 30 days in advance of the desired starting date. Part-time employees shall make all of their requests in writing 30 days in advance. The written approval of the senior pastor is required for all vacation requests. With the organist, youth director, and receptionist/office clerk, prior written approval of leave time must be secured from their immediate supervisor, before submission to the senior pastor for approval.

7. At termination of employment, annual leave earned but not used will be paid for by the church at the rate of pay current at the time of termination, if it has been six months or more since a pay-rate change, or at the previous rate of pay, if it has been less than six months since a pay-rate change.

## C. SICK LEAVE

Sick leave is considered a gratuity benefit and not an earned right. It is allowable only to employees when they are ill and unable to report for work, or when the illness is of such a nature it might be contagious to fellow employees. Illness in the family of an employee is normally not just cause for sick leave, unless due to exposure to a contagious disease, and the employee is restricted to the home. With these reservations, all persons employed on a regular basis will be granted sick leave with full pay as specified below:

1. *Full-time church employees* shall accrue sick leave at the rate of 5/6 of a day for each full month worked (10 working days per year), based on a 40-hour workweek and prorated for a regular workweek of less than 40 hours. Sick leave not needed will accrue from year to year, to a maximum of 50 work days.

   *Part-time employees* earn sick leave each year equaling two of their normal workweeks. Part-time employees' sick leave not needed will accrue year to year with a maximum of 10 working weeks.

2. Illnesses requiring absence of more than three consecutive workdays may require a written notice of illness, and a written release to return to work following illness from the physician treating the employee, for the employee to be eligible to claim sick leave. Specific instances that arise that are not covered by these Personnel Policies will be at the discretion of the Personnel Committee.

## D. JURY DUTY

If a regular employee is required to be absent during all or any portion of their normally scheduled working hours in the actual performance of jury duty (including a reasonable allowance for travel time to and/or from the place of jury duty), the employee shall receive their regular pay for the time they were required to be absent, less any fees paid for jury duty during the same period of time (above a reasonable allowance for food and travel), provided the employee has not chosen to serve voluntarily.

## E. LEAVE WITHOUT PAY

Approval of leave without pay shall depend upon the circumstances in each case, but the following general rules shall apply:

1. If a regular employee is required to remain away from work for a period of 10 working days or less because of illness or other justifiable cause, and does not have any, or enough accrued annual and/or sick leave to cover the full time they are absent, leave without pay may be granted by the senior pastor.

2. Requests for leave without pay shall not be granted for indefinite periods, but must state the anticipated inclusive dates, which shall not exceed 10 workdays in one continuous period.

3. Requests for leave without pay shall be made in writing and approved in writing, and a copy of the request and approval kept on file in the church office throughout the employee's term of employment. If the nature of the emergency makes it impractical to obtain written approval before commencing leave, verbal approval may be obtained by telephone, provided a written con-

firmation of the request and approval shall be filed before the employee will be eligible to return to work.

4. When leave without pay is granted for part of a pay period, pay shall be computed by dividing the salary for the pay period by the number of working days in a normal pay period, and multiplying this computed daily rate by the number of days worked in the pay period.

5. All paperwork must be completed and approved prior to receiving salary for the period affected.

6. The securing of substitutes for the director of music position is the responsibility of the director of music. The securing of substitutes for the organist for regular worship services, and for weddings, funerals, etc., is the sole responsibility of the organist and shall be from a substitute list approved by both the organist and director of music. This applies to all forms of leave.

### F. WORKERS' COMPENSATION INSURANCE

Workers' Compensation Insurance is provided to protect employees who are injured while on official duty.

### G. F.I.C.A.

F.I.C.A. benefits of the Social Security Administration must be participated in by those employees specified by law, through payroll deductions.

### H. HEALTH INSURANCE NOT PROVIDED

The church does not provide a group health insurance plan for lay personnel as an employee benefit. However, if a lay employee wishes to voluntarily participate in the denominational group health insurance plan at the employee's personal expense, they may do so.

## IX. Evaluation

All employees and their work will be evaluated annually, in written form, by the senior pastor. The employee will be requested to sign the performance evaluation and a copy will be given to the employee. Work may be assumed to be satisfactory unless advised otherwise. Work that is considered to be unsatisfactory will be discussed with the employee at the time, and if the work continues to be unsatisfactory, will constitute grounds for involuntary termination (see Part IV. B). A written evaluation will be made at the time of any involuntary termination, and kept in the individual's personnel file. Work that is considered to be outstanding will be given appropriate recognition. The PC will be kept advised of all employees' work that is typically unsatisfactory or outstanding, so that appropriate action may be taken.

## X. Grievances or Suggestions

### A. RIGHT OF EXPRESSION

Each employee has the privilege and will be provided the opportunity to express an opinion, suggestion, or grievance, in person, to the senior pastor.

## B. RIGHT OF APPEAL

Each employee, including involuntarily terminated employees, has the right to present a written appeal to the PC, with prior knowledge of the senior pastor, for a hearing in person on an unresolved complaint or grievance. The PC is the final authority.

## XI. General Disclaimer—Lay Personnel Policies

This document is intended to provide employees with a general understanding of the lay personnel policies of the church. Employees are encouraged to familiarize themselves with the contents of this policy for it will answer many common questions concerning employment by the church.

However, this policy cannot anticipate every situation or answer every question about employment. It is not an employment contract and is not intended to create contractual obligations of any kind. The senior pastor and Personnel Committee (PC) reserve the right to make employment decisions they believe to be in the best interest of the church. They also reserve the right to terminate any employee with or without cause or notice, and any employee may quit with or without cause or notice. This policy may be modified in writing only and any modifications must be approved by the senior pastor and Personnel Committee.

Approval date: _____

Revision date: _____

## Clergy Personnel Policies

Each denomination and church will have unique personnel policies concerning its pastors. Some denominations only make suggestions to local churches while others offer quite formalized policies, such as the Discipline of The United Methodist Church or the Canons of the Catholic Church. Likewise, local churches can vary significantly in the way they adopt clergy personnel policies. Because of these wide differences, we will not attempt to offer a sample clergy personnel policy statement.

We do firmly believe, however, that it is important that each church have a written policy statement or employment/assignment agreement (hereinafter called the "statement") which covers the following essential elements of personnel-related matters between the church and its pastors. Such a written statement should minimize future questions about what was agreed to at the time of employment or assignment. Of course, the statement would want to take into consideration what is already set in formal denominational policy and include those issues that are unique to the local church.

*Terms of employment or assignment.* The statement should clearly specify the process through which a pastor is employed/assigned, the term of employment or assignment if that is appropriate, and how the pastor is terminated or reassigned. It should name the responsible committee and what approval process must be followed. It should specify that a position description be written and agreed to and what evaluation process will be in effect. In the case of disagreements about an evaluation or any other terms of employment of assignment, the statement should specify what appeal process is available.

*Compensation.* The various parts of a pastor's compensation should be carefully documented. In addition to basic salary, there may be allowances, reimbursable expenses, medical coverage, and pension support as well as other such items.

1. Allowances will normally include (a) housing and living expenses, which clergy normally do not need to declare as income for federal tax reporting purposes; and (b) Social Security offset, which clergy are sometimes given to offset their self-employed Social Security and Medicare costs but which is considered as salary for federal income tax reporting. (Other parts of their compensation package which are sometimes handled as allowances, such as car allowance, are taxable.) The statement should specify that the amount of housing allowance must be declared and approved by the governing body annually, before the beginning of the tax year. The statement should clearly specify any other allowances that are to be paid.

2. Reimbursable expenses should be paid on an accountable basis whereby the pastor must turn in receipts and/or a record book before reimbursement, to take full advantage of tax laws. The statement should outline the procedure for reimbursement of automobile and other travel expenses, professional expenses, educational expenses, and other such reimbursements the church wishes to make. If a car is provided, the allowable use of the vehicle should be specified in the statement.

3. Medical care for the pastor and possibly the pastor's family may be paid for as a direct expense of the church. If so, the provisions of this compensation element should be covered in the statement.

4.  The type of pension plan and extent of coverage should be documented in the statement.

***Absences.*** The statement should be clear on the types of absences allowed and the length of time permitted for each type. In addition to annual and holiday leave, there may be sick leave, educational leave, termination/reassignment leave, and so forth. Also, the weekly "day off" should be specified so the congregation is clear about when the pastor is to have personal time. Compensation support for long-term absences such as illness or sabbaticals should be carefully specified in the statement.

***Denominational and community involvement.*** There may be other duties and responsibilities in which the church may want the pastor to become active that relate to denominational and community involvement outside the local church. The extent of the pastor's involvement should be discussed in the statement to document congregational support.

## Personnel Policy Acknowledgment

I,_____, acknowledge receipt of the _____ Church Personnel Policies and fully understand that I have a responsibility to read, understand, and comply with each and every policy and requirement. I have been given an opportunity to ask for clarification on any matter on which I am unclear.

I further understand that the Personnel Policies are not a contract, but rather, a guideline for policies, benefits, requirements, and procedures, which may, with or without notice, be changed, rescinded, amended, or added to at any time by the duly authorized administrative body of the church in its sole and absolute discretion.

I further understand and acknowledge that there is no agreement between me and the church for any definite period of employment and that I may quit at any time, with or without cause or notice, and that the church has the right to terminate my employment at any time, with or without cause or notice. I understand and acknowledge that this constitutes the entire agreement between me and the church regarding the term of my employment and that this agreement may not be altered, amended, modified, or otherwise changed except in writing which has been approved and signed by the authorized administrative body of the church.

Any dispute involving employment, including any State or Federal claim of any kind, shall be resolved by binding arbitration under the commercial arbitration rules of the American Arbitration Association.

Date: _____

Employee Signature: _____

Print Name: _____

# Sexual Harassment Policy

*(Note: This sample sexual harassment policy is intended as a general guide only and may not apply directly to every church or organization. Sexual harassment policies should be customized for each and every unique church organization and/or denomination.)*

## I. Theological Statement

We believe that God created and values human life, intending all men, women, and children to have worth and dignity in relationships with God and others.

[Name of church] commits itself to provide a friendly environment in which members, visitors, employees, and volunteers treat each other with respect, and to provide a collegial work environment.

We believe that sexual harassment is an unjust misuse of power which threatens a person's feelings of worth and dignity, and diminishes the quality of community within the church.

We believe that the caring community of the church cannot ignore or minimize the damage to the individual and to the community caused by sexual harassment, and must address itself to the healing of all persons involved.

We are committed to creating and maintaining a community within the church where persons can worship, participate in activities, and work together in an atmosphere free from all forms of sexual harassment, exploitation, or intimidation.

We are strongly opposed to sexual harassment; will do all we can to prevent it; will take whatever action may be needed to correct it; and if necessary, will discipline persons whose behavior violates this policy.

## II. Policy Statement

It is the policy of [name of church] that sexual harassment is wrong, that it is inappropriate in the church community, and that charges of sexual harassment will be carefully investigated according to procedures established herein. This policy applies to lay church staff, members, volunteers, and others working on behalf of the church. (Pastors are generally covered by the policy of their denomination as explained in Section VI.)

Sexual harassment is unacceptable at the church itself and at other church-related settings such as meetings, youth group events, trips, camps, etc.

## III. Definitions and Forms of Sexual Harassment

A. *Sexual Harassment:* Sexual harassment is any sexually related behavior that is unwelcome and/or offensive, or which fails to respect the rights of others. It includes any unwelcome advances, requests for sexual favors, and any other verbal or physical conduct which meets either of the following criteria:

1. Conduct which creates an intimidating, hostile, or offensive environment, or unreasonably interferes with an individual's participation in a church program, activity, or employment.

2. Submission to such conduct is made either explicitly or implicitly a term or condition of the individual's participation in a church program, activity, or employment; or such submission is used as a basis for a decision affecting an individual's participation in a church program, activity, or employment.

B. *Forms of Sexual Harassment:* Harassment may involve a wide range of behaviors from verbal innuendo and subtle suggestions, to overt demands and physical/sexual abuse. Sexual harassment is usually an exploitation of a power relationship or an attempt to gain power or intimidate another, and may not be solely a sexual issue. It may be behavior of a sexual nature directed at a person because they are male or female, such as jokes based on a stereotype of one sex, put-downs based on sex, or tasks assigned on the basis of sex, called "gender harassment."

## IV. Disseminating the Policy

This policy is to be disseminated to all staff and made widely available to all members of [name of church]; it shall be posted in at least one prominent place in the church.

## V. Responsibility for Implementing the Policy

The pastor-in-charge and the chair of the Personnel Committee are responsible for implementing the sexual harassment policy and ensuring that all allegations are investigated and resolved promptly and appropriately. All other employees are responsible, and all members are encouraged to inform the pastor-in-charge or the Personnel Committee chair of any incidents of sexual harassment.

## VI. Reporting Complaints of Sexual Harassment

We encourage individuals who believe they are being sexually harassed to promptly and firmly notify the offender that his or her behavior is unwelcome. In the event that such informal, direct communication is either impractical or ineffective, a complaint against anyone (other than clergy or diaconal ministers), should be made as soon as possible to the pastor-in-charge or the Personnel Committee chair.

Persons who believe they have been the subject of sexual harassment may be assisted by an advisor or advocate at all stages of the complaint procedure. Persons accused of sexual harassment may also be assisted by an advisor of their choosing.

Complaints against clergy and diaconal ministers should be made to the executive-in-charge of the denominational organization at the next level above the local church and shall be reviewed and/or investigated as set forth in the policy statement on ministerial sexual abuse.

## VII. Complaint Procedure

A. Complaints of sexual harassment will be investigated by the pastor-in-charge and/or Personnel Committee chair. In the event of a conflict of interest or time, one or more alternative investigators will be designated by the Personnel Committee.

B. Complaints of sexual harassment shall be promptly investigated. Confidentiality will be maintained throughout the investigatory process to the extent practical and possible.

C. The investigator will initially conduct an informal review that may include interviewing the complainant and the accused. If the complaint can be resolved informally to the satisfaction of the complainant and the accused at this stage of the process, no further action will be taken, and the matter will be considered closed.

D. If the matter is not resolved informally and there is substantial disagreement over what is alleged to have occurred, the investigator shall promptly investigate the complaint and the investigation shall include, at a minimum, interviewing the complainant, the accused, and any identified witnesses.

E. The results of the investigation shall be communicated to the complainant and the accused. If the investigator believes that sexual harassment has occurred as described in this policy, remedial action and/or discipline shall be taken as appropriate.

1. Remedial action may include, but is not limited to:

   a. Education or training;

   b. Referral to mediation or counseling; and/or

   c. Reparations, such as paying for counseling.

2. If the accused is an employee, disciplinary action may include, but is not limited to, verbal warning, written warning, suspension without pay, or termination.

3. In the case of a volunteer or member, disciplinary action may include, but is not limited to, verbal warning, written warning, removal from a position, or prohibiting participation in church programs or activities.

F. If the complainant or accused disputes the findings, is dissatisfied with the discipline imposed, or takes exception to the remedial actions taken, that person has 10 days, from the date the results of the investigation are communicated to him or her, to submit to the Personnel Committee a written request that such matters be reviewed.

Upon receipt of any such request, the Personnel Committee shall, as soon as practical, designate not more than three members of the Personnel Committee and not more than two members of the church at large to serve on a review board. To the extent practical the review board shall have equitable gender representation.

The review board shall review the original complaint, the investigative finding, and any disciplinary or remedial action and issue a final decision in the matter. Before making a final decision, the review board may meet with the complainant, the accused, and/or any other person it deems appropriate.

G. A summary of the complaint, investigative findings, and final action taken shall be prepared by the investigator and shall be maintained in a confidential file in the office of the pastor-in-charge.

If charges are substantiated against an employee, a sealed record shall be placed in the employee's personnel file, with an open notation in the file that confidential disciplinary information is on file, disclosure of which requires the staff person's permission.

*Note:* If at any time during the process the complainant believes the situation is not being taken as seriously as it should be, they should find another advocate, make a report to the chair of the Personnel Committee or another official of the church, or contact the executive-in-charge at the next level of the denomination or church.

## VIII. Retaliation and False Accusations

A. Retaliation against any individual for seeking assistance or bringing a sexual harassment complaint through the process as described in this policy is a violation of this policy. Similarly, any person who participates or cooperates in any manner in an investigation or any other aspect of the process described in this policy shall not be retaliated against. Any retaliation will be dealt with in the same manner as a charge of sexual harassment.

B. Deliberately false or reckless complaints will be dealt with in the same manner as a charge of sexual harassment.

## IX. Healing

The [name of church] will make every effort to provide ongoing ministry and pastoral support for all persons involved. The bonds of Christian love call us to effect healing for all persons.

## Sexual Harassment Policy Acknowledgment

I acknowledge receipt of the [name of church] Sexual Harassment Policy and fully understand that I have a responsibility to read, understand, and comply with each and every requirement contained therein. I have been given an opportunity to ask for clarification on any matter on which I am unclear.

Date: _____

Employee Signature: _____

Print Name: _____

# Injury/Illness Prevention Program

*(Note: This sample Injury/Illness Prevention Policy is intended as a guide only and may not apply directly to a given church or organization. This type of policy must be customized for each church organization.)*

Our church is committed to a goal of providing a safe workplace for all employees. To accomplish this goal, the following Injury/Illness Prevention Program was developed.

I.  The senior pastor, or a specifically designated representative, is directly responsible for implementing this Injury/Illness Prevention Program, and will perform the following duties:

   A. Oversee the church system for identifying and evaluating workplace hazards, and in so doing:

   1. Make scheduled periodic inspections to identify and evaluate unsafe conditions and work practices.

   2. Promptly investigate accidents and workplace injuries and illnesses.

   3. Conduct inspections when new, potentially hazardous substances, processes, procedures, or equipment are introduced to the workplace, or when new hazards are otherwise identified.

   B. Ensure that unsafe or unhealthy conditions or work practices are corrected as soon as possible after they are identified.

   C. Administer the Occupational Safety and Health Training Program. They will:

   1. Instruct employees, including supervisors, in safe work practices and provide instruction about hazards specific to each employee's job assignment.

   2. Provide training to all employees and supervisors (a) when employees are given new job assignments for which training has not previously been received, (b) whenever new potentially hazardous substances, processes, procedures, or equipment are introduced into the workplace, and (c) whenever the church is made aware of new or previously unrecognized hazards.

   D. Oversee the system for communicating with employees on occupational health and safety matters. They will:

   1. Encourage managers, supervisors, and employees to report workplace hazards, either directly to their supervisors or to the senior pastor.

   2. Ensure that employees and supervisors know that they will not be retaliated against for reporting workplace hazards.

   3. Communicate with employees as safety issues arise.

   4. Chair (no less than quarterly) meetings of the safety and health committee.

E. Maintain records concerning safety inspections and training.

II. Employees are required to observe the following safety rules, established after careful study of existing hazards, in the interests of providing a safe, healthful place in which to work.

    A. Unskilled persons shall not be permitted to operate or tamper with machines.

    B. Machines and their electrical cords shall be guarded as needed and required by law or regulation. No electrically operated machine or fan shall be used in a position or manner that would cause the cord to be stretched or otherwise extend across an aisle or passageway, or to be on the floor in a manner likely to create a tripping hazard. If temporary use across an aisle is required or necessary, portable barriers shall be erected. Frayed or badly worn cords shall be replaced. Cords should not be allowed to come in contact with heat-producing equipment such as portable heaters and the like.

    C. Machines shall never be cleaned or adjusted while in motion.

    D. Springs and fittings on swivel chairs shall be inspected frequently.

    E. Installation, repair, or maintenance of any equipment shall be done only by qualified persons.

    F. Guards on paper cutters shall be in place when the machine is being used; hand-power cutters shall have the blade in the "down" position at all times when not in use.

    G. Heavy filing cabinets shall be firmly based or attached to wall fitting(s) to prevent tipping.

    H. When not in actual physical use, all desk and file drawers shall be kept closed to avoid limiting safe use of aisles. Not more than one file drawer in one tier shall be opened at a time. Opening additional drawers could easily over-balance the file and cause tipping.

    I. Ladders or step stools designed to support an employee's weight and the material to be obtained shall be provided as a means of reaching high files and upper locker and/or storeroom shelves. No employee shall stand on a swivel or folding chair for any such purpose.

    J. Employees shall familiarize themselves with the location of fire extinguishers and shall know how to use them if required.

    K. A fully equipped first-aid kit is available if needed.

    L. Pens and sharp, pointed objects shall always be placed on a desk with the point away from the user and in a way that persons passing will not be endangered.

    M. Razor blades, knives, or other similar items shall not be used to sharpen pencils.

    N. All hazards, such as sharp file cabinet edges, slivered desk corners, broken chair casters, frayed electrical connections, loose linoleum and tiles, or any other conditions likely to do bodily harm, damage clothing, or constitute a fire hazard, shall be reported at once to the senior pastor *IN WRITING*.

O. Care shall be exercised at all times to avoid damage to tops of desks by storing or moving heavy or sharp objects on them.

P. Aisles shall be kept clear at all times of all obstructions. When supplies or other materials are received, they shall be placed in permanent, safe storage as quickly as possible.

Q. Care shall be exercised when matches are kept in desk drawers to avoid accidentally igniting them.

R. Correct positioning of arms, hands, and back when using typewriter or computer is essential to eliminate or reduce unnecessary muscle strain.

S. When employees leave their work at breaks, lunchtime, or when leaving work at the close of the day, they shall walk, not run, to avoid "slip and fall" accidents.

III. All employees shall observe all rules and instructions, both verbal and written, relating to safety in their work. Failure to comply with any safety rule or instruction is grounds for dismissal.

This program has been prepared in response to the requirements of [state]-OSHA.

Effective date: _____

# Memo of Employment, Full-Time

FROM:  [Authorized Hiring Person]

TO:

DATE:

SUBJECT:  Memorandum of Employment for Full-Time Position

We are pleased to confirm your hiring to the position of

_____.

A summary of the terms of the employment follows:

| | |
|---|---|
| Beginning date: | _____ |
| Salary: | _____ |
| Pay dates: | The 15th and last day of each month. |
| Vacation: | Earned at the rate of two work weeks per year. |
| Hours Worked: | Forty (40) hours per week. (8 a.m. to 5 p.m., an hour for lunch) |
| Sick Leave: | Earned at the rate of two work weeks per year. |
| Holidays: | 11.5 work periods per year, as per the current Personnel Policy. |
| Forms: | Completion of all requested employment forms, including acknowledging receiving and reading the Lay Personnel Policy, Sexual Harassment Policy, and the Position Description. |
| Personnel Policy: | The most current Personnel Policy is the final authority in employment matters. |

I understand that this employment, having no specified term, may be terminated at the will of either party on notice to the other under the provision of the [state] Labor Code, Section [        ].

_____          _____
(Employee)                                      (Authorized Hiring Person)

## *Memo of Employment, Part-Time*

**FROM:** [Authorized Hiring Person]

**TO:**

**DATE:**

**SUBJECT:** Memorandum of Employment for Part-Time Position

We are pleased to confirm your hiring to the position of

_____ .

A summary of the terms of the employment follows:

| | |
|---|---|
| Beginning date: | _____ |
| Salary/hourly rate: | _____ |
| Pay dates: | The 15th and last day of each month. |
| Vacation: | Earned at the rate of two work weeks per year. |
| Hours Worked: | Fifteen to twenty (15–20) hours per week. |
| Sick Leave: | Earned at the rate of two work weeks per year. |
| Holidays: | 11.5 work periods per year, as per the current Personnel Policy. |
| Forms: | Completion of all requested employment forms, including acknowledging receiving and reading the Lay Personnel Policy, Sexual Harassment Policy, and the Position Description. |
| Personnel Policy: | The most current Personnel Policy is the final authority in employment matters. |

I understand that this employment, having no specified term, may be terminated at the will of either party on notice to the other under the provision of the [state] Labor Code, Section [      ].

_____          _____
         (Employee)                                                    (Authorized Hiring Person)

# ENTITLEMENT RECORD

EMPLOYEE _____

DATE OF HIRE _____

ENTITLEMENT PER YEAR
VACATION _____
SICK LEAVE _____

| DATE | VACATION | | | COMPENSATORY TIME | | | SICK LEAVE | | |
|---|---|---|---|---|---|---|---|---|---|
| | EARNED | TAKEN | BALANCE | EARNED | TAKEN | BALANCE | EARNED | TAKEN | BALANCE |
| | | | | | | | | | |
| | | | | | | | | | |
| | | | | | | | | | |
| | | | | | | | | | |
| | | | | | | | | | |
| | | | | | | | | | |
| | | | | | | | | | |
| | | | | | | | | | |
| | | | | | | | | | |
| | | | | | | | | | |
| | | | | | | | | | |
| | | | | | | | | | |
| | | | | | | | | | |

## Vacation/Leave Of Absence/Compensatory Time-Off Application

I, _____, request the following for my vacation/leave of absence/
　　　Name of Employee

compensatory time off under _____ of the Personnel Policies.
　　　　　　　　　　　　　Paragraph/Section/Subsection

FIRST CHOICE: _____
　　　　　　　　　　　(From — To)

SECOND CHOICE: _____
　　　　　　　　　　　(From — To)

THIRD CHOICE: _____
　　　　　　　　　　　(From — To)

Date of Application: _____

Signature of Employee: _____ Date: _____

Signature of Approval: _____ Date: _____

### Office Use Only:

Number of days _____ (hours represented) working periods _____

Copies: Employee's Personnel File
　　　　Employee

................................................................

## Request for Sick Leave

I, _____, request _____ to be granted
　　　　　　　　　　　　　　　　　　Actual Date(s)

as paid sick leave under _____ of the Personnel Policies.
　　　　　　　　　　　Paragraph/Section/Subsection

Signature of Employee: _____ Date: _____

Approved By: _____ Date: _____

### Office Use Only:

Number of days _____ (hours represented) working periods _____

Copies: Employee's Personnel File
　　　　Employee
　　　　Treasurer

# Application for Employment

Applicant's Name: _____ Soc.Sec. #: _____
    (same as on Social Security card)

Address: _____ Home Phone: _____

_____ Business phone: _____
    (city)        (state)        (zip)

Person to notify in case of emergency: _____ Phone: _____

## Education

High School: _____ Dates attended: _____

Address: _____ Graduate? _____

Major subjects or courses: _____

University/College: _____ Dates attended: _____

Address: _____ Graduate? _____

Major subjects or courses: _____ Degree? _____

Trade or vocational schools attended _____

_____

## Work Experience

Please list each of your occupations or positions for the past 10 years, starting with the most recent, or present, employment.

| POSITION/TITLE | COMPANY | CO. ADDRESS | FROM | TO | REASON FOR LEAVING |
| --- | --- | --- | --- | --- | --- |
| | | | | | |
| | | | | | |
| | | | | | |
| | | | | | |
| | | | | | |
| | | | | | |
| | | | | | |
| | | | | | |

Please list your residence addresses for the past 10 years with the most current first.

_____

_____

_____

_____

Please list your affiliations with professional associations or organizations.

_____

_____

_____

Please tell us about your interests, your experience in those areas you consider to be your specialties, your achievements, objectives, personal plans, and/or any other information you feel may be helpful in evaluating your qualifications for this position.

_____

_____

_____

_____

_____

_____

I understand and am in agreement with the church's policy of hiring and promoting personnel on the basis of experience, qualifications, and capability—without regard to age, sex, religion, veteran status, marital status, handicap, color, race, national origin, or sexual preference. By virtue of my signature below, I authorize the church to obtain any relevant information concerning me from former employers or supervisors, references, associates, school officials, and others; and, it is understood that I release all concerned from any liability in connection therewith. I further certify that ALL information given on this Application for Employment is absolutely correct to the best of my knowledge. I understand that any willful omission, misrepresentation, or falsification will constitute valid grounds for immediate termination of employment.

I also agree to supply six (6) references that can verify my suitability for this position.

Signature: _____ Date: _____
(as on Social Security card)

## Telephone Reference Check

Applicant's name: _____ Date: _____ Interviewer: _____

Name of reference: _____ Phone: _____

Affiliation:_____

Position/title of reference:_____

How long have you known the applicant and in what capacity? _____

_____

_____

What was the applicant's position or title? _____

What were applicant's specific duties? _____

_____

_____

_____

Has applicant ever supervised or managed an activity?    ❏ Yes    ❏ No

If so, how many people did applicant supervise? _____

Do you consider the applicant a capable supervisor who can achieve desired results competently and efficiently? Please elaborate:

_____

_____

_____

How would you rate the applicant technically?

❏ Brilliant    ❏ Sharp    ❏ Average    ❏ Below Average

How would you rate the applicant compared to others with similar backgrounds?

❏ Upper 10%    ❏ Upper 25%    ❏ Other: _____

What are the applicant's strengths?

_____

_____

_____

_____

What characteristics, if any, does the applicant possess that have limited, or will limit, their performance or advancement?

_____

_____

_____

Describe the applicant's ability to interact/work with others in the workplace.

_____

_____

_____

Does applicant express ideas effectively, verbally, and in writing?

_____

_____

_____

Do you have any reservations in recommending the applicant?

_____

_____

_____

Can you tell me why the applicant left this position?

_____

_____

Would you rehire the applicant if you had a position available?

❏ Yes    ❏ No    ❏ If no, why not? _____

_____

Interviewer's comments and observations on the interview:

_____

_____

_____

_____

_____

## Employee Reprimand

Name of Employee: _____ Date: _____

It is necessary to warn you of the following:

❏ Absence    ❏ Smoking

❏ Tardiness    ❏ Carelessness

❏ Loafing    ❏ Refusal to obey orders

❏ Fighting    ❏ Use of abusive language

❏ Horseplay    ❏ Infraction of rules or policies

❏ Violation of safety rules

❏ Abuse of equipment and/or materials

❏ Leaving work without permission

❏ Performing poor work due to willful neglect

❏ Other

EXPLANATION OF OFFENSE: _____

_____

_____

_____

_____

_____

This warning will be made a part of your personnel record. The issuance of further warnings may subject you to disciplinary action such as suspension or discharge.

I acknowledge that this reprimand was discussed with me on this date and that a copy was given to me.

Supervisor's Signature: _____ Date: _____

Employee's Signature: _____ Date: _____

# Employee Warning Notice

Employee: _____ Position: _____

Time in present position: _____

Entry date: _____

Date of offense: _____

A. EXPLANATION OF OFFENSE: _____

_____

B. EMPLOYEE'S EXPLANATION: _____

_____

C. PRIOR WARNINGS: _____

_____

1. Active Warnings for This Offense?   ❑ Yes   ❑ No   Dates: _____

2. Prior Warnings for Other Infractions?   ❑ Yes   ❑ No   Dates: _____

Comments: _____

D. DISCIPLINARY ACTION TAKEN:

*Written Reprimand:* Immediate improvement in this area is required. Failure to do so may result in your suspension and/or final written warning.

Suspension of _____ days without pay.   Returned to work date: _____

*Final Written Warning:* A recurrence of this incident or failure to make the necessary improvements in your performance will result in your being discharged.

Suspension of _____ days without pay.   Returned to work date: _____

*Discharge*   Effective Date:_____

E. ITEMS DISCUSSED WITH EMPLOYEE: _____

_____

F. EMPLOYEE COMMENTS:_____

_____

I acknowledge that the above written warning has been discussed with me and a copy has been given to me on this date.

Employee's Signature:_____ Date: _____

Completed by: _____ Date: _____

# Employee Separation Report

Name: _____ Soc. Sec. #: _____

Date Hired: _____ Last Day Worked: _____

## Reason For Separation

**LAYOFF**

❏ Permanent    ❏ Temporary    Expected Date of Recall: _____

**RETIREMENT**

❏ Voluntary    ❏ Church Policy    ❏ Compulsory    Other: _____

**VOLUNTARY SEPARATION**

❏ No Notice       ❏ Other Work
❏ Left Area       ❏ Marriage or Domestic Obligation
❏ Pregnancy       ❏ Working Conditions
❏ Other: _____

**LEAVE OF ABSENCE**

From: _____ to _____ Reason: _____

**ILLNESS OR INJURY**

❏ Job related    ❏ Non-job related

**DISCHARGE**

❏ Chronic absence     ❏ Not qualified
❏ Chronic tardiness   ❏ Under Influence of Intoxicant
❏ Violation of rules/insubordination (explain):_____

_____

❏ Misconduct _____
❏ Refusal to Follow Instructions
❏ Other _____

Attach sheet with further explanation if necessary.

**SEPARATION PAYMENTS**

❏ In Lieu of Notice  $ _____
❏ Severance Pay      $ _____
❏ Vacation           $ _____

Supervisor's Signature: _____ Date: _____

Employee's Signature:_____ Date: _____

Complete this form upon separation of any employee for any reason. Give a copy to the employee and place a copy in the personnel file of the employee.

# Exit Interview

*(To be administered after the separation decision is made)*

Name: _____

Position: _____ Supervisor: _____

1. Why are you leaving this position? _____

_____

2. Do you have another job at this time?  ❑ Yes  ❑ No

   What will your job title be? _____

   Who is your new employer? _____

3. How do you feel about the supervision for the position you are leaving?_____

_____

4. How do you feel about the salary, benefits, and policies for this position? _____

_____

5. How do you feel about your fellow workers? _____

_____

6. How would you change the duties of the position you are leaving? _____

_____

7. How would you improve working conditions? _____

_____

8. How would you improve communications? _____

_____

9. Do you have any other suggestions? _____

_____

Interviewer comments: _____

_____

Interviewer: _____ Date: _____

# Legal Issues

A very important part of the organizing and staffing of today's church are the legal issues that surround its operations. There are structuring and zoning issues as well as rules about doing business. Employment laws are many and apply to a church as they do any other employer. Liability for one's actions also applies to a church, especially in counseling and sexual misconduct, as well as in real-estate liability.

While many of these legal concerns are discussed in various contexts throughout the manual, we felt it important to present a synopsis of the basic concerns at this point in our discussions. This is done through a reprint of a paper by Penelope Mercurio-Jennings, professor of business law, California State University, Northridge, California.[5]

*Please note: While most of the material presented in this paper is generally applicable, some of the information may be peculiar to California laws and regulations. It is recommended that local legal counsel be consulted where local or regional laws and regulations are involved.*

# Legal Issues Facing Churches
## Church Structuring

1. If the ministry is currently operating as a self-directed ministry or an unincorporated association of members, be aware of the potential liability to the pastor and the members. Consider limiting personal liability by incorporating as a nonprofit corporation.

2. After incorporation, the articles of incorporation, bylaws, and other rules for structuring or operating the church should be reviewed on a regular basis to make sure they are consistent with current legal requirements for nonprofit corporations as well as the actual current operation of the church. For example, at the time of incorporation the articles or bylaws may have given the original pastor almost total control over the operation of the church. However, as the church grows or if there is a change in pastors, the congregation (and possibly the new pastor) may want the congregation to have greater control over the management of the church.

3. When the articles of incorporation are filed, the church will be recognized as a nonprofit charitable corporation. However, the church should be operated and managed in a manner consistent with the fact of incorporation (i.e., treat the church as a legal entity separate from the members, officers, pastor, etc.) or there may be a "piercing of the corporate veil" which protects the members and others from personal liability. Common mistakes made by incorporated churches include:

   a. Failure to recognize the formal structure of the organization. For example, if there are formal procedures for meetings or decision making, they should be followed.

   b. Commingling the assets of the church with the assets of the pastor or members. In order to avoid personal liability, as well as misunderstandings, separate accounts for church business and personal expenses of the pastor should be maintained.

   c. Using church employees for personal business. Remember that church employees work for the church. They should not be directed to handle personal as opposed to church matters for the pastor or other management personnel.

4. Consider separate incorporation of businesses connected with the church such as schools, counseling centers, and special fund-raising organizations so that they will be separate nonprofit organizations with separate liability.

## Zoning

1. Be aware of zoning and land-use regulations in your area. These laws are generally local in origin (city and county rules) and are often very complicated. Furthermore, violations are often treated as quasi-criminal conduct resulting

in significant penalties and fines. Consequently, competent legal counsel with expertise in this area of the law should be sought in connection with any land-use decision.

2. Be sure that the church activities and operations are consistent with any special use permits or exemptions for "church activities." Zoning laws should be examined carefully before the addition of a school, counseling center, church store, etc.

## Doing Business

1. Know the businesses with which the church deals. Just as the pastor and members generally seek to avoid personal liability by incorporating, so too do the operators of small businesses. In such cases, consider securing the written personal guarantee of a majority shareholder (owner) of a small business before signing the contract. When dealing with contractors and other licensed professionals, check on whether they have the required state licenses.

2. Be aware of state laws regarding mechanics' liens on real property. For example, if payment for construction work on church property is made to the general contractor but payments are not made by the general contractor to the subcontractors, the church could be found liable for the nonpayment and then pay twice for repairs, improvements, or construction on real property.

3. Put contracts in writing.

   a. Although most oral contracts are valid, certain types of contracts must be in writing to be enforceable in a court of law. These include contracts for the sale of an interest in land (including many leases), personal guarantees to answer for the debt of another, contracts incapable of performance in one year or less, and contracts for the sale of goods for a price of $500 or more.

   b. Other contracts should also be in writing in order to reduce misunderstandings and to have better proof of the transactions. At the very least, begin to use confirmation letters. State your understanding of the oral agreement and send it to the other party to the contract.

   c. Always read what you are signing. If there are provisions which you do not understand (often a problem with "form" contracts) seek legal counsel.

## Employment

1. Be aware of state and federal employment rules.

   a. The federal Fair Labor Standards Act establishes rules for what is the minimum wage, payment for overtime, etc. However, there may also be state law requirements including higher minimum wages and different methods for calculating what is "overtime."

   b. Discrimination on the basis of race, color, national origin, gender, religion, age (over age 40 years), and disability is prohibited by federal and state statutes. However, a religious organization may consider and give preference to members of its faith who follow its theological principles when making employment decisions. For example, questions concerning an applicant's religious beliefs and practices are clearly appropriate when hiring a pastor or a Christian education director. The church may even consider the religious practices of those hired for secular positions such as janitors and bus drivers. However, remember that the exception for religious organizations only applies to questions of faith. The church employer may not discriminate on other grounds.

   c. Establish and enforce nondiscrimination policies including policies prohibiting sexual harassment.

2. Act carefully when hiring employees. An employer may be liable for "negligent hiring." For example if an employer fails to check the driving record of a person hired to drive a bus or to check references of people who will be working with children, there may be liability if injury occurs. Furthermore, in most states, churches (along with other employers) are vicariously liable for injuries to others resulting from negligent acts of employees committed "within the scope of employment." The possibility of "deep pocket" liability makes many churches attractive targets.

3. Maintain appropriate personnel files and records in writing. Many potential legal and personnel problems can be avoided or reduced by making use of established personnel policies such as periodic performance reviews. Be aware that one of the fastest growing areas of legal actions concerns wrongful termination of employees.

## Counseling Liability

1. Clergy often mistakenly believe that they are legally protected from liability in their roles as church counselors. However, many of the legal protections from liability have disappeared.

   a. In the past, many states had charitable immunity laws. However, in most states, charitable organizations are now liable to third parties under the usual rules of agency law.

   b. There is no Constitutional protection for counseling activities that go beyond issues of faith and belief. Counseling concerning general mental health issues will not be protected under the First Amendment.

2. State courts, including the California Supreme Court in the case of *Nally v. Grace Community Church* (1988), have ruled that there is no cause of action for "clergy malpractice" per se. However, if a pastor holds himself or herself out as being an expert in a field (or if the pastor is in fact such an expert) he or she will be held to an expert standard of care. For example, if a pastor claims to be a competent marital counselor, he or she will be required to act as such a competent, reasonable professional would have acted in that situation. Thus, unlicensed church counselors should make clear that they are not giving emotional, psychological, or other mental therapy.

3. Be aware of the limits of the pastor and other church counselors. When counseling starts to involve mental health counseling as opposed to pastoral (religious) counseling, be prepared to refer the counselee to a professional. Maintain a referral list of appropriate, competent, licensed mental health professionals.

4. Make sure that the staff and volunteers are appropriately hired, trained, and supervised.

5. Maintain confidentiality but be aware of exceptions to the requirement of confidentiality such as (a) the duty to warn of imminent harm and (2) the duty to report child abuse. Since a mistake in this area could create substantial legal and social risks, consult a lawyer if there are questions about whether to disclose information or maintain confidentiality.

6. Be careful about publicizing information (including through prayer requests or newsletters) that may be defamatory or may be a public disclosure of private embarrassing facts (note that a public disclosure of private facts is a type of invasion of privacy for which truth is *not* a defense).

## *Insurance*

1. Periodically review liability insurance policies to make sure coverage is appropriate to the current activities and assets of the church.

   a. Determine whether legal defense costs are included in the calculation of when policy limits have been reached.

   b. Examine whether the insurance company is given the right to settle the claim without the consent of the insured. Ask whether the carrier will be willing to go to trial instead of settling a case where the reputation of the pastor or the church is an issue.

   c. Determine whether the church or the pastor has the financial resources to cover the amount of a deductible.

2. Insurance policies often exclude many types of coverage.

   a. Many policies do not include coverage for directors or officers who are sued for their conduct in such capacity. Check on the addition of such coverage.

   b. Most policies do not insure against the award of punitive damages.

   c. Other common exclusions which may require additional coverage include (1) damages for child molestation and sexual misconduct, (2) damages for defamation and invasion of privacy, and (3) damages for loss of personal property of the staff.

3. Be prepared to cooperate actively in the defense of a lawsuit covered by insurance. For example, maintain accurate and up-to-date financial records, employment records, notes on meetings, etc.

4. Maintain proper real estate liability and fire insurance and appropriate vehicle insurance. Note that the actual uses of property and vehicles must be for uses

covered by the policy. For example, if the vehicle insurance only covers the church staff do not let others use the vehicle. If the property insurance does not cover a newly created church school, change the coverage to conform with the new use.

5. Be aware of the changing legal climate. The church has become an increasingly popular target for lawsuits. Consider obtaining "umbrella" or excess liability policy coverage to protect the church from potentially large legal losses.

## Choosing Legal Counsel

1. Budget legal reserves now and be prepared to pay reasonable fees to attorneys and other professionals.

2. Confer with a lawyer before making decisions which may have serious legal consequences.

3. Choose the lawyer who is best qualified to handle the legal issue faced by the church. As with all professions, not every lawyer is equally competent or equally well-qualified to handle every legal issue. Do not make the mistake of selecting a lawyer simply because he or she is a friend, relative, or member of the church. Remember that most legal issues facing the church will involve secular issues.

4. Don't be afraid to ask questions to determine the lawyer's expertise, experience, competence, caseload, and education. Also, if the church is hiring a firm, find out which lawyer or lawyers will actually be working on the case.

5. Discuss fee arrangements in advance including billing procedures and estimates of total fees. Legal fees are negotiable and fee reductions should be discussed in advance.

6. Be prepared to consider alternative methods of dispute resolution such as mediation and arbitrations.

## CHAPTER FOUR

# Leading

## Leadership and the Church

We have learned that *planning* is following a sequence of steps to create a documented plan that all can read and follow. *Organizing and staffing* is, to a great extent, applying rules and policies to achieve a functioning organization. We need to see that *leading* is an element of human behavior that, although it almost defies definition, is probably the most important among the managerial disciplines.

For our formal definition of leadership, we will accept the thoughts of another author who says, in essence, that leadership is the ability to get people to work together toward common objectives—with enthusiasm. It is the human factor that binds a group together and motivates it toward achievement.[1] This statement defines this important element of human behavior in somewhat tangible terms and indicates that there will be an end result. But what are the elements of leadership and how do you ensure its effectiveness in varying environments and situations?

### *Leadership Styles and Characteristics*

As we try to answer this question, especially in the context of the church, we will first list on page 250 the styles of supervisory leadership and discuss their characteristics. A comparison of these characteristics will lead us toward a suggestion of an optimum style. We then will list and discuss the leadership qualities which an effective leader of a "team" or group will need (page 250), and starting on page 253 is a self-evaluation to determine your tendencies as a team leader. This may, in turn, suggest some parts of your personal leadership style you may want to change to better fit the needs of your leadership responsibilities.

Since you cannot normally do all the work yourself, a cardinal rule is ***delegate, but don't abdicate.*** As leaders enlist help with the tasks at hand, they must delegate some of their duties. Beginning on page 259 we will examine basic principles of delegation and the reasons why, when delegating duties, you must never abdicate ultimate accountability. The result is always the leader's primary goal and responsibility. How to achieve a satisfactory result by providing a motivating environment, and the factors that motivate individuals, also will be considered. Beginning on page 262 we discuss team building and the characteristics of an effective team. Exceptional results are possible in a motivating environment in which a team can flourish. However, it seems conflict is always with us. An effective leader will need to recognize the reasons conflict occurs, to watch for flash points, and to know what steps to take to resolve differences. With satisfactory resolution, a team will be stronger for having gone through the disruption.

### Parish Leadership

Leadership in the church must be considered as part of an understanding of the nature of the church as a whole. We will look first at how leadership relates to the theological nature and purpose of the church (page 265). Parish leadership is meant to be a joint clergy and lay experience as we form the body of Christ. But what shape or direction should this joint form of leadership take? How are leadership styles and characteristics integrated into a church setting? These questions are addressed on page 266.

As is true in any organization, the staff of the church requires nurturing and counseling if it is to work as a team. The pastor is the most logical person to work with the staff in ensuring its effectiveness. Important points to consider are discussed on page 267. But we cannot forget that the church is composed of clergy, staff, and lay volunteers, all working together. Tapping into strong lay leadership and working with volunteers can sometimes be unique challenges. Ideas are found beginning on page 269.

Active, effective communication must be present in any church that desires energized leadership. Critical communication concerns are considered on page 271.

### Leadership in the Financial Function

Financial management is high on a church's list of important functions. Every church must have effective financial leadership if it is to properly support its mission. Key issues concerning the leadership in church financial management are discussed beginning on page 272. The finance committee, as the church group responsible for ensuring financial support for church programs, makes a significant contribution and must have effective leadership.

### Leading a Stewardship Program

A vital stewardship program, based on dynamic stewardship theology, attitudes, and leadership is necessary to support the financial needs of a church. Starting on page 274 are several discussion items about this important commitment, which all members make when becoming a part of Christ's church. Remember that stewardship is not just about money, but about the lives of its members.

## Leadership Styles and Characteristics

### Defining and Understanding Leadership

Possibly the best way to define and understand leadership is by examining the actions or characteristics of various leadership styles or patterns. If you were to study a variety of organizations, both religious and secular, for-profit and nonprofit, you would probably find a wide range of leadership styles. Indeed, you probably have experienced a variety of leadership, supervisory, or management styles in your own work situations. Not all of these leadership styles are considered successful or effective, but it is well to be aware of the different styles so that you can recognize them in yourself, or others, and then try to work toward the most effective style.

The following pages present a number of items that relate directly to defining and understanding leadership. First, there is a listing of six different leadership styles—from the autocrat to the easygoing. Note that none of these categories is absolute. Rather, the categories define leadership tendencies. In actuality, the styles presented can be considered a continuum with leaders moving easily between them. Study the elements of each leadership style. Think about several persons in leadership roles and put them in their appropriate place on the continuum. Some questions you might consider include: Why do different leaders seem to fit into different categories? Which style seems the most appropriate? Would this be different in a church setting?

Next is a listing of leadership qualities. Research has shown that successful and effective leaders exhibit most if not all of these qualities, suggesting that you may want to emulate or develop them if you aspire to be an effective leader. Answers to some of the questions posed in the previous paragraph may begin to emerge.

Have you decided what type of leader you are? One of the principles of planning is that you must know where you are before you can determine where you want to go. To aid you in this determination, a self-evaluation, "What Type of Team Leader Are You?" appears in the following pages. Completion of this evaluation in an honest and forthright manner may indicate the type of team leader you tend to be. Is this style of leadership the best for the leadership role you may be in now?

Where is all of this "leading" us? Hopefully, to being the most effective team leaders we can be. By being aware of and understanding the variety of leadership styles, and having determined our own tendencies, we can work toward what will be the most effective style.

Among the leadership styles suggested, the *consultive/participative* pattern is generally the most successful. People usually like to be involved in, participate in, and have ownership of decisions that impact them even in minor ways. They feel much better about the work situation if they are consulted and have the feeling of meaningful participation.

A leader does not always have the luxury of working with people who enjoy consulting and participating. In reality, several leadership styles may be required in almost any organization; thus, there tends to be a continuum among styles presented. Not all of the people the leader will be required to work with will want to consult and/or participate in the management process. Some may respond to a more authoritarian approach, while others may work better with greater freedom and less direct supervision. The most effective leader, therefore, must adopt a *situational* leadership style to bring out the individual best in a wide variety of people as they work together toward common objectives—with enthusiasm.

### STYLES OF SUPERVISORY LEADERSHIP

The following leadership styles have evolved over time. Look at them as a continuum, with each leader fitting into a style or styles according to their personal traits and leadership situations.

*Autocrat.* Leader makes all decisions unilaterally, then gives orders and expects compliance. Never consults and avoids praising. Communication is only downward. Feedback is not solicited or even tolerated. Quick to criticize. Would like to arbitrarily fire someone regularly just to keep the other people in line. Prefers to be surrounded with "yes" people. All that really matters are numbers and performance, and any means will be employed to achieve them. Generally works long hours and expects others to do the same.

*Benevolent Autocrat.* Leader is slightly more sensitive of employee feelings than the autocrat. Still makes all decisions unilaterally, then attempts to "sell" decisions. Rarely consults with subordinates and doesn't encourage or want much feedback.

*Authoritarian.* Leader will "pass down" decisions often made at higher management levels. Explains the basis for such decisions, encourages and answers all questions within the confines of the "top-down" structure. Supports the need for compliance with all management decisions. Does not encourage dissent about decisions or policies. Does not take any "guff" from subordinates and has a tendency to be ruthless.

*Consultive/participative.* Leader presents the challenge, solicits opinions, ideas, and suggestions from team members. Keeps an open mind, weighs all input and then makes and announces the decision. Provides details about how and why the decision was reached. Is quick to praise good work. Readily shares credit for accomplishments and acknowledges team and member contributions publicly. Is generally respected by colleagues for good judgment, conscientiousness, and for getting the job done effectively.

*Democratic.* Leader presents the challenge, then sets the limits within which the group is allowed to reach its own decision, with the understanding that the leader will accept and support the decision. Does not take part in the decision-making process per se.

*Easygoing.* Leader is usually insecure and weak. Does not really want to get involved with team members any more than necessary. Is dominated by subordinates and allows them great freedom to make their own decisions. The leader just goes along, provided the decisions are not too outlandish. Is often considered a "seat warmer" on the organization chart.

## LEADERSHIP QUALITIES

An effective leader of a team or group has a number of special qualities that result in mutual respect and cause group members to be willing to follow the leader's visions, hopes, and directions. Some of the most important qualities are listed below. Although this is not necessarily a complete list, it illustrates the qualities required for effective leadership. Additional qualities may certainly be added, as appropriate, within the context of a given organization or situation. Please note that we use the term "team" to describe any group or organization, such as a church staff, a task force, a program committee, a congregation, and so forth, that comes together to accomplish worthwhile tasks or objectives. That said, these are the characteristics of an effective leader:

Listens to multiple inputs

Establishes meaningful objectives

Affection for team members

Decisive

Encourages excellence—with enthusiasm

Responsible

Spiritual dimension apparent

Helps develop individuals

Integrity in everything

Participative in leadership style

*Listens to multiple inputs.* An effective team leader does not make decisions alone. Multiple inputs are sought from team members and from others outside the team who may have pertinent knowledge.

*Establishes meaningful objectives.* There is a saying: "If you don't know where you are going, any route will take you there, but you will never know when you have arrived." Goals and specific objectives set direction for a team and allow it to measure achievement and celebrate success. The most effective objectives are established jointly by team members, thus engendering a feeling of ownership in the objectives and the outcome.

*Affection for team members.* Affection is a term not often used in the workplace, especially in a secular setting. Yet there is ample research indicating that the most successful leaders have genuine affection for their team members. One author uses the word "love" when describing the feelings an effective leader has for their team.[2]

*Decisive.* After listening to pertinent input, the leader must articulate a clear and forceful course of action in pursuit of a vision or goal. Once the decision is communicated to the team, there should be no deviation from the course unless some major factor causes a rethinking of the decision.

*Encourages excellence—with enthusiasm.* We all need encouragement from time to time. This is a very important role of a team leader. But beyond just ordinary "pep talks," there must be the expectation and encouragement of excellence in all that the team does. The effective team leader is openly enthusiastic about team goals, tasks, and achievements.

*Responsible.* True leaders readily accept responsibility for actions of team members, for the tasks at hand, for the goals and objectives, and, most important, for themselves. They must be the Rock of Gibraltar around which the team can rally when encountering the inevitable rough spots. There must be no ambiguity about who is ultimately responsible for the successes, or failures, of the team's efforts.

*Spiritual dimension apparent.* A wise team leader realizes and acknowledges openly that there is a greater power guiding the team's efforts. This spiritual dimension is especially important for church leaders. Opening and closing a meeting with prayer is a way to seek divine guidance for the work of the team and leader.

*Helps develop individuals.* As Jethro so wisely counseled Moses, "You can't do it all alone," so team leaders must realize they can't do it all alone. Individual team members need to develop according to their desires and capabilities, so they can assume additional responsibilities. This development ultimately allows the leader to delegate work and empowers the organization to function effectively.

*Integrity in everything!* Integrity is defined as "moral soundness, honesty, uprightness." One manifestation of integrity in a team is that promises are kept. A team leader and team members must operate by the maxim, "My word is my bond!" Mutual respect between team members and the team leader must be based on total honesty. One way to achieve this level of honesty and trust is to have a "no surprises" covenant among team members. All agree that any matter that may surprise other members of the team will be revealed in a timely manner, even if the matter is unpleasant.

*Participative in leadership style.* It is generally accepted that the participative style of leadership will normally be the most successful. Team members are generally eager to share their inputs and insights with the team and leader. While the ultimate responsibility for a decision rests with the team leader, team members will have a better feeling about the final decision, should it differ from their opinion, if they have been fully heard and had an opportunity to participate in the decision process.

# What Type of Team Leader Are You?

*Instructions:* Answer the following questions by selecting the one response that best describes your feelings. Please restrict yourself to the given choices even though you may feel you have another, more appropriate response. Forthright answers should indicate the type of team leader you tend to be.

1. What would your attitude tend to be regarding employee working hours?

    _____ a. Be a "stickler" for established work hours.

    _____ b. Ignore latecomers and people who leave early, provided you know they are putting in the required hours.

    _____ c. Ignore time altogether as long as employees get their work done.

2. If one of your employees lost their temper with you, how would you respond?

    _____ a. Fire them.

    _____ b. Try to placate them and suggest you discuss the matter at a more appropriate time.

    _____ c. Let them know very firmly that you will not be talked to that way.

    _____ d. Treat the incident as if it never happened, but watch them closely in the future.

    _____ e. Treat them more cautiously in the future.

3. How would you treat minor but ongoing incidents of stealing of church and personal property?

    _____ a. Put up notices to tell people that incidents of theft were occurring.

    _____ b. Call in a security service.

    _____ c. Ask supervisors and employees to keep watch.

    _____ d. Ignore it and accept it as human nature.

    _____ e. All of the first three items.

4. If one of your employees asked to see you about an alleged act of harassment by a supervisor or fellow employee, how would you react?

    _____ a. Ignore it since it was probably just a simple misunderstanding.

    _____ b. Go to the person in question and have a quiet word with them.

    _____ c. Invite them both into your office to talk about the alleged incident.

5. How do you think it is best to lead?

_____ a. By example.

_____ b. By the rules.

_____ c. By common agreement or consensus.

_____ d. Depends on the situation.

6. What do you think the main purpose of any organization should be?

_____ a. To provide products and/or services to people.

_____ b. To provide people with employment and a livelihood.

_____ c. To survive.

7. Given two candidates of the same age, experience, and ability, which one would you tend to choose?

_____ a. The one who has the most knowledge of your church and its operation.

_____ b. The one who has the closest philosophy to your own.

_____ c. The one who seems to fit into the organization the best.

_____ d. The one who seems to need the job the most.

8. You are faced with declining worship attendance. How would you react?

_____ a. Change the worship support leadership.

_____ b. Offer incentives to the existing staff for ideas for increasing attendance that really work.

_____ c. Alter the service to be more attractive to the community.

_____ d. Both a and c.

_____ e. Both b and c.

9. What do you feel is the single most important factor in an employee's life?

_____ a. Success and achievement in the organization.

_____ b. Their personal life.

_____ c. Money.

10. As a newly selected pastor of a church, you find that it is failing. What action would you take?

_____ a. Reduce staff and expenses.

_____ b. Make plans to turn the church around while maintaining essentially the same staff and expense levels.

_____ c. Close the church and start over again somewhere else, if you have that option.

11. You are confronted with the need to fire a person. How would you proceed?

_____ a. Do it yourself.

_____ b. Authorize someone else to do it on your behalf.

_____ c. Make work life uncomfortable for the person so that they will resign.

12. What do you think wage increases should be based upon?

_____ a. On merit alone.

_____ b. On length of service.

_____ c. Equally distributed; i.e., everybody gets the same percentage.

13. On the whole, how do you feel about paperwork?

_____ a. It is necessary.

_____ b. It is wasteful of a lot of people's time.

_____ c. It tends to get overwhelming.

14. To which of the following philosophies would you tend to subscribe?

_____ a. The early bird gets the worm.

_____ b. Slow and steady wins the race.

_____ c. Make haste deliberately.

15. You have found that one of your employees has been lying to you regularly. How would you handle this situation?

_____ a. Confront them so they know you are aware of the practice.

_____ b. Fire them.

_____ c. Make allowances and check everything they tell you.

_____ d. Ask them to resign.

16. If your secretary complained of feeling ill and had not quite finished typing an urgent letter, what would you ask of him or her?

_____ a. To just finish the letter and then go home.

_____ b. To finish the letter and stay as long as possible.

_____ c. To go home right away and you will make other arrangements, recognizing that the letter probably won't get finished in time.

17. If one of your staff members periodically disagrees with you, what would you do?

_____ a. Begin to worry about your own judgment.

_____ b. Get rid of them as soon as possible.

_____ c. Regard their attitude as a sign of a healthy and constructive mind.

18. What type of directives do you tend to give your staff?

_____ a. Orders.

_____ b. Instructions.

_____ c. Suggestions.

_____ d. None or very few.

19. Which of the following do you feel is the main function of a team leader?

_____ a. Decision making.

_____ b. Personnel matters.

_____ c. Financial matters.

_____ d. All three.

20. If your church is running quite well, what action would you tend to take?

_____ a. Be content to let it continue that way.

_____ b. Take personal action to commit the church to expansion of services.

_____ c. Motivate the staff and laity to think growth and expansion.

Refer to the following page to score your responses.

*Scoring your responses.* Circle the number of points corresponding to your responses to the questions on the previous pages. Total your score. An evaluation of your leadership style follows.

| | | | | | |
|---|---|---|---|---|---|
| 1. | a. 5 | 8. | a. 5 | 16. | a. 3 |
| | b. 3 | | b. 2 | | b. 5 |
| | c. 0 | | c. 3 | | c. 0 |
| | | | d. 5 | | |
| 2. | a. 5 | | e. 3 | 17. | a. 0 |
| | b. 2 | | | | b. 5 |
| | c. 4 | 9. | a. 5 | | c. 2 |
| | d. 3 | | b. 1 | | |
| | e. 3 | | c. 3 | 18. | a. 5 |
| | | | | | b. 3 |
| 3. | a. 3 | 10. | a. 3 | | c. 1 |
| | b. 3 | | b. 2 | | d. 0 |
| | c. 0 | | c. 5 | | |
| | d. 0 | | | 19. | a. 4 |
| | e. 5 | 11. | a. 2 | | b. 2 |
| | | | b. 1 | | c. 3 |
| 4. | a. 5 | | c. 5 | | d. 5 |
| | b. 3 | | | | |
| | c. 0 | 12. | a. 5 | 20. | a. 0 |
| | | | b. 0 | | b. 5 |
| 5. | a. 3 | | c. 2 | | c. 3 |
| | b. 5 | | | | |
| | c. 0 | 13. | a. 0 | | |
| | d. 3 | | b. 5 | Total _____ |
| | | | c. 3 | |
| 6. | a. 3 | | | |
| | b. 0 | 14. | a. 5 | |
| | c. 2 | | b. 0 | |
| | | | c. 3 | |
| 7. | a. 3 | | | |
| | b. 5 | 15. | a. 3 | |
| | c. 2 | | b. 5 | |
| | d. 0 | | c. 0 | |
| | | | d. 3 | |

Refer to the following page for an evaluation of your leadership style.

*Your leadership style tends to be:*

A. (11–27 points) *Easygoing leader*—You are quite sociable. If the church closed its doors permanently, you would have plenty of friends around.

B. (28–50 points) *Democratic leader*—Your idea of a leader is someone friendly rather than astute, deliberate rather than quick, sensible if not imaginative—one who would do no more harm than good, but would hardly set the world on fire.

C. (51–72 points) *Consultive/participative leader*—You are well aware of the task at hand and are considered an effective leader. You are adaptable to individual situations, conscientious, have good judgment, and are respected by your colleagues.

D. (73–84 points) *Authoritarian leader*—You do not take any "guff" from subordinates; you are inclined to be ruthless, telling yourself that everyone tends to find their own level somewhere. You are not very popular but are thought of as efficient.

E. (85–100 points) *Autocratic/benevolent autocratic leader*—As an autocratic leader, you are power hungry. You prefer "yes" people around you. All that really matters are the numbers and performance. You tend to work long hours and expect others to do the same. As a benevolent autocratic leader, you may be slightly more sensitive to employee's feelings but still make all decisions unilaterally. You rarely consult with subordinates.

## Delegation but Not Abdication

Whenever more than one person is involved in an organization, a project, or even an activity, the work must be subdivided, either informally or formally. Informal division of work happens when two or more equals decide among themselves, "I will do this while you do that." This usually works quite well on small projects or activities. As projects and organizations become more complex and involve more than just a few people, more formal division of work is required if the group is to work together effectively and efficiently. In addition, someone must be in charge of the activity or organization—a leader of the group. This formal assignment of responsibilities in an organization is called *delegation*.

You may recall that in Exodus 18, Jethro advised Moses that he could not do his work all by himself. He needed to select capable people to help him with his task of resolving disputes. Jethro was suggesting organization and *delegation*. This relatively simple advice suggests the following basic principles.

### BASIC PRINCIPLES OF DELEGATION

1. First and foremost, leaders must realize and accept that they cannot do it all themselves. There just aren't enough hours in the day. If they try to do it all, the words of Jethro should ring loudly in their ears: "You will wear yourself out and then what will become of the people?"

2. A leader of a group of any size, even as small as two or three people, must learn to delegate as much as possible if the group is to function effectively and efficiently. Effective delegation allows the leader time to perform other leadership tasks of planning, organizing and staffing, and assessing and reporting on activities of the group.

3. When responsibility is delegated, the attendant authority to act must accompany that delegation. Relinquishing authority is often quite difficult for an inexperienced leader to do. You must realize, however, that the delegation of responsibility without the attendant authority is a useless act.

4. The leader must be certain that the person to whom responsibilities are delegated understands the responsibilities, accepts them, and realizes that there will be checkpoints and reports on performance.

5. The degree of delegation depends on the experience and competence of the person to whom a responsibility is being delegated. Delegating inappropriately can be a formula for failure as a person is asked to do things that are beyond their capabilities or experience. It is grossly unfair to put anyone in a position of almost certain failure.

6. The degree of control, such as checkpoints and frequency of progress reports, depends on the importance of the responsibility delegated and the competence, experience, and proven performance of the person to whom it is delegated. Obviously, a leader should follow a matter of great importance more closely because of the potential for adverse impact. One example might be a church's financial campaign. The various activities are subdivided, or delegated, to a number of people because the leader cannot do it all. Regular group

report meetings, or even one-on-one meetings, are required to assure that this important activity is moving along as planned. A slip in any of the several related activities of a financial campaign can have a negative impact on giving and church finances for the following year.

7. In general, it is most effective to delegate to the lowest level in the organization where there is competence to assume the responsibility. It is a waste of good talent to assign a task to a person who is overqualified to perform that task. You would not want a pastor, for example, typing and filing in the office if there is someone qualified to do these tasks. While this may be an extreme example, there are many other tasks that a pastor often does that could be delegated, thus providing more time for pastoral duties.

8. As discussed in the previous chapter, the position description and a list of attendant specific objectives are excellent communication tools. They assist the delegation process by defining boundaries, responsibilities, and expected performance.

9. In all cases where delegation occurs, periodic checkpoints or times for progress reports *must* be established. Without checkpoints, when the person to whom a task is delegated reports on progress, delegation becomes *abdication*. The result of abdication is an inevitable drifting of the organization from its goals and mission, and, ultimately, the waste of a great deal of time, talent, and effort. The final result could even be chaos.

10. ***The ultimate accountability of the leader cannot be delegated!*** The leader cannot use as a legitimate excuse the failure of someone to whom a task was delegated. It is the responsibility of the leader to ensure the performance of the person to whom a task has been delegated, or sensing a faltering, to assist that person to successfully complete the task. As a last resort, the task may need to be reassigned to someone who can perform it. As one who is ultimately accountable, it is up to the leader to do all within their power to see that the mission and goals of the organization are accomplished in a timely and credible manner.

## Motivation as Related to Leadership

The simplest definition of motivation is that which moves one to action. We all have a wide variety of needs, and at various times we are prompted, moved, or motivated to fulfill those needs. Abraham Maslow, in his theory of human motivation, postulates that there is a hierarchy of needs, and that as we fulfill a need it no longer moves us to action. For example, if you are hungry or thirsty, the need to partake of food and drink can become overwhelming, and possibly all-consuming. Once we have enjoyed a meal, the motivation to obtain sustenance is eclipsed by the need to fulfill other needs. And so, according to Maslow, as you fulfill the lower-level physiological needs, the higher-level psychological needs begin to take on more importance and become a driving or motivating force.[3]

In summary, here is a hierarchy of needs, with basic physiological needs listed at the bottom, ascending in order of complexity to the highest, self-actualization.

| Human Needs | Fulfilled By |
|---|---|
| Self-actualization | Attaining maximum potential |
| Esteem | Recognition, status, title |
| Social | Belonging, acceptance |
| Safety | Security, protection, comfort |
| Physiological | Food, water, shelter, rest, sex |

Frederick Herzberg, an industrial psychologist, relates Abraham Maslow's human motivation theory to the "promotion of health" in the workplace. His basic thesis is similar to that of Maslow in that he feels that various factors or needs in the work environment, *once satisfied, no longer motivate.*[4]

Herzberg divides influences in the work environment into two categories—hygiene factors and motivating factors. If the hygiene factors are present, the workplace is healthy. Since these factors are taken for granted, people are not necessarily motivated by them. If, however, these factors are absent or below standard, people will be continually dissatisfied, and the workplace will be unhealthy and demotivated. Herzberg summarizes by stating that *hygiene factors are not motivators, but they can be demotivators.*[5]

### Hygiene Factors

Reasonable policies

Good supervision

Reasonable working conditions

Fair wages and benefits

Good relationships

Note that hygiene factors are rather pragmatic and are therefore measured relatively easily. For example, reasonable policies are either present or they are not; wages and benefits are either fair or they are below average. Numerous studies and documents are available as references to determine how your policies, procedures, wages, and benefits compare to those of other organizations. Annual wage and benefit surveys are done in various regions of the country and are available for a reasonable fee. One of the authors uses the annual survey of the Center for Non-profit Management in Southern California in both his own church and at denominational headquarters to assure that wages and benefits are reasonable and competitive.

### Motivating Factors

Opportunity for achievement

Recognition of achievements

Interesting work

Responsibility

Opportunity for advancement

Opportunity for growth

Motivating factors are not quite as pragmatic and will generally take more time to develop and maintain. While hygiene factors generally apply to the organization as a whole, motivating factors, to a great extent, must be tailored to the individual. This fact requires the leader to be aware of each individual's needs. When well planned, individual tailoring can result in a synergistic effect. One achievement can lead to even greater achievement and responsibility, well discharged, can lead to even greater responsibility.

While these principles seem somewhat theoretical, they are generally accepted as quite practical. An understanding of the presentations by Maslow and Herzberg can help leaders better appreciate what makes their team members function as human beings, and what will motivate them in a work environment.

There is one overriding principle that comes out of this discussion. In the long term, *leaders or supervisors cannot motivate people.* Motivation comes from within a person. What leaders can and should provide is a motivating environment in which an individual can work with satisfaction and achievement, and thus flourish.

Some leaders, especially those who tend to be autocratic in their management style, mistakenly feel that pushing, cajoling, demanding, nagging, and so forth is providing motivation. Inducing people to action by inflicting mental or physical pain may have a short-term effect at best. In the long term it can be a demotivator and a source of great anxiety and dissatisfaction.

The following pages name the elements of a motivating environment in which a team can flourish and produce exceptional results. Effective leaders should work toward achieving this environment for themselves and for those they are leading.

## Elements of a Motivating Environment in Staff Team Building

A number of motivational elements describe the environment in which an effective team functions. The most significant factors are listed below. Even though these are the major points to consider, other factors may also come into play depending on the situation. Feel free to add to this list from your own experience.

*Clearly defined goals are known.* As we have said a number of times, the organization must have a clearly defined mission with specific objectives and goals. From these organizational goals, individual goals can be established for each team member in support of the overall mission.

*Communication is open.* Among many other items of information, the mission, objectives, and goals of the organization must be communicated to the team. Team members must be willing to listen to the input, and there must be a willingness to act on this input. A regular team meeting is an excellent way to foster open communications.

*Opinions and feelings are expressed freely.* A significant factor in promoting effective communication within a team is the knowledge that ideas, opinions, and feelings will be seriously considered. The team leader must ensure that judgmental comments like "That won't work" or "We tried that once before" are discouraged in team meetings and discussions.

*Information is shared readily.* A quotation often seen on desktops reads, "It is amazing how much can be accomplished if it doesn't matter who gets the credit."

The wise leader strives for team credit while recognizing and appreciating individual contributions.

*Activities are well planned and coordinated.* Good planning is the genesis of all effective activity. Once the plan is developed, preferably with input from team members, tasks must be delegated and coordinated. Each member of the team needs to know who is doing what, so there will be no duplication of effort or gaps in the tasks that need to be accomplished. Planning and coordination of activities at the outset will minimize team dissatisfaction later.

*Team members feel they are involved and contributing to team activities and decisions.* The leader promotes these feelings with a consultative and participatory style. Everyone must be encouraged to participate in discussions that lead to decisions which affect the team. Every effort must be made to engender a feeling of ownership in team decisions and activities.

*Team members are motivated.* The leader must be sensitive to each team member's relationship to the motivating factors listed earlier. The goal is to create an atmosphere in which each team member is self-motivated.

*Mutual trust exists among team members.* In a well-functioning and effective team, each member depends on others to accomplish their part of the task. There must be trust that each member will accomplish their delegated task as required and on schedule. The team leader can foster mutual trust by reviewing progress and ensuring that individuals are performing according to their commitments.

*Conflicts are quickly resolved.* Conflict is inevitable when two or more people interact. The team leader must work for resolution as quickly and as effectively as possible. The goal of conflict resolution is a solution that is of mutual satisfaction to all parties. (A more detailed discussion of conflict resolution begins below.)

*Mutual respect exists for individual differences.* We are all endowed with different talents and have had many different experiences. When these talents and experiences come together on a team, in a coordinated way, exceptional results can be achieved. An effective team leader recognizes and respects these individual differences.

*Achievement is recognized.* Few if any of us are so self-assured that we do not require a pat on the back from our peers and/or leaders. Recognition is our reward for work well done, sometimes called "mental wages." *The One-Minute Manager* capsulizes this well: "Help people reach their full potential. Catch them doing something right."[6]

*Opportunities are available for individual growth.* Both Maslow and Herzberg list the opportunity for growth as a motivating factor. It is up to the team leader to identify growth opportunities for each team member and then to bring these to the individual's attention. An outstanding leader will assist team members to excel by coaching, mentoring, and assisting at any time.

*All these elements add up to a motivating environment in which a team can flourish and produce exceptional results.*

## Conflict Resolution

According to the Gospel of Matthew, Jesus said, "Where two or three are gathered in my name, I will be there." The scriptures also tell us that when two or three or twelve of the disciples were gathered, conflict or disagreement was sometimes also present.

So it is to this day. When people gather for almost any purpose it seems that conflict is inevitable. Is the church organization and/or congregation immune from conflict? Obviously not, since these organizations are made up of people who differ on a wide variety of subjects, and who often express those strong opinions forcefully. Various religious news sources attest to conflicts arising for a variety of reasons. Just as Jesus addressed conflicts among the disciples, a leader must resolve conflict in a constructive and instructive way. The purpose of this section is to give guidance on how conflicts may be resolved.

There are at least two aspects to conflict or disagreement. Conflict can be disruptive and destructive to an organization if it is not quickly and effectively addressed. Conflict can also be constructive. Honest differences of opinion can often result in a better solution to a particular challenge or situation. It takes extraordinary leadership skills to convert destructive conflict into a constructive force.

Conflict can occur for many reasons and can be related to, among many other factors, differences in:

| | | |
|---|---|---|
| Opinion | Philosophy | Perceptions |
| Values | Education | Methods |
| Culture | Age | Responsibilities |
| Personality | Religion | Authority |

Conflict might also relate to misunderstandings, unclear instructions, or a lack of communication.

When leaders face conflict or disagreements in their organization, whether it be constructive or destructive, they must first recognize that conflict must not be ignored. Conflict usually will not go away, and it will probably get worse. The persons involved seldom resolve the disagreement among themselves. Conflict must be addressed promptly, openly, and honestly, involving all persons concerned, individually or collectively, as the situation dictates. With the involvement of competent leadership, conflict can quite often be resolved in a way satisfying to all parties. This should certainly be the objective. Unfortunately, however, sometimes the only way to resolve conflict is through drastic action: reprimand, suspension, and/or termination. Every leader must recognize these as alternatives, but only if all else fails.

The leader of any organization, including a church, is often cast as an "arbitrator" of conflict. For the leader to be effective in this role, the following steps should be taken, whether the disagreement is large or small. Quite often small and easily managed conflicts escalate into large disagreements that can become disruptive to the organization and consume an extraordinary amount of a leader's time.

*Steps to Conflict Resolution*

1. Be a good listener. Hear both sides in the conflict.

2. Buy some time to look into the issues thoroughly. Set a specific time for meeting again to discuss the issues. Make assignments to gather information if appropriate.

3. Involve as few people as possible, at least initially. There is no point to enlarging the "circle of conflict" and possibly causing other people to choose sides.

4. Be certain of the facts. Don't reach a conclusion too quickly.

5. Be as objective as humanly possible. It is not unusual for the leader to have an agenda and/or feelings about the conflicting parties that must be overcome if you are to be a truly impartial arbitrator.

6. Identify alternative ways to resolve the conflict and select one; or better yet, have the parties agree on one from the options available, or encourage them to develop an alternative solution.

7. Attempt to gain a consensus on the chosen alternative. This is important, since an imposed solution often is not effective.

8. Follow up periodically to determine if the solution is working. Don't assume that because the conflict resolution steps have been followed, the matter has been resolved. It may be festering, waiting to blow up again.

9. If the conflict still exists, go through the above process again until the conflict is finally resolved.

## Parish Leadership

Parish leadership begins with an understanding of a theology of leadership and how it relates to the nature and purpose of the church. Particular styles of leadership are desirable in a church in which the staff is to be nurtured and counseled, and strong lay leadership empowered. All parish leadership must be enveloped in a circle of complete and open communication.

### *Theology of Leadership*

To lead in the church you must know and understand the nature of the church. The primary purpose of the church is to be a worshiping community. Out of worship—the gathered body—all else grows. The worshiping community produces a sensitized and caring fellowship that encourages productive teaching, learning, and serving. Caring for others—inside and outside the immediate fellowship—becomes a natural outgrowth of the community. The worshiping community affects administration and leadership by what is done and by how it is done.

The community from the earliest times was called out to worship and to serve; it was equipped to be God's people in and to the world. The Bible is clear in its expectation that Christians are the Body of Christ and that we should "be doers of the word, and not hearers only" (James 1:22, RSV).

God calls leaders to serve the community and empowers them by the Holy Spirit. We may respond to this call in various ways, for each one of us is a unique creation with valuable gifts, some of which may take years to discover or to develop. We need only to recall the parable of the talents to illustrate that we each have varying talents entrusted to us. Some will be called to lead, some will be called to follow and support. But the main issue is we must use what we have and grow in what we have; otherwise we will not be faithful to what God calls us to be. Whatever our role, we must use our gifts to the glory of God.

As we look at leadership in the church, we believe that the priesthood of believers is made up of *all* involved in the life of the church—clergy and laity, without regard to gender or other artificial differentiations. While we recognize that the clergy have specific functions of Word, Sacrament, and Order, the community of believers is all the people of God, and so we hold that ministry is the work of all who are united in the church.

## *Leadership Styles in the Church*

Leadership, as the logical application of planning, organizing, and staffing, comes in many forms and is distinctly related to the personality of the leader. While you can legitimately argue that church leaders possess the same characteristics and have the same attributes as secular leaders, we propose that there is a Spirit-filled difference. The roots of this spiritual dimension lie in the mission of the church. We all, together, are in ministry as we are guided by the Great Commandment and Great Commission articulated by Jesus (Matthew 22:37; 28:19, 20).

How, then, are we to apply the leadership styles and characteristics we have just studied to a church setting? Are there differences in the way a "team" works in a church?

The first conclusion we could draw is that our previous observation that a consulting/participatory leader is generally the most successful holds just as true in most churches as in the secular world. But we must quickly add that the individual situation will dictate the style and success of a church leader. For example, the membership of a church filled with people who are leaders in their daily work will probably react to clergy and lay leadership quite differently from the members of a church located in a predominantly worker-oriented area. The leadership-filled church is blessed with people who understand and know how to apply leadership principles, and thus the pastor and lay leaders will need to spend much less time on leadership development, goal orientation, and follow-up. Conversely, the pastor or lay leaders of a follower-filled church may need to take a more active role in directing activities while training and developing leaders.

Problems arise in the examples just cited when the pastor and lay leaders are not sensitive to members' leadership capabilities. The pastor and lay leaders may find it necessary to use a leadership style that they find uncomfortable. An example comes to mind of a newly assigned pastor who was quick to let it be known that, "I preach and teach. Everything else is up to the lay people." This statement was particularly significant, because the pastor was charged with being the chief administrative officer of the local church, according to denominational procedure, and thus the local church leadership expected the pastor's involvement in administrative matters. Further, the new pastor replaced a much more leadership-oriented pastor, who had a style that was primarily consultive/participative. The lay leadership and members found themselves somewhat adrift without the active leadership to which they had become accustomed. It took considerable time for both the pastor and members to adjust to a new leadership style, with give and take necessary on both sides. The pastor did assume a somewhat more active leadership role in administrative matters, at the insistence of members, and the members learned to assume more responsibility than they had under the previous pastor.

This situation provides an example of the evolutionary process necessary in any leadership change. It took about two years for the discontent to settle down.

Another concern we need to recognize is that there may be a substantial difference between working with or for someone who is providing your livelihood, and working as a volunteer in a church because you want to and believe in the mission. It is likely that persons put up with situations in their daily work they may not be willing to put up with in a volunteer position. As leaders in a church, we must recognize that although working with volunteers may be a challenge, this offers an opportunity for real Christian growth for both the leaders and the volunteers. It may be that our church associations provide the environment for growth we may not have in our job associations, and church work may teach us the necessary tools to function better in our work relationships.

It is not likely that anyone would disagree with the premise that our churches need good solid leadership, just like any viable organization. We must still establish working relationships that result in active "teams" to accomplish our mission and to implement goals and objectives. In short, we use the same leadership qualities and methodologies in a church as in our secular lives. We plan, we organize, we delegate, we motivate, and we resolve conflicts in basically the same way, using established, time-proven techniques.

As we see it, the primary difference in church leadership is the acceptance of an intangible spiritual direction and recognition that God, through us, is in charge. As church leaders we still will want to have the same qualities as any good leader, and more, for the glory of God.

## Leadership and the Church Staff

In any church, small or large, there will be leadership opportunities and challenges. A small church will normally have few, if any, full-time paid staff members other than the pastor, but it may have several persons employed part-time. A large church can have an extensive staff of both full-time and part-time employees, and several clergy. Churches serving various ethnic groups, sometimes in the same facilities, may have unique staff associations and requirements for leadership. Obviously, there will be differing leadership needs depending on the size of the church staff and composition, and the pastor and lay leadership must be prepared for these challenges.

In all probability, supervision of the staff, as a whole, will fall to the pastor, assisted and counseled by a personnel committee. As we have previously discussed, there should be position descriptions for each staff position, full-time or part-time, and each staff member should have a clear understanding of their role in the mission of the church and how they are to interact with other members of the staff. Staff members, in concert with the pastor and personnel committee, will want to set annual individual goals and objectives which help implement church goals and objectives. Coordination among staff members and with the pastor will be required to varying degrees, depending on the size and complexity of the staff.

With the organization and operating process in place, the act of leading a church staff becomes one in which the pastor uses the basic leadership techniques and characteristics discussed in the previous section.

To work as a team, the leader must ensure full communication within the staff. At a minimum, there should be a staff meeting scheduled at a given time and day each week, even if some of the staff cannot attend. This weekly "touch point" is extremely important for a busy and often preoccupied staff. The agenda should primarily focus on individual reports of activities, progress on projects, and happenings in the church of interest to the whole staff. There should, of course, be the usual time for follow-up on items discussed previously, as well as discussion and consideration of new items. The church staff meeting will normally open with prayer, to request God's guidance for the staff, and it might close with prayer concerns, in which staff members have an opportunity to share matters in their lives that they might like their coworkers to pray about.

The staff meeting is also an opportunity for the pastor or other staff members to affirm individuals, or the staff as a whole, in the tasks which they are performing. Be sure to include part-time staff members performing specialized tasks in the staff meetings, such as those involved in the music program. All staff members must feel they are included to ensure as effective a program as possible.

Assessment of job performance, based on position descriptions and previously agreed-upon goals, objectives, and tasks, is essential. Although a formal evaluation will normally occur annually, there should be regular and frequent feedback to all staff members about their contributions. The pastor or supervisor should consciously plan to "catch them doing something right" and tell them about it immediately. Recognition for work well done might also include mention in the newsletter and in the Sunday morning order of worship. Public statements of support are important motivational tools when there has been outstanding work or significant accomplishment.

Conversely, problems should be addressed as soon as possible, in a private, compassionate, and instructive way. There is an old maxim: "Praise in public; reprimand in private." Don't forget to document in writing both good and substandard performance. How this can best be done will be covered in detail in the following chapter.

The pastor-leader will need to be aware of unique staff concerns. The needs of individual staff members can vary widely, and each must be addressed independently in a unique way, if necessary.

The involvement of the church personnel committee and other lay persons in staff matters should be clearly defined. Members of the personnel committee, as well as all members of the church, must be sensitive to the fact that a staff member cannot serve multiple masters. Member requests and concerns should be made through the pastor or immediate supervisor, if this is a different individual. The pastor and personnel committee, working together, can form a strong, affirmative force for dealing with personnel matters. One or the other usually will not be as effective as both working together. Members of the congregation will recognize their needs must be met in the context of all other needs, if they are reminded in a firm but polite way.

If the church is large enough to have more than one clergy on staff, the relationships and responsibilities must be clearly defined, not only among the clergy but with other staff members as well. Everyone needs to know from whom to take direction, in what program area. One of the clergy normally will be designated as senior. But unless there is close coordination among the clergy, each may naturally consider their activities and needs as having priority on the time other staff members may have available.

Problems arise quickly when time available does not meet need. This situation should be resolved at the next staff meeting, unless the need is so urgent that special action is required. The senior pastor may need to arbitrate and set priorities.

Similar leadership concerns can surface in a small church if staff is shared with another church, or if a part-time staff member needs to work extra time to finish a project but cannot do so for various reasons. Careful consideration of all needs, and planning ahead, can usually resolve these concerns.

In church facilities where different denominational or ethnic groups meet, there must be careful coordination of activities by the leadership. In many respects, these situations may require a high level of leadership skill to manage the multitude of challenges and potential conflicts which can occur. There may be need for the same space at the same time, a lack of understanding of unique practices or requirements of different denominational or ethnic groups, strong feelings of ownership by the host congregation, and so forth. The leaders will need to be sensitive to each other as well as with other staff members and the laity of all involved groups. Perhaps the best advice is to be an exceptional listener. Learn the facts. Bring disputing persons together for an opportunity to solve concerns jointly. Work for conciliation and win-win solutions.

Concerns are often expressed about members of the congregation working as church staff members. Perceptions of multiple loyalties can surface. The pastor may find it more difficult to be a supervisor of a parishioner who may require pastoral care and counseling. Church members may tend to "talk church business" with a staff member on Sunday when this should be a day for worship. While some say that these are valid reasons for not having church members on staff, we believe that excellent talent may be overlooked if church members are not considered for employment. With a professional leadership style that is consistent in keeping work and ownership separate, a pastor-leader can resolve almost any concern that arises from employing member–staff persons. When problems do arise, they must be dealt with immediately.

Perhaps the one situation in which a member does not belong on staff is when it is perceived that a candidate cannot maintain confidentiality or does not support the pastor and staff. There have been instances in which a member wants to join the church staff with a hidden agenda to "straighten them out." This situation will inevitably lead to dissatisfaction and even chaos among staff members. Astute inquiry and knowledge of congregational alliances can usually identify this type of member, and you can avoid adding them to the staff.

Staff leadership concerns, whatever they may be, are best approached if the leader will listen, study the facts, bring the parties together, work for consensus, and always try to reach a solution that solves the problem for all concerned—if at all possible.

## Tapping into Strong Lay Leadership

The pastor and lay leaders are in a crucial position to observe the overall lay leadership in the local church. They need to be working continuously to assess the existing leadership and be constantly looking for new and emerging leadership.

This can be done by observing people as they participate in the life of the church. What are their skills? How do they interface with other people? In social situations, how do they interact? Do they have leadership potential? Are they strong followers?

Are they supportive of a positive direction? Are they "yes" people, or are they able to represent a position which will be constructive to the growth of individuals and to the church? Since pastors may see people from a different perspective, it is important that both the clergy and laity watch for leadership potential.

All of the above requires knowing people. It means observing their strengths and their weaknesses. It means assessing how they are perceived by others. Both pastoral and lay leadership can reach this understanding by personal observation and conversation. Conclusions may be drawn by looking at a person's track record of leadership and ability to follow in the church, as well as in the community.

### FUNCTION OF THE NOMINATING COMMITTEE

Every church has some means to place persons into positions of leadership, and more often than not it is a nominating committee. Membership on the nominating committee depends on the official structure of the individual church. Each nominating committee should have a position description for its work. In addition, the various leadership roles for which it will be choosing persons should have position descriptions. This not only assists the committee in its work, but benefits persons considering taking on particular tasks. (Examples of position descriptions for most volunteer positions in a church can be found on pages 181–207.)

To guide the committee in its work, and to maintain credibility, the nominating committee must have policies of its own. Most important, the policies need to insist on confidentiality. They should deal with the potential for conflicts of interest on the committee, how to nominate members of the committee itself to other positions, or the nomination of relatives of members of the nominating committee. The tenure of persons in leadership positions ought to be a part of the policy, so that, unless intended, persons cannot retain a position for too long. With appropriate policies and procedures in place, the work of the nominating committee will have a better chance for credibility, integrity, and success.

### WORKING WITH VOLUNTEERS

The working heart of the church is volunteers. It behooves all persons in positions of leadership to understand what motivates a volunteer, and how to use these dedicated members well. It is important that volunteers understand what is expected of them, and that opportunities for training will be provided. Volunteers can have a sense of ownership in what happens in the church and an important opportunity to make a contribution. They should be supported and nurtured in much the same way as members of the staff. Volunteers need to be thanked, commended, and uplifted. Earned recognition cannot be overdone.

In a church familiar to one of the authors, volunteer leaders are appointed and trained to assure that all volunteers are effectively used and appreciated. This church has no problem recruiting volunteers. Perhaps the greatest demotivator for volunteers is to show up ready for work only to find that their time has been wasted because of poor planning or lack of resources. A second demotivator is lack of appreciation for their hard work and a job well done.

Pastors need to experience personally what it means to be a volunteer, to see the important work of a volunteer, and to focus on the servant role to which Christ calls them. Working as a volunteer will also give the pastor a sense of what it feels like to be under the leadership of someone else. From these experiences can come important ideas about cultivating, not alienating, volunteers.

Even the largest churches use volunteers. Some have volunteer coordinators on staff to guide individuals and groups working at all hours on prayer chains, crisis hot lines, suicide intervention, and so forth, in addition to administrative tasks and maintenance. A facilities maintenance group, for example, might meet weekly, start with Bible study and maybe breakfast, and contribute a significant amount of work each week while reducing maintenance expenses. These groups tend to develop bonds of friendship that sustain them in their personal lives.

Leadership takes on many forms in the life of a church, and as we have seen it takes on many facets of which the laity and the clergy both need to be aware.

## Communication

A high level of direct communication and understanding is absolutely essential if any form of leadership is to be effective. In addition to imparting ideas, communication reflects openness in the organization.

For there to be effective communication, leaders must be seen as credible. There needs to be a sense of consistency in what is written, spoken, and lived. If what is printed or said does not match what is done in the church, credibility will immediately be questioned, and people will doubt the leader's intentions. Any doubt undermines the church program and the opportunity for open communications.

We also need to recognize that it takes time to build relationships on which to base communication. As God's children we are all different. We must work at effective communication as we come to know each other. We need to commit ourselves to learning as much as we can about others with whom we will be working in the church. With this knowledge we can know how best to communicate with one another. We need to listen, carefully hearing what really is being said and not just what we want to hear. Since we can receive and process 400 to 500 words a minute, but talk at about 125 words a minute, we can easily get bored when listening to someone else, and our minds can wander. There are six important rules to good listening:

1. Stop talking!

2. Minimize thinking about what you are going to say in response.

3. Remove distractions; think only about what is being said.

4. Ask questions for clarification and understanding.

5. Summarize to clarify and to provide feedback; communication is not complete unless there is feedback to indicate understanding.

6. Stop talking!

We have discussed the need for effective communication throughout this manual, so we will not dwell on it further here. Suffice it to say, nothing can be accomplished on a team without clear and open communication.

# Leadership in the Financial Function

Financial leadership in the church serves one basic purpose: to ensure financial support for the mission, goals, objectives, activities, and even dreams of the program committees.

## Church Financial Management

Every church must have enlightened financial management leadership if it is to accomplish its mission and plans. Its organization will normally call for a finance committee, stewardship committee, or trustees who, as a group, oversee the financial health of the church. Working with or for this group will normally be a treasurer and possibly a financial secretary, depending on the size of the church and its needs. In large churches there may also be a church administrator or business administrator, who oversees the daily financial operations, acting as a liaison with lay leadership on an oversight committee.

While the size of the church may dictate the management organization and leadership required, any size church must have effective financial leadership if it is to survive. Contributions must still be accounted for and gifts used according to donor instructions. Bills must be paid. And someone must create the budget to guide the church as it supports its mission with financial resources.

Especially in small churches, financial leadership concerns center around turnover, training, burnout, and commitment. Long-tenured, dedicated people may become so attached to their role that they fear losing the role would mean losing their identity. To ensure system integrity, turnover may need to be required. Staying current on new approaches, especially computers, can transform a financial system. To avoid burnout and enhance commitment, you should show appreciation, encourage personal growth, and reward people. Although many financial leadership jobs in a church may naturally be long-tenured to facilitate continuity, the job should not be "forever."

Important leadership concerns of the finance committee are discussed in greater detail on the following pages. Most important, this oversight group must be one that works, synergistically, with all other groups and members of the church. All members and groups must have confidence that financial affairs are being handled with absolute integrity.

*Leadership in church financial management must be dynamic, responsive, mission oriented, and must maintain complete integrity.*

## The Finance Committee in Action

The finance committee (or stewardship committee, in some denominations) is one of the most important volunteer groups within a church. It not only funds the ministry of the church, but actively participates in forming plans and programs. Without financial input, plans may not be feasible.

The finance committee acts as the fiscal agent of the church and ensures gifts are managed impeccably. This gives credibility to the financial management system and gains the confidence of church members. More specifically, the finance committee normally performs the following functions:

- Ensures church programs and activities are properly funded, by requiring and preparing an annual budget. In preparing the budget, the finance committee works in concert with all committees, work areas, and boards to ensure their plans, programs, and activities are supported financially.

- Reviews giving to the church to ensure receipts will support the budget.

- Supports the financial stewardship program and may direct the annual-fund drive unless there is a separate stewardship committee.

- Ensures financial gifts are properly receipted and accounted for by the financial secretary.

- Monitors spending against the budget through review of the treasurer's reports.

- Keeps the congregation informed about the financial condition of the church through regular reports to the governing body and a summary statement to the congregation.

- Arranges for an annual independent financial review of financial records and procedures by either an internal audit committee or someone specifically designated to perform this review.

- Acts on recommendations related to financial policy and procedures to ensure a credible financial system with integrity that is always beyond question.

While performing these primary responsibilities, the committee must look beyond immediate needs, although the natural tendency will be to fix current problems. Some questions that need to be considered are:

- What about two years from now?

- What new programs may be next?

- What new equipment is needed?

- What future repairs are needed?

- Will there be educational changes?

To be all-encompassing in its outlook, the finance committee must be a part of basic planning and programming—*not to direct it but to support it.* The committee's inclusion will ensure fiscal concerns are part of the planning and programming process. Full coordination between and among all church groups is necessary if the full program is to be successful.

The danger is an actual or perceived idea that the finance committee wants to dictate what the church does because it holds the purse strings. *This puts a great additional responsibility on the finance committee to ensure that their actual or perceived power is not misused.* The pastor may need to ensure the finance committee does not abuse its power.

Members of the finance committee should be respected leaders of the church. In many church organizations, membership is to be broadly representative of the congregation and include each of the prime leaders of other units, as well as the treasurer and financial secretary. It may also include nonmembers of the church, for professional counsel.

The chairperson of the finance committee should be a unique individual able to

- Visualize the future, recognize the concerns of the present, and be a leader of leaders

- Clearly see the total mission of the church and realize dollars will come if the mission is clear and active

- Coordinate and cooperate with all, aiming always toward the good of the group

- Instill integrity and credibility beyond question

- Cause volunteers, always with limited time, to want to devote what effort is required to accomplish the task

- Always lead by example, using a participatory but active leadership style

## Leading a Stewardship Program

As one of the major emphases in a church, stewardship—in the broad sense of all we do in life—deserves a separate review within the context of important leadership needs. We will review the basic theology of stewardship and the attitude and leadership necessary to support it. We then take a practical view of financial stewardship by looking at how to raise giving levels, pledge campaigns and how to lead them, and stewardship models. We end with a look at how the small or ethnic local church may view stewardship.

### Developing a Theology of Stewardship

During a discussion between students and faculty at Perkins School of Theology, a question was asked of Dr. W. J. A. Power: "If the seminary offered a class on how to teach historical critical theory of the Bible, what might it include?" His answer may surprise more than a few: "Stewardship might be an interesting place to start. It would be relevant both to the clergy and to the congregation. The issue would open the whole matter of what various biblical traditions have to say about funding projects of one kind or another and then about what stewardship itself might mean *in toto*. It also comes up every year."[7]

There obviously is more to stewardship than you might think, including a deeply rooted theology. There certainly is a significant difference between "stewardship" and "finance." Church finance has to do with budgets; stewardship is "giving until it helps." Until it helps God's purposes. Until it helps other people. Until it helps the denomination. Until it helps the giver relate to God.

Historically, stewardship began early in biblical times when "stewards" were employees in charge of large households and acted as trusted agents of the owner. An early reference to a steward in the Bible appears in the Joseph stories in Genesis 40–46. Pharaoh entrusted Joseph, a Hebrew, to oversee the Egyptian storage and relief effort during a fourteen-year period of famine as one who had the knowledge and ability to do the job and as one who could be trusted. Joseph did not own the grain in storage. He managed it for the Pharaoh, as a trusted agent responsible only to Pharaoh.

In Luke 12:41–48, Jesus makes it clear that a faithful and wise steward is one who performs assigned duties in such a way that all receive their portion of food at the proper time. But a foolish or unfaithful steward was one who knew what was expected but did not perform the duties properly. This steward would be seriously disciplined.

Stewardship, then, has two conditions: (1) the steward is not the owner, but a responsible, powerful agent of the owner; and (2) the steward must perform the assigned duties properly to earn the respect and trust of the owner.

A serious student of the Bible knows there are many references to stewardship. On page 277 is a listing of fifty-five biblical references, demonstrating the breadth with which we should consider stewardship.

As time passed, the concept of what the term "stewardship" entailed changed. Contemporary theologians now use an image of *partner* as well as *steward*.

- As stewards, we are all created in the image of God, the owner. Thus, we are to exercise our individual stewardship as managers of God's creation—not owners—and in accordance with God's management policies.

- As a partner, the steward moves toward a joint or corporate effort. This image of partner better addresses the larger issues of the society we live in—public education, human rights, the environment—and allows us to become partners with God and one another.

The church, in a stewardship context, is not simply a collection of individuals but a body of believers who become the body of Christ in mission to the world.

Money has a theological basis, as well. Money was a favorite sermon topic of Jesus. He preached at least thirty-one sermons on the subject of money and possessions, and at least thirteen of the parables dealt directly with money. "For where your treasure is, there will your heart be also" (Matthew 6:21).

What is taught about stewardship in today's churches? Evaluate your church against the following:

*Environmental stewardship:*

- Does the congregation use only as much paper as necessary? Are both sides of the page used? Is recycled paper used for printed materials? Are aluminum cans recycled? Is a recycling center possible?

- Are dishes washed, or is paper and plastic tableware used? Are "coffee hour" cups either washed or recycled?

- Is the building temperature kept at an energy-saving level? Are utilities turned off when not in use?

*Stewardship of property:*

- Are church buildings used other than on Sunday morning? Are church programs planned for effective and efficient use of facilities, or are there rooms in the church dedicated to one use that could be opened for additional uses?

- Are outside groups seen as part of the church's mission and encouraged to use the facilities?

*Financial stewardship:*

- What percentage of the church budget goes to outreach and mission? Is it less than a tithe? Is it a percentage of ALL giving? Is outreach the first budget item to be cut in financially tough times?

- Does the congregation send its giving for outreach as soon as possible—monthly? Or, does it wait until the end of the year or when funds are available?

- When funds are invested, are nondiscrimination guidelines considered?

When we put stewardship in the context of the whole work of the church we find that evangelism calls people to commitment; worship celebrates the commitment; and stewardship acts out the commitment—from the heart.

***Stewardship responsibility is the essence of Christian living!***

# Biblical References for Stewardship[8]

|  |  |
|---|---|
| Genesis 1:1–2:25 | Creation: Stewards of Nature and Ecology |
| Genesis 4:3–5; 14:20 | Giving of First Fruits or Tenth |
| Leviticus 22:18–21; 23:9–21; 27:30 | Worship, First Fruits, and Tithes |
| Leviticus 25 | Jubilee Generosity |
| Deuteronomy 10:12–14; 12:5–7; 14:22–29; 18:4; 26:1–19 | Worship and Giving |
| Psalm 8:4–8 | Dominion Given the Created |
| Psalm 24:1,2 | The Earth Is the Lord's |
| Psalm 41:1 | Blessing to the One Caring for the Poor |
| Isaiah 11:6–10 | Stewardship of Peace |
| Isaiah 40:12–31 | God Is the Ultimate Source |
| Isaiah 58:6–9 | God's Kind of Fast |
| Isaiah 61:1–3 | Stewardship of Good News |
| Amos 5:7–15; 5:24; 8:4–6 | Stewardship of Justice |
| Malachi 3:8–10 | Robbing God or Bringing Tithes |
| Matthew 6:19–33 | Priority of Faith |
| Matthew 8:18–22 | Commitment and Simplicity |
| Matthew 19:16–30 | Stewardship of Resources |
| Matthew 20:1–16 | Grace Given by God |
| Matthew 23:1–13, 23,24 | Integrity in Stewardship |
| Matthew 25:1–13 | Stewardship of Time |
| Matthew 25:14–30 | Stewardship Demands Risk |
| Matthew 25:31–46 | Stewardship Meets Needs |
| Matthew 27:57–61 | Stewardship of Resources |
| Mark 8:27–38 | Cost of Gospel |
| Mark 11:15–19 | Stewardship of Prayer |
| Mark 12:28–34, 41–44 | Stewardship of Loving God |
| Mark 14:3–9 | Stewardship of Generosity |
| Luke 6:20–26 | Beatitudes and Woes |
| Luke 8:1–3 | Providing Out of Means |
| Luke 12:13–34 | Folly and Faith in Stewardship |
| Luke 10:29–37 | Stewardship of Love and Money |
| Luke 12:41–48 | Responsible Stewardship |
| Luke 16:1–13 | Practical Dimensions of Stewardship |
| Luke 16:19–31 | Stewardship Has Consequences |
| Luke 17:11–19 | Stewardship of Gratitude |
| Luke 19:1–10 | Stewardship of Justice |
| John 6:5–13 | Giving Is Multiplied |
| Acts 4:32–5:11 | Generosity and Empty Show |
| Acts 20:35 | Blessedness in Giving |
| Romans 12:1–8 | Commitment and Gifts |
| 1 Corinthians 3:5–9 | Partnership in Stewardship |
| 1 Corinthians 4:1,2 | Stewardship of Gospel |
| 1 Corinthians 12:1–12 | Stewardship of Gifts |
| 1 Corinthians 16:2 | Regular and Proportionate Stewardship |
| 2 Corinthians 5:1–21 | Stewardship of Reconciliation |
| 2 Corinthians 8:1–9:15 | Generosity and Cheerfulness in Giving |
| 2 Corinthians 12:1–10 | Stewardship in Ministry |
| Philippians 4:10–13 | Contentment in Life |
| 1 Timothy 6:10–19 | Value Formation |
| 2 Timothy 1:13,14 | Stewardship of Gospel |
| James 2:1–9 | Treatment of Rich and Poor |
| 1 Peter 2:9,10 | Stewardship of Grace |
| 1 Peter 4:10,11 | Stewardship of Gifts of Grace |
| 1 John 3:16–18 | Integrity in Stewardship and Love |
| 1 John 4:7–21 | Love Reflected |

## Developing a Healthy Climate and Attitude about Stewardship

For there to be a healthy attitude about stewardship, certain myths that inhibit our understanding must be addressed for what they are—myths.

*Myth:* "Stewardship begins with discussing church budgets and asking for funds to support the need." We seem naturally to want to start thinking about specific line items on a budget and how we are going to get the support we need—before we know *why* we need the funds.

*Reality:* Stewardship begins with living a Christian life and faith every day. When doing so, financial support of our ministerial mission will come naturally.

*Myth:* "The problems in the church are primarily financial. If there were just more income, things would be OK." When things are not going well, the first item we look to is lack of financial support.

*Reality:* Spiritual concerns may be the real problem. When Christians believe with all their heart that something is right, a spirit exists that can move mountains. There should be no financial problems.

*Myth:* "If the budget is presented clearly enough, people will respond with their giving." We want to see the facts. We like to deal with small, tangible items we can handle.

*Reality:* Instead of "line items," we need to present the vision of the church, its people, and the programs that need help and why. "Faith and facts" will raise the budget.

*Myth:* "Stewardship is a synonym for pledging." Once a year we "collect the pledges" and this is our stewardship drive.

*Reality:* Stewardship is *all* that we do throughout our lives. It is far more than just money. We need to emphasize stewardship throughout the year, and that includes the use of our time and natural resources as well as finances. Stewardship is the essence of Christian living.

*Myth:* "The members don't have money." There certainly are situations in which this is true and we must search for ways to determine the giving capability of members.

*Reality:* It seems fair to say that most of us find ways to afford the many "extras" of life. It also seems fair to conclude that we can include the church on our "extra" list. There are numerous examples of relatively poor churches giving a high percentage of their financial means to help others, while more affluent churches give a smaller percentage.

*Myth:* "To talk about money will offend people." That may be true in some instances, but it may also be appropriate to offend them.

*Reality:* Jesus dealt directly with the use of one's resources. He was not afraid to offend the rich young ruler (Matthew 19:16ff.), or anyone else. If we ask directly and personally, there should be little reason for a person to feel offended, unless they are already embarrassed about their lack of giving.

The final reality about stewardship is that there is a positive correlation between stewardship and the institutional health of the congregation, and the spiritual health of individual members and the pastor.

- Strong stewardship happens when people are encouraged by successes rather than threatened by failures.

- Levels of giving usually reflect the way people feel about the church and their faith.

- People increase giving when they believe the church has a plan for the future—a vision of what it is and where it is going.

- Giving is a function of the quality of parish life.

- Healthy congregational stewardship occurs when the pastor leads the giving.

- The amount of money a person gives to the work of the church probably has little to do with that person's income. *Faith and finances work together.*

## *Practical Principles about Raising Giving Levels*

The mission statement and implementation plans are complete and have been accepted by the congregation. The organization and leadership is sound and the financial system credible. Programs are inviting people to participate. Stewardship responsibility is understood. The budget is clear. Now, how does one raise the level of giving?

Local churches that emphasize ministry usually find they have little problem raising needed funds. People generally give based on their commitment, not based on their wealth. Churches that emphasize "raising the budget" often find they are unable to do so.

Four faith assumptions form a basis for a sound program of stewardship. Based on these assumptions, members are willing to raise their levels of giving: (1) God is adequate; (2) we are partners with God; (3) we need to be consistent in our stewardship, avoiding extremes; and (4) the outcome—the Kingdom of God—is certain. The result should be a positive climate in which the value of mission and program is emphasized while the budget is balanced and kept within spending guidelines.

The emphasis must be on people giving, rather than the church receiving. Offer multiple opportunities to give, in response to a person's need to give. Remember, *people give first to people,* then to purposes and causes, then to programs, and only lastly do they give to paper. And, of course, stewardship development is a year-round effort involving every dimension of church life.

Stewardship growth can be emphasized in many different ways. One very effective way has been through a "Grow One" percentage program, in which members are encouraged to move to the next percentage level of giving when compared to their income. Step increments in actual dollars also can be effective. Special envelope mailings (used as "Catch-Up") may be effective. Recognizing that people respond first to people, presentations from the pulpit during worship, usually by lay persons, may be most effective. Of course, the need must be clearly presented.

Since stewardship is a year-round event, a church should not forget new members who join after a pledge campaign. There should be a system that encourages these new members to make a stewardship pledge. That system needs to include follow-up and tracking of participation.

Feedback about giving is imperative. There should be monthly communication about the overall status of giving. This can be presented during worship, during a report to the governing body, during Sunday school class discussions, in the weekly newsletter, or in a monthly stewardship letter or report of giving. In these reports:

- Offer a positive parable (in person, from the pulpit).

- Lift up something happening at church or outreach that is being accomplished as a result of giving.

- Tell about the financial situation and the programs money enables. Be honest about finances.

- Distribute special offering information.

- Acknowledge significant gifts, but always in the context of what these gifts will accomplish.

Feedback about individual financial stewardship may be appropriate between the financial secretary and pastor so that the pastor is kept informed about changing trends in members' giving habits. These changes in giving may indicate changes in people's lives that require pastoral care.

Of course, there are financial stewardship opportunities beyond support for the general operating needs. A church should develop a clearly articulated policy for an endowment fund and provide education about this important means of giving. Every church should encourage wills and bequests, through an active educational program.

Stewardship concerns for peace, ecology, and time management should be considered within the context of a church's mission priorities. There certainly is strong theological support for doing so. Some congregations may be more ready for this step than others, but every congregation should challenge itself to move in this direction.

*The sooner we all consider our stewardship responsibilities as affecting everything that happens in our lives and as the ultimate fulfillment of all that is good, the sooner we will understand our place in God's plan.*

## Pledge Campaigns and How to Lead Them

Any congregation benefits from an effective stewardship drive, one that is well planned and based on actual need. The best campaigns emphasize positive mission and programming, are well organized, personal, and, as Dr. Callahan says, are built "on the relationships of respect, trust, and integrity that are already solidly in place in the congregation."[9]

Equally important, "most members need to be led from concepts to deed, from knowledge to action."[10] People need to be challenged to make a meaningful commitment so they can practice what they believe. A well-planned commitment procedure helps most people implement their convictions, and it may even lead others to new convictions. Practical reasons for an annual stewardship enlistment program include:

1. It focuses the congregation on its mission and ministry. Stewardship enlistment programs can naturally generate communication and excitement about the work of the congregation.

2. It encourages responsible budget preparation. Budget "goals" may lead members to greater stewardship and recognition of program needs, as opposed to an "expenditure-oriented" budget which may limit members' vision to what has been calculated as a need. Carrying out a stewardship enlistment program

will enable those responsible for the budgeting process to do their work responsibly.

3. A well-organized stewardship enlistment program increases giving because *people give when they are asked.* A documented study shows:[11]

   - Congregations that ask members to pledge report average giving levels as much as 30 percent higher than congregations that do not.

   - Congregations with a stewardship emphasis report average giving levels 23 percent higher than those that don't.

   - Congregations that ask members to consider tithing report average giving levels almost 20 percent higher than those that don't.

   - Congregations that use all three of these activities report giving levels 38 percent higher than those that use none of them.

When choosing a stewardship enlistment program, it is always best to assess the church's needs and the nature of the congregation. Every church is different. A successful program in one church may not fit another. Several questions should be posed before selecting a stewardship program:

1. What has been done in the past? Was it successful and why?

2. What should the focus be?

3. Whom do you plan to reach?

4. Should outside leadership be used?

5. How much time can be devoted?

6. How much congregational involvement is possible?

7. How does the congregation respond to training?

8. What is the budget? Is it easily attainable or a goal?

9. Are there internal church issues which may need to be considered?

Although there are a myriad of stewardship programs available in written material, several basic programs are discussed briefly on pages 282–286. Each includes a general description, discussion of the target, and a listing of strengths and limitations. Perhaps you will find this material useful as an introduction to stewardship programs, and then seek out additional material where appropriate.

When you have decided to conduct a stewardship enlistment campaign and selected the best program, the question of leadership still must be decided. Here are a few recommendations:

- Follow the selected program and get the whole congregation behind it.

- Choose a leader who is respected by the congregation and who will give the program the in-depth leadership it will need.

- Don't take shortcuts on detail or procedures; they exist for a purpose.

- See it through to the end—a commitment of faith by each member.

- Celebrate the success.

*"Ask, and you will receive."*

## Stewardship Models

The basics of ten different stewardship campaign approaches are outlined below.[12] These outlines should give readers some guidance, and perhaps lead to further study, as they select a stewardship program that will best fit a specific local church situation. Remember that the same stewardship approach probably should not be used each year.

### PERSONAL VISITS: EVERY-MEMBER VISITATION

A personal visit to each member provides an opportunity to share information about the church's local and wider ministries and budget, to get interpretive materials into the hands of members, to answer questions, to invite members to consider their financial commitment, and to give instructions about returning financial commitment cards. The focus is ministry and the audience is all members of the church. High congregational involvement should stimulate increased giving. The model offers high communication potential at a low cost.

*Strengths*

- carefully outlined manuals available
- includes all resident church members
- face-to-face discussion
- effective in achieving congregation's goals
- allows for personal growth and acceptance
- the starting point for stewardship education
- involves the total congregation
- helps update membership list
- follow-up usually included

*Limitations*

- requires time, leadership, and training
- difficult to recruit enough visitors
- variations in approach seldom provided
- little time to deal with motivation
- follow-up difficult to complete
- calls interpreted as asking for money

### DIRECT MAIL

The direct-mail approach is usually used for one appeal, if it can create an immediate, direct, and easily understood response. Conditions in the congregation must be favorable for this relatively low-key program. The focus is ministry and the audience is all members of the church, at a potentially low cost.

*Strengths*

- allows for much creativity in writing
- little time required
- includes all members
- easy to manage
- an efficient use of effort
- little leadership required
- nonconfrontive
- updates membership list

*Limitations*

- lacks face-to-face dialogue
- materials mailed must be top quality
- if discontent exists in the congregation, mail appeal often ineffective
- resembles secular appeal for funds
- requires an efficient way to receive pledges
- follow-up difficult

## TELEPHONE APPEAL

A telephone appeal offers an opportunity to talk, member-to-member, about the work of the church and the need for financial support. The focus is ministry and the audience is all members of the church, at a potentially low cost. However, training is required.

*Strengths*

- little time required
- low cost
- allows for questions, answers, and feelings
- easy to enlist callers

*Limitations*

- cannot show materials
- not face-to-face
- difficult to do in a caring manner
- does not involve the whole family
- lacks confidentiality
- associated with business solicitations
- calls too easily terminated
- requires careful training of callers
- calls sometimes irritate people
- strong motivation often lacking

## PERSONAL DELIVERY: "PONY EXPRESS"

The personal delivery stewardship program is designed to move interpretive materials and financial commitment cards from one household to another. Each member records their financial commitment and then passes the "bag" to the next member on the list. The focus is ministry and the audience is all members of the church. High congregational involvement should stimulate increased giving. It can be done at potentially low cost.

*Strengths*

- cuts down on travel time
- only limited training needed
- highlights confidentiality
- involves a large number of people
- little time required
- fun, often stimulating a creative, playful spirit
- reaches "uncommitted" members

*Limitations*

- can easily encounter delays and breakdowns in delivery system
- process can become more important than the objective
- difficult for shut-ins to participate
- little dialogue about the work of the church
- no training provided for "riders"
- little opportunity for stewardship education

## CONSECRATION SUNDAY

The emphasis of Consecration Sunday is on the need of the giver to give, not the church to receive. At the close of Sunday worship, members are invited, as an act of worship, to make their estimate of giving for the coming year. This can be an intensely meaningful personal worship event that is an act of dedication to God, and which acknowledges that we are partners in mission with God. There is usually no home solicitation for pledges. Each person completes their own pledge in worship, and no member calls on another member for a pledge. The focus is spiritual and the audience is active members of the church. Outside leadership is recommended, potentially increasing costs.

| *Strengths* | *Limitations* |
|---|---|
| • little time or training needed | • no chance of dialogue |
| • can distribute materials easily | • may not reach shut-ins, non-residents, or "uncommitted" members |
| • can be combined with other approaches | |
| • allows for a single, effective presentation | • weighted heavily toward mail and sermon |
| • can use a "guest leader" | • primarily reaches those in attendance |
| • little calling required | • effective "guest leaders" are hard to find |
| • involves celebration | |

## K*I*S*S: CONGREGATIONAL DINNER

K*I*S*S (Keep It Simple, Steward!) is a single congregational event that includes something to eat (free); a program that succinctly gives inspiration, information, and motivation; an opportunity to make a pledge, as a private act; and a closing service for the consecration of pledges. The focus is ministry and the audience is active members of the church.

| *Strengths* | *Limitations* |
|---|---|
| • provides face-to-face contact | • does not reach shut-ins |
| • can distribute materials easily | • a large crowd can inhibit sharing and questions |
| • can have several dinners to reach more members | |
| • low cost | • does not reach "uncommitted" members |
| • everyone hears the same presentation | • requires extensive follow-up |
| • strengthens fellowship | |
| • can make good use of audiovisuals | |

## A MAY THANKSGIVING

Although designed specially for those congregations that have a July–June fiscal year, and which therefore conduct their financial campaign in the spring, this program can be used in the fall and climax around Thanksgiving Sunday. Its basic approach is a letter campaign culminating on a designated "Thanksgiving Sunday," when the congregation hears a guest speaker, returns pledge cards (financial and time/talent), and participates in a free dinner after worship. The focus is spiritual and the audience active members. There is no follow-up except a personal letter of thanks to each person making an estimate of giving.

| *Strengths* | *Limitations* |
|---|---|
| • provides face-to-face contact | • does not reach shut-ins without follow-up |
| • can distribute materials easily | • requires advance informational letters, which may be ignored |
| • combines the best of other approaches | • does not reach "uncommitted" members |
| • low cost | • reaches only those in attendance |
| • uses an inspirational guest speaker | • no follow-up may reduce pledges |
| • strengthens fellowship | |
| • involves celebration | |

## FAITH PROMISE

Faith, not budget, is uppermost in this approach. The emphasis is on "What shall I promise?" in light of the giver's capability to give. When a congregation is well informed, and highly committed to the church's mission, little more needs to be said about why the church needs financial support. Giving, then, is a faith-inspired deed. The focus is spiritual and the audience is active members of the church. There is little associated cost. A variation to this approach could include some mission and program information, to effectively combine "faith and facts."

| *Strengths* | *Limitations* |
|---|---|
| • saves time, money, planning | • may reach only highly committed members |
| • appeals to the "best" in members | • no "binding" commitments made |
| • can have a strong, biblical motivation | • difficult for church to set goals and budget |
| • may help some grow toward a pledging tradition | • relies on clergy for motivation |
| • assures confidentiality | • temptation to misuse Bible; i.e., literalism |
| • can be used for special offerings | • can encourage a step away from responsible pledging, budgeting, etc. |
| • appeals to more "conservative" congregations | |

## SMALL-GROUP MEETINGS IN HOMES

This approach, if well organized, can very effectively communicate the church's message of mission and financial need while encouraging member fellowship. It allows for greater discussion and thus, potentially, a higher level of interest and response. It can easily be combined with other approaches for even greater responsiveness. The focus is ministry and the primary audience is active members of the church. High congregational involvement is paramount to success. Training of leaders is required, and the potential for increased giving is high at a relatively low cost.

| *Strengths* | *Limitations* |
| --- | --- |
| • allows for dialogue | • time consuming; could drag out |
| • can organize members by geographical area, age, interest, or time available | • need telephone callers to remind people to attend |
| • strengthens fellowship | • host/hostess training required |
| • creates high level of interest | • careful organization needed |
| | • does not reach "uncommitted" members |
| | • difficult for a large congregation |
| | • negative voices can dominate |
| | • reaches only those who attend meetings |
| | • requires extensive follow-up |

## MIRACLE SUNDAY

This approach is a highly intensive program in response to a cause or need that *everyone* believes in; you have to believe in miracles and be willing to ask people for the money. The pastor must be an enthusiastic supporter, and you must have a well-organized system for raising the money. The focus is ministry and the audience active members. Preparation can be considerable, but the payoff astounding—from one-third to three times the combined total for the operating budget and benevolences. Typically, the approach includes a carefully planned informational program defining the need, followed by an inspirational dinner, followed by face-to-face calling to secure commitments—all before the miracle Sunday. Variations include a combination of letters to all church members accompanied by personal visits to perhaps 20 percent of the member families.

| *Strengths* | *Limitations* |
| --- | --- |
| • can raise a large amount on one Sunday | • requires great preparation and organization |
| • excites members' imagination and enthusiasm | • must be done right to ensure success |
| • focuses members' interest and support | • purpose for drive must not be divisive |
| • may tap savings of aging members | • fund-raising appeal primary, rather than stewardship education |
| • approach includes characteristics of an ideal goal—specific, attainable, measurable, visible, unifying, satisfying, with an ending date | • requires significant time |
| | • could fall well below goal |
| • opportunity for unified celebration at end | • emphasis only on active members |
| • you can expect a miracle | • you must believe in miracles |

*Summary:* Any effective stewardship program must fit the local church and the place of members in their faith journeys. While you will want all members to enrich their stewardship, remember that frequently 80 percent of the dollars come from 20 percent of the contributors.

## Stewardship in a Small or Ethnic Local Church

Stewardship, as the essence of Christian living, is appropriate in any church setting. Although we generally discuss stewardship programs in the context of a medium or large church that is quite often primarily Anglo, there are just as many needs for enlightened stewardship considerations in a small or ethnic local church. In this setting, members quite often are incredibly responsible and creative in giving time and talent in shared ministry and mission. Although a budget is appreciated and needed as a planning tool and a way of setting commitments and priorities, it is only as complex as necessary to fit the need.

Stewardship campaigns are more "family-oriented" with one sermon and one letter to gain a pledge. Every need, in terms of its mission relationship, is clearly communicated. Since a higher percentage of members usually attend worship in a small church, the message gets through quickly. Commitment is usually high—members are good and faithful stewards when asked. Fund raisers can also be used to involve those still on the fringes of the church.

As more ethnic or mixed congregations emerge in our communities, stewardship approaches must respond to members' backgrounds and culture, as well as to their capabilities. An important part of understanding and clarifying diversity issues is listening to the stewardship journeys of persons claiming racial-ethnic identities. Perhaps we should consider the following:[13]

- What does cultural diversity look like in our local community, society, and in God's community as a whole? What are the myths we need to dispel?

- Can we share stories of cultural traditions and values passed down through generations and listen to other people's stories? A number of cultures have an extremely strong faith-oriented stewardship, which may direct people's entire lives.

- Can we advocate justice, and maintain dialogue with church leaders about opportunities for sharing the richness of various experiences and traditions, and about opportunities for celebrating differences?

To enhance our understanding of stewardship and what stewardship means to others, we need to answer these questions in the context of our own Christian stewardship and response to God's bountiful love.

*Listen, learn, share, and respond to God's calling to stewardship.*

## CHAPTER FIVE

# Assessing and Reporting

## The Importance of Assessing and Reporting

As you move through the process of planning, organizing, and leading, it becomes readily evident that a final and important discipline of church administration remains. There must be a positive means through which we can assess and report on the first three steps of administration, to ensure the integrity and effectiveness of the process.

Recall that to assess and report is to measure progress against objectives, to examine results, and then to take appropriate corrective action. If the church leadership team is to be effective, there must be an active assessing and reporting program so feedback can result in change when necessary. Another way of looking at this important discipline is to consider it a process of "controlling," and in fact much of the standard literature incorporates the term "control." However, to be successful, this concept of assessing or controlling must always be viewed in a positive, proactive way. Realistically, those "in control" will succeed only when the team allows it, when it is for the good of the team and the entire management process.

In this chapter, we will examine how programs and activities are reviewed and evaluated, and how results are communicated in three major areas: human resources management, financial management, and property management. We will also present several key management review checklists or surveys which can be used in any church setting to ensure the effectiveness of the management process.

In the area of human resources management, we will show the importance of

- Regular performance reviews to assess whether goals have been attained

- Detailed records to document all personnel actions

- Care in ensuring employees' legal and personal rights

Effective financial management will come naturally when the following are included:

- Simple but effective accounting for funds received and disbursed

- A budget to guide the financial affairs of the church

- Appropriate forms to organize and document the process

- Reports prepared to communicate effectively to the user

- Careful handling of tax considerations

- A financial control system, reviewed periodically to ensure integrity

Church property will be effectively managed when:

- It is well maintained, using standards, guidelines, and checklists.

- There is an economical and effective insurance program.

- There are inspections to recognize and correct problems, using a loss-prevention checklist.

- Inventory records are maintained.

Management review checklists and guides are helpful aids in ensuring an effective management system. Starting on page 363, are:

- A church administration and finance survey, which asks the user to assess their individual church's efforts as they plan, organize, lead, assess, and report.

- A parish checklist, which suggests specific tasks to accomplish annually, again to ensure effective planning, organizing, leading, assessing, and reporting.

- A guide to church financial management, in checklist format, which suggests procedures to evaluate the effectiveness and efficiency with which financial and managerial responsibilities and procedures are carried out.

Perhaps it seems that assessing and reporting will take an inordinate amount of effort and time. However, if done well this important step enhances the entire church administrative process and results in better planning, organizing, and leading. The management process we suggest in this manual is a synergistic process in which each discipline enhances the other disciplines. When joined, these disciplines become a solid framework for effective administration.

## Human Resources Management

For any church to operate effectively, the leaders must be energized toward attaining goals and objectives in an organized and efficient way. We have discussed the importance of personnel position descriptions as the best way to keep tasks organized and everyone headed in the same direction. Now we need to examine the importance of performance evaluations and how they can form a positive feedback system. This final step in the human resources management process is extremely important if people are to feel part of the team that leads and facilitates the activities of the church.

Immediately following this introduction we will discuss what makes a performance evaluation effective and the important purposes these evaluations serve. Beginning on page 292 we list guidelines for a competent and effective performance evaluation, followed by sample forms for several typical clergy and lay staff positions.

### Performance Evaluations

There are three key elements in an effective performance evaluation:

- *Position Description.* To evaluate a person meaningfully the performance requirements and standards must be defined. This process starts with a position description delineating the responsibilities. (Sample position descriptions for both staff and volunteers appear on pages 158–207.)

- *Specific Objectives.* Specific objectives, keyed to the major responsibilities in the position description, must be carefully identified for there to be a truly meaningful performance evaluation. The position incumbent and supervisor develop the objectives *jointly*. Objectives for the pastor would be developed in cooperation with the pastoral advisory or supervisory committee.

- *Performance Evaluation.* Performance evaluations, both formal and informal, document an individual's work performance. To be most effective, they must include positive and motivating feedback and a joint discussion of what was expected, compared to what was actually accomplished.

Although we have discussed position descriptions and specific objectives in chapter 3, it is appropriate to make a few additional comments about setting objectives and why people are often reluctant to do so. Perhaps the greatest reason for reluctance is the fear that objectives will not be met, and that this failure will result in criticism and a bad performance report. When jointly developing goals and objectives it might be helpful to explain that **goals are statements of faith.** They state expectations of future outcome and serve as an attempt to make a proposed action dynamic by defining it in specific terms. Nothing becomes dynamic until it becomes specific. Failure can result when people are not willing to set a goal or specific objective, since they are essentially saying that they are satisfied with the status quo and are not willing to take a risk to make improvements.

For the employee to have an opportunity to perform as anticipated and to be motivated, there must be an understanding about expectations. A complete understanding should exist between the supervisor and employee that, while specific objectives and their achievement are important, perfect performance is not usually within the realm of human behavior. Slippages will occur for any number of reasons within and beyond the control of the affected individual. As long as there is good reason for the slippage, and steps have been taken to reschedule and recover, performance will be considered acceptable. The key, always, is full communication between the supervisor and employee.

Performance evaluations serve a number of important purposes. They provide:

1. A formal, periodic, written review of performance that, if done properly, will generally improve performance, job satisfaction, and morale. People want to know what is expected of them and how they are performing to those expectations.

2. Communication regarding the job and its various responsibilities. While this is not an ideal or recommended procedure, all too often the annual performance evaluation provides the only meaningful and detailed dialogue between the two parties.

3. A means to measure, recognize, and reinforce achievement and to provide positive feedback, and, as necessary, corrective action. None of us is so self-reliant that we would intentionally pass up an occasional "pat on the back" for a job well done. Conversely, we sometimes are not as aware of deficiencies in our performance as we might be and should be amenable to constructive feedback.

4. A permanent record of performance, changes in performance, special talents and skills, progress, problems, and so forth. This written record is especially important in our litigious environment in which it seems that people bring lawsuits for what appear to be frivolous or unjustified reasons. Quite often these lawsuits, even though unjustified, are settled, because there is insufficient written evidence to refute the charges.

5. A basis that is *objective* for selecting people for promotions, merit increases, training opportunities, or, possibly, separation. The employer must be able to prove that the action was justified. For example, if an employee brings a grievance for not being selected for a promotion, there should be clear, written justification for the selection that was made if the grievance is to be processed properly.

In addition to formal performance evaluations, a good supervisor will seize every opportunity to praise an employee for work well done, or to offer constructive criticism. Feedback is most effective when done immediately, with praise in public and criticism in private. When offering constructive criticism, supervisors will be most effective when they go to an employee's work location, if it is private, or meet in a neutral spot. To call someone into an office usually results in the anticipation that something is wrong and may bring on defensiveness.

Proper evaluation of performance is hard work. A supervisor or advisory committee should strive to do it as objectively as possible, with the appropriate sensitivity and firmness that each situation dictates. Only through a complete process of establishing requirements and expectations, and then evaluating against those expectations, can a positive and effective team effort result.

## Guidelines for an Effective Performance Evaluation

Proper preparation for a performance evaluation is important for the supervisor, and possibly even more important for the employee who will be anticipating the evaluation, perhaps with trepidation. Supervisors should think carefully about what they will say to the employee and how they will say it, especially if there is a sensitive area to discuss. Plan the conversation with a particular outcome or goal in mind. The following are suggested guidelines that should make the evaluation process constructive and pleasant for all parties involved:

1. *Always* be prompt, if not early, with the performance evaluation. People know when the "annual" evaluation is due (anniversary date of hire, a set period from the last evaluation, etc.) and become anxious if it is delayed. If it is impossible to meet the due date, advise the person well in advance, and explain why the evaluation will be delayed. Set a new time and *do not* miss the revised date.

2. Set "quality time" aside for the evaluation. This may be one of the most important communications of the year with that person and should not be hurried.

3. Do not allow the evaluation to be interrupted, if possible. Hold all telephone calls and other possible intrusions.

4. Be candid in the appraisal of performance. Little is accomplished using the "halo effect," a natural tendency to minimize marginal or poor performance. It

is not easy to sit in judgment or to constructively criticize another person, but it is essential to be as honest as possible during the evaluation.

5. The evaluation should be oriented to objectives to a maximum extent, with a minimum of subjective input. If specific objectives have been mutually established, the focus of the evaluation should be how those objectives were accomplished, offering praise for those achieved and discussing in detail those missed. Examine why those objectives were not accomplished, not critically but constructively. If specific objectives have not been established, this is an excellent time to introduce and discuss this subject to prepare for the next evaluation period. Personal goals and objectives need to be reset annually; the process of setting goals together allows the manager to participate in and hear about the employee's hopes for growth and to talk about new opportunities. If time does not permit this discussion during the evaluation, set a time in the near future.

6. Always begin with positive reinforcement of good performance, being as specific as possible. *"Catch them doing something right!"*[1] List instances when exceptional performance was noted and appreciated, even if this reiterates earlier recognition. A record of these instances, as they occurred, should have been noted in writing and placed in the personnel folder.

7. Next, discuss performance that needs improvement, if any. Be specific about where and how changes must be made, and when results will be measured. Again, a written record should have been kept of substandard performance, and the record should be in the personnel folder. Instances in which corrective action is required should not be brought to the employee's attention at the performance evaluation, unless these instances have been discussed previously. It is grossly unfair for an employee to hear about substandard performance for the first time at the evaluation. This accomplishes nothing constructive and is inevitably destructive to morale and future performance.

8. Allow the person to discuss their reactions, concerns, and questions regarding the evaluation. Ask, "What can I do to help you in your job performance?" *Listen attentively and openly!* You may be part of the performance problem, if there is one.

9. Conclude the evaluation session with positive reinforcement about the employee and their part in the future of the team. Covenant to give that person, and all other people for whom you have an evaluation responsibility, input on performance between evaluation periods.

10. Both parties should sign and date the performance evaluation. For record-keeping purposes, it must be ascertainable that the performance evaluation was given and received.

11. If the person evaluated disagrees with part of the performance appraisal, they may state the disagreement in writing, either on the evaluation form or on a separate sheet stapled to the evaluation.

12. Give a copy of the completed evaluation form, along with any attachments, to the person evaluated.

13. Place the completed performance evaluation in the person's personnel file.

14. Be sure to follow up on any agreements that may have been made during the evaluation.

## Performance Evaluation Forms

The following pages present sample performance evaluation forms that may be adapted to the unique positions in almost any church. These sample forms range from comprehensive, detailed, and objective-oriented to fairly simple. The most effective performance evaluation, and the one usually most appreciated by the staff person, is detailed and objective-oriented, and that should be the goal in any organization.

Whether detailed or simple, an evaluation of performance is important to employees and the organization, and should be formally documented at least annually.

The sample performance evaluations presented on the following pages are intended as guidance only. Do not simply copy and use them as printed. Each organization should develop a unique evaluation form that follows the responsibilities listed on the position description developed for the specific position or individual.

# Performance Evaluation—Senior Pastor

Name: _____ Review Period: _____

Please comment on performance in each of the following areas and indicate an overall rating with an X on the line between O and BR. Where specific objectives exist, note the actual performance and the goal.

RATING: **O**—Outstanding   **AR**—Above Requirements
**MR**—Meets Requirements   **BR**—Below Requirements

## Worship

Rating: O — AR — MR — BR

Inspiring, meaningful, and orderly worship: _____

Preaching quality and skill: _____

Cooperation with Worship Committee: _____

Laity involvement in worship service: _____

Other comments: _____
_____
_____
_____

Worship attendance: _____ Goal: _____ Actual: _____
Specific: _____ Goal: _____ Actual: _____
Specific: _____ Goal: _____ Actual: _____

## Congregational Care

**NURTURE:**

Rating: O — AR — MR — BR

Calling program on those in need: _____

Calling program on members, constituents, and potential members: _____

Counseling availability and skill: _____

Officiating at weddings, funerals, and celebrations: _____

Other comments: _____
_____
_____
_____

Specific: _____ Goal: _____ Actual: _____
Specific: _____ Goal: _____ Actual: _____

**EVANGELISM AND MEMBERSHIP:**                    Rating: |——O——AR——MR——BR——|

New membership: _____

_____

Newcomer visitation: _____

_____

Public relations program: _____

_____

New member integration: _____

_____

Inactive member reactivation: _____

_____

Other comments: _____

_____

_____

Church Growth: _____ Goal: _____ Actual: _____
New member dropout: _____ Goal: _____ Actual: _____
Specific: _____ Goal: _____ Actual: _____

**CHRISTIAN EDUCATION:**                          Rating: |——O——AR——MR——BR——|

Christian education program: _____

_____

Teaching classes: _____

_____

Other comments: _____

_____

Church school attendance growth: _____ Goal: _____ Actual: _____
Adult education attendance growth: _____ Goal: _____ Actual: _____
Specific: _____ Goal: _____ Actual: _____

**PARISH LIFE:**                                  Rating: |——O——AR——MR——BR——|

All-church fellowship activity: _____

_____

Small-group involvement: _____

_____

Other comments: _____

_____

Small-group growth: _____ Goal: _____ Actual: _____
Specific: _____ Goal: _____ Actual: _____

**ADMINISTRATION:**                               Rating: |——O——AR——MR——BR——|

Effectiveness of Nominating Committee: _____

_____

Working relationship with key responsibility groups: _____

Contact with work areas: _____

Annual budget development: _____

Budget funding: _____

Annual Plan development/update: _____

Long-Range Plan development/update: _____

Fiscal controls in place: _____

Required reporting completed: _____

Personnel records maintained properly: _____
Other comments: _____

_____

_____

_____

_____

_____

_____

_____

Specific:_____ Goal: _____ Actual: _____
Specific:_____ Goal: _____ Actual: _____
Specific:_____ Goal: _____ Actual: _____
Outstanding accomplishments during this review period:_____

_____

_____

_____

_____

_____

_____

_____

Suggestions for improvement: _____

_____

_____

_____

_____

_____

Additional comments: _____

_____

_____

_____

_____

_____

_____

_____

Performance evaluation written by: _____ Date: _____

Received by: _____ Date: _____
　　　　　　　　　　　　　　　(Pastor)

Pastor's Comments: _____

_____

_____

_____

_____

_____

_____

_____

# Performance Evaluation—Secretary

Name: _____ Evaluation period: _____ to _____

RATING: **O**—Outstanding   **AR**—Above Requirements
         **MR**—Meets Requirements   **BR**—Below Requirements

Place an X on the line between O and BR that is indicative of the performance for the period.

1. Performance of secretarial duties as defined    Rating: O   AR   MR   BR
   in the position description.
   Comments: _____
   _____
   _____

2. Supervising of volunteer and office staff.    Rating: O   AR   MR   BR
   Comments: _____
   _____
   _____

3. Quality of work.    Rating: O   AR   MR   BR
   Comments: _____
   _____
   _____

4. Quantity of work/productivity.    Rating: O   AR   MR   BR
   Comments: _____
   _____
   _____

5. Maintaining confidentiality of conversations,    Rating: O   AR   MR   BR
   relationships, and records.
   Comments: _____
   _____
   _____

6. Cooperating/coordinating with pastor and    Rating: O   AR   MR   BR
   office staff.
   Comments: _____
   _____
   _____

7. Maintaining of church calendar and schedules.    Rating: O   AR   MR   BR
   Comments: _____
   _____
   _____

8. Maintaining of accurate records and reports.     Rating: |————|————|————|
                                                            O    AR   MR   BR
Comments: _____
_____
_____

9. Performance to established objectives.     Rating: |————|————|————|
                                                      O    AR   MR   BR
Objective: _____ Results: _____
Objective: _____ Results: _____
Objective: _____ Results: _____
Objective: _____ Results: _____
Comments: _____
_____
_____

Noteworthy performance during the review period: _____
_____
_____
_____
_____

Areas where improvement is needed: _____
_____
_____
_____
_____

Additional comments: _____
_____
_____
_____

Secretary's comments:_____
_____
_____
_____
_____
_____
_____
_____

Evaluator's signature: _____ Date: _____
Secretary's signature: _____ Date: _____
If space is required for additional evaluations or comments, please do so on an additional page and attach to this form.

# Performance Evaluation—Choir Director

Name: _____ Evaluation period: _____ to _____

RATING: **O**—Outstanding  **AR**—Above Requirements
  **MR**—Meets Requirements  **BR**—Below Requirements

Place an X on the line between O and BR that is indicative of the performance for the period.

1. Enhancing the spirit of worship and assisting the congregation in praising and serving God.

Rating: O — AR — MR — BR

Comments: _____
_____
_____

2. Selecting music appropriate to worship themes.

Rating: O — AR — MR — BR

Comments: _____
_____
_____

3. Providing quality music performances.

Rating: O — AR — MR — BR

Comments: _____
_____
_____

4. Promoting growth and stability of choir membership.

Rating: O — AR — MR — BR

Comments: _____
_____
_____

5. Developing musical skills of the choir.

Rating: O — AR — MR — BR

Comments: _____
_____
_____

6. Cooperating/coordinating with ministerial and office staff.

Rating: O — AR — MR — BR

Comments: _____
_____
_____

7. Cooperating/coordinating with choir officers, organist, pianist, and other music program personnel.

Rating: O — AR — MR — BR

Comments: _____
_____
_____

8. Performance to established objectives.                Rating: O ⊢———+———+———⊣ AR   MR   BR

Objective: _____ Results: _____

Objective: _____ Results: _____

Objective: _____ Results: _____

Comments: _____

_____

_____

9. Administering and caring for the physical        Rating: O ⊢———+———+———⊣ AR   MR   BR
   properties and materials related to the music program.

Comments: _____

_____

_____

Noteworthy performance during the review period: _____

_____

_____

_____

_____

Areas where improvement is needed: _____

_____

_____

_____

_____

Additional comments: _____

_____

_____

_____

Choir Director's comments: _____

_____

_____

_____

_____

_____

_____

Evaluator's signature: _____ Date: _____

Choir Director's signature: _____ Date: _____

If space is required for additional evaluations or comments, please do so on an additional page and attach to this form.

# Performance Evaluation—Organist

Name: _____ Evaluation period: _____ to _____

RATING: **O**—Outstanding   **AR**—Above Requirements
           **MR**—Meets Requirements   **BR**—Below Requirements

Place an X on the line between O and BR that is indicative of the performance for the period.

1. Enhancing the spirit of worship and assisting the congregation in praising and serving God.

   Rating: O ─── AR ─── MR ─── BR

   Comments: _____
   _____
   _____

2. Selecting music appropriate to worship themes.

   Rating: O ─── AR ─── MR ─── BR

   Comments: _____
   _____
   _____

3. Providing quality music performances.

   Rating: O ─── AR ─── MR ─── BR

   Comments: _____
   _____
   _____

4. Providing music for other occasions: weddings, funerals, celebrations.

   Rating: O ─── AR ─── MR ─── BR

   Comments: _____
   _____
   _____

5. Providing accompaniment for rehearsals of the choir amd other music groups in the church.

   Rating: O ─── AR ─── MR ─── BR

   Comments: _____
   _____
   _____

6. Cooperating/coordinating with ministerial and office staff.

   Rating: O ─── AR ─── MR ─── BR

   Comments: _____
   _____
   _____

7. Cooperating/coordinating with choir director and other music program personnel.

   Rating: O ─── AR ─── MR ─── BR

   Comments: _____
   _____

8. Performance to established objectives.  Rating: 
O    AR    MR    BR

Objective: _____ Results: _____

Objective: _____ Results: _____

Objective: _____ Results: _____

Objective: _____ Results: _____

Comments: _____

_____

_____

9. Caring for the physical properties and materials  Rating: 
O    AR    MR    BR
related to the music program.

Comments: _____

_____

_____

Noteworthy performance during the review period: _____

_____

_____

_____

_____

Areas where improvement is needed: _____

_____

_____

_____

_____

Additional comments: _____

_____

_____

_____

Organist's comments: _____

_____

_____

_____

_____

_____

_____

_____

Evaluator's signature: _____ Date: _____

Organist's signature: _____ Date: _____

If space is required for additional evaluations or comments, please do so on an additional page and attach to this form.

# Performance Evaluation—Supervisory Position

Name: _____ Evaluation period: _____ to _____
Position: _____

RATING: **O**—Outstanding   **AR**—Above Requirements
   **MR**—Meets Requirements   **BR**—Below Requirements

Place an X on the line between O and BR that is indicative of the performance for the period.

## Supervisory Skills

|   | O | AR | MR | BR |
|---|---|----|----|----|
| 1. Planning | | | | |
| 2. Organizing and staffing | | | | |
| 3. Leadership and supervision | | | | |
| 4. Assessing performance and reporting | | | | |
| 5. Maintenance of records and reports | | | | |
| 6. Scheduling and coordinating | | | | |
| 7. Delegating of responsibilities | | | | |
| 8. Judgment and decision making | | | | |

Comments: _____
_____
_____

## Work Habits

|   | O | AR | MR | BR |
|---|---|----|----|----|
| 9. Attendance | | | | |
| 10. Meeting schedules and deadlines | | | | |
| 11. Appearance of work area | | | | |
| 12. Operation and care of equipment | | | | |

Comments: _____
_____
_____

## Work Performance

|   | O | AR | MR | BR |
|---|---|----|----|----|
| 13. Quality of work | | | | |
| 14. Quantity of work/productivity | | | | |
| 15. Job skill level | | | | |

Comments: _____
_____
_____

## Adaptability and Initiative

|   | O | AR | MR | BR |
|---|---|----|----|----|
| 16. Accepts responsibility | | | | |
| 17. Adapts well to change | | | | |
| 18. Works effectively under pressure | | | | |

19. Initiative                 O     AR    MR    BR

20. Dependability

Comments: _____

_____

_____

## *Relationships*

                                                  O     AR    MR    BR

21. Working with staff and volunteers

22. Contacts with the public

23. Working as a team player

Comments: _____

_____

_____

## *Performance to Objectives*

24. Performance to established objectives

Objective: _____ Results: _____

Objective: _____ Results: _____

Objective: _____ Results: _____

Comments: _____

_____

Noteworthy performance during the evaluation period: _____

_____

_____

_____

Areas where improvement is needed: _____

_____

_____

_____

Additional comments: _____

_____

_____

_____

Employee's comments: _____

_____

_____

_____

Evaluator's signature: _____ Date: _____

Employee's signature: _____ Date: _____

If space is required for additional evaluations or comments, please do so on an additional page and attach to this form.

# *Performance Evaluation—General Form*

Name: _____ Evaluation period: _____ to _____

Position: _____

RATING: **O**—Outstanding   **AR**—Above Requirements

**MR**—Meets Requirements   **BR**—Below Requirements

Place an X on the line between O and BR that is indicative of the performance for the period.

## *Work Habits*

1. Attendance
2. Meeting schedules and deadlines
3. Appearance of work area
4. Operation and care of equipment

Comments: _____

_____

_____

## *Work Performance*

5. Quality of work
6. Quantity of work/productivity
7. Planning and organizing of work
8. Judgment and resourcefulness
9. Job skill level

Comments: _____

_____

_____

## *Adaptability and Initiative*

10. Accepts responsibility
11. Adapts well to change
12. Works effectively under pressure
13. Initiative
14. Dependability

Comments: _____

_____

_____

## *Relationships*

15. Working with staff and volunteers
16. Contacts with the public
17. Works as a team player

Comments: _____

_____

_____

## *Performance to Objectives*

|  | O | AR | MR | BR |
|---|---|---|---|---|

18. Performance to established objectives

Objective: _____ Results: _____

Objective: _____ Results: _____

Objective: _____ Results: _____

Objective: _____ Results: _____

Comments: _____

_____

_____

Noteworthy performance during the evaluation period: _____

_____

_____

_____

_____

Areas where improvement is needed: _____

_____

_____

_____

_____

_____

Additional comments: _____

_____

_____

_____

_____

Employee's comments: _____

_____

_____

_____

_____

_____

_____

_____

Evaluator's signature: _____ Date: _____

Employee's signature: _____ Date: _____

If space is required for additional evaluations or comments, please do so on an additional page and attach to this form.

# Financial Management

## Elements of an Effective Financial Control System

Although churches recognize conceptually that good financial management of resources is desirable, they may not always recognize what is required. An effective financial control system is imperative and facilitates financial management. But what constitutes an effective financial control system? The following comments summarize the important elements. Many of these elements are then discussed in greater detail in the pages that follow.

The essence of a church financial control system is that it is a "feedback" system. It alerts members about whether their goals are being attained; it ensures absolute integrity in the system; and it communicates credible information.

Most recognize that good use of money requires careful management. It must be gratefully received from wherever it may come. Then, once received, it should be carefully accounted for, and spent wisely for optimum benefit—including being shared with others for outreach ministry.

Trust and confidence in the financial management system is an absolute must and will enhance Christian participation and support. The system must, in fact and perception, be proper and sound. Every person trusted with financial management duties must appear to be trustworthy, and then demonstrate this trust. *There must be absolute integrity in every single action. Every transaction. Every decision. Every piece of paper. Every comment. Every human contact of any kind. Even when honest errors are made.*

An integral part of the trust that must be established is that financial personnel are seen as participating in a positive way in all phases of the church. First they should assist in any way necessary to ensure that plans and programs are known and understood, and then find ways to ensure that they are supported financially. There must be accurate feedback on contributions showing they are being used as donors intended. Understandable and complete financial reports, tailored to local needs and programs, should be used to convey confidence and to cause support. Audit or financial reviews support actions of financial personnel and instill confidence.

Specific policies and procedures must be clear, understood, and workable for the local church if there is to be an effective financial control system. These policies include:

- Bank accounts for general operations, as well as for special purposes. (Not too many; only what is needed to separate funds appropriately.)

- Savings and investment accounts for special purposes, not to hoard money, but to plan for the future.

- Bonding (as part of an insurance policy).

- Policies concerning who is responsible for what and who reports to whom (chain of command).

- Deposit procedures.

- Check-writing procedures, to include who is authorized to sign checks.

- Kinds of financial reports, frequency, and to whom made.

- Procedures in writing which can offer a clear road map, which can be reviewed and audited, and which can guide people who are new to the position.

We also must not forget that there should be adequate facilities and tools available to financial management personnel so they can properly protect, count, pay, report, and keep complete records.

Finally, audit reviews should be done annually, sometimes by external auditors, but more frequently by internal auditors, who perhaps are members of the church and who use an internal audit, systems-procedure approach. (See page 372.)

## Church Accounting (A Simplified Approach)

Accounting for the contributions of members and how these funds are used can be a simple but effective process.

In most instances, churches use a variation of traditional accounting methods which call for a financial statement showing how funds are received and spent, and perhaps a balance sheet showing asset values and liability balances. Some attempt is made to compare data between fiscal periods. However, many accounting approaches use standard presentations and do not show information in a way that church committees can easily use and understand. This especially may be true with standard computer software. Often the result is a tedious process which gives the church the right information, but not always in easily usable form. Members have a difficult time using the financial data to help them track programs.

Much more usable is a process that quickly, but accurately, gives members financial information. The keys to such a process are:

1. A "fund" approach, rather than a profit and loss approach; that is, receipts and expenditures are tracked by "fund" and by respective budgets rather than in total. You must ensure the integrity of each fund for which activity is recorded. "Due to" (liability) and "Due from" (receivable) accounts must be used between funds and should be reconciled monthly, unless all fund receipts and expenditures are handled through separate checking accounts—a cumbersome and unnecessary method.

2. Income and expense items which are recorded as carefully as possible, according to how the budget was prepared. For instance, if a member makes a special reimbursement against an expense item, it is recorded as a "negative" expense instead of other income. This procedure gives a more accurate picture of how much is really being spent for a particular budgeted item.

3. A monthly statement and analysis by the treasurer so all committee heads (as well as all other members) can see what is happening financially. Both the statement and analysis should compare actual results to budgets. An accounting, by individual fund, will lend credibility and integrity to the system and give members no cause for concern or hesitation about giving. Members will respond promptly to calls for more support knowing that what is asked for is really needed.

4. Record keeping that is complete and provides an audit trail, but still is simple. With a complete chart of accounts for each fund, checkbook stubs can serve as

the books of original entry, recording the account numbers to be charged when funds are received or as checks are written. Then, during or at the end of the accounting period (usually monthly), the checkbook entries are posted directly to a simple computer accounting program (or manual spreadsheets on accounting ledger paper). Member's gifts can be posted manually to forms printed for that purpose, or there is inexpensive computer software to record contributions. The financial statement is prepared directly from the computer input (or manual spreadsheets), as well as payroll data. If using a computer, a simple accounting program, perhaps a spreadsheet program, a program for recording contributions, and a printer are all that is needed.

5. Time of a devoted member, one who knows a "little" about basic accounting and who preferably has access to a computer. With 80–100 checks written each month, and an annual budget of up to $200,000, the time required monthly to write checks, do payroll, prepare financial statements, and analyze financial results should take an average of 35–40 hours. Recording contributions may take an additional six to eight hours monthly.

A simple system devoid of complicated accounting terminology and formats, and tailored to church needs, should allow members to get information they need. To establish and maintain such a system:

1. Review the organizational structure and develop an accounting system and chart of accounts that provides the information needed by each committee.

2. Number accounts so everyone can see how the system builds toward its totals while keeping funds and categories of receipts and committee expenditures separated.

3. Record the account number on the stub of each check, receipt, and deposit.

4. Summarize (post) receipts and checks on a spreadsheet or accounting program (manually or by computer); total each category and show a grand total received and spent.

5. Balance the checkbook to the accounting records to ensure accuracy of bank and cash balances.

6. Prepare a financial report from the spreadsheet or accounting program, comparing totals to budgeted amounts. Analyze variances.

7. Communicate the financial report to committee members and congregational members, using appropriate reporting media that fits the unique needs of the members. Be complete, accurate, and timely!

## A Basic Understanding of Accounting

Expecting that some readers may have little or no knowledge of basic accounting principles as they apply to a church, it may be well to offer a short explanation and practical exercise. Although pastors have little need for a detailed knowledge of accounting methodology, they do need enough understanding to ask the right question at the right time and to know when an expert is needed.

First, remember that in a church setting, the only things necessary are:

- A *fund accounting system* whereby cash received is added to cash balances and cash paid out (according to budget categories) is subtracted from cash balances, resulting in a running balance of cash on hand. The system can work with only a checkbook.

- A report of this cash activity, made to members.

- A listing of asset values and loan balances, for insurance and loan purposes.

Now, let's look at some basic accounting.

First, you must know algebra. However, you only need to know one formula and some derivations of the following formula:

$$A - L = E$$

or

$$ASSETS - LIABILITIES = EQUITY$$
(What you have) − (What you owe) = (What you own)

Church **assets** might include cash, investments, land, buildings, and furniture, but usually not accounts receivable.

**Liabilities** might include current bills, payroll taxes, mortgages, and money received for one purpose that is designated for another purpose, but usually not accounts payable.

**Equity** is the value of what you have, less what you owe.

You may have heard about "cash basis" versus "accrual basis" accounting. These terms are even on IRS Form 1040. Churches should be on a "cash basis" for 99 percent of their actions. This is especially true if bills are paid on time.

"Accrual accounting" is appropriate when one earns or owes something this month, but does not receive or pay for it until later. It's called matching income and expenses in the same period—a desirable procedure for precise accounting. Churches probably do not need to be that precise—except at the end of a fiscal year—as long as bills are paid on time. The most important task is to match receipts and expenditures with budgets so variances can be studied.

Depreciation of assets (or showing how an asset is used up, and recording this amount as part of monthly expenses) is not significant in a church setting. It generally only becomes relevant when taxes must be paid on income (or if you must borrow money and a bank will require a true value of church assets).

Two special accounting terms—**debits** and **credits**—confuse many people, because within the accounting discipline they take on unique definitions.

- Debit *means left side of the formula.*

- Credit *means right side of the formula.*

Remember that in algebra, if

$$A - L = E, \text{ then } A = L + E$$

or

Assets (debit balance) = Liabilities (credit balance) +

Equity (credit balance)

So, when *adding to a debit balance, you debit.* When *adding to a credit balance, you credit.* Conversely, when *subtracting from a debit balance, you credit.* When *subtracting from a credit balance, you debit.*

Now, let's expand the algebraic formula to include receipts (**R**) and expenditures (**X**) as they affect what we own (**E**).

$$A - L = [E + (R - X)] \qquad \text{or} \qquad A + X = L + E + R$$

Since you add to what you own (**E**) when you receive (**R**) something, you *credit the receipt.* Since you subtract from what you own (**E**) when you pay (**X**) something, you *debit the expenditure.*

For example, when receiving a contribution, you debit (add to) an **A**sset, such as cash, and credit (add to) **R**eceipts, such as contributions received. When paying a debt, you credit (subtract) an **A**sset, such as cash, and debit (subtract) e**X**penditures, such as telephone expense.

An important concept in church fund accounting must be *very* carefully handled: ensuring that money deposited in one fund account but belonging to another fund (e.g., general fund vs. building fund) is tracked and eventually transferred to the proper fund balances. "Due to" (liability) and "Due from" (receivable) accounts are usually used, and these accounts *must* be balanced at least monthly. Ensure the treasurer is properly handling these transfers!! A computer accounting program may track these transfers well if set up properly. Or, the treasurer will need to make separate transfer entries. In either case, it is imperative that the integrity of each fund be maintained.

In a nutshell, that is the basis of church accounting. Remember, however, accounting is not the gospel. It is simply the numerical recording and reporting of history. But without accurate accounting, the gospel can be distorted!

On the next page is an exercise to demonstrate the principles just presented. Try posting the four transactions to the individual accounts, being very careful to maintain the proper balances in each of the two funds. *After doing the exercise, compare your postings to those explained on the page following the exercise.*

## Fund Accounting (An Example)

(1) Sunday offering deposit of $1,000. $750 for General Fund Income, and $250 for Building Fund Income. Deposit made in General Fund Checking account.

(2) Transfer from General Fund Checking to Building Fund Savings of the $250 owed to the Building Fund.

(3) Purchase of two items costing $500; payment made from the General Fund Checking. One item was for a General Fund need of $300. One item was for a Building Fund need of $200.

(4) Transfer (clear) Building Fund of the $200 owed to the General Fund.

*Remember*

$$A = L + [E + (R - X)] \text{ or } A + X = L + E + R$$

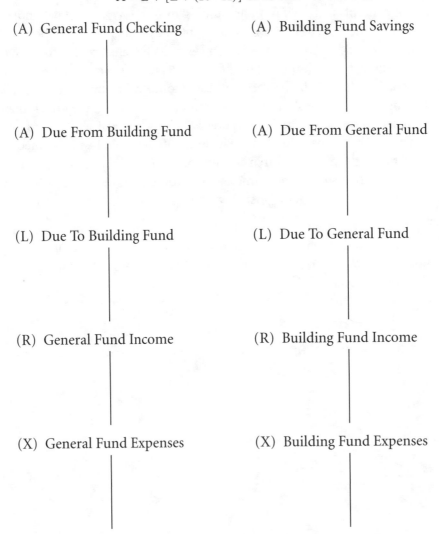

(A) General Fund Checking        (A) Building Fund Savings

(A) Due From Building Fund        (A) Due From General Fund

(L) Due To Building Fund          (L) Due To General Fund

(R) General Fund Income           (R) Building Fund Income

(X) General Fund Expenses         (X) Building Fund Expenses

*Questions pastor should ask treasurer about "Due To" and "Due From" accounts: Does the General Fund "Due From" account equal other fund's "Due To General Fund" account? When are these funds balanced? At least monthly?*

(1) $1,000 is debited to General Fund Checking, $750 is credited to General Fund Income, and $250 is credited to Building Fund Income. To complete the entry and maintain the integrity of the funds, the $250 deposited in the General Fund Checking but belonging to the Building Fund should be recorded as a credit to Due To Building Fund, and a debit to Due From General Fund.

(2) To clear the Due To and Due From accounts, usually at the end of the month, a check would be written from the General Fund to the Building Fund for $250 and a credit posted to the General Fund Checking and a debit to the Building Fund Savings. The Due To and Due From accounts would be cleared by posting a debit to the Due To Building Fund, and a credit to the Due From General Fund for $250.

(3) $500 is credited to General Fund Checking, $300 is debited to General Fund Expenses, and $200 is debited to Building Fund Expenses. $200 would be debited to Due From Building Fund and credited to Due To General Fund, to record the fact the Building Fund owed the General Fund $200.

(4) The Due To and Due From accounts are cleared with a check for $200 written from the Building Fund Savings to the General Fund Checking, and recorded as a credit to the Building Fund Savings and a debit to the General Fund Checking. The Due To and Due From accounts would be cleared by posting a debit to the Due To General Fund and a credit to the Due From Building Fund for $200.

If all posting has been done correctly, the accounts should have the following balances: General Fund Checking, debit of $450; Due From Building Fund, $0; Due To Building Fund, $0; General Fund Income, credit of $750; and General Fund Expenses, a debit of $300. The Building Fund Savings should show a debit balance of $50; Due From General Fund, $0; Due To General Fund, $0; Building Fund Income, a credit balance of $250; and Building Fund Expenses, a debit balance of $200.

## Recording of Contributions

There is probably nothing more sensitive in church financial management than how contributions by members are received, counted, deposited, and recorded. Members want to know their contribution is used in the way they designated. They want to know it is safe, as it is counted and deposited. They deserve to have their giving kept private. They want an accurate record of their contributions maintained and sent to them periodically.

The financial secretary should be primarily responsible for the entire process, a process that is clearly defined by a system of disciplined procedures and controls. Counting and depositing procedures need to be written and available for review by counters. Control procedures need to include safekeeping facilities, handling of keys, and who and how many people handle the money.

Necessary equipment includes collection plates, a lockable bank bag, a fireproof lockable storage cabinet or safe, bank deposit slips and endorsement stamp, and a copy machine to copy checks for more accurate recording by the financial secretary.

To ensure the integrity of the process and to protect those involved, the collection should be counted and prepared for deposit by teams of *two or more unrelated persons*. The duty should be rotated and performed as soon as possible after the last service, in a safe place, and the collection put into a bank's night deposit box that day, if possible. The routine of the counters should vary from week to week, to lessen the chance of robbery as they leave for the bank. Or, a team can perform the actual counting at the bank on Monday morning, after the collection is placed in a night deposit box. If the collection is retained at the church overnight, checks should be stamped "for deposit only" and copied before the collection is stored in a safe place.

Counting steps will vary at each church. But in all instances there must be detailed written procedures specifying what each teller does, when, and why. On page 320 is a sample teller procedure, which might be used by a medium-sized church. Note the importance of indicating the fund to be given credit for the contribution on either the offering envelope or check, and assuring that all checks are copied and the copies stored separately from the deposit bag. The financial secretary will need this information before accurate recording of the contribution can take place. Note also that the tellers are not expected to do anything more than prepare the collection for deposit and probably make the deposit. If documentation about the collection is complete, the financial secretary can determine later which fund should receive credit for the gift. In fact, this is probably a preferred procedure in that giving habits of members do not need to be known to more than a very few people. Additionally, this lessens the time needed to prepare the offering for deposit.

*There is no room for compromise in this important function!*

Adherence to the following cardinal rules is extremely important, since perceptions of impropriety often can hurt more than actual wrongdoing.

- No husband and wife teams should be allowed.

- No one should take the money home to count it.

- Pastors should never be involved.

- Treasurers should not be involved until after the collection is counted and posted.

Procedures for receipts in the office from mail, weddings, special projects, and so forth should be clear, and the funds should be kept in a safe place during the week. These receipts are then integrated into the Sunday collection and appropriately accounted for and deposited.

The "Teller Offerings Report" included on page 319 should be carefully prepared and balanced for the deposit being made. (Note that the detailed teller procedures can be printed on the back of the report so they are readily available for reference.) The financial secretary will use this report, along with offering envelopes and copies of the checks, to record receipts to various funds, according to the wishes of contributors.

A copy of the teller offerings report, showing the distribution made by the financial secretary, goes to the treasurer for recording in the checkbook and computer accounting records or manual cash receipts journal. Depending on the computer software being used, the contributions may enter accounting records directly from postings the financial secretary makes to members' records of giving.

Physical deposit is usually made to one bank account, with the treasurer making distribution later to other funds and/or bank accounts.

The financial secretary records individual contributions to records of giving, which may be kept manually or by using a computer contributions program. Totals of amounts posted must equal the total amount collected and deposited.

Statements should be sent to contributors, usually at least quarterly, and again in January of each year showing all gifts for the year (for substantiation of gifts for IRS purposes). There is evidence to support the belief that stewardship levels increase 5 to 15 percent when each donor begins receiving a periodic financial giving report. Such statements also serve to give further credibility to the church financial management system, since members can track the accuracy of gift recording.

The IRS rules for substantiating charitable contributions of $250 or more that took effect in 1994 require that a donor who gives $250 or more in cash or property in a single gift must now substantiate their contribution with a written acknowledgment from the church. Checks can still serve as proof of gifts for amounts under $250, but not for amounts of $250 or more. Practically, church members will expect to receive an itemized list of every donation for their IRS records at the end of each calendar year. (The law also contains other unique requirements about gifts that are partly related to goods or services received; church officials will need to be aware of these requirements.) The statement must be received by donors on or before the *earlier* of two dates: *before they file their income tax report, or by the due date (including extensions) for filing the return.* It should be signed by the financial secretary or other proper official of the church, and should indicate that *"no tangible goods or services were received by the donor in exchange for the gift other than intangible religious benefit."*

Due to the IRS rules, churches obviously will need to provide reports of contributions to members as soon after the end of the year as possible, but certainly not later than January 31. The report should consist of a listing of each contribution, regardless of amount, so that it can also serve as a record of the member's stewardship and confirm the integrity of the record of giving. There is no requirement for a standard format for reporting cash contributions, except that a statement that no tangible goods or services were received must be included. Manual records of giving usually list each gift, and computer-generated reports also can do this easily; the required "no tangible goods or services" statement will need to be added. A sample computer-generated report is included on page 321.

For noncash property contributions, IRS Form 8283, Part IV, should be completed by the church, when requested by the donor, as an acknowledgment for any gift valued more than $500. If the church sells, exchanges, consumes, or otherwise disposes of (other than for consumption for a charitable purpose) a noncash property gift valued more than $500 within two years of receiving the gift, IRS Form 8282 must be filed by the church within 125 days after the date of disposition.

To help members comply with the IRS rules, the following notice should be placed in the church bulletin or newsletter during the last few weeks of each year:

> *Important notice:* To ensure the deductibility of your church contributions, please do not file your income tax return until you have received a written acknowledgment of your contributions from the church. You may lose a deduction for some contributions if you file your tax return before receiving a written acknowledgment of your contributions from the church.

When sending giving reports, many congregations can save money by sending them bulk mail, if the following rules are followed:

- Reports are computer-generated.

- Reports include a line that says, "This is not a bill or statement."

- Reports do *not* indicate any balance-due amount.

- The envelope contains a letter or note indicating the member's contributions are greatly appreciated.

- Each mailing contains a minimum of two hundred pieces.

***Small-church procedures.*** Some of the above procedures will seem unnecessary or impractical in a small church since all financial record keeping may be done by one person, usually the treasurer. However, if possible, the principles discussed above should be followed—to ensure a perception of system integrity. If one person does everything, then the trustees should oversee this activity, or a full financial review should be conducted each year. The trustees possibly could act as an audit committee and do the bank statement reconciliation each month. This procedure would protect the credibility of the person doing the financial work and give absolute and impeccable credibility to the system.

# Teller Offerings Report

Date: _____ Teller Names: _____

## CASH RECEIPTS (Envelope and Loose)

| DONOR OR SOURCE | DESIGNATED FOR | CURRENCY | COIN |
|---|---|---|---|
| Plate Offering | General Fund | _____ | _____ |
| _____ | _____ | _____ | _____ |
| _____ | _____ | _____ | _____ |
| _____ | _____ | _____ | _____ |
| Envelope Offering | General Fund | _____ | _____ |
| Envelope Offering | Capital Improvement | _____ | _____ |
| Envelope Offering | Benevolences | _____ | _____ |

**Total Currency and Coin:** _____ _____

**Number of checks:** _____          **Total all Checks:** _____

**TOTAL DEPOSIT:** _____

## OFFERING DISTRIBUTION RECORD
*(To be completed by Financial Secretary)*

| DESIGNATION | AMOUNT | DESIGNATION | AMOUNT |
|---|---|---|---|
| General Fund Giving | _____ | _____ | _____ |
| Capital Improvement | _____ | _____ | _____ |
| Benevolences | _____ | _____ | _____ |
| Memorials (List below)* | _____ | _____ | _____ |
| Outreach (List below)** | _____ | _____ | _____ |
| Weddings | _____ | _____ | _____ |
| Facility Use | _____ | _____ | _____ |

**Totals:** _____

\* _____

\*\* _____

# Teller Procedure

## Preparation:

1. **Teller #1:** Gather together the second service offering plates. Gather Teller Offerings Report, endorsement stamp, calculator, and deposit slips from teller drawer. Organize table.

2. **Teller #2:** Remove from the locked file-cabinet drawer the money bag containing receipts gathered during the week and the offering from the first service. Look in drawer for any special containers that may have dinner receipts, etc. Empty all containers onto table.

3. **Teller #1:** Gather all loose currency and coin and put it aside; then, gather any special receipts that may be for special purposes such as dinner receipts. **Teller #2:** Gather all checks and offering envelopes together.

## Assembly and Counting:

1. **Teller #1:** Count loose currency and coin from offering plates and record total on Teller Offerings Report. Count any receipts for special purposes, segregating the currency/coin from checks. Record the currency and coin on the Teller Offerings Report, under Cash Receipts showing source and designation, if known. Verify the checks have a notation on them showing what they were for and set them aside.

2. **Teller #2:** Open all offering envelopes, and make sure the envelope total equals the contents. Set cash aside and *record gift designation and envelope number on the check,* if not already there. (If there is no designation, the gift is recorded as a general fund gift.) Mark on envelope whether cash or check was given. Run adding-machine tapes on the envelope checks and amount recorded on envelopes and compare; do the same for the envelope cash. For checks given loose and not in envelopes, look up envelope number and record on check.

3. **Teller #1:** Take envelope cash and envelopes and record totals on the Teller Offerings Report as Cash Receipts, according to the designated category. All cash is then counted together and the total compared to the Teller Offerings Report Total Currency and Coin. The cash is then com-mingled and made ready for deposit, ensuring all bills are put together by denomination.

4. **Teller #2:** Sort all checks by envelope number or by name, alphabetically, as the financial secretary directs, to ease later posting to giving records. If ready, **Teller #1** can stamp the checks with the deposit endorsement stamp as they are sorted. An adding-machine tape is run on the checks by **Teller #2** while **Teller #1** begins copying all checks on the copy machine, keeping them in order. **Teller #1:** Read the individual check totals to **Teller #2** who verifies tape accuracy.

## Deposit:

1. **Teller #1:** Count the number of checks on the copies. **Teller #2:** Count the number of actual checks and compare total with count of Teller #1. **Teller #1:** Record the total number of checks on the report, the dollar value of all checks, and total the deposit.

2. **Teller #1:** Complete the deposit slip. **Teller #2:** Place the deposit (cash, checks, tape of checks, and deposit slip) into the bank bag. The bag is locked and the key retained in the office. One of the tellers takes the bag to the bank for deposit while the other teller assembles all supporting envelopes, notes, tapes, etc., and attaches them to the Teller Offerings Report. All equipment and the Teller Offerings Report is returned to the teller drawer.

# Contribution Statement

## *for the year ending December 31,* _____

Mr. & Mrs. Church Contributor
1234 Street Road
Anytown, USA

| Designated Fund | Date | This Year's Contributions | |
|---|---|---:|---|
| General Fund | 01/07/_____ | 350.00 | check# 2476 |
| | 02/04/_____ | 350.00 | check# 2498 |
| | 03/03/_____ | 350.00 | check# 2522 |
| | 04/07/_____ | 350.00 | check# 2540 |
| | 05/05/_____ | 350.00 | check# 2561 |
| | 06/09/_____ | 350.00 | check# 2585 |
| | 07/28/_____ | 350.00 | check# 2611 |
| | 08/05/_____ | 350.00 | check# 2627 |
| | 09/08/_____ | 350.00 | check# 2648 |
| | 10/06/_____ | 350.00 | check# 2671 |
| | 11/03/_____ | 350.00 | check# 2699 |
| | 12/08/_____ | 350.00 | check# 2731 |
| | | $4,200.00 | |
| Flower Gifts | 12/08/_____ | 20.00 | check# 2731 |
| | | $   20.00 | |
| Library Fund | 04/21/_____ | 14.95 | check#  513 |
| | | $   14.95 | |
| Special Outreach | 02/18/_____ | 50.00 | check# 2514 |
| | 12/02/_____ | 50.00 | check# 2718 |
| | 12/08/_____ | 200.00 | check# 2736 |
| | | $  300.00 | |
| Special Projects Fund | 11/10/_____ | 50.00 | check# 2708 |
| | | $   50.00 | |
| Non-Deductible | 12/08/_____ | 58.00 | check# 2707 |
| | | $   58.00 | |
| Tax Deductible | | $4,584.95 | |
| Non–Tax Deductible | | 58.00 | |
| Gifts in Kind | | 0.00 | |
| Other | | 0.00 | |
| Total Received | | $4,642.95 | |

NOTE: This is to certify that no goods or services were received by you in exchange for the contributions listed above other than intangible religious benefits.

## Disbursements by Program Plan (Budget)

Although an approved budget normally gives committee chairpersons authority to spend, spending must be controlled by the budget. Recall that the budget normally is created as part of the church planning process and represents a consensus of what the church intends to spend on plans and programs. Even though we would like to believe there would always be sufficient funds available to meet needs, this is not always the case. Thus, spending limits (maybe no more than 10 percent in one month) help to control cash flow, spreading spending out over the year. Of course, some spending, such as for quarterly Sunday school materials and seasonal utility needs, should be planned for on a seasonal basis. During seasonal slumps in giving, it also may be necessary to closely control spending through coordination and cooperation. Special programs outside the budget should be funded only after review and approval of how funds can be made available.

Communication between the treasurer and chairpersons of the various committees is essential. The treasurer (or finance committee) gives feedback and controls the entire process, carefully using human relations skills to ensure a positive atmosphere. Stewards of the funds should always look for positive ways to fund, not ways to restrict spending. Adjustments to the budget may be necessary during the year for:

- Unanticipated costs
- New or changed programs
- Departmental budget shifts among accounts
- Large needs, for which governing-body approval should be sought

As long as members understand the need for careful budgetary control and are committed, emotionally and intellectually, to the mission and ministries of the congregation, their understanding and support should come eagerly.

Buying of equipment and supplies can be done effectively and economically if this function is centralized in a purchasing agent. This procedure should save money, in that various persons will not be buying from expensive catalogs and paying high shipping charges. A purchase request form (sample on page 324) can facilitate and organize this process. Note that simple instructions about how to use the form can be printed on the back.

Check requests, with committee approval, are facilitated by a simple check request form. (Sample on page 324.) Using check requests for all disbursements except routine monthly billings ensures the elimination of oral requests and proper documentation of transactions. Such procedures better organize this important function and allow the treasurer to manage time and job more effectively.

The treasurer can limit check-writing to once a week in most churches. This limit is especially important when a computer accounting system processes and prints payments. At times checks will be required between regular preparation periods, and these can be processed manually through the computer; however, this should be discouraged. The purchasing agent, secretary, and possibly a pastor can be signatory to a small "petty cash" checking account for daily purchases and outreach emergencies, with the treasurer reimbursing it as necessary. (Standard petty cash forms are available in any stationery store.) One signature on checks is adequate if other control features are present—separation of duties and audit review. Otherwise, two signatures are desirable *when both signatories verify payment authenticity.* Note that many banks will honor checks with one signature, even though two signatures may be required; thus, it is the responsibility of the church to ensure that two signatures are on each check before distribution.

Bank statement reconciliation is an important and required control feature, especially if only one signature is required. Someone other than the person who prepared the checks should perform the reconciliation. An effective control would be to have an audit committee reconcile the statement.

All invoices and check requests should be marked "Paid," initialed, dated, and the check number recorded by the person signing the check.

The church secretary or possibly a financial clerk will be directly involved in the disbursement process. They will open mail, prepare bills for payment, mail checks, post records to the computer, and file paid invoices in an organized way. The secretary may also keep a petty cash fund for small office needs.

To ensure a smooth, organized payment of obligations, the treasurer will need to track cash flow and control when bills can be paid. However, treasurers should not hold unpaid bills without informing responsible people about the shortage of funds. *The treasurer is not responsible for money not coming in when expected, nor is it the treasurer's responsibility to determine which bills to pay if there are insufficient funds to pay them all.*

Most important, an organized disbursement system will lend credibility and confidence to the financial management system.

## Check Request Form

Requestor: _____ Date: _____

Committee: _____ Amount $: _____

Payable to: _____

Address: _____

City: _____ State: _____ Zip: _____

Payable for: _____

_____

When needed: _____ Mail check?  ❏ Yes  ❏ No

Signed: _____ Approved: _____

**FOR ACCOUNTING USE ONLY**

Check#: _____ Issued by: _____ Date: _____ Acct. #: _____

## Purchase Request Form

Requestor: _____ Date: _____

Committee: _____ Date required: _____

| ITEM ID# | DESCRIPTION | QUANTITY | UNIT COST | TOTAL |
|---|---|---|---|---|
| _____ | _____ | _____ | _____ | _____ |
| _____ | _____ | _____ | _____ | _____ |
| _____ | _____ | _____ | _____ | _____ |

Suggested Supplier: _____

_____

Signature: _____ Approval: _____

**FOR ACCOUNTING USE ONLY**

Check#: _____ Issued by: _____ Date: _____ Acct. #: _____

## Instructions for Using Check Request Form

This form will be used for each check request. Proper and consistent use of this form will document payment of bills or invoices as well as reimbursement to individuals.

### Procedure:

- Complete form and leave with secretary or in treasurer's drawer.

- Note clearly the purpose for which the check is requested.

- Obtain approval of committee chairperson if a major expenditure; i.e., more than 10% of the annual budget.

- Attach invoice or receipts.

Checks normally will be written once each week.

Oral requests for a check without the check request form will not be honored.

## Instructions for Using Purchase Request Form

This form should be used whenever something needs to be ordered from an outside supplier; e.g., office supplies, Sunday school supplies, etc.

### Procedure:

- Fill in as much detail about the item/s as possible.

- Note the related committee or budget area.

- Be sure to indicate when item is needed.

- Obtain required approvals for the purchase.

- Leave form with secretary or give to the purchasing agent.

## Financial Reports Must Communicate

The primary function of financial reports is to communicate results of financial operations. Each report must be tailored to meet a certain purpose for a certain audience. Businesses may have as many as four different reports: (1) for management; (2) for stockholders; (3) for banks; (4) for the IRS. Even though each will portray the same basic facts, each may differ in presentation.

Likewise, church reports should portray the facts, but they need to be presented in a way that will be clear and understandable to members. Reports for churches normally need only show "cash" transactions; seldom do they need to worry about accruing expenses. Nor do they necessarily need to show property asset values or depreciation, except for insurance purposes or possibly as a guide for replacement need. To fully communicate, a church should adapt any computer software's standard financial report to respond to the unique needs of its members.

The basic questions church members usually ask are:

1. Did we collect enough to cover expenses?

2. How are we doing in total?

3. Are we collecting our estimates of giving?

4. How much of my committee budget do I have left?

The sample reports which begin on page 329 were developed over a period of several years and are designed to answer the above questions. As you study them, note the following:

- The cover page is a report to the congregation, which also appears in the church newsletter once a month. (The information can be summarized more briefly for a newsletter which offers only limited space for such information.) Notice that an analysis appears in positive terms, adding perspective about the overall monetary position and encouragement about the financial health of the church.

- On page 330 is a summary of the cash balances—both checking and savings—for the general fund and "funds held for others"; that is, money held in the general fund which belongs to other funds. Also shown is the long-term debt, so that this is not easily forgotten. Otherwise, there is no attempt to show any other asset or current liability information since church members are not, on a regular basis, interested in other asset or liability detail.

- Two pages of line item income and expense detail are included next, showing current month and year-to-date financial results compared to budgeted amounts, with resulting dollar variances. A final column shows the amount of the annual budget remaining for the year. (Other financial statements might show percentage variances between year-to-date actual spending and budgeted amounts.) This is probably far more information than most governing body members care to get, but it does give them an opportunity to track and study data that interests them. For example, each committee is able to track its own expenditures. You should also note the emphasis put on segregating program expenses from administration and property. This division conveys that contributions are being used toward program needs first, and then for administration or property.

- The building fund, van fund, and memorial fund statements on pages 333–334 are more typical statements of fund receipts and expenditures. They effectively communicate information about special funds. Note the listing of specific memorial fund designations at the bottom of that fund statement, showing the restrictions put on the fund. Notice also that the building fund and memorial and special project funds have separate checking or savings accounts, while the van fund balance is held by the general fund. This demonstrates the two basic ways monies are held by churches and how fund integrity is maintained even though the actual money may be held by another fund.

- The perpetual fund statement on page 335 emphasizes restriction of fund uses and shows total balances of both the unrestricted and restricted portions of the fund. Note that this is just a dollar balance summary; the perpetual fund committee would receive a more detailed statement.

- Graphs offer a pictorial view which can communicate effectively. With computer capabilities, graphs of all types can be created to better communicate to the congregation the monetary message it needs to hear. (Be careful about what data is shown; it probably would not be well to have a pie chart showing the pastor's salary as the largest expense item in the budget.)

In summary, ***do whatever is necessary to communicate.*** Make a report that will (1) give information members need; and (2) give credibility to the system.

# CREATING

# A

# CHRISTIAN COMMUNITY

## *Financial Summary*

### *Month and Year Ending January 19—*

| Giving Through | Budget January | Actual January | Budget Year to Date | Actual Year to Date |
|---|---|---|---|---|
| General Fund | $ 21,777 | $ 21,825 | $153,887 | $149,120 |
| Building Fund | | 500 | | 50,017 |
| Memorial Fund | | 45 | | 410 |
| Special Outreach | | 210 | | 1,627 |
| Van Fund | | 520 | | 520 |
| Special Projects | | 150 | | 5,859 |
| Perpetual Fund | | | | 60,000 |
| Total Giving | | $ 23,250 | | $267,553 |
| Total General Income | $ 22,767 | $ 20,254 | $160,118 | $155,557 |
| General Expenses | 23,311 | 22,958 | 144,595 | 155,750 |
| Reserve for Future Need | 2,563 | | 15,283 | 12,720 |
| Net Gain or Loss (−) | | $ −2,704 | | $ −193 |

**General Fund** gifts were about what we expected this month, but year to date we are below what we expected at this time by about 3 percent. Extra expenses for insurance, property taxes, office equipment maintenance, and office supplies caused an abnormally high expense month. Thus, we were not able to set aside anything this month for future needs. (We previously have set aside a year-to-date total of $12,720 for future needs.) As our program expenses now increase with added commitments, please remember we need the continuing support of everyone to attain our very positive goals.

Gifts of $500 were added to funds now available for other capital improvement areas.

**Special Project** gifts were received for bell choir equipment, library, and the van.

Treasurer

# General Fund

Financial Statement for January 19—

## CHECKING ACCOUNT SUMMARY

| Account | Current Month | Cumulative Year to Date |
|---|---|---|
| 50 Balance, Start of Month and Year | $ 9,925.54 | $ 11,435.34 |
| Add Total General Fund Income | 20,253.83 | 155,557.27 |
| Less Total General Fund Expense | −22,957.94 | −155,749.69 |
| 201 Funds Due from Others | −539.06 | −441.16 |
| Funds Held for Others: | | |
| 402 Memorial and Special Projects | | |
| 403 Building Fund | | |
| 404 Outreach | | |
| 405 Perpetual Fund | | 2,924.57 |
| 406 Van Fund | 520.00 | 1,180.66 |
| 407 Facility Use Deposits | −75.00 | 1,375.00 |
| 408 Youth Groups | | 747.87 |
| 409 Insurance Claim | | 1,952.67 |
| 410 Advance Pledges | −625.00 | 1,000.00 |
| 411 Crosspaths Class | | 231.86 |
| 412 Centennial Committee | −2,263.79 | −1,355.76 |
| 413 Singles Payable | | 20.00 |
| 420 Federal Taxes | 960.88 | 960.88 |
| Total Funds Held for Others | $ −1,482.91 | $ 9,037.75 |
| 861 Funds for General Fund Future Needs | | 12,720.00 |
| 576 Balance of Prior Year Funds Held (1) | | −11,435.34 |
| 100 General Fund Savings (2) | −89.25 | −16,013.96 |
| Withdrawals—Deposits (−) | | |
| 50 Balance, End of Month and Year to Date | $ 5,110.21 | $ 5,110.21 |

## SAVINGS AND INVESTMENTS

| | Balance July 1, 19— | Change During Year | Present Balance |
|---|---|---|---|
| 100 General Fund Savings | $ 22,832.88 | $ 16,013.96 | $ 38,846.84 |
| 51 Petty Cash Checking | 350.00 | | 350.00 |

## LONG-TERM DEBT

| | Balance July 1, 19— | Change During Year | Present Balance |
|---|---|---|---|
| 430 Jordon Property Mortgage | $ 23,869.03 | $ −1,708.65 | $ 22,160.38 |

(1) Balance of General Fund owed to Other Funds at July 1, 19—
(2) General Fund savings interest included in total income.

# Statement of Income and Expense

(Actual Compared to Budget and Variance of Actual to Budget)
Month of January 19—

| Account | Annual Budget | Month | | | Year to Date | | | Budget Left |
|---|---|---|---|---|---|---|---|---|
| | | Actual | Budget | Var | Actual | Budget | Var | |
| **INCOME** | | | | | | | | |
| **Gen Fund Giving** | | | | | | | | |
| 600 Gen Fund Gifts | 273,235 | 21,825 | 21,777 | 48 | 149,120 | 153,887 | −4,767 | 124,115 |
| **Other Gen Fund Inc** | | | | | | | | |
| 611 Interest Income | 1,000 | 126 | 83 | 43 | 719 | 583 | 135 | 281 |
| 612 Other Income | 9,000 | 350 | 417 | −67 | 4,202 | 6,917 | −2,715 | 4,798 |
| Subtotal | 10,000 | 476 | 500 | −24 | 4,921 | 7,500 | −2,579 | 5,079 |
| **Rental Property** | | | | | | | | |
| 610 Rental Income | 11,700 | 975 | 975 | | 6,825 | 6,825 | | 4,875 |
| 604 Prop Mortgage Exp | −4,318 | −360 | −360 | | −2,519 | −2,519 | | −1,799 |
| 605 Rental Repair Exp | −3,500 | | −125 | 125 | −127 | −2,875 | 2,748 | −3,373 |
| 606 Tax on Rentals Exp | −2,700 | −2,663 | | −2,663 | −2,663 | −2,700 | 37 | −37 |
| 607 Insurance Exp | −612 | | | | | | | −612 |
| Subtotal | 570 | −2,048 | 490 | −2,538 | 1,517 | −1,269 | 2,785 | −947 |
| **Total Income** | **283,805** | **20,254** | **22,767** | **−2,513** | **155,557** | **160,118** | **−4,561** | **128,248** |
| **EXPENSES** | | | | | | | | |
| **Budgeted Outreach** | | | | | | | | |
| 860 Budgeted Outreach | 30,208 | 2,401 | 2,395 | −6 | 16,403 | 17,079 | 676 | 13,805 |
| 861 Reserve for Future | 29,329 | | 2,563 | 2,563 | 12,720 | 15,283 | 2,563 | 16,609 |
| Subtotal | 59,537 | 2,401 | 4,958 | 2,557 | 29,123 | 32,362 | 3,239 | 30,414 |
| **Worship & Pastoring** | | | | | | | | |
| 800 Minister Sal & Allow | 61,764 | 5,147 | 5,147 | | 36,029 | 36,029 | | 25,735 |
| 801 Min Hospitalization | 6,193 | 462 | 555 | 93 | 3,234 | 3,419 | 185 | 2,959 |
| 802 Min Pension/Annuity | 10,856 | 905 | 905 | | 6,333 | 6,333 | | 4,523 |
| 804 Assoc Sal & Housing | 19,162 | 2,018 | 2,467 | 449 | 6,378 | 6,827 | 449 | 12,784 |
| 805 Assoc Pension | 2,391 | 264 | 321 | 57 | 730 | 787 | 57 | 1,661 |
| 837 Assoc Reimb Exp | 1,660 | | 277 | 277 | | 277 | 277 | 1,660 |
| 810 Guest Ministers | 200 | | 17 | 17 | | 117 | 117 | 200 |
| 807 Music Dir Salary | 9,200 | 767 | 767 | | 5,367 | 5,367 | | 3,833 |
| 808 Organist Salary | 7,136 | 595 | 595 | | 4,163 | 4,163 | | 2,973 |
| 811 Guest Musicians | 250 | | 21 | 21 | 116 | 146 | 30 | 134 |
| 812 Spc Ed Ministers | 750 | 55 | 63 | 8 | 324 | 438 | 114 | 426 |
| 813 Spc Ed Music Dpt | 100 | 125 | 8 | −117 | 125 | 58 | −67 | −25 |
| 870 Worship Sup & Prog | 350 | 42 | 29 | −13 | 365 | 204 | −161 | −15 |
| 871 Communion Sup | 400 | 30 | 33 | 4 | 195 | 233 | 38 | 205 |
| 872 Order of Worship | 800 | | 200 | 200 | 426 | 600 | 174 | 374 |
| 874 Music Supplies | 1,050 | | 88 | 88 | 882 | 613 | −270 | 168 |
| 875 Robe Maintenance | 300 | | | | 23 | 150 | 127 | 277 |
| Subtotal | 122,562 | 10,409 | 11,491 | 1,082 | 64,690 | 65,759 | 1,069 | 57,872 |

| Account | Annual Budget | Month | | | Year to Date | | | Budget Left |
|---|---|---|---|---|---|---|---|---|
| | | Actual | Budget | Var | Actual | Budget | Var | |
| **Christian Education** | | | | | | | | |
| 830 SS Supplies | 2,750 | 138 | | −138 | 1,865 | 1,325 | −540 | 885 |
| 832 Library Books/Sup | 150 | −83 | 13 | 96 | −85 | 88 | 173 | 235 |
| 833 Youth Activities | 1,500 | 18 | 125 | 108 | 840 | 875 | 35 | 660 |
| 834 Camp Scholarships | 1,500 | 731 | | −731 | 731 | 500 | −231 | 769 |
| 835 Nursery | 4,800 | 435 | 400 | −35 | 2,891 | 2,800 | −91 | 1,909 |
| 836 Vac Church School | 1,000 | | | | 11 | 175 | 164 | 989 |
| Subtotal | 11,700 | 1,238 | 538 | −701 | 6,252 | 5,763 | −489 | 5,448 |
| **Christian Witness & Fellowship** | | | | | | | | |
| 840 Evangelism Pub | 200 | | 17 | 17 | 75 | 117 | 42 | 125 |
| 841 Eva Lit & Supplies | 300 | | 25 | 25 | | 175 | 175 | 300 |
| 850 New Member Sup | 500 | | 42 | 42 | 117 | 292 | 175 | 383 |
| 852 Flowers & Cards | 100 | −6 | 8 | 14 | 145 | 58 | −87 | −45 |
| 831 Lay Programs | 1,500 | 18 | 125 | 107 | 946 | 875 | −71 | 554 |
| 838 Lay Delegates | 535 | | | | 572 | 535 | −37 | −37 |
| 851 Kitchen Supplies | 300 | 56 | 25 | −31 | 263 | 175 | −88 | 37 |
| 853 Fellowship Programs | 100 | | 8 | 8 | −177 | 58 | 236 | 277 |
| 858 Misc Member Exp | 50 | | 4 | 4 | 55 | 29 | −26 | −5 |
| 854 Stewardship Material | 300 | 13 | 100 | 87 | 13 | 100 | 87 | 287 |
| 859 Wellway | 200 | | 17 | 17 | −69 | 117 | 186 | 269 |
| 880 Video Supplies | 400 | 31 | 33 | 3 | 32 | 233 | 202 | 369 |
| 881 Video Equip & Maint | 200 | 180 | 17 | −163 | 180 | 117 | −63 | 20 |
| 857 Drink Machine Inc | −500 | −106 | −42 | 65 | −230 | −292 | −62 | −270 |
| Subtotal | 4,185 | 185 | 379 | 194 | 1,921 | 2,589 | 668 | 2,264 |
| **Total Program Exp** | **197,984** | **14,233** | **17,365** | **3,133** | **101,985** | **106,472** | **4,487** | **95,999** |
| **Church Administration** | | | | | | | | |
| 806 Admin Assist Salary | 17,372 | 1,448 | 1,448 | | 10,134 | 10,134 | | 7,238 |
| 809 Fin Mgt Service | 1,800 | 150 | 150 | | 1,050 | 1,050 | | 750 |
| 803 Denominational Meet | 1,500 | | | | 1,513 | 1,500 | −13 | −13 |
| 814 Soc Sec Taxes | 4,124 | 342 | 344 | 1 | 2,403 | 2,406 | 3 | 1,721 |
| 815 Worker's Comp Ins | 2,900 | 692 | 725 | 33 | 1,967 | 2,175 | 208 | 933 |
| 820 Postage | 2,750 | 265 | 229 | −36 | 1,594 | 1,604 | 11 | 1,156 |
| 821 Office Supplies | 2,100 | 85 | 175 | 90 | 1,492 | 1,225 | −267 | 608 |
| 822 Newsletter | 750 | 602 | 63 | −539 | 1,130 | 438 | −692 | −380 |
| 823 Office Eq/Maint | 2,500 | 646 | 208 | −438 | 2,302 | 1,458 | −844 | 198 |
| 824 Office Misc | 100 | | 8 | 8 | 40 | 58 | 18 | 60 |
| Subtotal | 35,896 | 4,230 | 3,350 | −880 | 23,624 | 22,048 | −1,576 | 12,272 |
| **Church Property** | | | | | | | | |
| 816 Custodian Sal, etc | 16,000 | 1,283 | 1,333 | 50 | 8,983 | 9,333 | 350 | 7,017 |
| 890 Water & Garbage | 3,500 | 218 | 241 | 23 | 1,986 | 2,294 | 308 | 1,514 |
| 891 Gas (Heating) | 2,000 | 365 | 503 | 139 | 790 | 1,037 | 247 | 1,210 |
| 892 Electricity | 16,500 | 1,094 | 1,261 | 167 | 9,302 | 10,374 | 1,072 | 7,198 |
| 893 Telephone | 1,100 | 81 | 92 | 11 | 613 | 642 | 28 | 487 |
| 894 Custodial Supplies | 750 | 30 | 63 | 33 | 318 | 438 | 120 | 432 |
| 895 Bld Maint & Equip | 4,075 | 56 | 250 | 194 | 3,951 | 2,825 | −1,126 | 124 |
| 896 Yard & Grounds | 500 | | 42 | 42 | 91 | 292 | 200 | 409 |
| 897 Church Insurance | 5,500 | 1,369 | 1,375 | 6 | 4,106 | 4,125 | 19 | 1,394 |
| Subtotal | 49,925 | 4,495 | 5,159 | 664 | 30,140 | 31,358 | 1,218 | 19,785 |
| **Tot Admin & Prop** | **85,821** | **8,725** | **8,509** | **−216** | **53,764** | **53,406** | **−358** | **32,057** |
| **Tot Gen Fd Exp** | **283,805** | **22,958** | **25,874** | **2,916** | **155,750** | **159,878** | **4,129** | **128,055** |
| **Income, less Exp** | **0** | **−2,704** | **−3,107** | **403** | **−193** | **240** | **−432** | **193** |

## Building Fund

Financial Statement for January 19—

| Account | Current Month | Cumulative Year to Date |
|---|---|---|
| Balance, Start of Month & Year 60 Building Fund Savings | $ 5,388.85 | $ 0.00 |
| **Add** Receipts from: | | |
| Pledge Contributions | 500.25 | 50,016.65 |
| Memorial Contributions | | 25.00 |
| Interest Income | 7.94 | 7.94 |
| Total Receipts | 508.19 | 50,049.59 |
| **Subtract** Expenditures for: | | |
| Loan Principle | | 43,579.90 |
| Loan Interest | | 572.65 |
| Total Expenditures | 0.00 | 44,152.55 |
| Balance, End of Month & Year-to-date | $ 5,897.04 | $ 5,897.04 |

## Van Fund

Financial Statement for January 19—

| Account | Current Month | Cumulative Year to Date |
|---|---|---|
| Balance, Start of Month & Year | $ 660.66 | $ 647.86 |
| **Add** Receipts from: | | |
| Van Fund Giving | 520.00 | 520.00 |
| Memorial Contributions | | |
| Van Use Fees | | |
| Total Receipts | 520.00 | 520.00 |
| **Subtract** Expenditures for: | | |
| Maintenance and Supplies | | −74.60 |
| Installed Equipment | | |
| Insurance | | |
| Registration | | 61.80 |
| Total Expenditures | | 61.80 |
| Balance, End of Month & Year-to-date | $ 1,180.66 | $ 1,180.66 |

# Memorial and Special Project Funds

Financial Statement for January 19—

| Account | Current Month | Cumulative Year to Date |
|---|---|---|
| Balance, Start of Month & Year<br>120 Memorial & Special Project Savings | $ 7,701.20 | $ 6,498.26 |
| **Add** Receipts from: | | |
| Memorial Contributions | 45.00 | 385.00 |
| Special Project Gifts | 150.00 | 5,858.69 |
| Interest Income | 19.69 | 121.62 |
| Total Receipts | 214.69 | 6,365.31 |
| **Subtract** Expenditures for: | | |
| Use of Memorial Funds | 424.97 | 1,764.38 |
| Special Projects | 3,494.07 | 7,102.34 |
| Total Expenditures | 3,919.04 | 8,866.72 |
| Balance, End of Month & Year-to-date | $ 3,996.85 | $ 3,996.85 |

## LISTING OF FUND DESIGNATIONS

**Memorial Fund Designations:**

| | | |
|---|---|---|
| Frances Playground Equipment | $ | $ 570.00 |
| Undesignated | −385.28 | 1,443.10 |
| Total Memorial | | 2,013.10 |

**Special Projects Designations:**

| | | |
|---|---|---|
| Bell Choir Equipment | −2,315.82 | −48.49 |
| Bell Choir Stoles | | 162.00 |
| Playground | | 1,405.72 |
| Library | | 0.00 |
| Other Music Dept Equipment | | 0.00 |
| New Hymnals | | 174.62 |
| Nursery | −200.00 | 18.15 |
| Vacation Church School | | 0.00 |
| Associate Minister Equipment | −803.25 | 271.75 |
| Total Special Projects | | 1,983.75 |
| Balance of Funds Available | | $ 3,996.85 |

# Perpetual Fund

January 19—

## SAVINGS AND INVESTMENTS

| Account | Balance July 1, 19— | Change During Year | Present Balance |
|---|---|---|---|
| **Unrestricted Funds:** | | | |
| 70 Perpetual Fund Checking | $ 2,133.00 | $ −2,133.00 | $ 0.00 |
| 131 CD, Local Savings | 25,000.00 | 583.13 | 25,583.13 |
| 132 Denominational Foundation | 77,345.90 | 62,652.01 | 139,997.91 |
| 205 Perpetual Fund Receivable | 784.23 | 2,140.34 | 2,924.57 |
| Total Unrestricted Funds | $105,263.13 | $ 63,242.48 | $168,505.61 |
| **Restricted Funds:** | | | |
| 107 Denominational Foundation (Betty XYZ Music Scholarship) | 7,897.05 | −93.41 | 7,803.64 |
| 108 Denominational Foundation (Sue ABC VCS Support) | 3,561.49 | −42.54 | 3,518.95 |
| Total Restricted Funds | 11,458.54 | −135.95 | 11,322.59 |
| Total All Perpetual Funds | $116,721.67 | $ 63,106.53 | $179,828.20 |

## Payroll Records and Reports

A church is required to keep the same payroll records and to make the same federal and state reports as any employer, with some unique exceptions. It is critical that the treasurer learn the tax rules and follow them closely. At the time of publication of this manual, IRS Circular E was the basic rule book, supplemented by IRS Publication 15A, which includes special rules and tables for churches. Please check with the IRS for possible updates.

Payroll records, kept in an individual folder for each employee or self-employed staff member—including the pastor—should include the following:

- A copy of the employment agreement showing the date and terms of employment (the original would be kept in the employee personnel file). (Examples on pages 228 and 229. )

- IRS Form W-4, withholding allowance certificate for employees (other than clergy, unless they request voluntary withholding of federal income taxes).

- IRS Form W-9, identification number and certification for those who are self-employed.

- INS Form I-9, immigration and naturalization certification for each employee hired on or after June 1, 1987.

- Payroll-related documents which may be required by individual states.

- Time sheets, if appropriate.

- Record of vacation, compensatory time, and sick leave earned and taken. (Example on page 230.)

- Record of earnings and taxes. (Usually this will be a computer record or a standard form available in any stationery store.)

- Copy of annual IRS W-2 or 1099-MISC, taxable compensation.

- A copy of resignation statement showing date and terms.

Basic tax rules and reports are discussed beginning on page 337, including special rules for clergy. Every church should be aware of the absolute importance of following tax rules closely. The IRS issues penalties for not doing so and collects them, quite often no matter what the circumstances.

Remember that these policies and tax requirements apply to all employees, including clergy and part-time personnel, such as custodians, nursery attendants, and so forth. The only exception is if a person is truly self-employed; however, this likely will be rare. If a staff member insists on being considered self-employed, a formal determination of status can be requested using IRS Form SS-8.

Computer payroll programs are available and may be useful to churches with a number of employees. However, one must use conventional software cautiously; it may not allow for the unique reporting for clergy and employees who earn less than $100 in a year.

In summary, payroll records and reports must be maintained and completed professionally. The alternative is not acceptable, considering potential legal and monetary penalties.

*Please note that these guidelines, and any others that discuss rules and regulations that different states and the federal government may apply to churches, were current at the time of printing of this manual and are only guidelines. They do not substitute for a full knowledge of the rules and regulations in a given state, area, and time, which should be thoroughly researched by the reader.*

## Tax Considerations for Church and Clergy

Concern by the IRS about certain nonprofit "church-related" activities make it imperative that all tax considerations are understood and calculated properly. Pastors and lay leaders need to understand the basic tax issues concerning a pastor's personal obligations and those of the church, so they can assist lay persons responsible for church tax reporting. Since it is improbable that church leaders can "keep up" with all tax ramifications without assistance, the church should have readily available the tax-related publications of its denomination, usually issued each year. Additionally, the tax guides listed at the end of this section are excellent.

### Primary church considerations for payroll taxes.

Employee versus contract personnel:

- Normally, personnel paid for services to and supervised by the church are classified as employees of the church, including clergy. This includes part-time personnel; for example, nursery attendants, custodians, music personnel.

- Regularly paid staff who could be considered independent contractors might include: music personnel, if they make their living as professional musicians, contracting their services; and custodial and other personnel serving a wedding party. If in doubt, the church should seek a ruling from the IRS using Form SS-8.

- IRS Form W-9 should be used to request the federal identification number for a self-employed person, needed to report payments to contract personnel.

Social Security and Medicare taxes:

- Unless previously declared exempt, all church employees (except clergy) are subject to Social Security and Medicare deductions.

- One-half of these two taxes is deducted from the employee's wages, and the church pays the other half.

- The employee must make $100 or more in a tax year before Social Security or Medicare taxes are assessed or withheld by the church.

Federal tax withholding:

- The church withholds according to IRS Circular E and Publication 15A.

- All employees (except clergy) are subject to federal tax withholding, according to their declaration on IRS Form W-4.

- Clergy may voluntarily have federal taxes withheld.

Taxes withheld and Social Security and Medicare amounts must be paid to a national bank monthly, by the fifteenth of the month following the end of the tax period when there is more than a $500 monthly tax liability (and a liability less than $50,000 in a previous "lookback" of four tax quarters), or any time during a tax quarter when the tax liability reaches $500. An employer must deposit its tax liability under a "semiweekly rule" if the tax liability for the lookback period was more than $50,000 (average $4,167 monthly).

A quarterly report, Form 941, must be submitted to the IRS by the end of the month following the tax quarter.

Annually, by January 31, all employees (normally including clergy) must receive a W-2 if their annual income was greater than $100, and contractors must receive a 1099-MISC if their compensation was greater than $600.

Employee clergy receive a W-2 showing only total salary paid (usually includes salary, Social Security offset, allowances other than housing, and any unused reimbursable expenses advanced to the clergy) and any federal tax voluntarily withheld. *Housing allowances and Social Security and Medicare wages should not appear on the W-2, except that the value of the housing allowance can be included in an "other" block, and a notation "minister" could also be shown there.*

***Primary church considerations for property taxes.*** Church property must be used regularly for worship and related activities to qualify for exemption, if an exemption is authorized by the state. Some tax districts allow only portions of a church's land to be exempt, depending on their definition of what portion of the property is needed to support the church's worship activities. "Dissolution" statements usually are required in the church constitution; that is, will the property be given to the state or another nonprofit entity if the church should cease to exist?

***Primary church considerations for state sales taxes.*** A congregation or entity within that congregation may be exempt from paying state sales taxes on purchases if allowed by the state, and if the congregation has a federal employee identification number and is listed in good standing in the directory of the denomination. This exemption also applies at hotels, but only for the state portion of the room tax. The church is *not* exempt from locally imposed taxes unless given an exemption by the local authority. (One should verify applicable state and local laws.)

***Primary clergy tax considerations for compensation.*** Even though clergy are self-employed for Social Security reasons, it is best they be considered an employee of the church if provided fringe benefits (such as medical or life insurance premiums). An accounting for reimbursable expenses should be made to the church, and the pastor should be reimbursed only for what is actually spent (this avoids employee expenses being considered as allowances and subject to tax).

The individual parts of a clergy compensation package should be clearly identified—salary, allowances, reimbursable expenses, and expenses paid directly by the church.

- The annual church budget should clearly identify the individual parts of the compensation package. The housing allowance, especially, must be designated as such before the start of a tax year. This designation must appear in official governing body records. (See page 340 for an example.)

- If reimbursable expenses (auto and professional expenses) are paid by the church, it is best for the church to adopt an "accountable reimbursement plan." The church governing body must pass an appropriate resolution adopting this plan which:

  a. Reimburses only those business expenses that an employee substantiates as to the date, amount, and business nature of each expense.

b. Requires any "excess reimbursements" to be returned to the employer.

c. Requires an accounting be made within a reasonable amount of time (sixty days) and done before reimbursement.

- If reimbursable expenses are paid and the church does not require an accounting of how they were used, then these are considered allowances, are fully taxable, and must be included on the pastor's Form W-2 as salary.

- Any Social Security offset allowance (an amount given the pastor to offset a portion of the cost of self-employed Social Security and Medicare taxes) must be reported as salary.

- Expenses paid directly by the church (e.g., pension, annuities, and hospitalization) are not included as salary or allowances, and no annual accounting is required.

Church-owned vehicles provided to clergy for church-related use carry special tax considerations.

- The simplest procedure is for the church to require the clergy to use the vehicle for official church business only.

- If commuting between home and church is required, this is considered to be personal use of a car, and some value of that commute must be included on the clergy W-2 as salary. The total can be an actual accounting of distance and value, or it can be a set amount for each commute, if the clergy person is required to commute in the church-owned vehicle for "noncompensatory" reasons; for example, security.

*Note: This discussion should not be considered to be a complete statement of all tax considerations. Detailed study of this area is the responsibility of the parties making a tax report, and although accuracy of the above has been sought, no responsibility will be accepted for any unintentional misstatement or misrepresentation.*

Two excellent tax guides for clergy, each published annually, are:

Hammar, Richard R. *Church Law & Tax Report: Church and Clergy Tax Guide.* Matthews, N.C.: Christian Ministry Resources.

Touche Ross & Co. *Abingdon Clergy Income Tax Guide.* Nashville: Abingdon Press.

## Housing Allowance Designation for Pastors: An Example

The IRS requires that a governing body designate pastor housing allowances on a calendar-year basis, to be made *before* the beginning of the year. The sample resolution below should satisfy this requirement for a calendar year—adjustable whenever required due to any change during the year. A new resolution is required annually in December and before any change in allowance is made.

The allowance figures include budgeted amounts for housing, utilities, and household expenses, if appropriate, since the total of these expenses is considered the housing allowance, according to the IRS. The pastors will need to provide the governing body a reasonable estimate of the expenses they will incur, stating that these amounts are not greater than the fair rental value of their homes, furnishings, utilities, and household expenses.

## Governing Body Resolution

I move the following resolution be accepted:

"Whereas, section 107 of the Internal Revenue Code permits ministers of the gospel to exclude from gross income a church-designated allowance paid to them as part of their compensation, to the extent that the *lesser* amount of the following is allowed to be excluded from a minister's reporting of gross income:

1. The amount of actual expenses in owning or renting a home, or

2. The amount of fair rental value of the home, furnishings, and utilities, or

3. The amount of the church-designated housing allowance.

"That the Board of the _____ Church of [city and state] affirms the following 'nonaccountable' ministerial housing and utility allowances for calendar year _____ for the following pastors who are compensated by the church exclusively for services as ministers of the gospel and for whom the church does not provide a parsonage:

[Pastor's Name]—Annual allowance of $ _____, paid _____.

[Pastor's Name]—Annual allowance of $ _____, paid _____.

"It is further resolved that the housing allowances cited above shall apply to calendar year _____ and all future years unless otherwise provided."

## Basic Administrative Record Keeping

It is imperative that administrative records maintained by a church, including important financial records, be kept in an organized, safe environment. Although we have addressed this subject briefly in several other places, here we bring these thoughts together and review some basic guidelines.

While the rule, "If it isn't written down, it didn't happen" can prove relevant many times, a rule just as relevant may be, "If you can't find it, it doesn't matter if it is written down." Church office files must be organized and user-friendly! A file structure plan and file retention plan should be two of the most important documents on file.

A file structure plan might include:

- A listing of file categories

- Location information about each file category and special storage items

- Maintenance responsibility for each category and special storage items

- Instructions for safekeeping of confidential files, and access authorization

A file retention plan is required to ensure legal and practical retention requirements are met. Below are suggested retention periods for most documents in a church. When developing your own record retention policy, think about where files will be kept, how secure they will be, and the conditions under which files will need to be stored (e.g., heat and dampness can be destructive). If computers store the bulk of your records, special access and backup procedures need to be documented and passwords used to protect their integrity.

Some of the reasons to keep files and records include legal requirements, potential relevance in future litigation, and special needs of the organization, as well as historic importance. Should there be threatened litigation or an investigation on a certain subject, no file or document relating to that matter should be destroyed.

Remember that a number of documents should be retained permanently in a safe-deposit box; for example, articles of incorporation, bylaws, mortgages and contracts and other related documents, possibly permanent accounting and contribution records, which can be stored on computer disk or tape, and other backup computer files.

An especially important financial record is one that lists all the church bank accounts, numbers, location, function, and the authorized signatures for each account.

In short, have file structure and retention plans, and then maintain the files according to the plan. The true test will come several years later when someone asks to see a particular document they know exists, and it can be found with relative ease.

## Church Record Retention

| Document | How Long to Keep (Minimum) |
| --- | --- |
| Articles of incorporation, amendments, bylaws | Permanently |
| Certificate of incorporation and corporate records | Permanently |
| Tax returns | Permanently |
| Tax return work sheets and related backup documents | 7 years |

| | |
|---|---|
| W-2 or 1099 forms and related payroll records | 7 years |
| Minutes of board and subcommittees | Permanently |
| Annual church and corporate reports | Permanently |
| Membership, property, and accounting records and budgets | Permanently |
| Mortgages | Permanently |
| Contracts and leases in effect | Permanently |
| Insurance policies (including expired policies) | Permanently |
| Insurance letters and correspondence | Permanently |
| Annual financial statements and audit reports | Permanently |
| List of bank accounts, numbers, location, and authorized signatures | Permanently |
| Bank statements and reconciliations | 7 years |
| Canceled checks for standard transactions | 4 years |
| Invoices from vendors | 3 years |
| Housing allowance designations | 7 years |
| Business correspondence | 3 years |
| Member giving records and contribution receipts | 7 years |
| Offering envelopes and/or check copies | 3 years |
| Employment applications (for current employees) | Permanently |
| Employee personnel records and contracts (after termination) | 3 years |

Some of the suggested retention periods are for legal reasons, while others are based on practical considerations.

The suggested retention time for tax returns, governmental reports affecting tax liability, and backup records applies because the IRS calls for a six-year statute of limitations. The IRS has three years from the date of when the income tax return is filed to question or audit the return. If the IRS can prove an omission of at least 25 percent of income, the time period doubles to six years. The seven-year period for retention gives a one-year cushion. While most churches are not required to file tax returns, these periods apply to any entity that must file, as well as to individual filers who may need help from the church to support their filings.

The retention of insurance policies and related documents is important since lawsuits reaching back many years are sometimes brought. In such instances, it is important to determine the policy in effect at the time a claim arose. Computer records pose unique concerns. As hardware and software change, some older records will not be able to be read; thus, it may be necessary to have hard copy of important documents that can be scanned into any new hardware and software.

## Audit—More Than a Financial Review

Even assuming proper record keeping and retention, church financial management procedures, accounts, and records should be audited or formally reviewed periodically, preferably annually. A complete review should include financial management procedures and internal controls as well as a financial review of account balances and records. For important loan applications or other significant financial reasons, outside auditors may need to be engaged to perform a full audit in accordance with generally accepted auditing standards, in which account balances are independently reviewed and confirmed. However, these audits are expensive. The church will want to weigh the risk it is taking by not undergoing the audit against the benefit it gains from the investment.

A suitable alternative to a full audit of church accounts and records may be a review by a Certified Internal Auditor. Although internal auditors do not issue an audit opinion about the formal adequacy of accounting records, in accordance with generally accepted auditing standards of the American Institute of Certified Public Accountants, they are formally certified and can perform a valuable review of the internal control system and comment on procedures that need to be strengthened or changed, and on accounts which may be out of balance. Internal auditors are professionally trained and certified to perform this broader review and can be found working for various firms or governmental agencies as the internal eyes and ears of management. The Institute of Internal Auditors can be contacted for a member reference.

Another realistic alternative is a review by an internal church audit committee using a well-prepared guide. This procedure allows a nonaudit professional to review the financial system and internal controls to test records prepared during the year, and to confirm bank balances through an independent bank statement reconciliation.

In the absence of an annual review, a church should at least review its internal controls periodically and have an audit committee responsible for reconciling the bank statement. This independence is important to ensure the integrity of the financial system. If done properly, real or perceived problems should not surface.

Beginning on page 372 is a "Guide to Church Financial Management (A Checklist)," prepared by a Certified Internal Auditor with a number of years of experience in church financial management. This guide is designed for use by professionals and nonprofessionals to review the completeness of a church financial management system. It is an excellent checklist for laity and includes audit review tests at the end.

## Property Management

### Maintenance of Property

The proper management of church property will consume a significant amount of the time and resources of every church. In addition to facility planning and maintenance organization and staffing, there are several important review procedures which should be followed. If church property is to be properly maintained:

- Responsibilities for maintenance, current and preventive, must be clear.

- Regular maintenance schedules must be established and kept.

- Periodic inspection of facilities must be completed.

- Replacement planning and programs must be active.

- Property and insurance inventory records need to be complete.

Who takes care of this important area? *"When everyone is in charge, no one is in charge."* Most churches have specific groups responsible for property maintenance, such as the trustees or a property committee. The ultimate responsibility will rest with these groups, and they must be proactive in their approach. Their part of the total mission of the church must be understood and specific action plans prepared. They must be fully supported by members and money as well as recognized periodically for their contribution to the life of the church. An active preventive maintenance program and involvement of church members in "work days" or a "weekly maintenance fellowship" of volunteers will help to cement the understanding of the congregation about this important area.

If the church has a custodian, this individual usually becomes the primary contact point for all custodial duties and minor repairs. The work of the custodian must be organized by schedules and checklists. The custodian must know when to inspect facilities and equipment and how to correct concerns. This individual must also be familiar with equipment and how it works, as well as with tools and how to use and store them. Congregation members must be encouraged to respect the work schedule of the custodian and refrain from requesting special work that has not been scheduled.

In a *small church,* volunteers will undoubtedly be directly involved in the day-to-day custodial duties. In this context it is even more important to stress schedules, who is in charge, when things will be done, and what funds are or are not available for needed maintenance. A schedule of maintenance needs is developed, posted, and items checked off as they are completed. Often the entire congregation is involved in work projects and is fully supportive of the efforts.

Because regular inspection to recognize problems and correct them is so important in any church, someone needs to ensure that maintenance has been done well, that items needing repair have been identified, that checklists are current and posted, and that there is follow-up on maintenance concerns.

Who inspects and follows up? In larger churches, a business manager may fill this need. Or, trustees or a property committee member may be responsible. In most churches, the custodian and church leaders who feel responsible may perform these reviews.

Once a need is identified the problem must be communicated to someone who is responsible for either fixing it or scheduling it to be done. One needs to be specific about who, how, and when! A simple, standard form can be used to record the problem, solution, when fixed, and a date for follow-up.

When major repairs are necessary, the trustees or property committee must take the lead, whether in a large or small church. There should always be a thorough assessment of the need to repair or replace.

Volunteers, in a church of any size, should be encouraged but held accountable to the trustees or property committee. Rules for equipment use should be established and posted. Volunteers should be encouraged to learn how to use equipment, activate utilities, clean up their areas, and so forth. They must know who can provide help and training. If no custodian is on duty, every volunteer must assume they are individually responsible for maintenance and security.

The church constantly needs to remind members to respect the need for good property use and maintenance, and to "turn off the lights and lock up." Repair needs should be monitored and communicated positively to trustees or the property committee for action. Members need to know where a "complaint sheet" is posted.

The pastor can't do it all. In fact, it probably is best for pastors *not* to get themselves involved in closing up on Sunday after services, opening up early, turning on the heat or air conditioning, checking the public address system, and so forth. Once this starts, everyone assumes the pastor will do it. The more the pastor does, the more the pastor will be expected to do, resulting in less time for primary pastoral duties. With proper leadership, responsible volunteers will take charge and take pride in the operation and upkeep of facilities and equipment.

This important area *needs to be organized.* Anticipate and prepare for major problems and replacement. Encourage participation by all, but have responsibility clearly set. The items which follow in this property management section of the manual will assist you with this process.

## Standards, Guidelines, and Checklists

Written standards and guidelines describing jobs, maintenance schedules, and disaster preparedness are invaluable, although in many churches these may be woefully lacking. Proper use of church property and a consideration for the safety of members requires a certain amount of paperwork—and some active organization.

A bulletin board might be provided in the custodial area for posting lists and schedules. It can also post names and telephone numbers of people to contact in case of problems. Specific guidelines might include:

- Inspection checklists
- Cleaning schedules (especially seasonal)
- Painting schedules
- Repair procedures
- Procedure to follow when problems arise

Custodial checklists include such things as what needs to be cleaned and when; what tools need to be used; and items to observe and check while cleaning. Detailed operating instructions for major equipment need to be posted near the equipment. Schedules for use of facilities need to be posted in a common area.

Guidelines for volunteer help should be available at the place where tools and equipment are kept and should include:

- Procedures for caring for certain space
- Clear instructions for the proper tools to use for a given job
- Times or schedules for doing certain tasks
- Checklists for inspections
- Instructions for operating tools and equipment

Guidelines for the general membership might be posted in individual rooms and include:

- What to do when entering the property, such as how to turn on the air conditioning, how to turn on the amplification system, and so forth

- What to do to secure the property when leaving, such as what doors to check, windows to close, electrical items to turn off, and so forth

- Procedures to follow in case of disasters

It is always best to *overuse checklists and procedural statements*. Equipment and facilities will be better used, maintained, and secured, and people kept safe.

## Contingency Plans for Potential Disasters

Procedures and guidelines for handling potential disasters could be some of the most important documents ever prepared by a church.[2] When a church opens its doors to the public, it assumes the legal, ethical, and moral responsibility for the safety and physical well-being of those who assemble. Churches and their schools, recreational facilities, day-care centers, and various shelters and camps are prime targets for lawsuits, especially if there is no evidence of carefully prepared up-to-date contingency plans.

Depending on local need, contingency plans should exist for fire-related disasters; bomb threats; natural disasters such as severe freezing weather, earthquakes, flooding, hurricanes, and tornadoes; power failures and interruption in telephone and utility services; and robbery. After plans are developed, they should be rehearsed, at least by the persons primarily involved in crowd control and facility maintenance and security.

The following information provides an awareness of what may be required. By working closely with the local fire and police departments, the utility companies, your insurance agent, and the local disaster preparedness agency, you can develop unique disaster plans and procedures which fit your church or church-related activity. All of these agencies will be more than willing to help as they recognize a "customer" wants to minimize the impact of potential disasters.

### FIRE-RELATED DISASTERS

At a minimum, the fire disaster plan must specify available exits, which need to be adequately marked with lighted signs, and ensure that escape route maps are posted in conspicuous places. The plan should specify leadership responsibility and functions. Adequate fire extinguishers need to be placed according to the local fire code, and other fire suppression equipment made available in high-risk areas. The church should consult the fire and police departments for other important fire disaster requirements, as well as reference material available from the National Fire Protection Association.[3] The loss prevention checklist beginning on page 351 also includes items related to fire that need to be checked annually.

### BOMB THREAT

The evacuation plan can be the same as for a fire, but specific procedures must be included in the bomb-threat contingency plan about who conveys the threat to the assembled group and how. For example, this responsibility might be entrusted to the head usher at Sunday worship. Everyone should be encouraged to remain calm and not panic, and the person in charge must do everything possible to ensure this calm. If a bomb threat comes in, one should get as much information as possible from the caller. The evacuation should include room-by-room checks for personnel who may have been left behind. Give special consideration and assistance to physically challenged persons and small children. Secure all monies. The senior person present should be the last person to leave the building.

## NATURAL DISASTERS

The contingency plan must include applicable procedures and assigned responsibilities for each of the following scenarios:

- *Severe freezing weather:*

    a. Keep a small amount of water running from the faucets of all sinks to prevent the pipes from freezing.

    b. Keep sidewalks clear and free of ice.

    c. Use ice-melting compounds if necessary.

- *Earthquakes:*

    a. Turn off open-flame gas appliances.

    b. Keep everyone away from windows and appliances or supplies which may slide or topple over.

    c. Direct people to a doorway or under a table.

    d. If outside, move to an open area.

    e. Keep everyone away from buildings, walls, power lines, and power poles.

    f. After a severe earthquake, evacuate the building, check for fires and structural damage. Shut off utility supplies.

- *Flooding:*

    a. When a flood warning is received, prepare the facility to lessen the possible damage.

    b. Store drinking water in closed sanitized containers normally used for food storage.

    c. Move everything off of the floor and low shelves.

    d. Secure all monies in the safe.

    e. Shut off the gas and electricity at the mains. If expected that electricity will be out for more than eight hours, move all perishables to another location.

    f. Do not reenter a flooded building until authorities have made a structural assessment.

- *Hurricanes:*

    a. Place masking tape on the windows from corner to corner, making an "X."

    b. Draw drapes or lower and close blinds to protect against flying glass.

    c. Secure anything on the roof that may be loose.

    d. Secure dumpster doors with rope.

    e. Put trash containers and all moveable furniture, toys, and so forth indoors.

f.  Keep everyone indoors.

g.  Follow all instructions issued by the local authorities.

- *Tornadoes:*

a.  Draw drapes or lower and close blinds to protect against flying glass.

b.  Have a radio available.

c.  Keep everyone away from outside walls and windows.

d.  Assume a kneeling position behind counters or under tables. Cover head and face with arms to protect yourself from flying glass or debris.

e.  After the tornado has passed, inspect the facility for damage.

f.  Follow all instructions issued by the local authorities.

## POWER FAILURES AND UTILITY INTERRUPTION

The contingency plans must address each of the following points, as they apply to the local church or church-related activity:

- *Power failure:*

a.  Turn off gas appliances.

b.  Turn off equipment that uses a lot of power, such as exhaust hoods, warming lights, fryers, grills, computers, air conditioners, and so forth.

c.  If your facility is equipped with a generator, it should be started.

d.  When power is restored, turn one piece of equipment on at a time to prevent damage from a power surge.

e.  Keep refrigerators and freezers closed to maintain a safe food temperature for a longer period of time.

f.  If dry ice is used, store it in an open, nonmetal container. Wear gloves or oven mitts and avoid skin contact. Carefully dispose of dry ice outside, under running water, where it will evaporate more quickly.

- *Telephone service interruption:*

a.  Find out if the outage is in your building or throughout the area. If service is available nearby, report the problem and arrange to use a nearby telephone or mobile phone in case of an emergency.

b.  Be sure that someone is available to go for help if no telephone service is available.

- *Interruption in water service:*

a.  Do not allow use of the rest rooms as use can pose a serious health risk.

b.  If warned of an interruption in water service, fill as many clean containers as possible with water, wash all dirty dishes, and turn off the ice machine at the breaker panel to prevent damage.

- *Gas leak:*

  a. If there is a gas smell, check pilots and related valves.

  b. If the smell persists, shut off the gas at the main and extinguish all open flames.

### ROBBERY

A robbery can be an extremely tense and dangerous time. Procedures should dictate:

- *During a robbery:*

  a. Stay calm.

  b. Be cooperative. Answer any questions promptly, but do not volunteer information. Follow the perpetrator's directions.

  c. Observe and mentally note any physical characteristics, but do not be obvious about it.

  d. If able, notice the direction the perpetrator takes when leaving. If possible, try to see the type and color of the vehicle and the license number.

- *Behavior to avoid:*

  a. *Never* try to be a hero.

  b. Do not make sudden moves that may startle the perpetrator.

  c. Try not to panic.

  d. Avoid staring at the perpetrator, which may cause them to be nervous or hostile.

- *Actions to take after a robbery:*

  a. Be ready to provide police with location, address, number of perpetrators involved, vehicle description, and so forth.

  b. Avoid discussing incident until authorities arrive, so that all happenings are not distorted.

  c. Do not allow anyone to enter the area, so physical evidence is undisturbed.

- *When the authorities arrive:*

  a. Cooperate fully. Be certain when answering questions to give only the facts.

  b. If perpetrators are still present when authorities arrive, remain calm. Continue to cooperate with perpetrators and stay away from windows. Avoid calling attention to the fact that the authorities have arrived. *Use good judgment.*

## *Effective and Economical Insurance*

Insurance on church property and services is essential, considering the liability risks for church employees and in unforeseen accidents, as well as for protection against losses from fire, theft, and natural disasters.

Although it needs to be comprehensive, church insurance can also be economical. The first step is to define the risks, and then manage them for better, more economical coverage. Obviously, the goal of any church is survival in the face of a catastrophic loss. But after basic survival has been addressed, the church will want to lessen accidental loss through a risk assessment program which in turn may lower insurance costs.

When dealing with loss exposure, a church should first look for ways to reduce or eliminate risk. For example, are there playground items that can be replaced with safer more modern equipment? Are there sprinkler systems, self-closing doors, handrails, and so forth, all of which enhance safety? Is there a regular program of maintenance inspection to ensure an optimum housekeeping program—and is something done about the problems found? The loss prevention checklist beginning on page 351 offers a systematic way of identifying exposure and the chance for loss through self-inspection. This review should be performed at least annually, with specific responsibility for the review clearly established.

A church intentionally may wish to accept some of the risk itself. It may be that many churches could take on far more risk than they do since most losses are partial losses. A higher deductible is an effective and normally economical way of accepting greater risk through some self-insurance. A church also should be clear on the value of its property, keeping some sort of inventory of property and furnishings. The form on pages 356–362 is one way to keep inventory, and many computers now come equipped with inventory programs suitable for a church. Videotaping the church and its contents is another excellent way of documentation. Don't forget to store the inventory and video in a safe place, preferably a safe-deposit box.

A church can also watch for opportunities to transfer some of its risk by requiring organizations using the church (e.g., a day-care program) to have their own insurance coverage.

The primary point of any active risk assessment program is that it allows for an organized approach to ascertaining what insurance coverage is needed, which then allows for purchasing only what is needed. Every church will differ; however, a risk assessment program will aid in identifying significant needs and differences.

When ready to purchase insurance, a church will want to carefully select an agent and company. One should examine whether the agency is knowledgeable about a church's unique needs and whether it insures a number of churches. Is the agency willing to cover all phases of risk, such as workers' compensation, pastor's professional liability, director's and officers' liability, and sexual abuse liability? Sometimes a church will find insurance agencies willing to write basic fire, theft, and liability coverage, but not interested or able to offer the unique coverages needed. Of course, claims responsiveness and billing procedures also may be important factors to consider.

The best coverage may be through group plans especially prepared for churches and often available through a church's denominational association. Substantial savings and greater coverage is often possible. These associations specialize in church coverage and may be able to isolate unique risks.

In summary, every church should review its risk, establish responsibility for risk assessment, use a loss prevention checklist, choose an insurance program and agent carefully, keep an up-to-date inventory of property, and carry enough insurance to cover acceptable risk at an optimum price.

# Loss Prevention Checklist

Every church must identify possible areas of exposure where losses can be minimized.[4] This self-inspection and review must be conducted as indicated, or at least annually for those items not specified. Each inspection must be fully documented. For each item in compliance, mark *Y for Yes* on the blank provided. For each item not in compliance, mark *N for No.* Bring that item into compliance by a specified date and document it. If an item does not apply, mark *N/A.*

## A. FIRE LOSSES

### General Prevention:

_____ 1. Does the local fire department inspect the church at least annually?

_____ 2. Has the insurance carrier inspected the facilities?

_____ 3. Is trash safely handled and accumulation not allowed?

_____ 4. Have all combustible decorations in assembly space been flameproofed?

_____ 5. Have all draperies and curtains been inspected, and are they flame-resistant?

_____ 6. Are spaces beneath stairs, etc., free from accumulation of combustible material?

_____ 7. Are metal cabinets used to store flammable liquids and floor polishing supplies?

_____ 8. Are all passageways well-lighted and kept free of obstructions?

_____ 9. Have Type ABC fire extinguishers been provided where not more than 75 feet of travel is required to reach the nearest unit?

_____ 10. Are fire extinguisher locations well marked and easily accessible?

_____ 11. Have fire extinguishers been inspected/recharged within the past year?

_____ 12. Is the date of inspection or recharge shown on the tag attached to each unit?

_____ 13. Is the building, particularly the steeples, spires, and towers, properly equipped with a certified system of lightning rod protection and inspected annually?

_____ 14. Where automatic sprinklers or standpipe and hose are installed, have these been thoroughly inspected within the past year and found to be operating?

_____ 15. Are there automatic fire detection devices or other means for warning of fire when buildings are unoccupied?

_____ 16. When candles are used, are they always used safely?

_____ 17. Are only approved, artificial, noncombustible Christmas trees used inside buildings?

_____ 18. Are Christmas lighting sets inspected prior to use, and defective sets discarded?

_____ 19. Are all Christmas tree lights turned off in unoccupied areas?

_____ 20. Are all doors kept closed when not being used, to impede the spread of fire?

_____ 21. Has a proactive liaison been established with the local fire department?

_____ 22. Is there adequate water (quantity, location, pressure) to fight a fire?

_____ 23. Are church grounds and landscaping maintained in a way that will minimize fire hazards associated with forest, brush, and grass?

### Electrical and Lighting Equipment:

_____ 24. If any fuses or circuit breakers require frequent replacement or resetting, have these circuits been checked by a competent electrician for overloading?

_____ 25. Are alterations of electrical installations made only by a qualified electrician?

_____ 26. Does all electric wiring installed within or in connection with organs, PA, or special lighting systems comply with appropriate government/industry codes?

_____ 27. Are all fixtures and outlets in safe condition?

_____ 28. Are extension cords used only when needed, and never in place of permanent wiring or run across aisles or under rugs?

_____ 29. Has the electrical system been inspected by a competent electrical contractor in the past year?

_____ 30. Is a smoke detection system wired to the building electrical system?

_____ 31. Are all electrical panels immediately accessible; i.e., not blocked/locked/latched?

_____ 32. Is there a master listing of all electrical panels by location and function?

_____ 33. Are all breakers or fuses properly labeled?

### Heating Equipment:

_____ 34. Is all heating equipment, including chimneys, flue connectors, hot air ducts, and building heating appliances, in good serviceable condition, well maintained, and inspected/serviced by a licensed service technician within the past year?

_____ 35. Is all heating equipment properly insulated and separated from all combustible material, and the furnace enclosed in a separate fire-resistive room?

_____ 36. Is there a self-closing fire door at the entrance to the furnace room?

_____ 37. Do boilers have pressure relief valves, water-level gauges, and low-water alarms?

_____ 38. Are all gas heating systems inspected regularly for leaks and cracks?

_____ 39. Are automatic limit controls provided on all heating equipment?

_____ 40. Do oil burners have a remote control switch?

_____ 41. Are exposed oil or gas lines protected from damage?

_____ 42. Is an approved type of fire extinguisher provided in the furnace room?

_____ 43. Has the custodian been fully trained on using heating and A/C equipment?

### Kitchen:

_____ 44. Are kitchen range ventilating hoods, filters, and ducts cleaned at least quarterly?

_____ 45. Is the kitchen kept free of all grease or cooking oil accumulation?

_____ 46. Is the range installed away from combustible material and is the floor protected?

_____ 47. Is a proper fire extinguisher (Type ABC) provided and in good working order?

_____ 48. Is the commercial refrigeration equipment properly maintained?

### B. CRIME

_____ 1. Is there nighttime surveillance of property by police or private security services?

_____ 2. If there have been any burglary losses, has an alarm system been considered?

_____ 3. Is exterior lighting adequate to deter vandalism and provide for personal safety?

_____ 4. Are adequate locking devices provided for doors and windows?

_____ 5. Has the number of door keys been controlled and key holders identified?

_____ 6. Are entrances monitored during business hours?

_____ 7. Is there a procedure to assure buildings are locked and secured when unoccupied?

_____ 8. Is little or no cash kept on the premises overnight?

_____ 9. Are double-cylinder, deadbolt locks installed on office doors to protect equipment?

_____ 10. Has office equipment been attached to a desk or table when possible?

_____ 11. Is there a protective covering over stained glass windows?

### C. WIND AND HAIL

_____ 1. Is the church roof inspected at least annually for loose shingles?

_____ 2. Is the church siding inspected at least annually to be sure it is secured properly?

_____ 3. Are small storage buildings secured properly?

_____ 4. Are all trees pruned properly?

### D. WATER DAMAGE

_____ 1. Is there an annual inspection of all plumbing by qualified technicians?

_____ 2. Is adequate building heat maintained on a 24-hour basis to prevent pipe freeze?

_____ 3. Are water lines located in unheated areas drained and outside faucets covered?

_____ 4. Are all sink drains kept clean of all foreign objects?

_____ 5. Are all building openings weathertight?

_____ 6. Is the baptistery monitored properly during use?

### E. PERSONAL INJURIES AND PUBLIC LIABILITY

_____ 1. Are stairways checked at least monthly to ensure adequate lighting and that steps are in good repair?

_____ 2. Are there handrails on all stairways?

_____ 3. Are all assembly areas properly maintained and never allowed to exceed posted occupancy levels?

_____ 4. Are building surfaces inspected at least semiannually to protect against falling parts?

_____ 5. Is snow and ice promptly removed from all surfaces?

_____ 6. Is all playground equipment regularly inspected and in good repair, in accordance with Consumer Product Safety Commission guidelines?

_____ 7. Are all sports and recreational activities adequately supervised?

_____ 8. Are only trained personnel allowed to operate power equipment such as lawn mowers, snow blowers, and power tools?

_____ 9. Are only non-slip Underwriters' Laboratories approved waxes used on floor surfaces?

_____ 10. Are runners used in aisles or entry areas on rainy days, and are cautionary signs posted?

_____ 11. Are all walkways free of holes, uneven sections, cracks, etc.?

_____ 12. Are all exits and fire escapes checked quarterly and maintained in good, safe, and usable condition and free from obstructions?

_____ 13. Are all exit doorways marked with operational illuminated exit signs, and do exit signs have battery backup power in case of loss of commercial power?

_____ 14. Are all doors at required exits provided with panic hardware or kept unlocked during occupancy?

_____ 15. Are all persons using their cars on church business required to furnish proof of automobile liability insurance?

_____ 16. Do drivers for any church event carry a valid driver's license?

_____ 17. If a church van is used, do only insurance company–certified drivers use it?

_____ 18. Are all contractors and other companies performing services for the church required to furnish proof of workers' compensation, general liability, and vehicle insurance which meets the required minimum level of coverage?

### F. SEXUAL ABUSE

_____ 1. Are selective hiring practices and detailed job applications required (including volunteers)?

_____ 2. Are job background statements checked and gaps in time watched for?

_____ 3. Is there a check of arrest and conviction records of "key" applicants?

_____ 4. Are supervisory guidelines established, to include a written standard of conduct for adult/children relationships?

_____ 5. Is a "confidential counselor" available to whom any student, camper, or other child can go at any time, without special permission, to discuss any problems they may be having?

_____ 6. Are employees and volunteers encouraged to limit their physical contact with children?

_____ 7. Is it required that activities be done in an open area or room, and not in private?

_____ 8. During youth activities, are bathrooms, closets, etc., checked regularly?

_____ 9. Do supervisors watch children for physical or behavioral indicators?

_____ 10. Is there an active educational program of sexual abuse awareness?

**REMARKS:**

_____

_____

_____

_____

_____

_____

_____

_____

_____

_____

_____

Inspector: _____ Date: _____

# Church Contents Inventory

Name of Church: _____

Address: _____ Inventory Date: _____

**Instructions:** Record as much information as you can about each item listed. Show condition under "Cond." as "N" for new, "E" for excellent, "G" for good, and "P" for poor. For items where there are more than one, show quantity. Record the cost and current replacement value. An addendum sheet should be used for model numbers, serial numbers, or other special data and additional notes; key your notes to the number recorded below in the "Notes" column. Review this inventory annually to ensure completeness and accuracy. File a copy in the church safe-deposit box along with a video record. Carefully preparing an inventory is clearly one of the best ways to get full value from insurance coverage in case of loss.

## *Sanctuary*

| ITEM | COND. | NUMBER | COST | VALUE | NOTES |
|---|---|---|---|---|---|
| Chancel Table/Chairs | _____ | _____ | _____ | _____ | _____ |
| Lectern (Unattached) | _____ | _____ | _____ | _____ | _____ |
| Pulpit (Unattached) | _____ | _____ | _____ | _____ | _____ |
| Baptismal Font | _____ | _____ | _____ | _____ | _____ |
| Communion Service | _____ | _____ | _____ | _____ | _____ |
| Offering Plates | _____ | _____ | _____ | _____ | _____ |
| Pews (Unattached) | _____ | _____ | _____ | _____ | _____ |
| Chairs | _____ | _____ | _____ | _____ | _____ |
| Draperies | _____ | _____ | _____ | _____ | _____ |
| Hymnals | _____ | _____ | _____ | _____ | _____ |
| Bibles | _____ | _____ | _____ | _____ | _____ |
| Textiles | _____ | _____ | _____ | _____ | _____ |
| Pictures and Paintings | _____ | _____ | _____ | _____ | _____ |
| Statuary | _____ | _____ | _____ | _____ | _____ |
| Pianos | _____ | _____ | _____ | _____ | _____ |
| Organ | _____ | _____ | _____ | _____ | _____ |
| Rugs (Unattached) | _____ | _____ | _____ | _____ | _____ |
| Candle Holders | _____ | _____ | _____ | _____ | _____ |
| Candle Lighters | _____ | _____ | _____ | _____ | _____ |
| PA System | _____ | _____ | _____ | _____ | _____ |
| Microphones | _____ | _____ | _____ | _____ | _____ |

| ITEM | COND. | NUMBER | COST | VALUE | NOTES |
|---|---|---|---|---|---|
| Video Equipment | | | | | |
| Decorations | | | | | |
| Pastoral Robes/Stoles | | | | | |
| Waders | | | | | |
| Acolyte Robes/Stoles | | | | | |
| Cry Room Furnishings | | | | | |

## Fellowship Hall

| | | | | | |
|---|---|---|---|---|---|
| Tables | | | | | |
| Chairs | | | | | |
| Carts | | | | | |
| Trays | | | | | |
| Linens | | | | | |
| Table Decorations | | | | | |
| Draperies | | | | | |
| Sound Equipment | | | | | |
| Soda Machine | | | | | |
| Athletic Equipment | | | | | |
| Stage Equipment | | | | | |

## Kitchen

| | | | | | |
|---|---|---|---|---|---|
| Stoves | | | | | |
| Refrigerators | | | | | |
| Dishwashers | | | | | |
| Serving Tables | | | | | |
| Steam Tables | | | | | |
| Pots and Pans | | | | | |
| Serving Dishes/Pans | | | | | |
| Cooking Utensils | | | | | |
| Mixers | | | | | |
| Dishes | | | | | |

| ITEM | COND. | NUMBER | COST | VALUE | NOTES |
|------|-------|--------|------|-------|-------|
| Silverware | _____ | _____ | _____ | _____ | _____ |
| Glassware | _____ | _____ | _____ | _____ | _____ |
| Warming Ovens | _____ | _____ | _____ | _____ | _____ |
| Coffee Makers | _____ | _____ | _____ | _____ | _____ |
| Ice Machine | _____ | _____ | _____ | _____ | _____ |
| Microwave | _____ | _____ | _____ | _____ | _____ |
| Toasters | _____ | _____ | _____ | _____ | _____ |
| Food & Supply Inventory | _____ | _____ | _____ | _____ | _____ |
| _____ | _____ | _____ | _____ | _____ | _____ |

## Church Office

| | COND. | NUMBER | COST | VALUE | NOTES |
|------|-------|--------|------|-------|-------|
| Desks & Chairs | _____ | _____ | _____ | _____ | _____ |
| Other Chairs | _____ | _____ | _____ | _____ | _____ |
| Sofa & Chairs | _____ | _____ | _____ | _____ | _____ |
| Tables | _____ | _____ | _____ | _____ | _____ |
| Filing Cabinets | _____ | _____ | _____ | _____ | _____ |
| Storage Cabinets | _____ | _____ | _____ | _____ | _____ |
| Draperies | _____ | _____ | _____ | _____ | _____ |
| Safe | _____ | _____ | _____ | _____ | _____ |
| Copy Machine | _____ | _____ | _____ | _____ | _____ |
| Computer Systems | _____ | _____ | _____ | _____ | _____ |
| Telephone System | _____ | _____ | _____ | _____ | _____ |
| Typewriter | _____ | _____ | _____ | _____ | _____ |
| Duplicating Machine | _____ | _____ | _____ | _____ | _____ |
| Folding Machine | _____ | _____ | _____ | _____ | _____ |
| Coffee Maker | _____ | _____ | _____ | _____ | _____ |
| Paper & Supplies | _____ | _____ | _____ | _____ | _____ |
| _____ | _____ | _____ | _____ | _____ | _____ |

## Pastor's Study

| | COND. | NUMBER | COST | VALUE | NOTES |
|------|-------|--------|------|-------|-------|
| Desk | _____ | _____ | _____ | _____ | _____ |
| Desk Chair | _____ | _____ | _____ | _____ | _____ |
| Sofa & Chairs | _____ | _____ | _____ | _____ | _____ |

| ITEM | COND. | NUMBER | COST | VALUE | NOTES |
|---|---|---|---|---|---|
| Other Chairs | | | | | |
| Lamp (desk) | | | | | |
| Lamp (floor) | | | | | |
| Filing Cabinet | | | | | |
| Bookshelf (Unattached) | | | | | |
| Books | | | | | |
| Draperies | | | | | |

## Parlor

| | | | | | |
|---|---|---|---|---|---|
| Sofa & Chairs | | | | | |
| Tables | | | | | |
| Lamps | | | | | |
| Mirrors | | | | | |
| Draperies | | | | | |

## Custodian Area

| | | | | | |
|---|---|---|---|---|---|
| Tools | | | | | |
| Floor Cleaning Equip. | | | | | |
| Vacuum Cleaners | | | | | |
| Brooms & Mops | | | | | |
| Electric Cords | | | | | |
| Window Cleaning Equip. | | | | | |
| Shelving (Unattached) | | | | | |
| Ladders | | | | | |
| Supplies | | | | | |

## Music Room

| | | | | | |
|---|---|---|---|---|---|
| Piano | | | | | |
| Desk & Chair | | | | | |
| Chairs | | | | | |

| ITEM | COND. | NUMBER | COST | VALUE | NOTES |
|------|-------|--------|------|-------|-------|
| Robes & Stoles | _____ | _____ | _____ | _____ | _____ |
| Music | _____ | _____ | _____ | _____ | _____ |
| Misc Instruments | _____ | _____ | _____ | _____ | _____ |
| Bells | _____ | _____ | _____ | _____ | _____ |
| Chimes | _____ | _____ | _____ | _____ | _____ |
| Draperies | _____ | _____ | _____ | _____ | _____ |
| _____ | _____ | _____ | _____ | _____ | _____ |
| _____ | _____ | _____ | _____ | _____ | _____ |

## Library

| ITEM | COND. | NUMBER | COST | VALUE | NOTES |
|------|-------|--------|------|-------|-------|
| Books | _____ | _____ | _____ | _____ | _____ |
| Videos | _____ | _____ | _____ | _____ | _____ |
| Tapes | _____ | _____ | _____ | _____ | _____ |
| Historical Items | _____ | _____ | _____ | _____ | _____ |
| Card Catalog | _____ | _____ | _____ | _____ | _____ |
| Computer System | _____ | _____ | _____ | _____ | _____ |
| Bible Study Software | _____ | _____ | _____ | _____ | _____ |
| Teaching Games | _____ | _____ | _____ | _____ | _____ |
| Draperies | _____ | _____ | _____ | _____ | _____ |
| Shelving (Unattached) | _____ | _____ | _____ | _____ | _____ |
| Desk & Chair | _____ | _____ | _____ | _____ | _____ |
| Tables & Chairs | _____ | _____ | _____ | _____ | _____ |
| _____ | _____ | _____ | _____ | _____ | _____ |
| _____ | _____ | _____ | _____ | _____ | _____ |

## High-Value Installed Items

| ITEM | COND. | NUMBER | COST | VALUE | NOTES |
|------|-------|--------|------|-------|-------|
| Pipe Organ | _____ | _____ | _____ | _____ | _____ |
| Chimes | _____ | _____ | _____ | _____ | _____ |
| Stained Glass Windows | _____ | _____ | _____ | _____ | _____ |
| Security Systems | _____ | _____ | _____ | _____ | _____ |
| Signs | _____ | _____ | _____ | _____ | _____ |
| _____ | _____ | _____ | _____ | _____ | _____ |
| _____ | _____ | _____ | _____ | _____ | _____ |

## Church School Classrooms and Nursery (Room: _____)
*(Use a separate sheet for each classroom or storage area)*

| ITEM | COND. | NUMBER | COST | VALUE | NOTES |
|------|-------|--------|------|-------|-------|
| Tables | _____ | _____ | _____ | _____ | _____ |
| Chairs | _____ | _____ | _____ | _____ | _____ |
| Draperies | _____ | _____ | _____ | _____ | _____ |
| Pictures | _____ | _____ | _____ | _____ | _____ |
| Chalkboard | _____ | _____ | _____ | _____ | _____ |
| Easels | _____ | _____ | _____ | _____ | _____ |
| Study Material | _____ | _____ | _____ | _____ | _____ |
| Bibles | _____ | _____ | _____ | _____ | _____ |
| TV Sets | _____ | _____ | _____ | _____ | _____ |
| Computer Systems | _____ | _____ | _____ | _____ | _____ |
| Radios | _____ | _____ | _____ | _____ | _____ |
| Recorders | _____ | _____ | _____ | _____ | _____ |
| Projection Equipment | _____ | _____ | _____ | _____ | _____ |
| Supplies | _____ | _____ | _____ | _____ | _____ |
| Cribs & Toys | _____ | _____ | _____ | _____ | _____ |
| _____ | _____ | _____ | _____ | _____ | _____ |
| _____ | _____ | _____ | _____ | _____ | _____ |

## Storage Areas (Area: _____)
*(Use a separate sheet for each classroom or storage area)*

| Decorations | _____ | _____ | _____ | _____ | _____ |
|-------------|-------|-----------|-----------|-----------|--------|
| Seasonal Equipment | _____ | _____ | _____ | _____ | _____ |
| Files | _____ | _____ | _____ | _____ | _____ |
| Lawnmowers | _____ | _____ | _____ | _____ | _____ |
| Electric Blower | _____ | _____ | _____ | _____ | _____ |
| Edger | _____ | _____ | _____ | _____ | _____ |
| Trimmers | _____ | _____ | _____ | _____ | _____ |
| Garden Tools | _____ | _____ | _____ | _____ | _____ |
| Snow Blower | _____ | _____ | _____ | _____ | _____ |
| Ladders | _____ | _____ | _____ | _____ | _____ |
| _____ | _____ | _____ | _____ | _____ | _____ |
| _____ | _____ | _____ | _____ | _____ | _____ |

# Addendum Sheet to Church Contents Inventory

| NOTE # | ITEM | MODEL # | SERIAL # | SPECIAL INFORMATION |
|--------|------|---------|----------|---------------------|
| | | | | |
| | | | | |
| | | | | |
| | | | | |
| | | | | |
| | | | | |
| | | | | |
| | | | | |
| | | | | |
| | | | | |
| | | | | |
| | | | | |
| | | | | |
| | | | | |
| | | | | |
| | | | | |
| | | | | |
| | | | | |
| | | | | |
| | | | | |
| | | | | |
| | | | | |
| | | | | |
| | | | | |
| | | | | |
| | | | | |
| | | | | |
| | | | | |
| | | | | |
| | | | | |
| | | | | |

# Management Review in the Local Church

We have covered a great deal of material about administration and finance in the local church. When this material is presented in a classroom setting, particularly with in-service pastors, a frequent concluding question is, "Where do we go from here?" A reasonable response might be, "You need to know where you are before you can plan to get to where you need to be." The surveys and checklists on the following pages represent ways of determining "where you are." Please note that if multiple copies of these surveys are needed they are available in a separate publication, *A Pastor's Survival Guide* (Morehouse Publishing).[5]

## *Church Administration and Finance Survey*

This survey asks a series of questions in each of the four disciplines of administration:

- Planning
- Organizing/Staffing
- Leading
- Assessing/Reporting

The primary purpose of this survey is to determine and document the administration and financial systems, records, and procedures that may or may not be in place at a given point in time. A survey of this type seems particularly appropriate and applicable when a pastor has been newly appointed or selected. It provides a reference point for implementation of a more complete and functional church administration program.

While all items in the survey may not be *equally* important, they *all* have implications for effective church administration.

Each of the questions in the survey should be answered with a Y for "Yes," or left blank for "No." In order to qualify for a Y, one should verify the area in question. In general, it is not sufficient to say, "Yes, we do that." For example, in order to answer Y to the question, "Does the church have a mission statement?" one should read a copy of the mission statement. If a question is left blank, this indicates the answer is "No" and that some work may be needed to achieve a Y answer.

When the survey is complete, priorities should be assigned to the blank items, with a planned completion date noted and a responsibility assigned for achieving a Y answer.

## *Annual Parish Checklist*

Numerous recurring and important tasks in the local church must be planned each year. If any of these items is omitted, frustration, dissatisfaction, or even panic can result in the daily life of the church. As the end of each year approaches, this Annual Parish Checklist should be consulted to ensure that all important tasks have been planned or accomplished. Since this list could vary somewhat by church or denomination, additions or deletions should be made as guided by unique situations.

### Guide to Church Financial Management (A Checklist)

The purpose of this checklist is to evaluate the effectiveness, efficiency, and completeness of the financial systems and procedures of the local church. Complete this checklist in the same manner suggested above and plan for a "Yes" answer for each question.

Without effective financial management and internal controls, every church is subjecting itself to unnecessary risk. Unfortunately there have been far too many instances of church financial mismanagement and even fraud and embezzlement. This guide is designed to detect the weaknesses in financial management procedure which, if conscientiously corrected, may lessen the opportunity for mismanagement and fraud.

# Church Administration and Finance Survey

**PLANNING**

### Mission Statement

_____ Does the church have a written mission statement?

_____ Has the mission statement been reviewed and affirmed within the past three years?

_____ Does the mission statement reflect a possible changing environment for the church?

_____ Is the mission statement published periodically in the church newsletter and/or order of worship? How frequently? _____ times per month

### Action Plans and Goals

_____ Does the church have written action plans with specific objectives or goals?

_____ Do the work areas of the church have written action plans and goals?

_____ Is there periodic review of performance to action plans and goals?

### Planning Process

_____ Is a long-range (three to five years) and short-range (one year) planning process in place and functioning?

_____ Do church leaders _participate_ in the planning process?

_____ Does the congregation have an opportunity to provide input to the planning process?

_____ Has there been a formal planning meeting held within the past two years?

### Financial Planning

_____ Has a budget been developed for the current year?

_____ Are church goals, plans, and programs fully considered?

_____ Are work areas/committees consulted about budget needs?

_____ Are realistic levels for potential income as well as expenses included?

_____ Are long-range replacement needs included?

_____ Is the budget accepted and supported by the congregation?

_____ Are trust and endowment funds encouraged?

_____ Do plans for borrowing funds carefully consider payback programs?

_____ Are church buildings and other assets adequately covered by insurance?

_____ Is there adequate liability insurance?

**ORGANIZING AND STAFFING**

_____ Does an organization chart or table exist?

_____ Has this chart or table been updated within the past two years?

_____ Do written personnel policies exist?

_____ Have these policies been reviewed and updated within the past two years?

_____ Does a sexual harassment policy exist?

_____ Have position (job) descriptions been written for all lay personnel?

_____ Have position (job) descriptions been written for all professional personnel?

_____ Have these position descriptions been reviewed and updated within the past two years?

_____ Do lay personnel have specific, measurable objectives or goals established?

_____ Do professional personnel have specific and measurable objectives or goals established?

_____ Is performance of lay personnel evaluated at least annually?

_____ Is performance of professional personnel evaluated at least annually?

_____ Are financial responsibilities divided such that the same person is not doing all functions?

_____ Is there an expectation that the pastor(s) *will not* handle church funds?

_____ Is a personnel file established for each employee?

_____ Is the personnel file kept current?

_____ Does the personnel file contain the following *minimum* information?

    _____ Employment application

    _____ Interview notes

    _____ Reference-check notes

    _____ Correspondence with employee

    _____ Record of attendance, illness, vacations, leaves, etc.

    _____ Performance reviews signed by the employee and supervisor

    _____ Wage and benefit records

    _____ Commendation and promotion information

    _____ Warnings, reprimands, suspensions, etc.

    _____ Separation report and exit interview

_____ Do committee folders/files contain the following information?

    _____ Church constitution

    _____ Church bylaws

    _____ Mission statement

    _____ Action plans

    _____ Responsibility statement

    _____ Church calendar

    _____ Current budget

    _____ Financial reports

    _____ List of committee members

_____ Check/purchase request forms

_____ Minutes of previous meetings

## LEADING

_____ Does the pastor-in-charge hold *regular,* preferably weekly, staff meetings?

_____ Are staff inputs welcomed, listened to, and acted on as appropriate?

_____ Do other supervisors hold regular staff meetings?

_____ Is delegation of responsibility encouraged and practiced throughout the church organization?

_____ Do supervisors have counseling sessions with staff, as required?

_____ Are new employees oriented and trained?

_____ Do existing employees receive orientation and training, as required?

_____ Does every employee have a copy of their position description?

_____ Has the position description been discussed with the employee?

_____ Has the employee signed a form indicating understanding and acceptance of the position description?

_____ Has the church identified and utilized competent lay leadership?

_____ Is lay leadership provided an opportunity for orientation and training, particularly when assuming new responsibilities?

_____ Does the pastor-in-charge meet regularly with the lay leadership?

_____ Does the church have a well-established communication system, including the following?

    _____ Prayer chain

    _____ Newsletter

    _____ Periodic informative mailings

    _____ Periodic informational meetings

    _____ Order of worship inserts

    _____ Printed membership directory (no more than two years old)

    _____ Pictorial membership directory (no more than five years old)

_____ Are members being led to a healthy theology of stewardship—beyond money and budgets and into time and talent stewardship?

_____ Is there a positive program to raise the levels of giving, including the following?

    _____ Recognized and publicized value of mission and programs?

    _____ Complete and clear communication about the status of giving?

    _____ A pledge campaign to fit needs and the local environment?

_____ Is the pastor showing positive leadership in personal stewardship of time, talent, and resources?

## ASSESSING AND REPORTING

_____ Are there written policies and procedures for the following?

    _____ Facility use policies for both church and nonchurch groups

    _____ Facility opening and closing checklist

    _____ Facility use scheduling and priorities

    _____ Security and safety self-inspection checklists

    _____ Key control and checkout procedures

    _____ Equipment use directions

    _____ Equipment use rules (for those not members of the church)

    _____ Maintenance and repair scheduling

    _____ Complete membership records that are periodically reviewed

    _____ Attendance and financial giving records

    _____ Visitor and evangelism call records

    _____ Work, purchase, and payment request forms

    _____ File maintenance plan and annual review

    _____ Seasonal worship items' storage location and inventory

    _____ Fixed asset inventory and valuation (written and video for insurance purposes)

_____ Do committees responsible for church property and finances, such as the finance committee and trustees, meet regularly, preferably monthly?

_____ Are required church reports completed and filed in a timely manner with government agencies, connectional entities, etc., as applicable?

_____ Are required federal government forms filed as required, especially any form related to taxes?

_____ Are required state and municipal government forms filed as required?

_____ Is there a complete and adequate financial control system with policies and procedures that are clear, understood, and workable for the local church?

_____ Is there an adequate feedback system to report goal attainment, to ensure absolute integrity, and to fully communicate information?

_____ Are separate bank accounts used for general operations and for special purposes—but only enough different accounts for proper separation of funds?

_____ Are special savings/investment accounts used only for special purposes?

_____ Are financial personnel bonded as part of the insurance program?

_____ Is there a clear organizational understanding of who is responsible for what and who is accountable to whom?

_____ Is there a proper separation of financial duties; i.e., the person receiving money does not disburse it?

_____ Are there written procedures for receiving and depositing cash?

_____ Are there clear check-writing procedures—checks signed only after review of supporting documentation?

_____ Are financial reports tailored to local needs?

_____ Are financial results compared to budgeted amounts and presented to committees and the governing body monthly?

_____ Does the treasurer or finance chairperson analyze results, compare with previous periods and/or budgets, and report findings?

_____ Is a periodic financial report made to the entire congregation, perhaps in a newsletter or informational meeting?

_____ Do adequate facilities and tools exist for counting, protecting, paying, reporting, and keeping funds?

_____ Is an annual financial management review of the financial control systems and records performed, preferably by members not directly involved in the financial matters of the church, using an internal audit, systems-procedure checklist?

For more detailed and comprehensive information on the financial functions in the church, see the "Guide to Church Financial Management (A Checklist)" on the following pages.

# *Annual Parish Checklist*

As the end of each year approaches, make plans to assure that all of the important tasks presented on this checklist are accomplished. As each is completed, initial and note the completion date on the line provided.

## PLANNING

_____ Plan for budget development and all related input required for the budget.

_____ Set annual stewardship program and organize.

_____ Project need to purchase and replace equipment for one, two, and five years.

_____ Set an annual planning event for the church leadership and members.

_____ Establish an annual calendar of major events, including liturgical year celebrations (Advent, Lent, etc.).

_____ Set Christian Education Sunday, Bible presentations, Promotion Sunday, and other special emphasis dates.

_____ Set dates for membership classes.

_____ Establish dates for continuing-education leave, camps/retreats, etc., for which the pastor has responsibility.

_____ Establish vacation times for the pastor and employees.

## ORGANIZING AND STAFFING

_____ Review position descriptions for all employees, including the pastor.

_____ Receive performance goals from all employees, including the pastor.

_____ Review personnel policies as well as any other written policies and modify as appropriate.

_____ Ensure committee records are passed on when new committees and chairpersons are impaneled.

## LEADING

_____ Set planning retreat/meeting for church staff.

_____ Set training events for new chairpersons and committee members.

_____ Set training events for new and incumbent employees as required.

## ASSESSING AND REPORTING

_____ Schedule employee performance evaluations, including the pastor's.

_____ Assure that all employee W-4 forms are current.

_____ Assure that the Articles of Incorporation adequately reflect the current role of the church.

_____ Assure that all legal aspects of employment are being maintained.

_____ Assure that personnel records of all employees are current.

_____ Schedule audit committee to perform an internal financial review and control-system check.

_____ Assure that all required denominational reports are completed and submitted.

_____ Have membership rolls reviewed for accuracy and currency.

_____ Set dates to have all gas-heating pilot lights turned off, if applicable.

_____ Set dates to inspect, relight pilots, and turn on/off heating and cooling systems, as applicable.

_____ Arrange to have trustees check:

    _____ Insurance coverage and needed changes

    _____ Inventory records, including video of property and premises

    _____ Heating and air conditioning equipment

    _____ Roofing

    _____ Door and window locking mechanisms

    _____ Plumbing, including landscape and fire sprinkler systems

    _____ Parking lot paving and sidewalks

_____ Arrange for check of premises for safety concerns.

_____ Arrange for fire extinguishers and other fire abatement equipment to be checked by a licensed company.

_____ Arrange for a loss-prevention review.

_Note:_ This is not intended to be an all-inclusive list. This list may vary from church to church and from congregation to congregation. Please use this list as a starting point and modify it to suit specific needs.

# Guide to Church Financial Management (A Checklist)

*Procedure:* Use this checklist to evaluate the effectiveness and efficiency with which financial and managerial responsibilities and procedures are carried out, as well as to verify completeness of the financial management system. Many of the questions relate directly to detailed material covered elsewhere in the manual, and you are encouraged to use this material as reference for a complete understanding of the questions.

As each question or group of questions is answered, initial and date the item to show it was completed. If an item is left blank, indicating noncompliance, make plans to complete or correct that item by a future date.

## I. RESPONSIBILITIES (A REVIEW OF FINANCIAL PROCEDURES)

### A. Division of responsibilities

_____ 1. Are financial responsibilities divided; i.e., collecting, paying, and accounting? (If possible, the same person should not be doing all functions.)

_____ 2. Is the person(s) signing checks carefully selected to ensure system integrity, and authorized by the governing body to do so?

_____ 3. Are nonrecurring expenditures made only after approval by a committee chairperson?

_____ 4. Are accounting records kept by a person not involved in collecting or handling cash? (If one person does do all functions, as may be necessary in small churches, note more carefully the bank reconciliation procedures.)

### B. Organizational procedures

_____ 1. Are clear organizational lines of authority for all administrative and financial matters established, understood, and functioning?

_____ 2. Are written procedures used to ensure system integrity?

_____ 3. Are all financial actions directed by the governing body completed on a timely basis?

_____ 4. When the treasurer, church secretary, or a teller is changed, is the combination or keys to the safe changed, and is there a current record of who has access to the safe?

## II. CASH RECEIPTS

### A. Receiving and Counting

_____ 1. Are two or more *unrelated* persons involved in each stage of handling offerings?

_____ 2. Are there written procedures for handling offerings and do they include the following?

_____ a. Are offering plates taken to the counting area immediately after each service?

_____ b. If counting will not be done until after the second service, are the offerings from the first service kept in a locked area with limited access?

_____ c. Do counters carefully segregate offerings of cash or check, and by fund?

_____ d. Are mail receipts gathered during the week integrated into the Sunday offerings and included?

_____ e. Are checks alphabetized (or arranged by envelope number) and copied on a copy machine (or listed on a counting sheet if a copy machine is not available)? (These steps will make reconciliation and future posting by the financial secretary much easier.)

_____ f. Is cash received from a known giver listed for future posting by the financial secretary?

_____ g. If money is given for special funds or activities, is this carefully noted?

_____ h. Is an adding-machine tape made of the checks, verified against the checks for accuracy, and then included with the deposit so checks don't need to be listed for the bank?

_____ i. Are the totals of all cash and checks posted separately on the counting sheet and reconciled to the items to be deposited?

_____ j. Are the names of the counters noted on the counting sheet?

_____ k. Is the deposit completed immediately after the last Sunday morning service and deposited in a bank's night-deposit box? (One person can take the deposit to the bank if the bag key is left at the church.)

(This counting and depositing procedure should not take too long if the reconciliation by fund takes place after the deposit. Reconciliation is possible if a complete set of documentation is kept, including copies of checks and all offering envelopes.)

_____ 3. Are mail receipts either recorded in a mail-receipts book or placed intact in a bag or box in a safe?

_____ 4. Are personal acknowledgments sent for gifts such as memorials?

_____ 5. Are interest and other miscellaneous receipts properly accounted for and recorded on the financial statements?

### B. Recording

_____ 1. Does the financial secretary verify weekly totals of entries made to records of giving with cash-counter records?

_____ 2. Does the treasurer maintain individual records for each of the different funds (e.g., general, building, benevolent, memorial, or special funds)?

_____ 3. Do the totals of amounts received by the financial secretary match the amounts recorded by the treasurer?

### C. Accounting for pledges

_____ 1. Are pledges recorded by the financial secretary as part of a members' record of giving and pledge cards retained for future reference?

_____ 2. Is the posting of records of giving up to date?

_____ 3. Are contribution statements given to members on a regular basis (perhaps quarterly or every two months; they must be provided at the end of the tax year)?

_____ 4. Is a total of active pledges calculated, after considering the pledges that need to be dropped or added during the year?

## III. CASH DISBURSEMENT

### A. *General operating expenditures*

_____ 1. Was a budget prepared and properly approved, and then used as a basis for expenditures during the year?

_____ 2. Are budget limitations tracked and not surpassed without proper approval?

_____ 3. Is there a general rule about how much can be spent against the budget during any specific period; e.g., not more than 10 percent in any one month without coordination with the treasurer?

_____ 4. Is an unpaid-invoice file used to ensure bills are paid on time?

_____ 5. Are discounts taken if available?

_____ 6. Are invoices for nonrecurring items (i.e., other than salaries, utilities, or other regular monthly billings) approved by the responsible committee chairperson before they are paid, using a check request form for ease of documentation?

_____ 7. Are check payment procedures proper?

_____ a. Are checks prenumbered and used in sequence?

_____ b. Are blank checks adequately protected in a fireproof safe or locked cabinet?

_____ c. Are payments made based on a valid invoice or other approved statement?

_____ d. Are signatures proper? (If two or more signatures are required, complete documentation should be presented to the additional signatory.)

_____ e. Are invoices or check requests marked "Paid" and the date of payment and check number shown?

_____ 8. Are capital expenditures or unusual billings paid only with proper approval?

### B. *Payroll*

_____ 1. Are payments in accordance with authorized, budgeted amounts and is a supervisor approving deviations, such as sick time or extra vacation?

_____ 2. Are all persons paid by the church properly classified as employee or contract?

_____ 3. Are complete and permanent records maintained for each employee, including regular part-time employees; e.g., W-4 and I-9?

_____ 4. Are proper and required amounts withheld from wages for taxes, Social Security, Medicare, health insurance, etc., for *all* employees, including part-time?

_____ 5. Is the church's share of Social Security and Medicare taxes being paid, along with that withheld from employees, on a timely basis?

_____ 6. Is the quarterly IRS 941 form prepared correctly and submitted on a timely basis?

_____ 7. Are W-2s, 1099s, and a separate statement of earnings prepared correctly for each employee at the end of the year, and is the W-3 and 1096 correct?

_____ 8. If a part-time employee or contract person does not earn enough for the church to make a formal reporting to the IRS, is an informal statement of earnings given the person for their voluntary reporting?

### C. *Petty cash*

_____ 1. Is the amount of petty cash maintained reasonable for the need?

_____ 2. Are the funds safeguarded and an approval-and-use policy in place?

_____ 3. Are receipt slips kept to support expenditures?

_____ 4. Is complete documentation submitted with the request for replenishment, including the budget accounts to be charged?

### D. *Benevolences*

_____ 1. Does the budget properly show the planned or levied benevolent giving, and do these amounts agree with governing body action or church headquarters authority?

_____ 2. Are the budgeted or planned benevolences to be taken from general fund giving disbursed on a timely basis?

_____ 3. Are special collections disbursed for the intended purpose?

### E. *Other funds*

_____ 1. If disbursements are made for building, memorial, or other special purposes, are these expenditures accounted for properly, if done through a central checking account?

_____ 2. Is there a "due to" (liability) or "due from" (receivable) system to facilitate this fund accounting?

_____ 3. Are church officers and the pastor aware of any funds "owed" to other funds?

_____ 4. Are disbursements made only with specific designation and authorization?

## IV. FIXED ASSET ACCOUNTING

### A. *Mortgage records*

_____ 1. Are mortgage records maintained and kept in a safe-deposit box?

_____ 2. Do mortgage records agree with financial records?

### B. *Insurance records*

_____ 1. Are insurance records complete, including an assessment of property values?

_____ 2. Is required employment information posted and claim forms available?

_____ 3. Is insurance coverage and risk reviewed regularly, and has one person or committee been given this responsibility to ensure that it is done?

### C. Inventory

_____ 1. Is there an inventory record of fixed assets, and is it complete?

_____ 2. Is the inventory record used to establish insurance needs?

### D. Financial reporting

_____ 1. Has a conscious decision been made about how fixed asset values should be shown on financial reports?

_____ 2. As a minimum, is long-term mortgage debt shown on financial reports?

## V. SUMMARIES, REPORTS, RECORDS, AND FILES

### A. Bank statement reconciliation

_____ 1. Are bank statement reconciliations done monthly on all accounts? (Ensure that regular reconciliations have been made throughout the period by persons other than those handling cash or making check payments. Note that, depending on the separation of duties, an audit committee might be made responsible for regular bank statement reconciliations, and thus perform a continuing review throughout the year.)

_____ 2. Are the individual records kept for benevolent, memorial, or special funds reconciled to appropriate savings or checking account statements from depositories?

### B. Monthly financial reports

_____ 1. Is there complete reporting; i.e., significant amounts owed and selected assets other than cash, etc., in addition to receipts and disbursements?

_____ 2. Are the reports useful to church members; i.e., are income and expenses tracked against the budget and reported by committee?

_____ 3. Is there a separate report made for each fund, to ensure fund integrity?

### C. Financial records

_____ 1. Are the formal financial accounting records adequate to provide a permanent, complete record of church financial transactions?

_____ 2. Are the formal accounting records balanced each month?

_____ 3. Is substantiating documentation for the individual records kept for special funds adequate to show designation, purpose, etc., for gifts given?

_____ 4. Are adequate financial records kept for miscellaneous church activities; e.g., outreach, women's and men's organizations, youth groups, Sunday school classes? (At least a simple in-out balance record of transactions should be kept.)

### D. Files

_____ 1. Are files systematically maintained for easy reference and use?

_____ 2. Are complete retention and destruction requirements set and followed?

_____ 3. Are the following types of data and files maintained: financial statements, accounting records, asset records, employees' earnings records, insurance records, and mortgages and related records? (This may simply be a computer disk in a safe-deposit box.)

_____ 4. Are appropriate personnel records on file, such as performance and evaluation records, time and attendance records, etc.?

## VI. ANNUAL FINANCIAL REVIEW OR AUDIT

Although formal audits are generally performed by CPAs, a church may wish to have a less formal independent review that will still ensure that basic controls are in place and that the financial records are reliable. As a minimum, an independent reconciliation of checking and savings account balances should be done. An audit committee of lay persons could be assigned to receive account statements directly from the financial institutions, before they are opened by the church treasurer, and then to perform the reconciliation. In addition, it would be highly desirable for this audit committee or some other independent group in the church to perform a financial review of all the items listed above to ensure the integrity of the financial management system, and to test several specific areas to a limited extent. Some of these tests might include:

_____ 1. Test the accuracy of collection counters; i.e., how many times did the bank report an error?

_____ 2. Select a small sample (perhaps three to five weeks of the year) of weekly counter sheets and trace the information recorded on the sheets to:

    _____ a. A bank deposit slip receipt, to ensure the total amount recorded is the same as the amount shown as deposited.

    _____ b. The financial secretary's records of giving, as to proper fund distribution and totals posted.

    _____ c. The checkbook, for accurate recording of the deposit.

    _____ d. The treasurer's financial records, for accurate recording of the funds into proper accounts and to ensure separation of funds.

_____ 3. Select a small sample of canceled checks (perhaps two or three from maybe six different months) and trace them to substantiating documentation (usually invoices or check requests) for propriety. Include in the sample all checks made payable to the treasurer or pastor (other than salary).

_____ 4. Select any unusual disbursement for other funds and review it for propriety, to ensure that proper funds were used.

_____ 5. Test the computation of payroll and tax amounts and confirm that they are proper and timely payment has been made.

## VII. FINANCIAL REVIEW OR AUDIT REPORT

1. Completely discuss all findings or concerns from the audit review with the responsible persons, ensuring that they fully understand the concerns. There should be no disagreement on facts! There may be differences about how a concern should be corrected, and if so, the best solution should be sought.

2. After complete discussion, write at least a simple report of audit review findings to the stewardship committee, finance committee, trustees, or governing body. Share the report with the responsible persons before it is formally presented to a committee or the governing body, so everyone can respond positively to the concerns as they are presented.

3. Ensure someone is assigned to follow up on agreed-upon actions required to correct any serious concerns or adverse findings in the review/audit.

## VIII. ADDITIONAL RESOURCE

Vargo, Richard J. *The Church Guide to Internal Controls.* Matthews, N.C.: Christian Ministry Resources (Church Law & Tax Report), 1995.

# Resources
# for Various
# Church Activities

The information in this resource section includes forms, sample letters, instructions, announcements, brochures, policies, and procedures that apply to most church activities and situations. Many of these items can simply be copied and used as is, perhaps with the name of the church added for identification. Other items will need to be modified and customized to fit the individual church.

## *Contents*

## Worship Attendance Record Procedure

1. Attendance registration slips will be found in the church office.

2. Separate into single slips.

3. Separate slips for visitors and give these to secretary to compose welcome letters.

4. Any registration slips with special notes or comments should be copied and routed to persons who may have an interest in the comments.

5. Alphabetize remaining slips.

6. Note any changes of name, address, or phone number and make these changes on the individual membership record forms or computer membership record.

7. Record member and constituent attendance on the computerized "Attendance Record."

8. Recorded member and constituent registration slips are banded together, dated, and filed.

9. Save computer record of attendance on the hard drive and back up on a diskette. Give "Attendance Record" disk to secretary for safekeeping.

For churches that may not be computerized, the following worship attendance record form can track attendance as well as quarterly totals of pledged financial support and gifts received.

# Worship Attendance Record Form

Name: _____

## WORSHIP ATTENDANCE RECORD

| Sunday | 1 | 2 | 3 | 4 | 5 | 6 | 7 | 8 | 9 | 10 | 11 | 12 | 13 | 14 | Total |
|---|---|---|---|---|---|---|---|---|---|---|---|---|---|---|---|
| **YEAR** Jan., Feb., March | | | | | | | | | | | | | | | |
| April, May, June | | | | | | | | | | | | | | | |
| July, Aug., Sept. | | | | | | | | | | | | | | | |
| Oct., Nov., Dec. | | | | | | | | | | | | | | | |
| **YEAR** Jan., Feb., March | | | | | | | | | | | | | | | |
| April, May, June | | | | | | | | | | | | | | | |
| July, Aug., Sept. | | | | | | | | | | | | | | | |
| Oct., Nov., Dec. | | | | | | | | | | | | | | | |
| **YEAR** Jan., Feb., March | | | | | | | | | | | | | | | |
| April, May, June | | | | | | | | | | | | | | | |
| July, Aug., Sept. | | | | | | | | | | | | | | | |
| Oct., Nov., Dec. | | | | | | | | | | | | | | | |
| **YEAR** Jan., Feb., March | | | | | | | | | | | | | | | |
| April, May, June | | | | | | | | | | | | | | | |
| July, Aug., Sept. | | | | | | | | | | | | | | | |
| Oct., Nov., Dec. | | | | | | | | | | | | | | | |
| **YEAR** Jan., Feb., March | | | | | | | | | | | | | | | |
| April, May, June | | | | | | | | | | | | | | | |
| July, Aug., Sept. | | | | | | | | | | | | | | | |
| Oct., Nov., Dec. | | | | | | | | | | | | | | | |
| **YEAR** Jan., Feb., March | | | | | | | | | | | | | | | |
| April, May, June | | | | | | | | | | | | | | | |
| July, Aug., Sept. | | | | | | | | | | | | | | | |
| Oct., Nov., Dec. | | | | | | | | | | | | | | | |

| Year | Current Budget Pledge | Current Budget Received | Specials Received | Building Fund Pledge | Building Fund Received |
|---|---|---|---|---|---|
| | | | | | |
| | | | | | |
| | | | | | |
| | | | | | |
| | | | | | |
| | | | | | |

## *Flower Donation Form*

Sample letter acknowledging the donation of a flower arrangement for the Sunday worship service.

[Date]

Dear Dorothy:

Thank you for donating a flower arrangement for Sunday, _____ .

Your flowers will enhance our worship atmosphere in a very special way!

Would you please complete the following sentence.

A donation has been made to the Altar Flower Fund in:
( ) honor of        ( ) memory of        ( ) thanksgiving for        ( ) celebration of

_____

_____ .

Given by _____

_____ .

The above statement will appear in the Order of Worship unless you indicate otherwise.

Enclosed is a return envelope. Send this completed form with your donation for flowers to the church office. Your check should be made out to the church.

We need the above information and your check by *TUESDAY, 4:30 p.m., preceding* the Sunday the flowers will be presented for the worship service.

If you have any questions, please feel free to contact me.

Thank you!

Flower Coordinator

Enclosure

# *Visitor Sample Letter: In-Town Visitor*

Sample letter welcoming a person who has not been in worship for a significant period of time. This letter can be modified to welcome a first-time visitor by removing the word "back" from the first sentence.

[Date]

Dear _____ ,

We are so pleased that you were back in worship with us Sunday.

The Sunday morning worship is a rich experience for us all and we trust that it was meaningful for you also.

We extend our hands to welcome you into the warmth of our fellowship, and shall always welcome your participation! Please feel free to call upon the ministry of our church to meet your individual needs.

Sincerely,

Pastor Jones

## *Visitor Sample Letter: Out-of-Town Visitor*

A sample letter of welcome to an out-of-town visitor to the Sunday worship service.


[Date]


Dear _____ ,

It was our privilege to have you in worship with us on Sunday. We hope that the experience was meaningful, and that you found a warm welcome.

The next time you are in worship in your home church, please give the members of that fellowship our warm greetings.

Anytime you are back in our area, we will be happy to see you and to have you join with us in worship!


Together, in God's service.


Pastor Jones

## *Confirmation Letter*

Letter welcoming a new member to the church through confirmation or baptism, after the person has attended a new-member study course:

[Date]

Dear _____ ,

It was an exciting time for all of us on Sunday, as we shared in [confirming you as a full member of the Church!] or [your baptism!] It is a real joy to welcome you into our fellowship in this way!

We have had a great opportunity to study and share together. We hope that you will continue to evaluate and put into practice what Jesus means to you in what you do, think and say!

Your church family wants to help you in any way that we can! Please let us know if there are any needs which you have. Be assured that our prayers are with you as you enter into the life of this church as a full member.

Together, in God's service.

Pastor Jones                                        Director of Christian Education

## *New-Member Class Sample Letter*

Letter announcing the schedule for a new church member orientation class.

[Date]


Dear _____ ,

We are pleased that you have indicated an interest in uniting with our church, and we invite you to attend an orientation class for new members.

The new-membership class is provided as preparation for persons who wish to join our church. The schedule for these classes is as follows:

Sunday, October 29—8:30 a.m. Continental breakfast and class at 9 a.m. in the Fireside Room. (This is a good chance to get acquainted.)

Sundays, November 5 and 12—9 a.m.

Saturday, November 18, 5:00–7:45 p.m., potluck dinner and closing session.

Sunday, November 19—Reception into church membership for those making that decision.

Childcare is provided for all sessions.

We look forward to your attendance at these classes.


Sincerely,


Pastor Jones

## New-Member Class Evaluation Form

1. Do you feel that this class was valuable to you in terms of gaining new information and insight about the church?   ❑ Yes   ❑ No

2. Do you think the class helped you to feel that you are a part of this congregation even prior to uniting with the church?   ❑ Yes   ❑ No

3. Do you think that three class sessions and the potluck were:
   ❑ Just the right amount of time.
   ❑ Not quite enough time—I would have felt more comfortable with more.
   ❑ More time than was really necessary.

Comments: _____

_____

_____

_____

4. What did you like about the class sessions?_____

_____

_____

5. What did you like about the evening session? _____

_____

_____

6. What would you suggest in the way of improvements to the program? _____

_____

_____

7. Were class materials helpful?  Easy to read (i.e., not too time-consuming)?_____

_____

_____

8. Have you ever participated in membership classes in any other church?   ❑ Yes ❑ No

   How would you compare class content? _____

_____

_____

*Thank you very much for your input!*
(use back if necessary)

## *Welcome to Membership Letter*

Letter welcoming a new member into the fellowship of the church


[Date]


Dear _____ ,

It is a real joy to welcome you as a member of our church. It is our prayer that you will find here a warmth of fellowship and depth of Christian faith that will help make your life complete.

Christian fellowship is best known by those who acquaint themselves with others and are, in turn, sought out. We know that you will rejoice in your new fellowship on this basis.

If there is any doubt as to where you feel you can fit in, by all means contact us. We are a working church. In the vows that you took to support the church with your prayers, your attendance, your gifts and your service, you indicated your willingness to be an active part of this church.

Above all, feel free to call upon the ministry of your church in any time of crisis. We cherish the opportunity to be a supportive fellowship—in joy or grief, in health or illness—allowing us the privilege of being your companions. We are ready to serve you at any time of the day or night. Please know that it is our prime purpose to do so.

Again, welcome into the life of our Christian fellowship!


Together, in God's service,


Pastor Jones

# My Personal Record

Name: _____

Street Address: _____

City: _____ State: _____ Zip: _____

Telephone: _____ Unlisted?  ❏ Yes  ❏ No
If yes, may we publish it?  ❏ Yes  ❏ No

Birthdate: (Optional) _____

Wedding Anniversary Date: (Optional) _____

Occupation: _____

Employed by: _____

Major Interests and Hobbies: _____

_____

Community Involvement: _____

_____

Children at Home:

| Full Name | Birthdate | | | Baptized | Grade | School |
|---|---|---|---|---|---|---|
| | Month | Day | Year | | | |
| | | | | | | |
| | | | | | | |
| | | | | | | |
| | | | | | | |
| | | | | | | |
| | | | | | | |
| | | | | | | |

I plan to join on:_____
                        (date)

❏ on profession of faith
❏ reaffirmation of faith
❏ by transfer _____
                              name of church

_____
    street address            city            state        zip

If by transfer, what name is your membership under? (Maiden or married name)

_____

# Survey of Personal Resources

In accepting membership in the Church, I pledged my life, my talents, my money, and my time. I indicate below the activities in my church in which I am most interested as a fulfillment of my tithe of time and talents.

Check (x) for interest, skill, experience, and/or willingness to serve.

## Work Areas
- ❏ Education
- ❏ Evangelism
- ❏ Finance
- ❏ Membership
- ❏ Parish Life
- ❏ Communications Committee
- ❏ Worship
- ❏ Outreach
  (Missions/Social Concerns)

## Special Services
- ❏ Auditing
- ❏ Bookkeeping
- ❏ Treasurer
- ❏ Secretary
- ❏ Prayer Group Leader
- ❏ Fellowship Friend
- ❏ News Writing, Editing
- ❏ Legal Counseling
- ❏ Ushering
- ❏ Receptionist ("Greeter")
- ❏ Calling on Home Members
- ❏ Visitation Evangelism
- ❏ Every Member Commitment
  (Finance)

## Property Care
- ❏ Grounds
- ❏ Painting
- ❏ Plumbing
- ❏ Electrical

## Sunday School
- ❏ Administration
- ❏ Teaching: level _____
- ❏ Youth Counselor
- ❏ Camp Counselor
- ❏ Librarian
- ❏ Maintaining Records
- ❏ Nursery and Childcare
- ❏ Vacation Bible School
- ❏ Leadership Education
- ❏ Youth Club

## Skills and Other Interests
- ❏ Cooking
- ❏ Serving in Dining Hall
- ❏ Transportation (your car)
- ❏ Transportation (bus driver)
- ❏ Typing
- ❏ Telephoning
- ❏ Running the Copier, etc.
- ❏ Addressing, Folding, etc.
- ❏ Nursing
- ❏ Men's Groups
- ❏ Women's Groups
- ❏ Word Processing Skills
- ❏ Office Help
- ❏ Receptionist (Office Substitute)
- ❏ Teller (Counting weekly offering
  for limited periods)
- ❏ Church Newsletter mailings
- ❏ Church Newsletter mailings
  (Substitute)

## Recreation, Arts, Crafts
- ❏ Planning Parties
- ❏ Folk Games and Dances
- ❏ Leading Other Games
- ❏ Drama and Stagecraft
- ❏ Costuming
- ❏ Woodworking
- ❏ Leathercraft
- ❏ Ceramics
- ❏ Metal Crafts
- ❏ Poster Making
- ❏ Photography
- ❏ Nature Lore
- ❏ Flower Arranging

## Music
- ❏ Choir
- ❏ Choral Direction
- ❏ Leading Group Singing
- ❏ Pianist
- ❏ Instrumentalist
- ❏ Soloist

Other: _____

# *Master File—Families*

| Family Name | | | Dates | | | | Transferred Membership Here From (City and Church) | When? | Listed in Which Church Groups | Removed | |
|---|---|---|---|---|---|---|---|---|---|---|---|
| First Name | Middle | Birth | Baptism | Prep. Mem. | Full Mem. | | | | | How? | When? |
| | | | | | | | | | | | |
| | | | | | | | | | | | |
| | | | | | | | | | | | |
| | | | | | | | | | | | |
| | | | | | | | | | | | |
| | | | | | | | | | | | |
| | | | | | | | | | | | |
| | | | | | | | | | | | |

Family Connections: _____

_____

Lived Here Since: _____

Previous Residences: _____

_____

_____

Occupation—Employer—Income Source: _____

_____

Facts and Events of Importance: _____

_____

_____

Send Family Mail To: _____

Address: _____

City: _____ State: _____ Zip: _____ Phone: _____

This is a form which can be used to record and maintain the vital statistics of a church member family. If church membership records are computerized, this form can be used as a guide to the type of data which should be recorded in the computer file for each member family.

## *Guidelines for Fellowship Friends*

1. Thank you for your willingness to serve as a Fellowship Friend to a new church member. You can become a vital ingredient in that person's active participation in our church fellowship. Please plan to continue in this role for at least four months.

2. The dinner session of the new-member orientation class is an important time for you to have fellowship and discussion time with your new member and others in the class. This dinner is scheduled for Saturday, _____, at 5 p.m. in the social hall. You will be contacted about your contribution to the planned potluck. Childcare will be available if needed. Please get in touch with your new member before the dinner.

3. Plan to sit with your new member during the 10 a.m. worship service on Membership Sunday and stand with them as they are received into membership.

4. During the fellowship time following worship, make an effort to introduce the new members to others in the congregation.

5. You may want to find a time for you and your new member to become better acquainted, such as a dessert evening in your home, brunch after worship—whatever works for you.

6. Encourage the new members to become active participants in church life. Invite them to attend events with you, such as Lenten dinners, special worship, and social events. Invite them to the small groups in which you participate, such as Sunday school, men's and women's groups, youth fellowship, etc.

7. Make yourself a source of information for the new member—call someone else if you don't have answers to their questions.

8. Keep in touch with the new member by phone. Perhaps you have not seen them in church for two or three Sundays. Let them know that you are concerned about them and want to help in any way that you can.

9. Be a good friend!

---

**YOUR FELLOWSHIP FRIEND NEW MEMBER**

Name _____

Address_____

_____

Phone _____

---

## MEMBERSHIP TALLY

**YEAR** _____

| Month | Profession of Faith | Reaffirmation of Faith | Restored | Transfer from Other Churches (Same Denomination) | Transfer from Other Denominations | ADD TOTAL | Transfer to Other Churches (Same Denomination) | Transfer to Other Denominations | Removal by Church Conference | Removal by Own Request | Deaths (Members) | LOSS TOTAL | Deaths (Constituents) | GAIN/LOSS | Baptisms | MONTHLY BALANCE Carry Forward: _____ |
|---|---|---|---|---|---|---|---|---|---|---|---|---|---|---|---|---|
| January | | | | | | | | | | | | | | | | |
| February | | | | | | | | | | | | | | | | |
| March | | | | | | | | | | | | | | | | |
| April | | | | | | | | | | | | | | | | |
| May | | | | | | | | | | | | | | | | |
| June | | | | | | | | | | | | | | | | |
| July | | | | | | | | | | | | | | | | |
| August | | | | | | | | | | | | | | | | |
| September | | | | | | | | | | | | | | | | |
| October | | | | | | | | | | | | | | | | |
| November | | | | | | | | | | | | | | | | |
| December | | | | | | | | | | | | | | | | |
| **TOTALS** | | | | | | | | | | | | | | | | |

## Sunday School Information

Greetings, and welcome to our church!

We're excited that you've chosen to join us for Sunday school this morning and would like to extend a *very* warm welcome to you! Christian education is an important component of our ministry to our members, visitors, and community, and we're proud of the ways we've been growing and developing in this area. We provide a number of opportunities for Christian growth and fellowship on Sunday morning and during the week, and we invite you to take advantage of the ones that meet your particular needs.

This registration packet has been designed to acquaint you with just a few of the many programs offered at our church. In it you will find information related to:

- **SUNDAY SCHOOL AT OUR CHURCH**

- **OTHER CHRISTIAN EDUCATION OPPORTUNITIES**

We hope your morning with us is a good one, and that you'll make plans to join us on a regular basis. If you have questions, comments, or would like more information regarding Christian education at our church, feel free to stop by the Sunday school office between 9 and 10 a.m. each Sunday, or contact me at the church office during the week.

We're glad you are here—enjoy your morning, and come back soon!


In Christ's Service,


Director of Education

# Sunday School at _____

*9:00 a.m.–9:45 a.m.*
*Every Sunday Morning*

**CLASSES FOR ALL AGES, PRESCHOOL THROUGH ADULTS.**

**CHILDCARE FOR INFANTS AND UNDER 2'S IN THE NURSERY AND CRIB ROOM**

Our Sunday school offering money goes to help fund Heifer Fund International. This group helps to fight world hunger by working with small groups of farmers throughout the world, supplying them with farm animals and the training necessary to raise them as a way to have food and increase income. One unique aspect of this project is "passing on the gift," whereby a recipient agrees to pass on offspring of his or her animal to help a neighbor in need.

**FOR CHILDREN:**

*Preschool 2 and 3* meet in Room 2.

*Preschool 4* meet in Room 3.

*Kindergarten* meets in Room 4.

*First and Second grade* meet in Room 12.

*Third and Fourth grade* meet in Room 10.

**FOR YOUTH:**

*Fifth and Sixth grade* in Room 9.

*Junior High* in Room 5.

*Senior High* in Room 8.

**FOR POST-HIGH SCHOOL THROUGH ADULTS:**

*Introduction to the Bible,* Room 11, is a Bible study class for beginners! Designed as an open-entry study class, this class includes a summary of the Old Testament, the life and teachings of Jesus, and the life and teachings of Paul. Lecture, open discussion, and student participation are to be expected!

*Growing Christians,* Room 7, is an open-entry study class formed to strengthen the faith of Christians and challenge them to broaden their Christian perspectives by focusing on studies of persisting social issues. Lively discussion on issues pertinent to today's problems is to be expected!

*"What Is A Christian?,"* Fireside Room, is a class for individuals interested in learning more about the Christian faith, as well as for people interested in becoming members of the church. This class is offered five times yearly, so check with the Sunday school office for dates.

*Selected Video Offerings* are regularly scheduled during the year and meet in Witman Hall. These reflect a variety of issues of current interest, so prepare yourself for open and lively discussion! Because these change on a regular basis, we suggest that you check the marquee by the Sunday school office for current and upcoming titles.

*Sunday school is for everyone, and we have classes for every age group! Newcomers are* **always** *welcome, so come and see what we have to offer!*

# Other Opportunities in Christian Education

## For Children:

**CHILDREN'S MESSAGE**

Midway through 10 a.m. worship, the children are invited to come to the front of the Sanctuary to hear a short but special message just for them! Presented each Sunday by a different member of our congregation, these messages are enjoyed by young and old alike!

**JUNIOR CHURCH FOR GRADES KINDERGARTEN THRU 2ND GRADE**

Held in the Chapel at the conclusion of our Children's Message time, this provides children in this age range with an opportunity to experience a special worship time geared to their energy level and attention span! Music, prayer, a brief story or message, and some movement activities help make this a special time. Aspects of worship such as the lighting of the candles, reciting of the Lord's Prayer, and a special offering are incorporated so the children begin to be familiar and comfortable with these. Staffed on a rotating basis by several of the parents, this has become a special time of sharing each Sunday morning!

## For Youth:

**YOUTH FELLOWSHIP**

This lively group of Jr. and Sr. High youth meet on Sunday evenings from 6:30–8 p.m. in the Fireside Room. Dinner is served at 6 p.m. for a cost of $1.50. What is Youth Fellowship? It's study time and recreation time, service projects and fun outings, work trips and retreats, quiet times of reflection and faith growth, and crazy, hilarious times of laughter, friendship, and food! Join us—new faces are always welcome! Interested? Contact the Youth Director.

**CONFIRMATION CLASS FOR 7TH THRU 12TH GRADE**

Held once yearly in early spring, Confirmation is a 12–13 week time of study, reflection, and interaction with other youth and the pastors/staff of our church. It's a time to take a mature look at the Christian faith and make a decision about a personal commitment to God and to the church. It's also a time to make new friends, have fun, and learn more about God's plan for you! At the end of this time the youth involved are invited to unite with the Church as full members on Confirmation Sunday. Interested? Questions? Contact the Director of Education.

## For Post-High School Through Adults:

**DISCIPLE BIBLE STUDY:** Contact Director of Education.

**WOMEN'S BIBLE STUDY:** Twice monthly on Monday evening. Contact _____ . Childcare is provided.

**ADVENT AND LENTEN STUDY CLASSES:** Offered twice a year as special seasonal study opportunities, a weekly evening study and a midweek breakfast study provide times of fellowship, discussion, and spiritual growth for youth, young adults, and adults. Subject material is identical, so you are encouraged to choose the time that best fits your schedule. Preregistration is necessary so that enough study materials can be ordered. Childcare is provided for the evening study.

## For All Ages:

**VACATION BIBLE SCHOOL:** Held in August in the evening for all ages, this has become a much-anticipated event! Study classes for all ages, fun elective course offerings for 5th grade through adults, recreation, music, fellowship, sharing, and growth are to be anticipated! Watch for more details as summertime approaches.

# QUARTERLY MEETING AGENDA
# SUMMER QUARTER

### *SATURDAY, MAY 30*
### *9 A.M.–11 A.M.*
### *Fireside Room*

**9–9:45 A.M.**   **STAFF MEETING FOR TEACHERS & WORKERS**

a) Introductions and Overview
b) General Information
c) Sunday School Registration Packets
d) Emergency Evacuation Procedures
e) Promotion Sunday—June 7

**9:45–11 A.M.**   **TRAINING SESSION**

"The C, D, E's of Teaching Sunday School—
Caring, Discipline, & Environment"

**11 A.M.–?**   **INDIVIDUAL AND TEAMWORK TIME IN CLASSROOMS**

*Please fill out an evaluation form before you leave the session.*

*Thank you!*

## *Evaluation—Training Session*

1. I would rate this training session as:

   GREAT          GOOD          OK          POOR

   Comments: _____

   _____

   _____

2. The staff meeting portion was:

   HELPFUL          OK          NOT NECESSARY

   Comments: _____

   _____

   _____

3. The information packets and handouts we were given were:

   GREAT          GOOD          OK          POOR

4. The all-group training session was:

   GREAT          GOOD          OK          POOR

   Comments: _____

   _____

   _____

5. In the future, I would like to see training sessions held on the following topics:

   _____

   _____

   _____

6. Additional comments or suggestions I have are:

   _____

   _____

   _____

Name (optional) _____

# A Note to Sunday School Teachers

How many of you have children? How many of you ask them "What did you learn in Sunday school today?" after church each week? I know I ask my boys that question weekly—and their teachers can relax, because they always tell me at length, in positive terms, all that they have done! For, you see, the answers children give their parents in most cases depend largely on their teachers. Teachers who are *enthusiastically caring*, *adequately trained*, and *well-prepared* will cause a flood of happy stories as members of their classes (no matter what their age!) answer that question!

We would probably all agree that learning takes place most effectively when it is carefully planned. I firmly believe that Christ called **YOU** specifically to work in the area of Christian education, but faithful and effective teaching doesn't just happen. In my own teaching, I've found that you can deepen your own faith and that of your students, as well as increase your effectiveness, by following four basic steps:

1. **CAREFULLY PREPARE**

   You might think this first one would pertain to lesson planning, but SUR-PRISE—it doesn't! It pertains to **YOU,** as a person! In Luke 11:9 Jesus said to his disciples, "Ask, and it will be given you; seek, and you will find; knock, and it will be opened to you." Now you might be asking, "How does this apply to my teaching each week?!" Well, it's quite simple:

   First, **ASK** in prayer that God will work through you, and then expect God's guidance in your teaching and in the rest of your life.

   Second, **SEEK** the word of God by studying the Bible, reading commentaries, and by asking questions. Careful regular Bible study or private devotional time will enrich your faith as well as strengthen your teaching.

   Third, **KNOCK** in the name of Christ. Knock on the doors of your students' lives by knowing them as individuals and as an age group. Knowing them individually takes time and love. But investing this time and love will bring rich dividends to you all, teachers and students alike. Knowing them as an age-level group helps you to understand what is "normal" or appropriate for the age you teach. I encourage you to talk to the other Christian educators at our church about problems you may be having, and then work toward solutions together. Share ideas for things that you've come up with. Be a support group for each other, no matter what age level you teach!

2. **ACTIVELY LISTEN**

   This consists of asking questions and then listening **with your whole person.** Ask questions that are open-ended; ones that can't easily be answered by a yes or a no. Questions like "How would you have felt if you were _____ and faced the decision of _____ ?" are more thought-provoking and generally prompt more learning to take place.

   In listening actively, use all of your senses and intuition. Words are important, yes, and make sure you listen for what the words are, but also listen to the tone of voice (how it is said), what the eyes might tell you, and what is being said with body movements and posture (body language).

3. **REALISTICALLY PLAN**

   This includes both long-term and short-term planning. Take the time to familiarize yourself with the curriculum for each quarter. Make shifts in activities or projects that will fit the needs of your individual classes. Attend our quarterly training sessions and other training opportunities that may arise through district and conference sources, as well as other study opportunities during the year, so that you can continue to grow in your teaching skills and your own personal faith. Finally, each week plan for the following Sunday using your Teacher's Guide and any related materials. Individuals vary in how they most effectively plan, so use what works best for you, but do find a system that works.

4. **EMPATHETICALLY RESPOND**

   You respond to your students empathetically when you know them well enough to be flexible, timely, and conscious of their needs. Be flexible. Plan your lesson well enough that you are able to change it to meet unforeseen circumstances—even *over* plan. That is, have alternate activities planned and know what activities take priority if you have to eliminate some. For example, if Josh's favorite pet just died on Friday and he brings it up, you'll want to take some time to talk about his feelings and let other students share how they may have felt similarly.

   Be timely. Part of timeliness is taking time to do what needs doing—like talking about the death of Josh's pet. Or if a craft activity is taking longer than you'd expected, don't rush on to the next project just because it's in your lesson plan. Take your time.

   Be conscious about special needs or events in your students' lives by talking to them about what's going on in their lives and sharing what's going on in yours. They will respond to your openness and caring.

In addition to these four steps there is one other thing you need to consider, and that's **Room Arrangement.** The room you teach in and how you display the resources you may have says as much to your students as the words that you say. Look for ways to say through your room arrangement, "Come in, we're ready to do something!" and "I'm glad you're here!" Some of our rooms have more flexibility in this respect than others because of our shared facilities, but we can all always be sure that our bulletin boards are attractive and pertinent to what we're teaching. They can be used to help focus on an area of Scripture we're studying and/or to display projects the class has made around a lesson or concept. Look at your room with a critical eye and then plan accordingly.

And that's basically it! In closing I'd like to stress one more thing. ***Don't be afraid to ask if you need help in ANY way!*** We've all had lessons that have failed miserably, children who we've just NOT gotten along with, times when we've felt VERY discouraged, but we're all in this together and we need to act as a support group for each other. We need to work together and help support each other, and if we do that we'll act to form a solid base for the Christian education program at our church.

God bless you for accepting the very special call to be workers in the area of Christian education! I'm very honored to have the chance to work with you!

Director of Christian Education

# *Suggestions for Sunday School Learning Activities*

- Reading a Scripture
- Hearing a Bible story read from different versions of the Bible
- Telling a Bible story using a flannelboard
- Discussing the Bible stories
- Listing ideas by brainstorming
- Listening to tapes
- Watching videos, films, or filmstrips
- Playing computer Bible games
- Writing a play based on the Bible lesson
- Writing poetry or psalms
- Paraphrasing the Bible story
- Creative story based on a Bible story but set in modern times
- Making videos
- Dramatizing a Bible story
- Developing a choral reading
- Constructing puppets and a stage to perform Bible stories
- Making a mobile
- Role-playing Bible characters
- Using playdough
- Playing active games
- Singing songs or hymns
- Playing musical instruments
- Playing rhythm instruments
- Tracing pictures
- Taking a listening walk (no talking allowed)
- Creating a diorama or a Bible scene
- Making a mural of Bible scenes
- Doing a tabletop model

# How to Be an Invitational Teacher

**INVITE YOUR STUDENTS INTO COMMUNITY**

- by creating a welcoming and inclusive environment;
- by recognizing each person's gifts;
- by providing opportunities for students to develop self-esteem;
- by offering activities that foster cooperation rather than competition;
- by including many creative activities that encourage students to express their feelings;
- by providing opportunities for students to talk about their own ideas and experiences;
- by emphasizing that each student is a part of the church.

**INVITE YOUR STUDENTS INTO RELATIONSHIP WITH JESUS CHRIST**

- by including times for worship and prayer;
- by increasing their familiarity with the Bible;
- by providing opportunities to learn, and sometimes memorize, Bible verses that tell about God's love and care;
- by using language that is appropriate for the age level when talking about religious or theological concepts;
- by helping them see how biblical concepts are related to experiences in their own lives;
- by leading them to realize that each one of them is special in God's eyes, and that God has a special plan for each one of them, a special direction that each is to go in their life.

**INVITE YOUR STUDENTS INTO ACTION**

- by using stories, activities, and projects that involve responding to the needs of others;
- by encouraging them to invite others to Sunday school and to share their faith in ways that are appropriate for their age level;
- by helping them learn to make choices.

**INVITE YOUR STUDENTS INTO CONTINUING GROWTH**

- by nurturing your own spiritual growth;
- by improving your teaching skills and by making the class time inviting to your students;
- by being loving, kind, and caring in your interaction with students to model what Christians are like;
- by talking about your faith with your students and by helping them to talk about their own developing faith;
- by taking advantage of "teachable moments" as well as moments for meaningful worship.

# Suggested Weekly Planning Schedule

**SUNDAY**      Evaluate and celebrate today's lesson.

**MONDAY**      Read the Bible verses and the surrounding verses for next week's lesson. Scan the lesson in your Teacher's Guide.

**TUESDAY**     Reflect on the Bible verses. Ask yourself, "What does this mean to me? What might it mean for persons in my class?"

**WEDNESDAY**   Read a commentary on the Scripture passages that you'll be teaching about next Sunday (these are available in the church office).

**THURSDAY**    Read the lesson in your Teacher's Guide thoroughly. Read the lesson in both the student and teacher resources. Examine any supporting curriculum materials for this lesson (flannelboard figures, activity books, etc.).

**FRIDAY**      Choose which activities you'll use with your class. Prepare for the activities by gathering any materials that you will need.

**SATURDAY**    Review the lesson, then preview the lesson through "visioning" in your mind, moving through the lesson step-by-step as you will teach it.

**SUNDAY**      Pray for God's guidance before teaching. Teach the lesson. Begin the process again for next week.

# *What about Discipline?*

**RIGHT AWAY YOU CAN ...**

- Set up simple class standards for acceptable behavior. Let the children help make the rules if their age permits—try to keep to about five or six basic rules of politeness ("THE FIVE COMMANDMENTS FOR ROOM 2").

- Post these rules in a visible spot in the room.

- Catch children being good. Reward them for following the rules.

- Build on positives whenever you can. Most children respond quite readily to praise!

- Tell parents what a good job their child has been doing when you see them, or call them at home to brighten their day with the good news!

**IF A CHILD CONTINUES TO MISBEHAVE YOU CAN ...**

- State firmly "(Name), you need to stop what you're doing right now!"

- Establish eye contact and quietly but firmly say, "That's enough!"

- Move closer to the child; this sometimes has a calming effect.

- Praise those who are behaving appropriately; maybe even reward them with a small treat.

- Get the rest of the class involved in an activity and then take the offender outside and speak to them.

- Provide a "Time Out" area, either a chair in a corner or outside the door (with older children only).

- Talk with parents and let them know what's been happening. Ask for their support in helping change the behavior.

- Ask other teachers for assistance in dealing with the problem. Perhaps they can offer some insight into a solution.

**REMEMBER—**

- Deal in positives whenever possible.

- Never ridicule or belittle a child.

- Always treat children the way you would want your child to be treated, or better yet the way you yourself would want to be treated in similar circumstances!

- Ask for help before you get too frustrated!!!

## *Fire/Earthquake Preparedness and Emergency Evacuation Plan for Sunday Morning Church School and Childcare*

The Education Committee (EC) has developed an emergency plan to be used on Sunday mornings should a fire, earthquake, or other disaster strike while we are at church. It is important that you be aware of this plan and available to help should the need arise. This plan includes the following:

**FOR FIRE:**

1. *Sunday School Office Person/Superintendent*—Will sound alarm, direct evacuation, and check preschool rooms and bathrooms.

2. *EC Members, Adult Class Members, and other willing church members*—If on site, should report to the preschool classrooms and to the Nursery/Crib Room to help evacuate infants and young children.

3. *Trustees on site*—Shut off electric, gas, and water only if necessary.

4. *Sunday School Teachers*—Will stay with their class and proceed to the *grass area in the west parking lot by designated evacuation routes,* unless unusable (see map). Attendance sheets and clipboards will be with them, and attendance will be taken. Teachers will stay with their students until all are released. No child will be released to anyone under 16 without a picture I.D.

**FOR EARTHQUAKE:**

1. The "Duck, Cover, and Hold" command will be given by the teacher. Students and staff will immediately duck under a desk or table and, with both hands, hold onto the desk or table leg, moving with the desk or table if necessary.

2. After all movement has stopped, students are to stay under the desk or table until the teacher gives them instructions.

3. If directed to evacuate, all classes will follow the same procedure as for fire (#4 above).

**PROCEDURES FOR CHILDCARE:**

*8 a.m. and 9 a.m.—Nursery/Crib Room*
*10 a.m.—Nursery/Crib Room for 2's and younger*
*　　　—Room 2 for Preschool age children*

During the 8 a.m. and 10 a.m. childcare time, most of the classrooms are unoccupied. The individuals involved in childcare during these two time periods will not have a designated person available to sound the alarm and direct evacuation in case of fire. Therefore, they will need to be aware of their surroundings and react to any emergencies that might arise, *considering the safety of the children in their care at all times.* If evacuation becomes necessary, they will follow the same procedures and evacuation routes outlined above, depending on the emergency. They are to stay with the children and proceed to the grass area in the west parking lot. As soon as possible, someone in the main sanctuary should be alerted to the situation, but the children will be moved to a safe place first.

Periodic practice sessions, or "Fire Drills," will be held during Sunday school on a regular basis so that everyone knows what to do if an emergency strikes. One of our main concerns is for the safety of all individuals on church grounds should an emergency arise, but we have special concerns for the infants, toddlers, and young children involved in childcare and/or Sunday school. If people are aware of what has been planned and practiced, are willing to help out if needed, and adhere to the above procedures, then panic and injury should be minimal, if at all.

## Fire Drill/Evacuation Procedures

1. Continuous intermittent ringing of the bell constitutes a fire alarm/evacuation signal.

2. First person out opens door and secures it in the open position. Class proceeds to designated area under the instruction of the teacher.

3. Take attendance sheets with you.

4. Teacher's Aide is the last one to leave the room and assures everyone is out.

5. Senior Teacher's Aide for each hall checks restrooms and closets, closes doors, and leaves building.

6. Wait for steady all-clear bell before returning to building.


(To be posted on the bulletin board of every classroom in the church)

## Sample Recruitment Letter

[Date]

Dear Church Family,

During the next few weeks, you will be hearing and seeing a lot about recruitment for Sunday school teachers and support staff. Next year we will need about forty people to commit to teach or work in other positions in order to fully meet the needs of our Christian education program. We will also be asking people to make a one-week commitment to teaching Vacation Bible School.

Our church school classrooms are filled each week with the sounds of children, youth, and adults laughing, singing, sharing, and learning. The people who provide these opportunities for Christian growth are many, and the need for additional support is ever present. The educational ministries of our church will only continue to grow stronger if we as a congregation support them with our time and our talents.

On two Sundays this month, *May 3 and May 17,* there will be an *Education Recruitment Table* set up outside the sanctuary following both services where you can sign up to serve in some capacity of Christian education beginning this June.

When you read this letter, we hope you will consider what your role in Christian education will be, and either stop by the Recruitment Table or call to offer your time. We want you to have the chance to say "yes." That is the purpose of this letter. Before you say "no," we challenge you to consider the following points.

1) All of us are teachers. We teach by the actions of our lives. What are you teaching? Are you suggesting by your life that Sunday school is important? That teaching or working to support Christian education is a high priority? That you are concerned that all classes have teachers? That all children, youth, and adults experience someone who cares?

2) As a Sunday school teacher, you help people know about Jesus Christ. You encourage children, youth, and adults to follow Him. You help people make commitments to become faithful in their daily lives.

3) When a child is baptized in our church, as a congregation we take corporate vows to bring the child up in the faith. Have you helped keep the vows you have repeated many times?

4) When we join the church, each of us promises to give our gifts, prayers, presence, and service. Do you take that promise seriously?

Sunday school and other facets of our educational ministry are vital to the life of this church. After you have given prayerful thought to this letter and decided on an area in which you might serve, stop by the *Education Recruitment Table* on *May 3 or May 17.*

Our needs are listed on the attached list of position descriptions.

If you have questions about any of these positions, stop by the *Education Recruitment Table* on *May 3 or May 17* and we'll share more specific information with you. As you can see, there are many needs—we hope you'll consider your personal situation and time commitments and pray about the role you can play in the educational ministry at our church. There is a place for your particular skills, your enthusiasm, and especially your love!

In Christ's Name

Director of Education        Christian Education Chairperson        Sunday School Superintendent

# Recruitment of Christian Education Workers

**BRIEF POSITION DESCRIPTIONS**

*SUNDAY SCHOOL TEACHER*

1. Possesses a growing knowledge and profession of the Christian faith.

2. Has an interest in and love for children, youth, or adults.

3. Actively participates in worship at our church.

4. Has a willingness to work with others.

5. Possesses organizational skills.

6. Uses curriculum provided. Is responsible for planning, preparing, and teaching. Works to meet individual class needs within this framework.

7. Arrives early to class and readies the room for students.

8. Welcomes students and takes attendance.

9. Follows up on attendance by contacting absentees.

10. Leaves the classroom clean and ready for use by others.

11. Is active in all facets of the Sunday school program.

12. Attends teacher-training meetings and workshops.

*ASSISTANT SUNDAY SCHOOL TEACHER*

1. Possesses same qualities as Sunday school teacher (as outlined above), but works in assisting in the areas of planning, preparation, teaching, attendance, cleanup, bulletin board design, etc.

2. Is active in all facets of the Sunday school program.

3. Attends teacher training meetings and workshops.

*SUBSTITUTE SUNDAY SCHOOL TEACHER*

1. Be available and willing to fill in for teachers on Sunday morning if regular teacher(s) cannot be there. (Indicate age and/or grade level preferences.)

2. Have a short lesson and accompanying materials ready to use if called at the last minute.

3. Arrive early and ready the room for students.

4. Leave the room clean and ready for use by others.

5. Attend teacher training meetings and workshops.

*SUNDAY SCHOOL OFFICE WORKER*

1. Arrive early.

2. Check attendance sheets to make sure they are in proper boxes.

3. Assist teachers in gathering materials.

4. Register new students—answer questions about Sunday school and church programs.

5. Answer phone.

6. Ring bell for class start and finish.

7. Gather attendance sheets, tabulate attendance, fill out master attendance sheet, and collect offering for Sunday school classes.

## CHILDCARE VOLUNTEER—8 A.M., 10 A.M., AND/OR 5 P.M.

*For infants and toddlers in Nursery:*

1. Arrive 15 minutes early and prepare to greet children and parents.

2. Supervise sign-in and sign-out system.

3. Provide loving care and supervision of children.

4. Assist parents in picking up children and children's belongings (i.e. bottles, diaper bags, jackets, etc.).

5. Tidy up room—put toys away, vacuum up any crumbs, empty trash, turn off heat, and lock doors.

*For preschoolers in Room 2:*

1. Arrive 15 minutes early and prepare to greet children and parents.

2. Supervise sign-in and sign-out system.

3. Provide loving care and supervision of children.

   Note: There is a general "lesson plan" provided which may include storytime, singing, simple indoor or outdoor games, a short project, and a snack.

4. Tidy up room—put toys away, wipe off tables, put chairs up on tables, turn off heat, and lock doors.

## JUNIOR CHURCH ASSISTANT/LEADER

1. Assist lead person first week—act as lead person following week.

2. Fill in when needed.

3. Promote Junior Church.

4. Help with staffing.

5. Be available to the children who get involved with Junior Church.

## JR. HIGH/SR. HIGH YOUTH GROUP COUNSELORS

Fun, dedicated, friendly, responsible adults ages 25 and older who possess leadership qualities, are active in worship, and who care about youth. Counselors attend and facilitate Sunday evening youth group meetings from 6–8:30 p.m. Short- or long-term commitments welcome.

## JR. HIGH/SR. HIGH YOUTH GROUP APPRENTICE COUNSELORS

Fun, dedicated, friendly, responsible young people ages 18 to 24 who possess leadership qualities, are active in worship, and who care about youth. Apprentice counselors attend and assist youth group counselors during Sunday evening meetings with youth from 6–8:30 p.m. Short- or long-term commitments welcome.

*CURRICULUM SUPPLY AIDE*

1. Be responsible for putting supplies back in designated places as they are returned to the Sunday school office each Sunday.

2. Assist Supply Coordinator in keeping supplies neat and clean.

3. Alert Supply Coordinator when certain supplies are running low and need to be ordered.

*LIBRARIAN FOR SUNDAY SCHOOL OFFICE*

1. Catalog books.

2. Organize shelves.

3. Clean and maintain shelves.

4. Set up check-out system and follow up on books checked out for an extended time.

5. Purchase new books.

6. Set up displays for teachers with books appropriate for the season (Christmas, Easter, etc.).

7. Promote the library.

*LIBRARIAN FOR CHURCH OFFICE*

1. Catalog books.

2. Organize shelves.

3. Clean and maintain shelves.

4. Set up check-out system and follow up on books checked out for an extended time.

5. Purchase new books.

6. Set up displays for congregation with books appropriate for the season (Christmas, Easter, etc.).

7. Promote the church library.

*AUDIOVISUAL MATERIALS COORDINATOR*

1. Identify, organize, and catalog audiovisual materials and equipment available (such as filmstrip projectors, screens, record players, tape recorders, VCRs, filmstrips, records, videotape cassettes, audio tapes, pictures, etc.).

2. Devise system to inform teachers of what is available.

3. Devise check-out system, monitor equipment checkout and return.

4. Make sure all equipment is in good working order.

5. Train people how to correctly use what we have available.

6. Clean, dust, and keep track of equipment and materials.

7. Share at teacher training meetings AV materials available for use and instruct in how to use them.

# Childcare Policies and Procedures

**GENERAL SETUP AND SECURING OF CHILDCARE PROVIDERS:**

1. The Childcare Coordinator will arrange for all childcare provided on church grounds for church events.

2. Groups requiring childcare will route all requests through the Childcare Coordinator with as much advance notice as possible.

3. *If a caregiver hired for a certain event cannot be there, contact should be made with the Childcare Coordinator ASAP,* and the Coordinator arrange for a substitute caregiver. At no time should a caregiver be engaged without the knowledge and approval of the Childcare Coordinator.

4. Parents are required to be on church grounds at all times while their children are placed in a church childcare setting.

**QUALIFICATIONS OF CAREGIVERS:**

1. All caregivers should be post–high school or older, or at least be in grades 9–12.

2. Youth in grades 7 and 8 may volunteer as unpaid childcare assistants. Although many youth this age are quite responsible, they should not be left in charge without an adult caregiver being present. This is for their own safety, as well as the safety of the children in their care, should an emergency arise.

3. At least once a year, youth interested in becoming involved in childcare will be encouraged to attend a Red Cross Babysitting Class offered through the church. A list of youth having completed this class will be maintained. Youth volunteers will be selected from this list whenever possible.

**PAYMENT METHOD AND TRACKING OF HOURS:**

1. Payment of childcare providers will be at the rate of:

   $ _____ per hour for adult caregivers (post–high school through adults)

   $ _____ per hour for youth caregivers (9th–12th grade)*

   *Note: Youth in 9th–12th grade may choose to be paid by check, or may request to earn credits to be applied toward camperships. Youth in grades 7 and 8 volunteering as unpaid childcare assistants will also be eligible to earn credits toward camperships, if they so desire.

2. A form will be completed by each caregiver at each event noting the actual hours involved in childcare. The Childcare Coordinator will keep accurate records on a weekly basis using these forms, keeping track of the actual hours and payments to be made to each caregiver during any given month.

3. All monthly childcare costs will initially be paid out of the general budget based on slips submitted before the end of the month by the Childcare Coordinator. For those groups preferring to pay for childcare out of their own

funds, the Childcare Coordinator will send itemized, monthly "bills" requesting reimbursement to the general budget for childcare for that group during that month.

4. All payment to caregivers will be made once a month by checks made out by the church.

5. A monthly statement will be sent by the Childcare Coordinator to any youth having requested campership credits, informing them of the amount they have earned.

6. If a caregiver is hired for an event, but no children show up, the caregiver will be paid for one full hour's work.

**LAUNDRY/TOY CLEANING PROCEDURES:**

1. At the end of each childcare session all used linens are to be placed in the hamper in the Crib Room. Arrangements for laundering of these linens will be made by the Childcare Coordinator.

2. All toys used during a childcare session will be wiped down with the disinfectant solution. Once a month, the Childcare Coordinator will arrange for all toys to be cleaned in a thorough manner by youth or other volunteers. Youth involved in this may earn credits toward camperships.

*Preschool-Age Childcare Schedule*

## Preschool-Age Childcare Schedule for Sunday Mornings

**9:45 A.M.—11:15 A.M.**

The childcare provider is responsible each Sunday to:

1) Arrive at church by 9:30 a.m.

2) Pick up boxes with toys, supplies, books, and snacks from the Sunday school office and take to the childcare room, arriving at the room by 9:40 a.m.

3) Set up two different activity tables for the children to involve themselves with at the beginning of this childcare hour. Materials for these will be in the boxes mentioned above and might include:

   a) Table 1—Playdoh

   b) Table 2—Art activity, such as paper and crayons, coloring pictures, or a simple craft project such as a collage on paper plates, etc.

   It is the responsibility of the provider to plan for these activities. These should be changed from time to time to provide new opportunities for exploration and involvement. Planning ahead is important—many supplies are available in the Sunday school office, but special supplies can be purchased by the Supply Coordinator, if advance notice is given.

4) A suggested schedule for each Sunday morning:

   a) Arrive early and have the room set up by 9:45 a.m.

   b) Have parents sign children in as they drop them off.

   c) Activity tables and free choice time with toys.

   d) Group activity such as Bible story time, finger plays, singing, movement activities, group games such as "Simon Says," "Duck, Duck, Goose," "Ring Around the Rosy," etc. If weather permits, occasional outdoor play is acceptable also.

   e) Cleanup of room should be at 10:45–10:50 a.m. Be sure to involve the children in helping to clean up. Serving snacks after all is clean is a great incentive and works well to get this done on time!

   f) If time permits, close with everyone on the rug listening to a fun story. This is calming, and also allows for children to be involved in an activity while waiting to be picked up. Volunteer helper(s) must be sure the children are signed out by the appropriate adult while this is occurring.

   g) After all children are picked up, straighten the room. Be sure all preschool toys and areas are straight, pick up and discard any unclaimed projects or Sunday school papers, wipe off tables, sweep floor, empty trash, turn off heat and lights, and be sure doors and windows are closed and locked. Return box with toys, supplies, books, etc., to Sunday school office— unused juice should be taken home or discarded.

# Guidelines for Caregivers

It is to be expected that all groups using childcare at our church will follow the current procedures, policies, and guidelines related to childcare to assure both safety and consistency of care for the infants, toddlers, and young children entrusted to us.

**GENERAL GUIDELINE:**

Parents are required to be on church grounds at all times while their children are in a church childcare setting.

**NURSERY CARE GUIDELINES:**

1) Before Nursery-Use Time:

    a) Turn thermostat on if weather is chilly.

    b) Place clean sheets on cribs and playpens.

    c) Take chairs off table.

    d) Place a few toys around the room to make it look inviting.

2) As Parents Arrive:

    a) Have parent sign child in on clipboard.

    b) Have parent make out two sticky name tags—one for the child and one for diaper bag or other items being left. *Place one tag on the child's back.*

    c) Take child from the parent and help child to adjust to the surroundings (you may use conversation, toys, or, as a last resort, crackers or Cheerios).

3) During Nursery Care Time:

    a) Keep gate locked at all times.

    b) Periodically (at least every half hour) check diapers and change if wet or dirty.

    c) Use changing table in Crib Room and follow posted diaper changing procedure (on wall in Crib Room).

    d) In case of accident or injury of child:

        i) If at all serious, send for parent—*do not leave other children alone to do this.*

        ii) For minor scrapes and cuts use First Aid materials in cupboard in Crib Room.

        iii) Notify parent when child is picked up as to what occurred and what was done.

    e) As departure time nears, begin picking up and putting away toys. Encourage children to help.

    f) Release children to parent only, unless otherwise arranged. *Have parents sign out.*

4) At End of Nursery Care Time:

    a) Remove all sheets and blankets from used cribs and playpens.

    b) Place used sheets and blankets in dirty clothes basket.

    c) Pick up and put away all toys.

    d) Pick up litter.

    e) Vacuum carpet.

    f) Put chairs up on table.

    g) Turn thermostat to "OFF."

    h) Check all doors and windows to be sure they're closed and locked. *Empty trash.*

    i) Turn lights out and lock door.

5) Diaper Changing Procedure:

    a) Place child on changing counter.

    b) Never let go of the child. They can move fast!

    c) Remove diaper and place on sink counter next to changing counter.

    d) Place clean diaper on child. Use diaper provided by parent or one from the cupboard under changing table.

    e) Dress the child and take or send them back to Nursery area.

    f) Clean up changing area. Place soiled materials in plastic bags provided and put in trash can. Wipe off the counter area. Pull down a new length of paper on changing area and discard the used section in the trash.

    g) *Wash hands thoroughly with disinfecting soap and water.*

**PRESCHOOL-AGE CHILDCARE GUIDELINES FOR SUNDAY MORNING:**

1) During Care Time:

    a) Have parent sign child in on clipboard.

    b) Help the child to adjust to the surroundings if necessary using conversation, a toy, etc.

    c) Interact with the children; talk to them, know their names, join in their games.

    d) Watch for safety hazards. *Do not* allow any running, hitting, or horseplay.

    e) The playground may be used in good weather, but children should not be left unsupervised at any time in either the classroom or on the playground.

    f) Provide a snack about halfway through the care time. Snacks should be eaten at the table.

    g) As departure time nears, begin picking up and putting away toys. Encourage the children to help.

h) Release the children to parent only, unless otherwise arranged. *Have parents sign out.*

2) After The Children Have Been Picked Up:

   a) Discard all Sunday school papers, crafts, etc., left by the children.

   b) Wipe off tables, pick up cups and napkins and throw them away. Chairs should be put up on the tables.

   c) Check to be sure heat and lights are turned off, and all doors and windows are closed and locked.

   d) Take one last look. Is everything put away and are the cupboards closed up?

   e) Empty trash on the way out if it contains food items.

**INSTRUCTIONS FOR YOUTH DOING CHILDCARE:**

1) Be sure you interact with each child—know their names, talk to them, and join in their games.

2) Watch for safety hazards—*do not* allow any running, hitting, or horseplay.

3) Check every 30 minutes to see if any younger children need to use the restroom or need a diaper change.

4) *Please do not do homework!* Your primary responsibility is being with the children and caring for them. Group games such as "Simon Says" or "Duck, Duck, Goose," etc., or reading to the group are great and provide positive, structured experiences.

5) Provide a snack about halfway through the time schedule. Snacks should be eaten at the table. *Do not* allow the children to get up and wander with food or drink.

6) At the end of childcare time be sure that:

   a) Toys/games are put away;

   b) Chairs are put up on the table;

   c) Carpet is vacuumed;

   d) Trash is emptied;

   e) Heater is turned off, doors and windows locked, and lights turned off.

**GUIDELINES FOR LAUNDRY/TOY CLEANING:**

1) At the end of each childcare session all used linens should be placed in the dirty clothes basket in the Crib Room. Arrangements for weekly laundering of these linens will be made by the Childcare Coordinator.

2) All toys used during a childcare session should be wiped off with the disinfectant solution found under the sink in the Crib Room.

# Nursery Care Provider Agreement

**The responsibility of a Nursery Care Provider is an important one. It is often the first contact new or visiting individuals with children have with someone at our church. Our main objective is to provide a clean, safe, happy, and loving environment for our little ones while they are in our care.**

The Nursery Care Provider position description states that I need to show the following characteristics:

(1) A willingness and ability to follow the instructions and policy of the church, especially as they are related to this position; and

(2) A strong commitment to providing regular, dependable, loving, quality childcare.

General policies I need to follow include those listed below:

(a) Arrive 15–20 minutes before any scheduled event to ready the Nursery and to receive the children as they are dropped off;

(b) Follow the prescribed sign-in/sign-out procedures;

(c) Clean and straighten the room after all children are gone, following the procedures listed on the instruction sheet(s) found in the room;

(d) Make the Childcare Coordinator aware as soon as possible if unable to fulfill a responsibility, so they can arrange for another provider in a timely fashion.

In assuming the part-time position of Nursery Care Provider, I have gone over the current policies and procedures of the church related to childcare, and I understand what is expected of me. *I am aware that if I am late or fail to show up for two scheduled childcare functions that we will mutually agree my performance is not meeting the needs of the church as outlined above and a replacement will be sought.* I am also aware that I am under a probationary period of three months, during which time my performance will be monitored and evaluated. If I fail to meet the above specifications, and do not show improvement after having been counseled regarding this, I am aware that my services can be terminated without notice. I sign this willingly, and with the best interests in mind of the little ones entrusted to my care.

_____

Signature of Provider           Date

# Childcare Sign-in Sheet for _____

| Child's Name | Age | Parent's Name | In | Out | Signature Upon Pick-up |
|---|---|---|---|---|---|
| | | | | | |
| | | | | | |
| | | | | | |
| | | | | | |
| | | | | | |
| | | | | | |
| | | | | | |
| | | | | | |
| | | | | | |
| | | | | | |
| | | | | | |
| | | | | | |
| | | | | | |
| | | | | | |
| | | | | | |
| | | | | | |

## Childcare Time Log

Name: _____

❏ Youth (7–8)   ❏ Youth (9–12)   ❏ Adult

Date: _____

Time In: _____

Time Out: _____

Event: _____

Signature of Caregiver: _____

Coordinator's Signature: _____

**PLEASE CIRCLE:**

Volunteer     Campership     Monthly
Service       Credit         Check

## Childcare Time Log

Name: _____

❏ Youth (7–8)   ❏ Youth (9–12)   ❏ Adult

Date: _____

Time In: _____

Time Out: _____

Event: _____

Signature of Caregiver: _____

Coordinator's Signature: _____

**PLEASE CIRCLE:**

Volunteer     Campership     Monthly
Service       Credit         Check

## Childcare Time Log

Name: _____

❏ Youth (7–8)   ❏ Youth (9–12)   ❏ Adult

Date: _____

Time In: _____

Time Out: _____

Event: _____

Signature of Caregiver: _____

Coordinator's Signature: _____

**PLEASE CIRCLE:**

Volunteer     Campership     Monthly
Service       Credit         Check

## Childcare Time Log

Name: _____

❏ Youth (7–8)   ❏ Youth (9–12)   ❏ Adult

Date: _____

Time In: _____

Time Out: _____

Event: _____

Signature of Caregiver: _____

Coordinator's Signature: _____

**PLEASE CIRCLE:**

Volunteer     Campership     Monthly
Service       Credit         Check

# Bible Presentation Sunday Guidelines

It has been the practice of our church for many years to present our current 3rd graders, plus 4th, 5th, and 6th graders new to our church since the last presentation, with Bibles on a special Sunday. To ensure that the Bible presentation goes smoothly and is generally the same each year the following procedures shall be followed:

Beginning in September, the Bibles will be presented as follows: from a representative of the church to the parent(s) to the child. This will include the parents in this very special process and symbolize the responsibility of both the church and the home in passing on the stories of the Bible to our children. However, no child will be excluded or made to feel inferior if their parent(s) cannot be a part of this process.

Generally, Bible Presentation Sunday should be held sometime in September (as a part of Christian Education Month activities), or in early November (to coincide with Bible Sunday). Both times are appropriate, but consistency from year to year is desirable. The date should be calendared early in the year, and the pastor should be kept aware of all plans.

*Two months prior to Bible Presentation Sunday:*

1. Prepare a list of all children eligible to receive Bibles (current 3rd graders in the church, plus 4th through 6th graders new since the last presentation).

    a. Check Sunday school class rosters for names

    b. Run publicity in the newsletter and orders of worship asking parents of eligible children who do not attend Sunday school to make contact with a designated individual (director of education or Sunday school superintendent, etc.) with names and grades of the children.

2. Begin running periodic articles in the newsletter and order of worship about Bible Presentation Sunday to keep this event before the congregation.

*One month prior to Bible Presentation Sunday:*

1. Order Bibles. The New Revised Standard Version (NRSV) should be used since this goes along with the curriculum being used in our Sunday school.

2. Have names calligraphied on a separate insert page, or typed on an adhesive-backed Bible nameplate. These inserts should not be placed in the Bibles until after the presentation so Bibles can be used in future presentations in the event the intended child did not receive the Bible for some reason.

3. Alert Sunday school teachers to the process.

4. Send letters to parents of children receiving Bibles informing them of the date, etc., and inviting them to attend and be a part of this special morning.

*On the morning of Bible Presentation Sunday:*

1. Have the children who are to receive Bibles and their parents sit together in the front two pews of the church at the 10 a.m. worship service. Alert the ushers to this special seating arrangement in advance.

2. At the time of the presentation, a short background should be given on the Bible, its importance to us as a people of God, reasons why we present Bibles to our children, etc. Recipients will then be called forward alphabetically to be presented with their Bibles, following the procedure recommended above.

# BIBLE

# PRESENTATION

# SUNDAY

## *is next Sunday!*

Bibles will be presented
at the 10 A.M. worship service
to all 3rd graders,
as well as 4th, 5th, and 6th graders
new to our church and
Sunday school classes
since last November.

## *Don't miss this exciting event!*

## *Letter to Parents: Bible Presentation Sunday*

[Date]


Dear _____ ,

Sunday, September 20, is Bible Presentation Sunday at our church. As a special part of the 10 a. m. worship service that morning we will be presenting Bibles to all of our third-grade Sunday school students, including your [son/daughter], [name].

As the Word of God, the Bible contains much that your child will draw from and build upon both now and in the years to come. We hope you will place this date on your calendar and plan on being present with your child during that worship service. Each child will be called forward individually to receive this special gift from our church—their very own Bible. This is always an exciting event for those involved, and one we are sure you won't want to miss.


Yours in Christ,



Director of Education

# Letter to Teachers: Bible Presentation Sunday

## BIBLE SUNDAY IS COMING!

Dear Teachers,

Sunday, September 20, will be Bible Presentation Sunday at our church! As a special part of the 10 a.m. worship service that morning, we will be presenting Bibles to all of the 3rd graders at our church, as well as 4th, 5th, and 6th graders new to our church and Sunday school classes since last November. The children will be called forward by name to receive their own special Bible as a gift from our church, and this is always an exciting event for those involved!

Letters are being mailed to the parents of the following children inviting them to be in attendance at 10 a.m. worship on that Sunday. Please check the names listed below and add any we might have missed. Then initial and return this sheet to the Sunday school office.

Thanks for your help. You play such a vital role in the Christian education of our youngsters, and you are always in my prayers. God bless you in all that you do to bring the light of Christ into our world and into the lives of our children!

Collect a hug when you see me!

Yours In Christ,

Director of Education

# Promotion Sunday: Letter to Students and Parents

## PROMOTION SUNDAY
## JUNE 7
## 9–9:45 A.M. SUNDAY SCHOOL HOUR

Dear Sunday School Students and Parents,

The school year is almost over, and plans are once again being made to celebrate the endings and the beginnings that this transition provides. Life itself is a series of progressive steps, and our church feels it is very important that we pause to recognize these steps in the faith journeys of the children and youth who attend our Sunday school. Every student moving up an age- or grade-level will receive a special promotion certificate, and those involved in changing classrooms due to an age- or grade-level shift will receive an additional special something as well.

Please mark your calendars now for Sunday, June 7th, from 9 a.m.–9:45 a.m. and plan to share in our annual Promotion Sunday Assembly. We will be honoring our Sunday school students from 2 years old up through senior high, and it's an event you won't want to miss!

Yours in Christ,

Director of Education

Education Committee Chairperson

Sunday School Superintendent

# Confirmation Program Letter

Sample first letter to be sent to potential participants in the Confirmation class, with schedules and discussion topics attached.

*Note:* It is recognized that the term "Confirmation" may not apply in all denominations to the process of orienting young people in the requirements and obligations of church membership. When using the materials dealing with "Confirmation" as guidelines, the applicable term should be substituted.

[Date]

Greetings!

Plans for our Confirmation program are well underway, and I am excited to be involved in both the teaching and planning of this! Confirmation involves 12 weeks of classes and activities designed to assist you as youth in exploring not only your faith, but what it means to be a Christian disciple. The Confirmation program culminates with the opportunity for you to unite with the church in full membership on May 31 at the Confirmation Sunday worship service. This is an important and exciting step in your personal journey of faith, and I am hoping you will make the decision to join with me in this venture.

Enclosed you will find a list of dates and times for all Confirmation class sessions. Please go over these with your parents and decide whether or not you will be a part of this year's Confirmation class. If you do choose to be confirmed this year, it will be necessary for you to regularly attend the scheduled class sessions or arrange for a make-up session should an emergency arise.

As I said, I am *very* excited to be leading Confirmation this year! I will be contacting you within the next couple of weeks to discuss your decision, or you may contact me at the church office. You are in my prayers as you make this exciting and important decision.

Peace and Grace,

Director of Education

# Confirmation Class Schedule and Discussion Topics

| Day/Date | Topic | Time |
|---|---|---|
| Friday, 3–6 | Confirmation Kickoff Potluck | 6:30–8 p.m. |
| Saturday, 3–7 | "With God and the Spirit" | 3–4:30 p.m. |
| Saturday, 3–14 | "With Jesus Christ" | 3–4:30 p.m. |
| Saturday, 3–21 | "With the Bible: The Great Story" | 3–4:30 p.m. |
| Saturday, 3–28 | "With the Bible: How to Read the Great Story" | 3–4:30 p.m. |
| Saturday, 4–4 | "With the People of God: In Ministry" | 3–4:30 p.m. |
| Tuesday, 4–7 | Trip to Jewish Temple | 4–6:30 p.m. |
| Wednesday, 4–8 | Observing Commission/Committee Meetings | 7:30–9:15 p.m. |
| Saturday, 4–11 | "With the People of God: From Simon Peter . . ." | 3–4:30 p.m. |
| Wednesday, 4–15 | Confirmation Trip | 5 p.m.–1 a.m. |
| Saturday , 4–18 | "With the People of God" | 3–4:30 p.m. |
| Saturday, 4–25 | "With the People of God: In Worship" | 3–4:30 p.m. |
| Friday, 5–1 | "With Your Life: Decision Making" | 4–6 p.m. |
| *Sunday, 5–3* | *Sunday Evening Worship (Youth Sunday)* | *5 p.m.* |
| Saturday, 5–9 | "With Your Life: The Spiritual Life" | 3–4:30 p.m. |
| Friday–Saturday, 5–15/5–16 | Confirmation Overnight at the Church "With Your Life: The Life of a Servant" "With Christian Hope" | 6 p.m–11:30 a.m. |
| Saturday, 5–23 | **NO CONFIRMATION CLASS DUE TO MEMORIAL DAY HOLIDAY** | |
| Saturday, 5–30 | "With Your Decision About Confirmation" (Final Class) | 3–4:30 p.m. |
| | Closing Potluck for Confirmands | 6:30–8 p.m. |
| Sunday, 5–31 | Confirmation Sunday | 10 a.m. |

# *Letter for Confirmands*

Sample second letter to be sent to all youth who have decided to participate in the Confirmation Class.

[Date]

Greetings!

Confirmation classes will be starting soon, and I'm getting really excited about sharing in this process with you and your families! Our *Confirmation Kickoff Potluck* has been scheduled for *Friday evening, March 6, from 6:30–8:00 p.m.* This will be an enjoyable evening of food and fellowship, and will include a brief orientation session regarding Confirmation schedules, requirements, field trips and outings, etc. Families of all the youth taking part in Confirmation are invited, and childcare will be provided after dinner for younger brothers and sisters.

Since this is a potluck meal, I am asking that each family *bring either a main dish or salad for eight to share.* Drinks, rolls, and dessert will be provided. *RSVPs are necessary only if you and your family will be unable to attend, or if childcare will be needed.* Please let me know no later than Sunday, March 1.

As I said, I am *very* excited that you have chosen to take part in Confirmation this year! I hold each of you in my prayers as we begin this exciting journey in faith together!

See you and your families on Friday, March 6, at 6:30 p.m.!

Peace and Grace,

Director of Education

# *Letter for Church Leaders: Confirmation*

Sample letter to be sent to the leadership of the church that have been invited to participate in the Confirmation process.

[Date]

Greetings!

Confirmation classes will be starting soon, and I'm getting really excited about sharing in this process with the youth of our church! As of this date, we have 15 youth who have signed up to participate in the Confirmation class—what a tremendous joy it will be to lead them through this journey in faith assisted by many of the leaders in our church!

I am writing to ask for both your prayers and your participation as we move through Confirmation. As leaders of our church in a variety of capacities, your presence, your prayers, your interest, and your support can have a significant impact on the lives of the youth involved. For that reason, I would like to invite you and your family to our *Confirmation Kickoff Potluck for Friday evening, March 6, from 6:30–8:00 p.m.* This will be an enjoyable evening of food and fellowship, and will include a brief orientation session regarding Confirmation schedules, requirements, field trips and outings, etc. The families of all the youth taking part in Confirmation have been invited, and childcare will be provided after dinner for younger brothers and sisters. This will be a great opportunity for you to meet the youth taking part in Confirmation and allow them to begin to get to know you, as well!

Since this is a potluck meal, I am asking each family or individual attending to *bring either a main dish or salad for eight to share.* Drinks, rolls, and dessert will be provided. *RSVPs are necessary only if you will be unable to attend, or will need childcare.* Please let me know no later than Sunday, March 1.

Thank you in advance for the support I know you will lend—I look forward to seeing you and your families on Friday, March 6, at 6:30 p.m.!

Peace and Grace,

Director of Education

# CONFIRMATION CLASS

**WELCOME TO THE CLASS:**

(NAMES OF PARTICIPANTS)

**PURPOSE:**

Confirmation provides a time for exploring, questioning, and choosing. It is a setting within which you can say "yes" to the touch of God in your lives and affirm all that is good. Through confirmation, you have the opportunity to examine and decide what your relationship with the church will be, now and in the years to come . . . for you will begin to explore what it means to live life as a journey into faith and to make important decisions along that journey's way! Confirmation is an initial step you take toward really informing yourself and getting involved in developing your faith.

**RESPONSIBILITIES OF CONFIRMANDS:**

- To be in attendance at all sessions.
- To complete all reading assignments and to come prepared to participate in all discussions.
- To offer support, acceptance, and understanding to your fellow confirmands at all times, and to share openly and honestly in the fun and laughter, new discoveries and ideas, and pain and struggle of growth.

**RESPONSIBILITIES OF PARENTS AND CONGREGATION:**

- To be visible in support of confirmands by your prayers and signs of love.
- To discuss with the confirmands their impressions, experiences, hopes, and dreams.

**RESPONSIBILITIES OF INSTRUCTOR AND FACILITATORS:**

- To creatively prepare and communicate lessons.
- To be patient with confirmands.
- To encourage confirmands to give their best to the journey.
- To be attentive to, supportive of, and compassionate with the joys and needs of the confirmands.

## *Ending Letter and Schedule—Confirmands*

Sample letter to be sent to all participants that have completed the Confirmation class requirements.

[Date]

Greetings!

It's hard to believe, but this Confirmation class is almost at an end! It seems like just yesterday that we started this journey together—we've learned a lot and shared a lot, had fun together, laughed, cried some, and even gotten upset at each other a few times. But through all of this I think we've also grown a lot, as individuals and as Christians on a faith journey together. I've enjoyed sharing this process of growth with you, and you will continue to be in my prayers and my heart long after our class times together have ended—each of you has become very special to me, and I'll never forget you and the ways you've helped me grow in my own faith!

Our *Closing Potluck and Celebration* has been scheduled for *Saturday evening, May 30, from 6:30–8:30 p.m.* This will be an enjoyable evening of food and fellowship, and will include a time of reflection on what Confirmation has meant to us as individuals, as well as a time for some special recognition for each of you as confirmands. There will also be a short practice time in the sanctuary in preparation for Confirmation Sunday. Families are invited, and childcare will be provided after dinner for younger brothers and sisters.

Since this is a potluck meal, I am asking that each family once again *bring either a main dish or salad for eight to share.* Drinks, rolls, and dessert will be provided. *RSVPs are necessary only if you and your family will be unable to attend, or if childcare will be needed.* Please let me know no later than Tuesday, May 26.

I look forward to seeing you and your families on Saturday, May 30, at 6:30 p.m.!

Peace and Grace,

Director of Education

## Ending Letter and Schedule—Leadership

Sample thank-you letter to be sent to the leadership and volunteers of the church who participated in the Confirmation class.

[Date]

Greetings!

It's hard to believe, but this Confirmation class is almost at an end. It has been a tremendous joy to lead our youth through this journey in faith assisted by many of the leaders in our church, and has provided me with a number of experiences I will not soon forget!

I am writing to thank you for both your prayers and your participation as we have moved through the Confirmation process during the past 12 weeks. As leaders of our church in a variety of capacities, your presence, your prayers, your interest, and your support have had a significant impact on the lives of the youth involved. For that reason, I would like to invite you and your family to our *Closing Potluck and Celebration* scheduled for *Saturday evening, May 30, from 6:30–8:30 p.m.* This will be an enjoyable evening of food and fellowship, and will include a time of reflection on what Confirmation has meant to the youth involved, as well as a time for some special recognition for each of our confirmands. The families of the youth taking part in Confirmation have been invited, and childcare will be provided after dinner for younger brothers and sisters. This will be a great opportunity for you to congratulate the youth who have taken part in confirmation and wish them well on their continuing faith journeys!

Since this is a potluck meal, I am asking each family or individual attending to *bring either a main dish or salad for eight to share.* Drinks, rolls, and dessert will be provided. *RSVPs are necessary only if you will be unable to attend, or will need childcare.* Please let me know no later than Tuesday, May 26.

Thank you again for the prayers and support you have provided—I look forward to seeing you and your families on Saturday, May 30, at 6:30 p.m.!

Peace and Grace,

Director of Education

## Adult Education Survey Form

Adult Sunday School (9:00–9:45 a.m.) provides a unique opportunity for Christians to share their joys as well as their struggles in following God's plan. Sunday morning classes can make a difference for you.

1. Listed below are possible topics for the development of *new* adult classes on Sunday mornings. Which of these topics would interest you enough to actually *attend a Sunday morning class?* (Check as many as you wish.)

❏ Bible Study for Beginners
❏ Men and Women of the Bible
❏ Caring for Aging Parents
❏ Death, Dying, and Grief
❏ Developing Strong Families
❏ Personal Growth—
   Where Does God Fit In?
❏ Marriage Enrichment
❏ Christian Disciplines

❏ Doctrines and Duties of
   the Christian Faith
❏ Single Again—Life after Divorce,
   Separation, or Death of a Spouse
❏ Social Issues (e.g., Abortion, Homo-
   sexuality, AIDS, Drug Abuse, etc.)
❏ Parenting Issues (e.g., Discipline,
   Developing Self-Esteem,
   Sexuality, etc.)
❏ Ages & Stages—Life Transitions
❏ Study of Islam

❏ Other Ideas (please list below): _____

_____

_____

_____

2. Would a short-term series (4–6 weeks) be appealing to you?
   ❏ Yes   ❏ No   ❏ Maybe

3. Would coffee fellowship before the Sunday school hour be appealing to you?
   ❏ Yes   ❏ No

4. If you are NOT interested in attending adult Sunday school at this time, please tell us why. Your ideas will help us as we plan:

I'm not interested in an adult Sunday morning class at this time because:
   ❏ The worship service(s) meets my needs.
   ❏ The time commitment is too much.
   ❏ The topics are not of interest to me.
   ❏ Other: _____

_____

_____

*Please drop this survey in the offering plate or in the basket marked "Survey"
in the narthex as you exit the sanctuary today. Thank you for your help
in making our Sunday school better meet your needs!*

*Study Announcement*

We're offering two Lenten Study opportunities during the week
for **Adults and Youth** this year!

Identical studies,
just held on different days and at different times
to better accommodate your busy schedules!

Make plans now to join us as together we

# "Journey to Calvary"
## during a special
## 7-week Lenten Study

## *Monday Evening Study*
7–8 p.m.
**Fireside Room**
Dates: March 2, 9, 16, 23, 30, April 6, and 13
Childcare available on request

## *Tuesday Breakfast Study*
6–7 a.m.
**Fireside Room**
Dates: March 3, 10, 17, 24, 31, April 7, and 14
A light breakfast will be served at this study.

*Join us for fellowship, reflection, and sharing*

# "Journey to Calvary"
# Monday Evening Lenten Study
### March 2, 9, 16, 23, 30, April 6, and 13
### 7–8 p.m. in Fireside Room

NAME                                                    PHONE NO.

_____

_____

_____

_____

_____

_____

_____

_____

_____

_____

_____

_____

_____

_____

_____

_____

_____

_____

_____

_____

## *Letter to Registrants*

Sample letter to be sent to participants in the Lenten Study class.

[Date]

Greetings!

I am really excited you have signed up to participate in this year's special Lenten Study class! Our Advent studies were well received, and I anticipate our Lenten studies will be as well. It's a special opportunity to expand and deepen our understandings, to progress in our individual faith journeys, and to share in a time of fellowship and discussion together. I know I'm really looking forward to our time together, and I trust you are too!

Study booklets will be available at the first class session, or you can make arrangements with me to pick yours up early. This year's study is entitled "Journey to Calvary" and promises to be a special way to remember and renew our relationship with God as we move through the season of Lent toward the promise that is Easter! Other items you will probably want to bring to class each week include your Bible, a tablet or paper for taking notes, and pencils or pens.

Let me know if there is anything I can do for you. I look forward to the unique insights and contributions you will bring to our time together. As we study and pray together, may your life be touched with a deeper understanding of how very much God loves you, as well as what He is calling you to do in His name! God bless you, and I'll see you this Sunday, if not sooner!

In His Service,

Director of Education

# Vacation Bible School: Planning Time Line

## Suggested Planning Time Line for Vacation Bible School

1. Begin planning early, by late January or early February.

2. Secure a Vacation Bible School (VBS) director and assistant director, or two co-directors.

3. Set first planning meeting date. Have the VBS director, assistant director, last year's director, education committee chairperson, and pastor be a part of this meeting. Discuss the following:

    a. General Format and Schedule—daytime or evening, children only or cross-generational, dates and times for VBS, staff meeting dates and times, length of VBS (1 week or 2), curriculum materials. Also plan closing potluck, picnic, or BBQ, as well as the closing program.

    b. Brainstorm names of possible people for different age-level classes, workshops, etc. Divide list of names and begin calling. Meet again and report on progress, add names to list of possibles, etc.

    c. Continue to meet every 2 weeks or so to keep up on recruitment, continue planning, and make sure things are running smoothly, etc.

4. Take recommendations to the education committee and governing body for approval.

5. Order teacher curriculum materials and sample student materials ASAP—be sure to have them by the first VBS staff meeting.

6. Hold first staff meeting, possibly in conjunction with a staff dinner, to go over schedules and general information and instructions with everyone, and then divide into age-level groups for some training with the curriculum materials.

7. Preregister 7–8 weeks ahead (at least by early June, before school is out and people begin to leave on vacations). Set up tables in the patio area after worship for several Sundays. Take registrations up to and during the first couple of days of VBS.

8. Order student curriculum materials about 5 weeks ahead.

9. Begin publicity in the church newsletter, order of worship, and the community several weeks in advance. Posters in local businesses as well as around the church keep VBS in people's minds. Have minute-speakers during worship on Sunday morning.

10. Hold second staff meeting to go over last-minute instructions, answer questions, pass out student curriculum materials, etc. Make this a time of fellowship and inspiration as well, so your staff leaves motivated and ready to begin!

11. Have a VBS staff dedication service during one of the worship services the Sunday before. It is really important to recognize and to lift up the hardworking and committed people who have said yes to staffing VBS, so make this an integral part of your planning!

12. Enjoy VBS and reap the benefits of your hard work and planning!

13. Evaluate your VBS program with participants and staff. Pass out evaluation forms to students in grades five through adults, as well as staff. Evaluations are a good source of great ideas for making next year's VBS even better!!!

14. Be sure to thank the staff in some way once VBS is over. Possibly have the director write thank-you notes to each staff member, and perhaps put a special thank-you in the church newsletter with all VBS staff names listed, or both.

15. A written report with attendance figures, etc., should be compiled by the director of VBS and presented to the education committee and governing body. A copy should be kept in the VBS file for future reference.

16. Send letters out to children/youth/adults who are not members of the church but who were in attendance at VBS. This is an invaluable form of outreach and evangelism to the community, and this step should not be overlooked. The pastor should also follow up this letter with a personal contact within a week of VBS completion.

# OUR CHURCH

*Invites You to the Third Annual*

# EVENING VACATION BIBLE SCHOOL
# AUGUST 3–7
# 6:30 to 8:30 P.M.

*Study classes for ages 2 through adults*

*Workshops for grade 5 through adults during second hour*

Childcare provided in the nursery
for children under 2

*Picnic style dinner each evening
from 5:45 p.m.–6:15 p.m.*

Registration forms available
in the church office

# Class and Workshop Information

## FESTIVAL!
### *WORSHIP WITH JESUS, WORSHIP TODAY*

Vacation Bible School—August 3 to August 7

Dinner:    5:45 to 6:15 p.m.

Full Gathering in the Sanctuary with Music and Singing    6:30 to 6:45 p.m.

Classes for children 4th grade and younger:    6:45 to 8:30 p.m.

Classes for 5th grade through adults:    6:45 to 7:35 p.m.

Elective Workshops:    7:40 to 8:30 p.m.

Vacation Bible School offers an exciting opportunity for adults and children to learn and grow in fellowship with one another and with Christ. Each evening a simple picnic-style meal will be prepared and served by one of the groups in our church. Our children's program will be centered around the theme "FESTIVAL! Worship With Jesus, Worship Today." Adults are invited to choose one of four study classes listed below. Youth in grades 5 and up plus our adults are also invited to select one of our many interesting and fun workshops. We will conclude the week with a Dessert Social and Closing Program on Saturday, August 8, in the social hall. Please fill out a registration form for each person who will be attending Vacation Bible School. We look forward to seeing you!

If you have any questions, please call our Registrar, _____, or our Education Director.

Cost for one full week of classes and workshops is $3 per person or $5 per family, unless otherwise noted in the workshop descriptions. Payment may be made in cash, or by check payable to the church.

---

Adult Study Classes—6:45 p.m. to 7:35 p.m. (Select one)

### *The Parables*

Through the stories that Jesus told—the parables—we can see how He used the events of everyday life to teach us how we are to live in the kingdom of God. This 5-night video-enhanced study class features Dr. Maxie Dunnam, popular writer, preacher, and Bible-study leader. Join other adults in hearing what Jesus has to say to you, today!

### The Holy Spirit

"Nevertheless I tell you the truth. It is to your advantage that I go away; for if I do not go away, the Helper will not come to you; but if I depart, I will send Him to you."

(John 16 : 7)

This was what Jesus said when He promised that he would not leave us alone, but would send the Holy Spirit to help us. The third member of the Trinity is known by many names—*Helper, Comforter, Counselor, Advocate.* But who exactly is the Holy Spirit? You are invited to join us for this 5-night study class aimed at deepening your understanding of the powerful presence of the Holy Spirit, "God present with us for guidance, for comfort, and for strength."

### Jewish Festivals and Celebrations

This class will tell the colorful story of the Jewish holidays and their development. The symbolism, ritual practices, ceremonial objects, and special foods will be traced to their historical roots. We will discuss the joys, the struggles, and the courage of a people who, through the living reminders of their spiritual essence, have carried on with their festivals and celebrations for over 2000 years.

### Father John Powell's "Faith" Series

This dynamic video series features Father John Powell, a powerful teacher, lecturer, and writer on both theological and psychological issues. This 5-night study class features videos and discussion on different aspects of FAITH, such as "The God Connection," "Comfort and Challenge," "God's Gift," "A New Vision," and "Prelude to Prayer." Join others in this stimulating and thought-provoking series, as Powell touches on the everyday realities of our faith in ways you will respond to and remember!

---

Elective Workshops—7:40 p.m. to 8:30 p.m. (Select one)

### "Free to Be Me — Likable, Lovable Me!" (Grades 5 & 6 only)

Choose your thoughts . . . Choose your feelings . . . Choose the behavior that makes you a winner! Come and find out more about this terrific person—YOU!

### Babysitting Clinic (Age 11 and up)

This workshop is designed for 11-year-olds and up. Basic child care, accident prevention, simple first aid, child sexual abuse information, as well as activities for young children will be discussed during this week-long course. Do you have a babysitter who would benefit from this class? Or perhaps an older son or daughter who babysits the other children in the family? Invite them to participate! This class has lots of helpful information to help the babysitter in all areas of childcare.

**Stained Glass**  (Age 13 and up)                                    Fee:  $15.00

Open to 13-year-olds and up, *this workshop will be limited to the first 12 who sign up.* This class will offer the beginner an opportunity to learn the basics of stained glass. Tools will be provided, but if you have a 40-watt soldering iron of your own it would be a big help to have you bring it. You will learn the basics of glass cutting, leading or foiling, and design, and will make a window-hanging or sun-catcher as your week's project. *Money is payable at time of registration.*

**Puppetry** (All ages)

Come find out what puppets can do and be! Handle all kinds of puppets—see puppets that can help make books come alive—make different kinds of puppets and take them home, use them, or give them as gifts. You'll enjoy this "no strings attached" workshop, so join us!

**3 Make-and-Take Crafts**  (All ages)                                  Fee:  $10.00

Open to anyone from 5th grade up to adults, *this workshop will be limited to the first 15 who sign up.* The materials fee will cover most of the necessary supplies, but some items will need to be brought from home. Three different holiday projects will be taught—Stiffy Ghosts, a Country Rag Heart Wreath, and Broom Reindeer. Supplies needed from home include: Scissors; 3 different colored fabrics for Heart Wreath at 1/4 yd. each; different-sized bottles for ghost bodies (ketchup, grape juice, or Martinelli Sparkling Cider bottles work well); and golf balls or tennis balls for ghost heads. *Money is payable at time of registration*—space is limited, so sign up and don't be left out of the fun!

**Cooking—Bible Foods Exploratory** (All ages)                          Fee:  $2.00

This class will focus on the different types of food found in the Bible, and is suitable for all ages. We'll be preparing these foods in class to experience the holidays and traditions set forth in the Old and New Testaments. Sign up for good food and good fellowship, and learn more about our culinary heritage! *Money is payable at time of registration.*

**Ballroom Dancing** (All ages)

This class is open to all ages and couples are not a requirement. We will be learning basic steps to the Foxtrot, Waltz, Swing, Rumba, and Cha-Cha. Different music styles will be used to appeal to different age groups. Come and swing with us!

*Introduction to CPR*  (All ages)
Learn basic CPR instruction under the guidance of a registered nurse. Choking and other life threatening situations will be reviewed along with practice time on mannequins to help prepare you for any situation. This is not a certification course, but it will enable you to respond to most emergencies with knowledgeable assistance. Whether you've taken CPR courses before or are just interested in learning what CPR is all about, come and join this valuable workshop. It could save a life! All ages are welcome.

*Personal Growth—5 Mini-Workshops with Varied Facilitators*  (Ages 18 and older)
This class will explore a variety of topics related to individual, personal growth and psychological and physical well-being. Come for one, two, three or all five nights—you'll be glad you did! Topics to be covered include: Behavior Modification, Self-Defense, Dental Health Issues, "Loving Others by Loving Yourself," and Personal Awareness and Self-Esteem.

*Banner Art*  (All ages)
The banners in our sanctuary add a special touch to each Sunday's worship time and always generate special words of praise! Over the years, many members of our church have worked together to create the banners we currently use—but there are many seasons and special situations we don't yet have banners for! Why not spend the week helping design and create some brand new banners for our church to use at different times during the year?! You'll be learning the art of banner making, serving the Lord, and enriching our worship time with your finished products! What a great way to relax, enjoy the fellowship of others, and create something beautiful and useful that will be enjoyed by many, both this year and in the years to come! Join us, won't you?

*JOIN US FOR DINNER?*  Each evening from 5:45–6:15 p.m. a simple dinner will be prepared and served picnic-style by one of the groups in our church. A free-will donation will be accepted to cover the cost of the food. Plan now to join us for one or more evenings! The menu will include:

| Monday | Sandwich Bar | Circle of Love |
| Tuesday | Super Nachos | Men's Fellowship |
| Wednesday | Hot Dogs | Fireside Friends Circle |
| Thursday | Sloppy Joes | Youth Group |
| Friday | Hamburgers | Evangelism Committee |

# Vacation Bible School Registration Form

Please fill out one form for each person registering for Vacation Bible School. Registration open from June 28 through August 2, unless otherwise noted.

Name: _____

Address: _____

Home Phone: _____

❏ Adult ❏ Child    Age: _____ Grade: _____

## Study Classes *(Adults choose one)* 6:45 p.m. to 7:35 p.m.

❏ The Parables (video)

❏ Jewish Festivals and Celebrations

❏ The Holy Spirit

❏ "Faith" Series (video)

## Elective Workshops *(Grades 5 up through Adults)* 7:40 p.m. to 8:30 p.m.

❏ Ballroom Dancing (all ages)

❏ Babysitting (age 11 and up)

❏ Craft Class (all ages) *Fee*

❏ Cooking (all ages)

❏ Banner Making (all ages)

❏ CPR Introduction (all ages)

❏ Puppetry (all ages)

❏ Stained Glass (age 13 and up) *Fee*

❏ "Free To Be Me" (Grades 5 & 6)

❏ Personal Growth (age 18 & up) *Fee*

## Join Us For Dinner? 5:45 to 6:15 p.m.
*Check the nights you will be with us. (Free-will offering.)*

❏ Monday (Sandwich Bar)

❏ Tuesday (Super Nachos)

❏ Wednesday (Hot Dogs)

❏ Thursday (Sloppy Joes)

❏ Friday (Hamburgers)

Parent's Name: (If Registering Child) _____

Address: _____

_____

Does your family currently have a church home?    ❏ Yes    ❏ No

# Youth Ministries: Covenant Agreement

## COVENANT AGREEMENT

### I. PURPOSE

The Youth Fellowship shall be a group of youth and adult leaders whose purpose is to learn, to know, to share, and to love God, and to develop into responsible persons through Jesus Christ and to work within the community to make it a better place in which to live.

### II. THE ROLE OF THE COVENANT

To achieve this purpose, a covenant relationship will be established between the church, the clergy, the parents, the youth, and the counselors. The success of the program will be determined by the sincerity of the covenant relationship.

### III. RESPONSIBILITIES

#### A. THE RESPONSIBILITY OF THE CHURCH

The church will provide a place for meetings, equipment, and whatever administration that is necessary for the success of the program. The youth ministries committee and the governing body have already committed themselves to do everything in their power to provide leadership and resources for carrying out this important work.

#### B. THE RESPONSIBILITIES OF THE YOUTH DIRECTOR AND PASTORS

It will be the responsibility of the youth director and/or clergy to carry out the administrative work done for the youth programs. In consultation with the youth council and the parents, they will submit, plan, and execute those programs which will achieve the purpose of the group.

The youth director and/or clergy will work with the youth during the weekends; will contact the families represented in the groups, making them aware of activities in the life of the church and inviting them to participate whenever possible; and will provide supervision of all outings which the groups undertake.

#### C. THE RESPONSIBILITIES OF THE PARENTS

It is our hope and prayer that all parents will want to attend and enroll their youth at the first parents' meeting. However, the church will accept into the youth program any responsible youth regardless of parent support and attendance. The church, the youth director, and clergy will seek to establish with those parents who are interested a voluntary covenant relationship.

Parents who wish to voluntarily associate with other parents in building a foundation for the youth program are asked to support the program in the following ways:

1. Parents are encouraged to make a commitment to the church and the program. Parents are encouraged to attend worship services and parents' meetings. They may also provide evening dinners and/or refreshments, as needed, and necessary transportation on a scheduled basis.

2. We urge parents not to sign up for the voluntary commitment unless they freely accept this as meaningful and as a challenge to them.

3. The youth director and/or clergy will be working with those parents who are involved in the covenant relationship.

D.  THE RESPONSIBILITIES OF THE YOUTH

It is the responsibility of the youth to attend the weekly meeting as often as possible.

Each youth will abide by the Youth Group Rules.

Each youth is required to function as a responsible member of the group. Disruptive behavior and/or violation of the covenant will result in disciplinary action as the youth director and/or the clergy may deem appropriate. Repetition of disruptive behavior will be adequate reason for a member to be called into a meeting with counselor(s), youth director, clergy, and parents of member. (Refer to Youth Group Rules.)

Each youth is encouraged to regularly attend, and support financially, the church school and worship.

Each youth is asked to read the covenant agreement, which signifies the commitment as well as their understanding of the requirements and discipline. Since we welcome youth, irrespective of parental support, it is necessary for the youth to establish the basic covenant relationship with the church. This is a firm commitment on the part of the youth and must be kept if the youth is to continue in the program.

E.  THE RESPONSIBILITIES OF THE COUNSELORS

It will be the responsibility of the counselors to direct and assist the youth in the youth fellowship program of the church. Counselors will be committed Christians, and will demonstrate their loyalty to the church by their regular attendance in worship. They will support the youth by being available to them for guidance, helping to plan meaningful programs and activities, and encouraging the young persons to grow in Christ.

Counselors will present ideas and wishes to the youth coordinator, youth director, and/or clergy for consideration on behalf of the youth program, and will attend regular planning meetings.

Counselors will show respect, consideration, and courtesy toward the youth as individuals and as a fellowship group.

F.  THE RESPONSIBILITY OF THE YOUTH COORDINATOR

It will be the responsibility of the youth coordinator to interface with all youth and counselors, youth director, and the governing body, and to provide leadership, inspiration, and enthusiasm to the total youth program.

## Youth Fellowship Counselor Covenant Agreement

Name of Counselor: _____

Group: _____

### For the Counselor—I promise

To be a committed Christian.

To demonstrate my loyalty to the church by my attendance and support.

To show respect, consideration, and courtesy toward the youth, as individuals, and as a fellowship group.

To support the youth by being available to them for guidance; by planning meaningful programs and by encouraging the young persons to grow in Christ.

To direct and assist the youth in the Youth Fellowship program.

To present ideas and wishes to the youth coordinator and/or pastors for consideration on behalf of the youth program.

To prepare the fellowship room each week and to straighten the room after meetings, including: turning off lights and heat, closing windows, arranging tables or chairs, and reporting any nonfunctioning equipment to the youth coordinator and/or pastors.

Signature—Counselor: _____

Date: _____

### For the Church—We promise

To provide leadership, inspiration, and enthusiasm to the total youth program.

To provide a place of meeting, equipment, and whatever administration is necessary for the success of the program.

To set aside the necessary finances for providing resource speakers and materials.

To have knowledge of all youth functions.

To interface with youth and counselors.

To work with the youth during the week and contact the families represented in the groups, making them aware of activities in the life of the church and inviting them to participate whenever possible.

Signature—Pastor: _____

Date: _____

# Youth Fellowship Parent's Covenant

Name of Youth: _____

Address: _____ Phone: _____

## Parents' Church Membership (Check one)

❏ Our Church

❏ Other: _____

## Covenant

It is my understanding that for my youth to be a part of the Youth Fellowship, I need to provide support in the following way:

1. I have read, and I understand, my youth's covenant. I am in agreement with its principles and give it my support.

2. I will be willing to occasionally provide refreshments, help cook dinner, and/or provide transportation as needed.

3. I will strive to become involved in the daily affairs concerning my youth in our home and in the community in general. I will endeavor to be aware of their personal motivations and counsel them accordingly.

Parents' Signatures: _____

_____

## Youth Covenant

Name of Youth: _____ Grade in School: _____

Address: _____ Phone: _____

Birthdate: _____

Church Membership (check one)

❏ Our church

❏ Other: _____

Father's Name: _____ Mother's Name: _____

Father's Vocation and Place of Employment: _____

Mother's Vocation and Place of Employment: _____

### Covenant

It is my commitment to join the youth fellowship. It is my understanding that to be a part of this group I shall need to support my covenant relationship with the church and the group in the following way:

1. I shall love the Lord with all my mind, soul, heart, and strength.

2. I shall love my neighbor (fellow member of the Youth Fellowship) as I love myself. Therefore, I shall be kind to others, help others, avoid forming exclusive groups, and accept newcomers.

3. I shall attend worship services and Sunday school regularly.

4. I shall attend the Youth Fellowship regularly.

5. I shall resist all forms of evil as represented in harmful gossip, disrespect of others, and selfishness.

6. I shall participate fully in the weekly scheduled programs which usually involve games, study, and worship, by remaining attentive, exhibiting courtesy to others and abiding by the leadership of the counselors.

7. I shall encourage my fellow youth to do their best and shall accept the same encouragement from them.

8. I shall enjoy myself. I shall laugh, love, exhibit sincerity and seriousness, and work toward the total enjoyment on behalf of others.

9. I have read the Covenant Agreement and understand my responsibilities as a member of the group.

10. I commit myself to be a responsible member of the fellowship. I agree to abide by the Youth Group Rules.

Youth Signature: _____

Parent's Signature: _____ Phone: _____

Address: _____

## Youth Activity Parent Consent Form and Emergency Medical Release

Group:  ❑ Senior High  ❑ Junior High  ❑ Sunday School  ❑ Other

Name of Event: _____ Date(s) of Event: _____

Departure Time: _____ Return Time: _____

Contact Person (not on activity): _____ Phone: _____

### Emergency Medical Release (to be completed by parent or guardian)

My son/daughter, _____, has my permission to participate in the activity listed above, sponsored by the [name of church], being held on the date listed above. I do further give my permission to teachers, leaders, or other adult staff to obtain and administer such medical aid as might be required for the immediate care of my son/daughter in the event such help of an emergency nature becomes necessary. I also give my permission to include the administration of such medicines or treatment as might be ordered or administered by a duly licensed physician. It is further understood that the church, its officers, pastors, counselors, leaders, or agents will not be held liable for any first-aid rendered, or treatment, drugs, or medicines administered, or surgical procedure performed pursuant to this consent.

My son/daughter is allergic to the following: _____

_____

_____

My son/daughter has the following medical conditions: _____

_____

_____

Parent or Guardian Signature: _____ Date: _____

Name: _____ Phone: _____

Address: _____

_____

Alternate emergency contact person and phone number if you are unavailable:

_____

_____

# Youth Group Rules

## I. *Respect*

A. Respect and obedience will be shown at all time to counselors, adults, and each other.

   1. The counselors, youth director, and/or pastors have agreed to show you respect and consideration. They will expect respect and courtesy in return.

   2. Courtesy to each other is expected at all times.

   3. Small groups and cliques make some people feel unwelcome and are discouraged.

B. Respect your church. Remember—this is the house of God. Clean up after yourself; and don't be afraid to help clean up after others.

## II. *Conduct*

A. The youth group will be fun if you give it a chance. No one has the right to interfere with another person's experiences.

B. Dangerous objects will not be permitted at any youth group gathering. Skateboards and bikes are great for transportation to church, but don't ride them on the parking lot, walkways, and corridors.

C. Unnecessary trips to the restroom disrupt youth group meetings.

D. It is important to stay with your counselors/adults during all youth group activities. Leaving church grounds during activities will not be permitted.

E. Disruptive behavior will not be permitted. Repetition of disruptive behavior will be adequate reason for a member to have their parents notified and a counseling session arranged. Continued disruption and disregard of rules may cause a youth to be suspended from the fellowship program.

F. Dress should be appropriate for the activity which is being engaged in by the group.

# Planning Your Wedding

[Name of Church]

## PLANNING YOUR WEDDING

This brochure is designed to help couples from the church and community prepare for their wedding. For more information, please contact the church's Wedding Hostess.

### WHAT IS CHRISTIAN MARRIAGE?

Christian marriage begins with a decision of two persons to spend the remainder of their lives together as husband and wife, sharing the joys and cares, the loves, and responsibilities of interdependent living.

More than just a physical union, Christian marriage is the uniting of two spirits, two children of God. Through mutual trust and faith, the two can achieve a sense of oneness that will touch every element of their lives. Marriage is a partnership in which each person respects the rights and privileges of the other. It is a skilled oneness which comes with practice and patience. It is a love which grows.

Christian marriage is a big step—and it can be a wonderful one! "No other human ties are more tender, no other vows more sacred than these you now assume."

### WHO MAY BE MARRIED IN THE CHURCH?

The Sanctuary and Chapel are dedicated to the glory of God, and used for the administration of the Christian sacraments, public worship, and private prayer, for weddings and funerals, and for activities of the church and its organizations. To all who desire to use the worship facilities for any of these purposes, a cordial invitation is extended. Please remember to treat them with reverence and good taste.

### THE CHURCH

The church is happy to make its facilities available to all who desire a wedding service which emphasizes the sacredness of Christian marriage. The staff wants to do everything within its power to make marriage a deeply religious experience.

In keeping with its mission, the church does not rent its facilities for weddings. There are, however, fees involved in the use of church facilities, equipment, and personnel. The furnishings and the equipment in the Sanctuary are part of the primary function of worship, and therefore are not to be moved without permission.

### EVALUATION

Following the wedding, couples will receive an evaluation form regarding the services and facilities provided by the church. Your frank response is invited.

## *NOTES*

In keeping with the purpose and policy of the church, SMOKING IS NOT PERMITTED IN THE BUILDINGS; AND ALCOHOLIC BEVERAGES ARE NOT TO BE BROUGHT ON, CONSUMED, OR SERVED ANYWHERE ON THE PROPERTY.

## SCHEDULING

Weddings on Saturdays may be scheduled at 10:00 a.m., 1:00 p.m., or 4 p.m.

The two hours allotted for a wedding includes one hour prior to the scheduled beginning of the service and one hour after the scheduled beginning of the service. (Example: If the service were scheduled to begin at 10:00 a.m., the church would be open to the wedding party from 9:00 a.m. to 11:00 a.m.)

The timing of weddings scheduled on a day other than Saturday is dependent upon available facilities and personnel.

## THE PASTOR

One of the pastors of our church officiates at all weddings, although a pastor from another church may assist at the discretion of the senior pastor. WEDDINGS MUST BE SCHEDULED WITH THE PASTOR-IN-CHARGE BEFORE SETTING A DATE, OR MAKING DETAILED ARRANGEMENTS. Counseling interviews with the pastor-in-charge are required at least a month prior to the wedding. The pastor may direct a couple to other counseling sessions.

A valid marriage license, issued within the state, and acceptable for use in the county, must be presented to the pastor before the marriage service will take place.

The license and the marriage certificate are signed by the best man and maid or matron of honor, in the presence of the pastor, just prior to the service.

## INVITATIONS

The name and address of the church is as follows:

3. The throwing of rice, confetti, or bird seed, the consumption of alcoholic beverages in any form, and smoking are not permitted in the church buildings or on the grounds.
4. If children will be included in the wedding ceremony (flower girls, ring bearers, candle lighters, etc.), please clear their participation with the pastor before asking the children.
5. ALL SCHEDULED MEETINGS—interviews, rehearsal, and wedding service—MUST BEGIN ON TIME.
6. No food or beverage may be consumed in the Sanctuary, Bride's Room, or office area.
7. The church does not allow rehearsals or weddings to take place when ANY member of the wedding party is under the influence of drugs or alcohol.
8. Any cancellation of wedding plans must be made in writing as soon as possible.

## REHEARSAL

During the carefully outlined rehearsal, details of the wedding are reviewed. The marriage service shall be conducted according to the customs and practices of our church. The rehearsal is to be attended by all members of the wedding party, the ushers, the parents of the bride, and the parents of the groom.

## WEDDING

*Arriving at the church:*
- 1 hour before: bride, maid of honor (with groom's ring), attendants, and mother of the bride.
- 45 minutes before: Ushers
- 30 minutes before: Groom (with license), best man (with bride's ring) and other family members.

## WEDDING HOSTESS

After the application for the wedding has been approved, the Wedding Hostess will call the bride to assist with detailed arrangements for the wedding and for the reception, if held at the church.

_____
(Hostess' name and phone number)

The fee for hostess services is indicated on page 4. This staff person is not optional.

## MUSIC

Music arrangements must be cleared first by the pastor and then the organist. The church has an organist on the staff who provides the organ or piano music at ALL weddings. Soloists also are available through the church. The Wedding Hostess will provide the name and number of the organist.

## THE CHOICE OF MUSIC

Since a wedding is a service of worship, use care in selecting music. The music should be consistent with the religious character of matrimony. It is not to be assumed that just any music may be used. It is appropriate for the congregation to sing.

## FLOWERS AND CANDLES, ETC.

Arrangements for flowers are the responsibility of the couple. Enclosed is an instruction sheet for your florist. Aisle runners are not permitted. Alternating pews have rings for attaching decorations.

The use of candles is limited by the fire department to the Chancel area. Only the church candelabra may be used. The Cross, Bible, and candles must remain in position, and must not be covered or hidden.

## PHOTOGRAPHS

The church is open for taking pictures one hour before the service is scheduled to begin. Photography is not allowed during the service, but the ceremony may be videotaped from the east upper room. Details about when and where pictures are to be taken should be discussed in advance with the photographer. An instruction sheet for the photographer is enclosed.

3

## APPLICATION FOR SERVICE

In order to confirm a wedding date and time, a written and signed application and a nonrefundable deposit of $100 must be submitted to the church office.

## COST

*Deposit:*

A nonrefundable deposit of $100, applied to the total cost, must be paid upon applying for a wedding service.

*Facilities:*

| | |
|---|---|
| Sanctuary (non-members), | $200.00 |
| Chapel (non-members), | $100.00 |
| Use of appropriate facilities is included. | |

*Equipment: (optional)*

Includes candelabra, marriage (unity) candle candelabra, kneeling bench, flower baskets, etc. $20.00

*Assistants:*

| | |
|---|---|
| Custodian | $40.00 |
| Organist | $50.00 |
| with rehearsal and/or soloist | $75.00 |
| Soloist (optional) | $50.00 |
| Wedding Hostess | $75.00 |
| Sound Technician (optional) | $25.00 |

*Note:* Prices quoted here are subject to change. Please check with hostess.

## PAYMENT

The balance of all fees must be paid two weeks prior to the wedding. Checks should be payable to the church. Please include all fees in one check.

*Note:* The pastor's honorarium is not included in the charges listed above and should be presented to the pastor prior to the service.

## OTHER MATTERS OF IMPORTANCE

1. For a more relaxed and enjoyable experience, please schedule wedding plans at least six months in advance.
2. The wedding service will not begin until all fees are paid in full.

4

# Application for Wedding Service

**Bride's Name:** _____

   Address: _____

   City: _____ State: _____ Zip: _____

   Phone: _____ Work Phone: _____

**Groom's Name:** _____

   Address: _____

   City: _____ State: _____ Zip: _____

   Phone: _____ Work Phone: _____

Pastor: _____ Number of Guests: _____

Desired Wedding Date: _____ Time: _____ a.m./p.m.
             Month   Date   Year

Is either the Bride or Groom under the age of 18?  ❑ Yes  ❑ No

**I understand and agree that:**

1. I am responsible for making the appointment(s) for premarital counseling at least one month before the wedding with the pastor who is conducting the service.
2. The deposit to reserve the date is nonrefundable.
3. I will personally make any changes in date and time of wedding with the pastor conducting the service.
4. I agree to read and abide by the content and policies of the wedding brochure, "Planning Your Wedding," and will be responsible for the wedding party abiding by policies and instructions.
5. Two hours' time will be allotted for wedding service: beginning 1 hour prior to the service (for preparation), and ending 1 hour after (including the concluding of photographs) the scheduled service time.
6. On rare occasion it may be necessary for the church to substitute pastors.
7. I agree, that all fees are to be paid two weeks prior to the wedding date. The service will not take place until all fees are paid in full.
8. I agree if cancellation of wedding plans is necessary, that it must be made in writing.

Applicant's signature: _____ Date: _____

## CHURCH OFFICE USE ONLY

Date Application Received: _____ Time: _____ a.m./p.m.  By: _____

Non-Refundable Deposit Received by: _____ Date: _____

Amount of Non-Refundable Deposit $ ____ Receipt # ____ Use of Facilities $ _____

Pastor's Approval: _____ Date: _____

Referred to Wedding Hostess: _____ Prospective Bride/Groom Given Book: _____
                   Date                                Date

Entered In: Church Use Calendar: _____ Pastor's Calendar: _____
                         Initials/Date                     Initials/Date

# *Wedding Information Sheet*

Bride's Name: _____

Bride's Address: _____

Bride's Phone: _____ Work Phone: _____

Groom's Name: _____

Groom's Address: _____

Groom's Phone: _____ Work Phone: _____

**Wedding Date:** _____ **Time:** _____

Rehearsal Date: _____ Time: _____

Location:  ❏ Sanctuary  ❏ Chapel  ❏ Other:_____

Reception at Church:  ❏ Yes  ❏ No  Number of Guests:_____

| SERVICES REQUIRED | AMOUNT | PERSON/GROUP RESPONSIBLE |
|---|---|---|
| Use of Church Building/s | $ _____ | _____ |
| Use of Church Equipment | $ _____ | _____ |
| Reception | $ _____ | _____ |
| Organist | $ _____ | _____ |
| Soloist | $ _____ | _____ |
| Wedding Hostess | $ _____ | _____ |
| Sound Technician | $ _____ | _____ |
| Custodian | $ _____ | _____ |
| TOTAL | $ _____ | |

Amount of Deposit: _____ Receipt #: _____ Received by: _____

Date Balance Paid: _____ Receipt #: _____ Received by: _____

Distribution:
❏ Pastor          ❏ Wedding Coordinator   ❏ Church Office   ❏ Sound
❏ Bride and Groom ❏ Organist              ❏ Soloist         ❏ Custodian

❏ Other: _____

## Instructions for Florist

In keeping with the policy of our church, florists shall observe the following general instructions:

1. Flowers may be placed on the floor in front of the altar, the pulpit, and lectern, or on top of the altar, or on pedestals supplied by the florist.

2. The only candelabras that may be used are those supplied by the church.

3. Care must be taken not to obscure the altar or cross with floral arrangements.

4. No aisle runner may be used.

5. No item may be attached to any furniture or fixture, or any part of the building.

6. Glitter may not be used with any of the floral or associated decorations.

7. Pew bows, etc., may be attached to the built-in rings that are provided on each alternate pew.

# Instructions for Photographers

1. These instructions apply to still photographers, motion-picture photographers, and those making video recordings.

2. It is important to note that all wedding services will begin at the appointed time.

3. Pictures taken during the service must be done only from the back of the sanctuary, and with existing light only.

4. Photographs may be taken before and after the service.

5. Definition of the beginning of the service is when the bride enters the sanctuary from the narthex, and the end of the service is marked at the time when the couple begins to come back up the aisle from the chancel area.

6. No flash, or additional lights, etc., may be used during the service itself.

NOTE: Because weddings are scheduled at 10:00 a.m., 1:00 p.m., and 4:00 p.m., the sanctuary must be ready for the next wedding party and therefore cleared by one hour prior to any of those times. Any picture-taking after the wedding service must be concluded by one hour after the announced wedding starting time. (Example: If the wedding is at 1:00 p.m., pictures may be taken in the sanctuary up until 12:40 p.m., and all picture-taking must be concluded by 2:00 p.m.)

# Instructions for Ushers

1. YOUR WORK AS AN USHER IS MOST IMPORTANT. *What you do helps set the tone for the entire service of worship* during which your friends are to be married.

2. It is important that you be present no later than 45 minutes before the service, ready to carry out your responsibilities. It is quite appropriate that the wedding service is an occasion of joy. As people enter the Narthex (the Lobby), they will want to have the opportunity to prepare themselves for this worship experience. It is ADVISABLE, therefore, for the ushers NOT TO ENTER INTO A GREAT DEAL OF CONVERSATION—OTHER THAN A GREETING—WITH THE GUESTS, in order that the mood of quiet and worshipful anticipation may be set. Discussion among yourselves as ushers should be limited to the solution of possible problems involved with the service.

3. It is important to keep the narthex of the church as clear as possible BY SEATING GUESTS AS THEY ARRIVE. This will assist in reducing noise and confusion.

4. You may be asked, so be sure you know where the restrooms are located.

5. Escort only the adult women of a family.

6. The general pattern is to seat persons from the center aisle only. However, friends of the GROOM ARE SEATED ON THE RIGHT, and the friends of the BRIDE ON THE LEFT, if this is requested. It is best to keep the sides balanced with approximately the same number of people on each side, and not to rigidly adhere to the above seating pattern.

7. No pictures are to be taken during the service. You are asked to advise persons with cameras of this, and to advise persons carrying rice, confetti, and bird seed that it is not to be thrown anywhere on the property.

8. Two ushers may be chosen to light the candles. Instructions will be provided to them at the rehearsal.

9. Ushers will be chosen to seat the bride's mother, the groom's mother, and grandmothers (if in attendance), just prior to the service. They will also escort them from their seats at the close of the service.

10. Following the service, two ushers are asked to release one pew of persons at a time into the center aisle, beginning at the front. This provides a much more orderly dismissal of the congregation.

## *Wedding Fee Letter*

Reminder letter that wedding fees need to be paid.

[Date]

Dear _____ ,

It is hard to believe that the time has passed so quickly and your wedding date is almost here!

I hope that everything is going well with your wedding plans, and that you have not encountered any major difficulties which cause you anxiety. It is quite normal to have loose ends to tie together at this stage, but I hope that everything else has gone well for you.

We have noted that the balance of your wedding fees, $_____ , has not yet been paid in full. It is church policy that all fees must be in the church office two weeks prior to your wedding date.

For your convenience, we are enclosing a self-addressed envelope which you may use to send us a check for the balance of your wedding fees. If you find it more convenient, you may bring a check to the church office. Thank you!

Sincerely,

Pastor

# *Wedding Service Evaluation Letter*

Cover letter asking a newlywed couple to complete the wedding ceremony evaluation form found on the following pages.

[Date]

Dear _____ ,

We hope that the time since your marriage has been a very meaningful and productive time for you!

We are always trying to improve what we do in terms of helping couples in the process of getting married. One of the best ways we have found to do this is to ask for an evaluation of the services which we have provided for your wedding.

Enclosed is a brief questionnaire which we would appreciate your completing and returning to us as soon as possible. To facilitate this, we have also enclosed a self-addressed and stamped envelope.

Most of the questionnaire simply involves making check marks, and of course there is also opportunity for you to make whatever comments you feel are important to you.

The questionnaire is confidential, and therefore we do not provide a space for you to indicate your name. If, however, you wish to provide your name so we can clarify any issues with you, we would be happy to have you do that and assure you that confidentiality will be maintained between yourselves and the undersigned.

Thank you very much for your assistance, and best wishes always!

God's Blessings,

Pastor

# Wedding Services Evaluation Form

Thank you for your willingness to provide some helpful information for us, as you look at what was provided for you, and as we look toward serving others.

## I. Facilities Which You Used

A. Space for the service (check one)
- ❏ Sanctuary
- ❏ Chapel
- ❏ Church Hall
- ❏ Outside on the grounds

Comments: _____

_____

_____

B. Other space used (check as many as used)
- ❏ Lounge
- ❏ Rooms to dress
- ❏ Restrooms

Comments: _____

_____

_____

C. Were the facilities you used
- ❏ Unlocked?
- ❏ Ready for use?
- ❏ Clean?
- ❏ Adequate?

Comments: _____

_____

_____

## II. Equipment used which belongs to the church (check all that you used)

- ❏ Two seven-branch candelabra
- ❏ One three-branch candelabra
- ❏ Kneeling bench
- ❏ Artificial flowers
- ❏ Sound system
- ❏ Pew bows

Equipment Comments: _____

_____

## III. Services

### A. PERSONS

1. *Church office personnel*—scheduling, information, etc. (check one)

   Name: _____ ❏ Excellent  ❏ Good  ❏ Improve

2. *Wedding Coordinator*   Name: _____

|  | (check one) | Excellent | Good | Needs to Improve |
|---|---|---|---|---|
| a. Prior to the wedding | | ❏ | ❏ | ❏ |
| b. Rehearsal | | ❏ | ❏ | ❏ |
| c. Wedding service | | ❏ | ❏ | ❏ |
| 3. *Organist*   Name: _____ | | ❏ | ❏ | ❏ |
| 4. *Soloist*   Name: _____ | | ❏ | ❏ | ❏ |
| 5. *Custodian*   Name: _____ | | ❏ | ❏ | ❏ |
| 6. *Pastor*   Name: _____ | | ❏ | ❏ | ❏ |
| a. Premarital Interview | | ❏ | ❏ | ❏ |
| b. Service | | ❏ | ❏ | ❏ |

Comments: _____

_____

### B. RECEPTION

1. (Check one)   ❏ We used this service   ❏ We did not use this service

2. If you used this service, please comment: _____

_____

## IV. Miscellaneous

A. Was the brochure "Planning Your Wedding" helpful? _____

_____

B. Was the application form helpful to you? _____

_____

C. Was the cost reasonable in relationship to value received? _____

_____

D. Rehearsal

    1. Was wedding party present at scheduled time?   ❑ Yes   ❑ No

    2. Did rehearsal begin on time?   ❑ Yes   ❑ No

    3. Was the rehearsal helpful?   ❑ Yes   ❑ No

    4. Was the rehearsal too long?   ❑ Yes   ❑ No

    5. Was the rehearsal too short?   ❑ Yes   ❑ No

Comment:_____

_____

_____

_____

In regard to the whole process:

I liked: _____

_____

_____

_____

_____

_____

An improvement would be: _____

_____

_____

_____

_____

_____

*Please use the attached, self-addressed, stamped envelope to return this evaluation.*

**THANK YOU!**

# WHEN DEATH COMES

*A Guide to be Studied and Discussed
Before the
Crisis of Death Comes*

## LOCATION OF MY IMPORTANT PAPERS

Will: _____

Insurance: _____

Checking Account: _____

Savings Account: _____

Safe Deposit Box: _____

Other Important Documents: _____

_____

_____

_____

Power of Attorney for Health Care: _____

My Attorney: _____

12

*Table of Contents*

## MY IMPORTANT DATA

Birth Date: _____

Birth Place: _____

Names of:

Father _____

Mother _____

Spouse _____

Children _____

_____

_____

_____

Church membership: _____

Military service: _____

Occupation _____

Place and length of residence _____

11

# WHEN DEATH COMES

## 1. LOOK TO THE MINISTRY OF THE CHURCH

At no time in life is the Christian faith more meaningful than when death comes. In the loneliness of separation, the presence of the living God is glorious. In the emptiness of farewell, the lively hope of the eternal life is like a sunrise.

How we are prepared spiritually, mentally, and emotionally will have a direct effect on how we handle the unavoidable loneliness that we or our loved ones must endure.

The love of God and the understanding sympathy of a Christian ministry are most reassuring. With the understanding that all God does is good, and with Christ as our guide, the suggestions on the following pages are offered in Christian love.

Persons can expect the continuing ministry of the church when death comes. Turning to the pastor, they will receive guidance and comfort. Assistance will be inspirational and practical. As a minister of Jesus Christ, the pastor is appointed to guide people through all passages of life, and especially when death comes.

The pastor proclaims the convictions of the Christian faith that death is not the end, but the doorway to another part of life eternal. Though sorrow is inevitable, there is also joy in the assurance that death brings us into a closer association with the Heavenly Father. The words of Christ take on a very personal meaning; "I go to prepare a place for you, that where I am, there you may be also." Therefore, those who hold the Christian faith are encouraged to relate the event of death to that faith.

The Scriptures provide strength, comfort, and meaning at death. Some which might be used by family and friends include: Psalm 23; Psalm 27; Psalm 46; Psalm 90; Psalm 100; Psalm 121; II Corinthians 4:16–18; John 14:1–7, 15–17, and 27; Romans 8:14–18, 28, 31, 35, 37–39; Ephesians 3:14–21; Isaiah 35:4. Some of these Scriptures may be used in the funeral or memorial service.

Death is very much a part of life. It is important that death be a thoughtful part of family discussion prior to the experience coming into the circle of family or friends. Decisions as to what you want for the service of worship, the extent to which you want to be committed financially

1

---

# INSTRUCTIONS FOR MY SERVICE AND BURIAL

On this date, _____ - _____ - _____ , my wishes are:

that interment be in _____ ,

that the pastor conducting my service be _____ ,

that the music include _____
_____ ,

that the following Scriptures be read: _____
_____
_____

and that the funeral director be _____ ,

Other instructions: _____ .

_____
(signature)

10

in funeral arrangements, and the thoughtful personal preparation of body, mind, and spirit for the experience, are extremely important. If time and effort are given to this prior to the event of death, the experience will be more meaningful and acceptable.

## II. THE CHURCH IS HERE TO SERVE YOU

### A. Call the Pastor

The service of pastors at time of death is a regular part of their ministry. Thus, at the time of death, your pastor should be notified, regardless of the time. Your pastor stands ready to share God's comfort and is available for any service. For the same reason your pastor should be called in time of serious illness, whether or not it appears terminal. Do not assume that others will call the pastor.

### B. Call the Mortician

A call to the mortician will set in motion the excellent and necessary service performed by these professionals. As you prepare for arrangements, have basic information and statistics concerning the deceased ready at hand, such as: church membership, birth date and place, name of father and mother, and other family relationships, social security number, insurance information, military service, marital status, occupation, length of residence in the community, and a statement regarding gifts to a memorial fund in the name of the deceased, in lieu of lowers, if this is desired. (Completion of pages 10 and 11 of this brochure will provide this information.) If you do not wish the body to be viewed at any time following death, this can be indicated.

Where burial is to be in a national cemetery, make certain that the time you wish is agreeable to their schedule before establishing other times and dates.

### C. Consider a Church Funeral

Christian families should give serious consideration to having the funeral service in their church. The resources of love and guidance, of hope and strength, are continually present in the church for all the crises of life. The last crisis—death—is a natural part of that fellowship.

The funeral is a service of worship in the sanctuary or chapel, wherein hymns of faith may be sung, prayers for God's guidance are offered, the Scriptures are read, and an inspirational message is given. In this, the congregation may fully participate. The pastor will plan such a service in consultation with the family, and with the cooperation of the mortician.

2

—such things as eyes, kidneys, hearts—parts of which may assist the blind to see or the living to live with less pain. If you are interested in this, contact your physician or local hospital, and advise your family and close friends. These are things to think on and anticipate.

## III. GO FORTH IN HOPE AND ASSURANCE

Whether in a funeral or a memorial service, the pastor will be conducting a service of worship. Final rites for the Christian are far more than the human expression of respect for the deceased. Praise to God, the giver of life, affirmation of belief in immortality, prayer for God-given comfort—these are the sacred purposes of the service at the time of death. In this spirit, the church offers its ministry.

## AT TIME OF DEATH

1. Call pastor.
2. Call mortician.
   Arrangements:
   - selection of casket
   - selection of cemetery plot (if not already selected)
   - cemetery arrangements
   - cremation
3. Advise relatives, friends, neighbors.
4. Select date, time, and place for service (after consulting with pastor).
5. Select pallbearers.
6. If desired, establish Memorial Fund.

## IV. INFORMATION TO HELP YOUR FAMILY TO BE PREPARED

On the following three pages are informational forms you can use to record data about yourself, your desires, and the location of important papers. You are urged to complete these forms now, and keep them updated.

9

D. *Types of Other Funerals—Organizational, Fraternal, etc.*

The mortician is dedicated to fulfilling the wishes of the family, and although customs often determine the procedure, it is entirely in order for changes to be made to better express our Christian faith.

The Christian funeral, as a sacred service, is conducted by the pastor, in cooperation with the mortician, and after consultation with the family.

Many organizations, service and fraternal, have complete plans for a funeral service. If this kind of service is desired, it is suggested that it be held at a separate and earlier time.

E. *Plan the Service*

Consult your pastor concerning the service. It is important that the pastor work with the families in planning the service with the mortician. Of critical importance is the need to discuss your desired arrangements with the pastor prior to announcements regarding the service, so that there will be no conflict in schedules. The time and place should be confirmed with the pastor before newspaper notices are released.

Your pastor will want to meet with the family. At that time the pastor will learn more concerning the deceased, and will interpret the meaning and form of the service.

If possible, check with near and dear relatives to coordinate desires for the service. There are always a variety of options in the kinds of services available; never feel you must conform only to "tradition" or are not free to discuss new ideas with those who are close to you. For example: the choir of the church might sing; congregational hymns could be employed; the committal service at the cemetery could precede the memorial service; a coffee-hour fellowship time could follow the funeral or memorial service; and individuals from the congregation could participate in the service. These are but just a few of the almost infinite number of possibilities.

F. *The Memorial Service*

Definite consideration should be given to the memorial service. The plan generally consists of two services: (1) the committal service, and (2) the memorial service.

able. Many different kinds of caskets are available at varying costs. Generally, the services of the mortician are the same, regardless of the cost of the casket. Many persons are beginning, well in advance, to discuss plans with their pastor for their funeral service, to make arrangements with insurance carriers and/or funeral directors, and to make plans for the time of death. This is best done after thorough discussion with family and by putting your desires in writing so there is no misunderstanding.

Burial, vault internment, or cremation are commonly acceptable. The choice and the decision of a place of burial or of interment of the ashes are made by the family. Cremation is, in effect, the hastening of the processes of nature. Cremated remains are placed in crypts or urns provided by cemeteries and mausoleums, or are sometimes buried in cemeteries. The ashes may also be scattered in accordance with prevailing laws.

Beautiful flowers are most appropriate at the time of death. However, huge masses of flowers become an unworthy display. Increasingly, it is becoming a practice that the flowers on the casket are provided by the family, and the family requests that a memorial fund be established, in lieu of flowers, to serve the living.

K. *Autopsies and the Living*

Sometimes, at the time of death, the family is asked for permission to perform an autopsy. The conduct of an autopsy is important, and persons are urged to cooperate with their physicians because of the following factors: autopsies are sometimes performed to determine the cause of death; they are important for the advancement of medical knowledge and for the assistance in better diagnosing; and they help to alert living family members in cases where communicable diseases are involved or diseases for which living members might be more susceptible because of heredity. The autopsy utilizes good surgical discipline, and maintains an attitude of respect for the physical body.

L. *The Use of One's Physical Body*

Some persons have given serious consideration to the use their physical bodies can give to others after death. Increasingly, it is becoming practice for persons to will their whole body to a medical or dental school, or similar institution, to assist in the training of physicians, nurses, dentists, and others in the skills necessary to better care for the living. In addition, persons will sometimes will portions of their body

1. Often on the second or third day after death, a private committal service is held, attended by members of the family—and often close friends. The committal service may precede or follow the burial, vault interment, or memorial service. If the weather is favorable, this service is held at the cemetery or mausoleum—the mortician and the pastor meeting the family there. If desired, they may meet at the mortuary and accompany the funeral coach to the cemetery. In case of bad weather, the service may be held at the church or mortuary, followed by the committal at the cemetery, if desired.

2. A memorial service is one of high faith. It may be held in the church at a time selected by the family and the pastor. It may include the singing of hymns, Scriptures, prayer, and a brief meditation. Members of the family may be seated with the congregation. Thanks are given to God for the life He has given for a season, but which is once more committed to Him in trust and confidence.

   A memorial service, meaning literally beyond the grave, can be a glorious experience of comfort, and the assurance of God's gift of eternal life.

   This procedure involves very little change in the work of the mortician and can be arranged after consultation with the pastor. Explanation of procedure can be made in the public notices so friends will be informed.

G. *The "Traditional" Service*

Often this service is conducted in the mortuary, or in the church. Content of the service is somewhat similar to that of a memorial service, except that the participation of the congregation is often lacking unless the service is in the church.

1. Open or Closed Casket

   The value of the Christian service would be greatly increased by changing the custom of viewing the deceased after the funeral. Many pastors and lay people feel that this custom lessens the meaning, comfort, and strength of the service.

   a. The casket is closed to the public entirely. This is quite consistent with good taste and consideration. Many people prefer to remember friends as they have known them in life. The pastor will simply close the service with the benediction and the wor-

*4*

H. *Coffee Hour Fellowship Time*

Increasingly, families are taking advantage of the opportunity to close the service at the church, which makes it possible to have a coffee hour fellowship time during which family and friends may greet each other. This time offers a wonderful opportunity to assist family and friends in making the transition from the experience of death back to the realm of normal living. This reflects the church at its best as it moves from worship to continue to be a supportive community.

I. *Memorials*

Memorial gifts at the time of death have been used as a means of tribute. It is always appropriate to make such a gift to the church, or to a recognized worthy charity, in memory of a loved one. Normally, these gifts are gratefully acknowledged when received. The pastor and the mortician will assist in making arrangements for an appropriate memorial at the request of the family.

When a family desires that memorials be given in lieu of flowers, this should be made through the first public announcement in the newspapers. The decision must be made as soon as the time of service has been set. When selecting your local church to receive the Memorial Fund, it should be designated as (name of deceased) Memorial Fund of (name of church). These gifts are tax-deductible and become the property of the church. They are administered by the trustees of the church, in consultation with the family.

It may be that you would want to establish a memorial by including your church and its work in your will. This can be done at your convenience, away from the possible highly emotional feelings at the time of death.

J. *Costs and Fees*

The costs of a funeral should be in proportion to the resources of the family. It would be unwise to deprive the living because of the manner of burying the dead. Remember the Christian attitude toward the mortal body and the immortal spirit. The casket is used to lay the body to rest . . . not an attempt to shield it against time and nature.

Under any circumstance, pretentious display is inconsistent with our faith. The admonition "Let all be done decently and in order" is a helpful guide.

The cost of the casket, the grave, and the various services performed by the mortician and cemetery management can be consider-

*7*

shipers will be dismissed. In this case, the family should view the body for the last time on the preceding evening or before the service.

b. The casket is open prior to the service, and then closed before the service begins. The casket is so arranged that friends may pass by as they enter the chapel. The family should view the body for the last time at some prior hour apart from the emotional strain of the service and the pressure of having to move on to the cemetery.

c. The members of the family may desire to have the casket open at the conclusion of the service. They may ask the pastor or mortician to indicate that those who wish to view the deceased may do so by coming forward. Those who wish to remember the deceased as when that person was alive should feel free to leave as directed.

d. Historically, the funeral service has been concluded with a committal at the cemetery. Some families may wish to have the service close at the church or mortuary. Others may wish to have a private committal service, either before or after the funeral or memorial service, including the family and close friends. The increasing traffic hazards of long funeral processions should be considered in planning the funeral.

2. Use Appropriate Music

Organ music, as prelude and postlude, can add a great deal. It should be profoundly sacred music for it is part of Christian worship. Sentimental songs have little place in the funeral, even though favorites of the deceased. Songs or hymns should be chosen in consultation with the pastor. The hymns which fit with the rest of the service will bring hope, strength, comfort, and understanding to the congregation. In addition, the choir of the church may be invited to sing.

When the funeral service or memorial service is held in the church, the use of appropriate congregational hymns is often desirable. The voices of Christian friends, raised in hymns of trust and victory, can mean much. The death of a practicing Christian is a time of triumph and should be accompanied by the great hymns of the church. Examples of hymns for use at a funeral worship service could include:

A Mighty Fortress Is Our God
All Creatures of Our God and King
All Hail the Power of Jesus' Name
Amazing Grace
Ask Ye What Great Things I Know
Blessed Assurance, Jesus Is Mine
Christ for the World We Sing
Christ Is Made the Sure Foundation
Close to Thee
Come, Let Us Tune Our Loftiest Song
Come, Thou Fount
From All That Dwell
Glorious Things of Thee Are Spoken
God Is My Strong Salvation
Guide Me, O Thou Great Jehovah
He Leadeth Me, O Blessed Thought
Holy, Holy, Holy! Lord God Almighty
How Firm a Foundation
I Am the Light of the World
I Am Thine, O Lord
I'll Praise My Maker
I Will Arise and Go to Jesus
Jesus Calls Us O'er the Tumult
Lead on, O King Eternal
My Hope Is Built on Nothing Less
O Could I Speak the Matchless Worth
O God Our Help in Ages Past
O for a Thousand Tongues to Sing
O Worship the King, All Glorious Above
Rise Up, O Men of God
Savior, Like a Shepherd Lead Us
Standing on the Promises
The Church's One Foundation
The Lord Is My Shepherd
When Morning Gilds the Skies

# Death in Family Follow-Up Form

Periodic follow-up with the loved ones of a person who has died is a very important congregational care function of the pastor. This action indicates in a very loving way that the deceased has not been forgotten, and even more importantly, that the survivors, who may be in a world of hurt, are remembered. One of the authors recalls a rather poignant comment by a friend who said, "It has been a year today since my son died, and no one from the church has called."

This form can be completed and placed in the follow-up or "tickler" file, where it will be retrieved as a reminder to make a call on family members of the deceased at the appropriate time interval.

## Death In The Church Family Follow-Up

Name of deceased: _____ Date of death: _____

Person to contact: _____ Phone #: _____

Relationship to deceased: _____

Person to contact: _____ Phone #: _____

Relationship to deceased: _____

Person to contact: _____ Phone #: _____

Relationship to deceased: _____

Information about deceased: _____

_____

Service conducted by: _____

Burial location: _____

Comments: _____

_____

Relationship to the church:   ❏ Member   ❏ Constituent   ❏ Not related

| FOLLOW-UP | DATE | BY WHOM |
|---|---|---|
| 3 months | _____ | _____ |
| 6 months | _____ | _____ |
| 12 months | _____ | _____ |
| Other: | _____ | _____ |

# Application for Use of Church Facilities

Name of Group: _____

Date of Application: _____  ❏ Single Event   ❏ Regularly Scheduled Program

Time Facilities Required: From: _____ am/pm  to: _____ am/pm

Description of Activities: _____

Other Particulars: _____

Contact Person (if other than applicant): _____ Phone #: _____

If there is a member of our church who is also a member of the applying group and who will accept responsibility for directing the proper use of the facilities, please note:

Church Member: _____ Phone #: _____

Is childcare at our church required during the event/s?   ❏ Yes   ❏ No

The applicant and the individual executing this application hereby waive any and all claims, demands, and causes of action which they may have against [name of church] as a result of the use of church facilities pursuant to this application. The applicant and the individuals executing this application shall indemnify and hold harmless [name of church] and its officers, agents, and employees from and against any and all claims, demands, causes of action, and all other loss and expense, including reasonable costs of litigation arising out of or associated with the use of church property by the applicant group and its members, guests, employees, and agents pursuant to this application. Further, the user group will provide a certificate of liability insurance in favor of [name of church] in the amount of at least $500,000.

We have read and agree to comply with the "POLICIES AND REGULATIONS REGARDING USE OF CHURCH FACILITIES BY NONCHURCH GROUPS."

Signature of Applicant: _____

Address: _____ Phone #: _____

## FOR OFFICE USE ONLY

Approved:   ❏ Yes   ❏ No   Date of Approval: _____

Room/s to be used: _____

Donations/Fees Paid $_____ Receipt No.: _____

*Note: Copy to be given to applicant after approval.*
*Original application to be retained in the church office files.*

## Key-Deposit Policy

1. All nonchurch groups or individuals who wish to use rooms in the church facilities are required to obtain keys prior to the day of room use.

2. A deposit of $40 per key must be made. When keys are returned, all deposits for keys will be refunded.

Key accepted by: _____ Date: _____

Key returned by: _____ Date: _____

Deposit refunded by: _____ Date: _____

## Policies and Regulations Regarding Use of Church Facilities by Nonchurch Groups

### POLICIES

[Name of church] recognizes that its outreach and ministry can be increased by providing its physical facilities in support of other organizations and programs designed to serve the community. At the same time, it is necessary that such use of facilities and equipment be controlled in the best interests of the church. The intent of this statement is to establish consistent requirements for nonchurch group use of our church facilities.

All nonchurch groups (any group not sponsored by or related to [name of church]) desiring to use church facilities must confirm acceptance of the terms herein specified. All required application forms must be completed and approved by the church; all key deposits, fees, etc., must be paid not less than two days before use of the facilities shall begin. Donations may be made, or fees paid, in cash. If a check is used, it shall be made out to [name of church]. Renewal of permission to use stated church facilities will depend, in part, on satisfactory compliance with requirements during the previous period of use. Groups which use the facilities on a year-round basis must renew their application each January 1.

The governing body of [name of church] reserves the right to accept or deny requests for use of church facilities and to cancel or modify established agreements in the church's best interests regarding property management, requirements for use of the facilities for church activities *(which shall always have priority),* and church relationships with governmental regulations.

### REGULATIONS

1. The using group must be a nonprofit organization whose purposes and activities contribute to the welfare of the community.

2. The objectives of the using group and the activities conducted on church property must not be in conflict with the mission of [name of church].

3. Sponsors or leaders of a group may not charge a fee or receive monetary remuneration for services rendered to the group on church property unless specific exception to this rule has been granted in writing by the governing body of the church. This, however, does not mean that using groups may not have organizational dues or assessments to meet operating expenses.

4. Alcoholic beverages, liquors, or other non-physician-prescribed drugs will not be permitted on church property at any time.

5. Smoking will not be permitted inside any church building.

6. Social dancing is permitted only in the social hall.

7. Decorations used must be flameproof, and shall not be attached to fixed portions of the facilities without specific approval in writing.

8. The use of candles or open flames is prohibited. Ceremonial use of candles may be permitted on occasion, with specific written approval.

9. Evening events will be concluded and the building closed by 10:00 p.m., unless special arrangements have been made.

10. User groups will be responsible for leaving the facilities used in such condition that another group may comfortably use them; i.e., furniture and equipment will be replaced in customary position, kitchen or kitchenette equipment left in clean condition, dishes washed and put away, floors swept, filled waste baskets emptied into the trash bin, etc.

11. The using group shall be held responsible for all loss or damage to church property during periods when they are using the facilities.

12. No equipment or facilities shall be added, modified, moved, or removed without prior written approval.

13. At no time shall equipment or facilities other than those covered by prior approval be used.

14. Permission to use church facilities or equipment shall not include liability on the part of the church for property damage or personal injuries resulting from user-group activities.

15. While no rental fees are charged user groups, donations to cover utilities and other expenses are anticipated and appreciated.

16. At the inception of the use of facilities, a key deposit of $40.00 will be paid. This sum provides from one to three keys. Any additional keys needed (more than three) will require an additional deposit of $5.00 per key. When the group terminates use of the facilities and all keys it is charged with are returned, all deposits paid for keys will be returned except for a $5.00 service charge. Any keys which are not returned will be charged at the rate of $5.00 per key. If the user group fails to secure a return of the key deposit, this deposit shall be transferred into the church general funds at the end of six months.

17. "Single-Use Events," that is those which occur no more frequently than once each calendar year, will be issued keys at no charge, but a $25.00 deposit must be made to ensure the return of the keys.

18. When meals are served to a nonchurch group by a church group, the total financial obligation of the user group is included in the per-plate charge for the meal, according to the agreement arrived at by the groups.

19. Donations, fees, and personnel required for use of facilities:

Use of social hall (three-hour minimum)       $85.00

Services of authorized person to *direct* setting up and putting away of tables, chairs, etc., *said labor to be provided by user group.*       $25.00

# Food Handling

While food-related functions are at the very heart of religious fellowship in any church, they can hold the highest potential for foodborne disaster if sanitation and safety rules are not followed.[1] Mass food poisoning with its attendant suffering and occasional death is a constant danger.

Although little control is possible over the sanitary preparation of dishes served at "potluck suppers," as a minimum the church must keep cold food below forty degrees Fahrenheit and hot food above 140 degrees Fahrenheit after it is brought to the church and before it is served. The church also should discuss the importance of sanitation in food handling with all members, as it is about the only possible means to enhance the quality of food prepared in other than church facilities.

Within church food-handling facilities, there is no room for error and no acceptable excuse for unsanitary or unsafe conditions. The following sections discuss the minimum policies and procedures that must be in place.

## SANITATION

There must be a strict cleaning schedule for all facilities and operations. Dirty, greasy floors, open containers in stock rooms, food debris on floors, dirty equipment, and so forth are all unsanitary. These conditions can cause bugs and disease and are potential hazards. All facilities must maintain standards of sanitation at or above those mandated by state sanitary codes. Ensure that the cleaning schedule is followed and monitor daily cleaning to assure that all areas of operation are cleaned, stocked, and properly maintained.

The food handling or kitchen committee chairperson must conduct a periodic sanitation inspection which should be dated, contain the action planned to correct unsanitary conditions, and indicate that follow-up is performed. The attached sanitation checklist can help document this inspection. All sanitation inspections conducted by the church or by a State Health Department representative should be posted, and any violations noted must be corrected immediately.

## FOOD SAFETY

The mishandling of food in receiving, storing, preparation, and cooling can lead to foodborne illness. Good personal hygiene practices are a critical protective measure against foodborne illness. Remember that *people* in one way or another are the primary cause of foodborne contamination.

The basic control measures you can take against dangers in handling food are as follows:

- Purchase food only from approved suppliers.

- Store, prepare, and cool foods properly to prevent bacterial growth.

- Prevent cross-contamination.

- Follow good personal hygiene practices.

- Chemical and metal products should be used only for their intended purposes.

- Properly inspect incoming food items for physical contaminants, temperature abuse, or signs of tampering.

## FOOD SAFETY AND SANITATION RULES

- Hands must be washed often and thoroughly, especially anytime there is possible contamination.

- Food handlers with cuts or open sores on their hands must not touch food. If there is a lesion on hands or fingers it must be antiseptically covered, and plastic gloves must be worn.

- Food should be handled as little as possible. Use tongs, forks, and spatulas and always use plastic gloves.

- When handling dishes, keep hands and fingers off eating or drinking surfaces.

- When sampling food, ladle some into a small dish using a separate spoon and, when finished, remove sampling dish and utensil to the dishwashing room immediately.

- Discard all food dropped on the floor.

- Do not use any food if there is any doubt about its freshness or wholesomeness.

- Keep all perishable foods at forty degrees Fahrenheit or below until ready for use.

- Keep all cold food cold, forty degrees Fahrenheit and below, and all hot food hot, 140 degrees Fahrenheit and above. *Hot food hot—cold food cold. When in doubt, throw it out.*

- Do not place cooked food on shelves under raw meat. Raw meat should always be stored on bottom shelves.

- There must be no smoking in the kitchen or serving area. If it is allowed, it should only be done in a designated smoking area, and hands must be washed thoroughly after smoking.

- All food handlers must be taught correct food handling procedures.

- All food stock should be used on a first in, first out (FIFO) basis.

- A cleaning schedule for the food facility and all equipment must be established and strictly enforced.

## RODENT AND INSECT CONTROL

For the most effective rodent and insect control, there should be an integrated pest management system, whereby preventive tactics and control methods are both used. The church must concentrate on the following areas:

- Eliminate sources of food and water, as well as breeding and hiding places, through good sanitation, housekeeping, and food safety practices.

- Physically prevent pests from entering the facility by closing off any openings in the building, practicing good grounds maintenance, and by inspecting incoming supplies.

- If insect or rodent pests are detected, a reliable pest control service should be used. A pest control service should always be employed for the more complex or hazardous extermination tasks.

- The food-handling manager must establish close communication with the pest control personnel so that faulty sanitary procedures and structural faults are promptly corrected.

# Food-Service Sanitation Checklist

Date: _____ Location: _____

Person Responsible: _____ Evaluator: _____

Each item on this checklist will be evaluated and marked as "OK" or "No" and referenced to an explanatory note below.

## FOOD PROTECTION
_____ 1. Clean receiving area
_____ 2. Cleaning supplies stored separately from food items

## FOOD STORAGE
_____ 3. Refrigerator temperature at 36°–45° Accurate thermometers?
_____ 4. Hot food temperature warmers 160°

## PERSONNEL:
### Employee Practices
_____ 5. Use of plastic gloves, spoons, scrapers, and tongs to minimize food contact
_____ 6. Employee food/beverage consumption not in work areas

### Personal Cleanliness
_____ 7. Employee hands washed and clean
_____ 8. Fingernails clean and trimmed

### Clothing
_____ 9. Clean uniform/apron before serving
_____ 10. Hats, hair nets, or restraints in use

### Health
_____ 11. No open sores or infections

## RESTROOMS
_____ 12. Men's room clean, with soap/towels
_____ 13. Women's room clean, with soap and towels, etc.

## EQUIPMENT & UTENSILS
_____ 14. Tables & legs, drawers, shelving
_____ 15. Sinks
_____ 16. Trash or garbage cans
_____ 17. Food carts
_____ 18. Walkin freezer: clean, minimal ice buildup, food 6″ off floor
_____ 19. Reach-in freezer

_____ 20. Walk-in refrigerator—clean, including fan, food 6″ off floor
_____ 21. Reach-in refrigerator
_____ 22. Pass through cooler
_____ 23. Pass through warmer—holding boxes
_____ 24. Ice machine inside, outside, scoop
_____ 25. Storage
_____ 26. Kitchen walls, ceiling, lighting
_____ 27. Kitchen floors, baseboards
_____ 28. Kitchen hood over the range
_____ 29. Hood filters
_____ 30. Stove tops
_____ 31. Grill
_____ 32. French fryer
_____ 33. Oven—inside and out
_____ 34. Steam kettles
_____ 35. Steamers
_____ 36. Mixer and attachments
_____ 37. Slicing machine
_____ 38. Chopper
_____ 39. Can opener
_____ 40. Portion scales
_____ 41. Cutting boards
_____ 42. Knife holder

## DINING AREA
_____ 43. Orderly arrangement of tables
_____ 44. Clean tables and chairs
_____ 45. Clean walls
_____ 46. Clean floor and baseboards
_____ 47. Neat, clean condiment area
_____ 48. Clean tray stands
_____ 49. Clean silverware dispensers
_____ 50. Clean silverware utensils
_____ 51. Clean napkin dispensers
_____ 52. Clean salt & pepper containers
_____ 53. Sanitizing solution used for cleaning

## DISHROOM

_____ 54. Clean dishwashing machine—inside and out; delimed, clear jets and nozzles; clean trays

_____ 55. Proper washing temperatures (Prewash 120°/wash 160°/rinse 180°)

_____ 56. Proper dishwashing techniques; (Racking, loading, silverware washing, clean/dirty loading, unloading)

_____ 57. Clean dish carts

_____ 58. Clean counters, shelves, and legs

_____ 59. Clean conveyor belt

_____ 60. Clean sink

_____ 61. Walls clean; no dirt buildup

_____ 62. Floor/baseboards clean; no water

_____ 63. Orderly & proper dish storage

## POT WASHING AREA

_____ 64. Pots scraped, washed, sanitized

_____ 65. Clean pot/pan/utensil area

## STOREROOM

_____ 66. Orderly & free of empty cartons/boxes

_____ 67. Supplies 6″ off floor, 2″ from walls

_____ 68. No open containers with unwrapped food products

_____ 69. Storage containers for rice, flour, beans, etc., covered and labeled

_____ 70. Clean storeroom shelving

_____ 71. Clean storeroom floor/baseboards

_____ 72. FIFO use of all stock

## SERVICE AREA

_____ 73. Clean counters & tray slides

_____ 74. Clean & orderly shelves under counters

_____ 75. Clean display shelving

_____ 76. Sneeze guards clean

_____ 77. Clean & accurate menu boards

_____ 78. Posters clean and neatly posted

_____ 79. Clean cash register/box and stand

_____ 80. Clean coffee urns—inside & out; clean gaskets & tubing

_____ 81. Clean cold-drink dispensers

_____ 82. Syrup/salad dressing tanks clean

_____ 83. Clean hot food wells

## OTHER

_____ 84. _____

_____ 85. _____

_____ 86. _____

_____ 87. _____

_____ 88. _____

| ITEM NO. | NOTE COMMENTS ON DEFICIENCES | ASSIGNED TO (NAME) | COMPLETION DATE |
|---|---|---|---|
| | | | |
| | | | |
| | | | |
| | | | |
| | | | |
| | | | |
| | | | |
| | | | |
| | | | |

# Safety in Church Facilities

Churches of any size have many opportunities to enhance safety in their facilities and activities.[2] It is not a question of whether an accident will happen, but when and how the effect of it can be minimized. The challenge for each church is to do everything it can to ensure its facilities and activities are as safe as possible. To assist with this considerable challenge, there are a number of checklists and forms included here and elsewhere in the manual which should be used regularly to inspect church facilities and report on accidents.

Facility and use policies must include essential points concerning safety. Employees and volunteers must always be aware of conditions that may need revision to make church facilities and activities safe. Since each church situation is unique, each must develop its own safety policies and guidelines. (In chapter 3 of this manual, beginning on page 225, we included a sample Injury/Illness Prevention Policy.) After developing its policy, each church should require all employees and volunteers involved in activities in which safety is important to be briefed on their roles in the church-safety program, basic safety rules, how to handle and report accidents, and how to report unsafe conditions or practices. The Safety Orientation Checklist which immediately follows these comments can help document and thus emphasize the importance of safety.

In addition to safety factors included previously in our discussion about contingency plans for potential disasters (pages 346–349), the loss prevention checklist (pages 351–355), and safety in handling food (pages 482–486), there are other important areas of concern. On page 489 is an example of an effective playground safety checklist which should be used by every church. On page 490 we present some important considerations about how to lift an object and save a person much pain and suffering.

On page 491 are accident reporting procedures for vehicles, which every church must supply to all those who transport members in either a church or personal vehicle. Following this document are a number of suggested forms for reporting vehicle accidents, personal injury, or property damage.

We end this important discussion by pointing out the requirements of the Occupational Safety and Health Act (OSHA) and how it applies to churches (page 496).

# *Safety Orientation Checklist*

| Topic | Initials |
|-------|----------|
| Employee/Volunteer Role in Safety | _____ |
| Employee/Volunteer Safety Rules | _____ |
| Use of Personal Protective Equipment | _____ |
| Equipment Training | _____ |
| Safety Rules for Specific Jobs | _____ |
| Reporting Accidents | _____ |
| Reporting Unsafe Conditions or Practices | _____ |
| Workers' Compensation | _____ |
| Sanitation | _____ |

**SAFETY EXPECTATIONS CONTRACT**

The preceding list of topics has been fully discussed with me, and I understand that I am to perform my duties or participate in activities in the safest possible way.

_____    _____    _____
Employee/Volunteer Name          Signature                       Date

_____    _____    _____
Church Representative             Signature                       Date
    Name

# Playground-Safety Checklist

There is nothing more enjoyable, but possibly more dangerous, than a well-equipped church playground. All equipment must be in excellent working order at all times and installed in a safe way to ensure the continued joy of our church children. The area must be fenced and gates locked when not in use, hopefully to ensure that all play is supervised. The following questions represent the minimum that must be considered and acted on if a playground is to be considered safe. Any question which cannot be answered "Yes" during a periodic inspection must be given immediate priority for repair.

**YES    NO**

____ ____   1. Is the sand or resilient ground cover (8"–10" deep) around and under play equipment compacted or displaced in heavy-use areas so as to increase the possibility of injury from a fall?

____ ____   2. Are there any climbing areas that would allow children (ages 3–8) to fall more than six or seven feet?

____ ____   3. Are there any foreign objects or obstructions in the fall zones under and around play equipment that is anchored in place?

____ ____   4. Are any concrete footings for fixed equipment sticking out above the ground cover? Are footings loose or no longer secure?

____ ____   5. Are there any obstructions in the normal traffic patterns?

____ ____   6. Are there any sharp edges, broken parts, or loose fasteners?

____ ____   7. Are there any openings between 5" and 9" that can trap a child's head?

____ ____   8. Are there any frayed cables, worn ropes, or chains that can pinch? S-hooks must be closed.

____ ____   9. Are there any excessively worn mechanisms, including swing swivels and merry-go-round axles?

____ ____  10. Are there any crush points or shearing actions, including hinges of seesaws and undercarriages of revolving equipment?

____ ____  11. Are any timbers rotting, splitting, termite-infested, or excessively worn? Are toxic materials used as preservatives?

____ ____  12. Does any equipment need refinishing, such as sanding or painting?

____ ____  13. Are any swing seats made of hard or heavy material, e.g., steel, wood?

____ ____  14. Is any portable play equipment, such as wagons or tricycles, in need of repair?

____ ____  15. Are there any gates that cannot be locked?

____ ____  16. Are there any electrical hazards in the playground?

____ ____  17. Are there any collections of contaminated water in the playground?

____ ____  18. Do the grass, trees, and shrubs need care?

____ ____  19. Are there any other fixtures in the playground that are not in good repair?

## *Lifting Safely*

1. Plan a route that is free from tripping and slipping hazards.

2. Determine the weight, and check for sharp edges. Check to see if the load is stable and equally distributed. Decide how to hold the object.

3. Use palms and fingers to make carrying easier and to protect hands and feet. If you wear gloves to prevent cuts, be sure they fit properly and won't slip.

4. Ask for help (or a mechanical aid) if you have any doubt about moving the object yourself.

5. Stand as close to the load as possible, feet spread apart.

6. Bend at the knees, keeping your back straight and stomach tucked in.

7. Grasp the load firmly.

8. Lift smoothly with your legs.

9. Hold the load close to the center of your body.

10. Avoid twisting your body. If you must change direction, move feet instead.

11. Do not block your vision.

12. Bend your knees to lower the load. Keep your back straight and the weight close to your body.

13. Be careful with fingers and toes. Allow enough room for them when the load is set down.

14. Be sure the load is secure wherever you place it. Make certain it won't fall, tip over, roll, or block someone's way.

# Vehicle Accident Reporting Procedures

Many churches own or lease vans or other vehicles, and all churches use private vehicles to support their activities. In all cases, the church must know about any accident and be involved in reporting the accident to appropriate authorities and insurance agents. All accidents, injuries, and thefts of vehicles should be reported within twenty-four hours. The following procedures should be followed by the driver:

1. First check for injures and call for help if there are injuries of any kind.

2. Comply with state laws about moving the vehicle, if it can be moved, to avoid impeding traffic and possibly causing further injury or damage.

3. Remain at the scene, if possible, and obtain the information needed to complete the attached accident form. Notify the police, unless the accident is of such a minor nature that local laws encourage that the police not be notified. In this case, go to the local police station and file a report, to ensure that the facts of the incident are properly documented.

4. Complete the church accident form at the scene of the accident or as soon as possible thereafter. After completing the accident form, report the accident by telephone or in person to the responsible church officer as soon as possible. Complete the property damage report.

5. If there were injuries, contact the responsible church officer immediately, and complete the employee report of injury or the nonemployee incident report.

6. Do not admit fault. Be courteous at all times, but do not talk about the accident to anyone except representatives of the church or police officers.

7. You may exhibit your driver's license and you may show your insurance card to the officer or the other party involved. Be sure to obtain the other party's insurance information.

8. Review the accident circumstances to determine if anything could have been done to prevent the accident.

The responsible church representative should notify the church insurance agency and follow its reporting procedure. A copy of the police report should be obtained and submitted with any insurance claim. Make sure the police report has a "report number." If a private vehicle on church business is involved, file an informational report to the church insurance agency even though private insurance may handle the claim, in case of future liability claims against the church.

## *Accident Report*

Date: _____ Time: _____

Location: _____
(street/road/route)

_____
| (City/Town) | (State) | (Zip) |

Number of vehicles involved: _____

Police report:  ❏ Yes  ❏ No  Police department: _____

Were you charged by the police  ❏ Yes  ❏ No  Type of charges: _____

_____

Driver's name: _____ Lic. #: _____

Address: _____

Home telephone: _____ Work telephone: _____

Other driver: _____ Lic. #: _____

Address: _____

Home telephone: _____ Work telephone: _____

Insurance company: _____ Policy number: _____

Describe accident: _____

_____

_____

_____

_____

## *Persons Injured*   ❏ Yes  ❏ No

Name: _____ Telephone: _____

Address: _____

_____

Name: _____ Telephone: _____

Address: _____

_____

# *Report of Employee Injury*

*(Retain this form in Employee's Personnel File)*

Date: _____ Time: _____

Person completing form: _____

Name of injured employee: _____

Home address: _____

_____

Home telephone: _____ Social Security #: _____

Sex: _____ Date of birth: _____ Date of hire: _____

Job Title: _____

Salary/pay data: _____

Date of injury: _____ Time of injury: _____

Day of week: _____ Date reported: _____

Area where injury occurred: _____

Describe in detail how accident happened, what employee was doing, and where employee was injured and the extent of the injury: _____

_____

_____

What was object or substance that caused injury? _____

_____

_____

Were safety regulations followed?  ❑ Yes  ❑ No   If no, what rules were not observed? _____

What has been done to prevent this type of accident from reoccurring? _____

_____

Has injured returned to work? _____ If yes, date returned: _____

If no, when expected back? _____

Name and complete address of medical facility: _____

_____

_____

# Member or Guest Incident Report

*(Retain in Incident File)*

Date of incident: _____ Time of incident: _____

Location of incident and condition of floor, if applicable: _____

_____

Name of injured: _____ Age: _____

If minor, parent's name: _____

Address: _____

_____

Home telephone: _____ Work telephone: _____

Witness name: _____

Witness address: _____

_____

Home telephone: _____ Work telephone: _____

Detailed description of incident and possible cause: _____

_____

_____

_____

_____

_____

_____

_____

_____

Person making report: _____

Action taken, or assistance given by church representative: _____

_____

_____

# *Property Damage Report*

*(Retain in Incident File)*

(Report all damage of any kind, including that caused by others, to property owned and operated by the church.)

Date of incident: _____ Time of incident: _____

Location of incident: _____

Detailed description of incident: _____

_____

_____

_____

_____

_____

_____

_____

_____

Name of person doing damage: _____

Address: _____

Home telephone: _____ Work telephone: _____

If vehicle involved, owner: _____

Address: _____

Home telephone: _____ Work telephone: _____

Driver's/Owner's insurance company: _____

Insurance company address: _____

_____

Policy #:_____ License #: _____ Tag #: _____ State: _____

Police department investigating incident: _____

Date reported to insurance company: _____

Company repairing damage: _____ Cost: _____

## OSHA Requirements

In 1970, Congress enacted the Occupational Safety and Health Act (OSHA) to assure every working person in the country safe and healthful working conditions. Employers engaged in a business affecting commerce, who have employees, must perform certain duties under the act. Records must be kept concerning employee injuries and illnesses.

Religious organizations are subject to the act if they engage in commerce and have employees. While most churches may not engage in activities that might be thought of as commerce, it has been ruled that churches that have attendees from out of state, purchase material from an out-of-state source, or even make out-of-state telephone calls are considered to be engaging in commerce. Church-operated preschools are enterprises considered to be engaged in commerce. Further, the term *preschool* includes childcare facilities that are primarily custodial in nature. Thus many, if not most, churches are covered by the act.

As a minimum, any church offering childcare or schooling, or if engaged in some other type of commerce, will need to report to OSHA employee fatalities or accidents requiring multiple hospitalizations, as well as to display the OSHA poster. Lesser injuries should be documented for later examination by OSHA, if they so desire. Additional specific requirements in individual church situations can be determined by contacting the U.S. Department of Labor, Occupational Safety and Health Administration Regional Office, as well as the participating state agency, in that many states have supplemented the act and have other requirements. A good place to start is the OSHA World Wide Web page on the Internet; the current address is http://www.osha.gov.

Regardless of legal requirements, we urge that every church respond positively to the OSHA standards, and stress that employees become knowledgeable about safety and health considerations in their work. In chapter 3 of this manual, beginning on page 225, we include sample policy statements about administering the OSHA training and communication program.

Accept the challenge. Make your facilities and activities as safe and healthful as possible.

# Notes

## Chapter One

1. Provided by Virginia Bihler. Developed while an administrative assistant at The United Methodist Church of Simi Valley, California, 1993.

2. Provided by Opie TerMeer, a member of The United Methodist Church in Rialto, California, 1993.

3. *The Book of Discipline of The United Methodist Church* (Nashville: United Methodist Publishing House, 1996).

4. Ibid., p. 202.

5. Ibid., p. 205.

6. Ibid., p. 204.

7. Exodus 18:18, The Living Bible (New York: American Bible Society, 1976).

8. New Revised Standard Version (Nashville: Thomas Nelson, 1989). This scripture quotation is used by permission of the Division of Christian Education of the National Council of Churches in the USA, with all rights reserved.

## Chapter Two

1. These considerations for study are based partially on Kennon L. Callahan, *Twelve Keys to an Effective Church* (San Francisco: Harper & Row, 1983).

2. Ibid.

3. See Joe Harding and Ralph Mohney, *Vision 2000—Planning for Ministry into the Next Century* (Nashville: Discipleship Resources, 1991).

4. Callahan, *Twelve Keys*.

5. Edgar Walz, *How to Manage Your Church* (St. Louis: Concordia, 1987), pp. 114–115.

6. Christian Church Foundation, Christian Church (Disciples of Christ), *How Firm a Foundation* (130 East Washington Street, Indianapolis, Ind. 46206–1986, self-published, non-copyrighted), pp. 23–24.

7. Ibid.

8. Culver Heaton, FAIA, and Thomas Zartl, AIA, and Associates, Pasadena, Calif., 1994.

9. This section, in edited form, was taken from an unpublished paper prepared by Culver Heaton, FAIA, and Thomas Zartl, AIA, and Associates, Pasadena, Calif., 1985.

10. Excerpted from Dr. Richard Jones, "Fourteen Lessons Learned in Becoming a Growing Church," *Circuit Rider,* March 1994, pp. 4–6.

11. *A Guide to Church Growth: Summary of a Study of Growing United Methodist Churches in the California-Pacific Annual Conference* (Santa Monica, Calif., 1994), commissioned by the Y. S. Mae Foundation and conducted by the Claremont School of Theology, Claremont, California.

## Chapter Three

1. Ralph Hardee, "Church Organization," in Bruce P. Powers, ed., *Church Administration Handbook* (Nashville: Broadman Press, 1985), p. 32.

2. Keith Davis, *Human Behavior at Work: Organizational Behavior* (New York: McGraw-Hill, 1977), p. 195.

3. George S. Odiorne, *Management Decisions by Objectives* (Englewood Cliffs, N. J.: Prentice-Hall, 1968).

4. Penelope Mercurio-Jennings, "Legal Issues Facing Churches" (paper prepared while a professor of business law, California State University, Northridge Calif., 1997).

5. Ibid.

## Chapter Four

1. Davis, *Human Behavior at Work,* p. 107.

2. James A. Autry, *Love and Profit: The Art of Caring Leadership* (New York: Morrow and Co., 1991), p. 13.

3. Abraham H. Maslow, *Movivation and Personality* (New York: Harper and Row, 1954).

4. Frederick Herzberg, *Work and the Nature of Man* (Cleveland: World Publishing Company, 1966).

5. Ibid.

6. Kenneth Blanchard and Spencer Johnson, *The One-Minute Manager* (New York: Morrow and Co., 1982), p. 39.

7. Dr. W. J. A. Power, "Asking the Question," *Perspective* (Perkins School of Theology, Southern Methodist University, Fall 1994), p. 24.

8. Dr. Harold E. Cline, "Effective Techniques for Stewardship Development," an unpublished article, 1990.

9. Callahan, *Twelve Keys*, p. 113.

10. Paula Ritchie, *Stewardship* (St. Louis: Christian Board of Publication, 1991), p. 15.

11. Information gathered by Ed Uthe from ten thousand Lutheran congregations; published in *Inside Information* by the Alban Institute, Summer 1991, and edited by Harold E. Cline, who held the stewardship portfolio for the Christian Church (Disciples of Christ) in the Southwest, (in a letter to pastors from Dr. Cline, dated July 8, 1991).

12. Models adapted from Robert J. Hempfling, "Finding the Enlistment Plan Which Fits Your Congregation," in *Stewardship Sampler: Overview* (Christian Church [Disciples of Christ], undated, uncopyrighted pamphlet), pp. 13A–16A.

13. Helen Davis Bell, "Stewardship and the Ethnic Local Church," in *Celebrate Stewardship* (Nashville: General Board of Discipleship, The United Methodist Church, 1993), p. 2.

## *Chapter Five*

1. Blanchard and Johnson, *The One-Minute Manager*, p. 39.

2. David B. Bates, Safety Engineer, PE, contributed to this section. He is a lifelong member of the Christian Church (Disciples of Christ) and active in the First Christian Church of Duncanville, Texas.

3. NFPA 912, "Recommended Practice for Fire Protection in Places of Worship" (National Fire Protection Association, Inc., 1993, and approved by the American National Standards Institute). Additional information is available in NFPA 101, "Life Safety Code." Local fire departments should be able to assist in acquiring these source documents.

4. Contributions to checklist by David B. Bates, Safety Engineer, PE.

5. Otto Crumroy, Jr., Stanley J. Kukawka, and Frank M. Witman, *A Pastor's Survival Guide* (Harrisburg, Pa., Morehouse Publishing, 1998).

## *Resources for Various Church Activities*

1. David B. Bates, Safety Engineer, PE, contributed to this section.

2. All articles, checklists, and forms included subsequent to this introduction received contributions from David B. Bates, Safety Engineer, PE.

# Bibliography

Autry, James A. *Love and Profit: The Art of Caring Leadership.* New York: William Morrow and Company, 1991.

Blanchard, Kenneth, and Spencer Johnson. *The One-Minute Manager.* West Caldwell, N. J.: William Morrow and Company, 1982.

Blanchard, Kenneth, and Norman Vincent Peale, *The Power of Ethical Management.* New York: William Morrow and Company, 1988.

Callahan, Kennon L. *Effective Church Finances: Fund-Raising and Budgeting for Church Leaders.* San Francisco: Harper SanFrancisco, 1992.

————. *Effective Church Leadership: Building on the Twelve Keys.* San Francisco: Harper & Row, 1990.

————. *Giving and Stewardship in an Effective Church.* San Francisco: Harper San-Francisco, 1992.

————. *Twelve Keys to an Effective Church.* San Francisco: Harper & Row, 1983.

Campbell, Thomas C., and Gary B. Reierson, *The Gift of Administration: Theological Bases for Ministry.* Philadelphia: Westminster Press, 1981

Cone, James H. *God of the Oppressed.* San Francisco: Harper, 1975.

Dale, Robert D. *Surviving Difficult Church Members.* Creative Leadership Series, ed. Lyle E. Schaller. Nashville: Abingdon Press, 1984.

DePree, Max. *Leadership Is an Art.* New York: Dell Publishing, 1989.

Dulles, Avery. *Models of The Church.* Garden City, N.Y.: Doubleday, 1974.

Drucker, Peter F. *Managing the Non-profit Organization.* New York: Harper Business, 1990.

Engstrom, Ted W., and Edward R. Dayton, *The Art of Management for Christian Leaders.* Waco, Tex.: Word Books, 1976.

Glasse, James D. *Putting It Together in the Parish.* Nashville: Abingdon Press, 1972.

Hammar, Richard R. *Church Law & Tax Report: Church and Clergy Tax Guide.* Matthews, N.C.: Christian Ministry Resources. Updated annually.

Harding, Joe A. and Ralph W. Mohney, *Vision 2000: Planning for Ministry into the Next Century.* Nashville: Discipleship Resources, 1991.

Johnson, Douglas W. *The Care and Feeding of Volunteers.* Nashville: Abingdon Press, 1982.

———. *Finance in Your Church.* Nashville: Abingdon Press, 1986.

Kennedy, Gerald. *The Seven Worlds of the Minister.* New York: Harper and Row, 1968.

Lee, Harris W. *Effective Church Leadership: A Practical Source Book.* Minneapolis: Augsburg Fortress, 1989.

———. *Theology of Administration.* Minneapolis: Augsburg Publishing House, 1981.

Lincoln, Eric C., and Lawrence H. Mamiya, *The Black Church in the African American Experience.* Durham, N.C.: Duke University Press, 1990.

Logan, Robert E. *Beyond Church Growth: Action Plan for Developing a Dynamic Church.* Terrytown, N.Y.: Fleming H. Revell Co., 1989.

Massey, Floyd, Jr., and Samuel Berry McKinney, *Church Administration in the Black Perspective.* Valley Forge, Pa.: Judson Press, 1976.

Pappas, Anthony. *Money, Motivation, and Mission in the Small Church.* Valley Forge Pa.: Judson Press, 1989.

Pollock, David R. *Business Management in the Local Church.* Chicago: Moody Press, 1992.

Powers, Bruce P., ed. *Church Administration Handbook.* Nashville: Broadman Press, 1985.

Radford Ruether, Rosemary. *Liberation Theology.* New York: Harper, 1972.

Ray, David R. *The Big Small Church Book.* Cleveland: Pilgrim Press, 1992.

Ritchie, Paula. *Stewardship.* St. Louis: Christian Board of Publication, 1991.

Russell, Letty M. *Household of Freedom.* Philadelphia: Westminster Press, 1986.

Schaller, Lyle E. *Effective Church Planning.* Nashville: Abingdon Press, 1979.

———. *Forty-Four Ways to Expand the Financial Base of Your Congregation.* Nashville: Abingdon Press, 1989.

———. *The Multiple Staff and the Larger Church.* Nashville: Abingdon Press, 1980.

———. *The Seven-Day-a-Week Church.* Nashville: Abingdon Press, 1992.

———. *The Small Church Is Different!* Nashville: Abingdon Press, 1982.

Shearn, Carol R. *The Church Office Handbook.* Wilton, Conn.: Morehouse-Barlow, 1986.

Suchocki, Marjorie Hewitt. *God, Christ, Church.* New York: Crossroad, 1993.

Swan, William S. *How to Do a Superior Performance Appraisal.* New York: John Wiley and Sons, 1991.

Touche Ross and Co. *Abingdon Clergy Income Tax Guide.* Nashville: Abingdon Press, published each year.

Vargo, Richard J. *The Church Guide to Financial Reporting.* Matthews, N.C.: Christian Ministry Resources, 1995.

————. *The Church Guide to Internal Controls.* Matthews, N.C.: Christian Ministry Resources, 1995.

————. *The Church Guide to Planning and Budgeting.* Matthews, N.C.: Christian Ministry Resources, 1995.

Walz, Edgar. *How to Manage Your Church: A Manual For Pastors and Lay Leaders.* St. Louis: Concordia, 1987.

White, Robert N. ed. *Managing Today's Church.* Valley Forge, Pa.: Judson Press, 1981.

Wilson, Marlene. *How to Mobilize Church Volunteers.* Minneapolis: Augsburg Publishing House, 1983.

# Special Resource Groups

Alban Institute, The. 4125 Nebraska Ave., N.W., Washington, DC 20016. 1-800-457-2674. Books, tapes, courses, consulting.

Christian Ministries Management Association (CMMA). P.O. Box 4638, Diamond Bar, CA 91765. Open to ministers. Publications, reference for questions, workshops, tapes.

*Christian Computing Magazine.* Hewlen, Inc., P.O. Box 198, 406 Pine St. Center/Ste. L-M, Raymore, MO 64083. Computing advice and software reviews.

Church Management, Inc. P.O. Box 162527, Austin, TX 78716. Magazine, books, booklets, and tapes.

Christian Ministry Resources. P.O. Box 1098, Matthews, NC 28106. Publishes bimonthly *Church Law & Tax Report,* a review of legal and tax developments affecting ministers and churches. Markets an annual church and clergy tax guide and other related church administrative aids.

National Association of Church Business Administrators (NACBA). 7001 Grapevine Highway, Suite 324, Fort Worth, TX 76180. Publications, tapes, questions, workshops.

Net Results. 5001 Avenue N., Lubbock, TX 79412–2993. Editor, Herb Miller. A resource for congregations that work—"New Ideas in Church Vitality & Leadership." Also, there is a Net Results Resource Center at the same address, from which one can obtain items authored or edited by Herb Miller and published by Net Press.

# About the
# Authors

## Otto F. Crumroy, Jr.

Otto Crumroy serves as an independent financial management consultant to churches and their headquarters and teaches church administration and finance. To prepare for this role of service, he completed thirty years in the Air Force with increasingly responsible positions in internal audit, culminating his career as director of a sixty-five-member audit group for the Army and Air Force Exchange Service (a $10 billion retailer). He earned a B.B.A. in accounting from the University of Oregon and an M.B.A. from Oklahoma University. He holds the professional certification of Certified Internal Auditor and is a member of the Institute of Internal Auditors.

Crumroy has been active in financial management positions in a number of different local churches, with much of his experience being with United Methodist and Disciples congregations. He has developed detailed accounting and financial management systems for several churches and his consulting services have given him a wide range of experience. He revised the financial systems for three Disciples regional and area offices while also serving a five-year term as business administrator for the Christian Church (Disciples of Christ) in the Southwest and a fourteen-year term as treasurer of his local Disciples church in Duncanville, Texas. Crumroy is also an adjunct faculty member at the Claremont School of Theology in California.

## Stan Kukawka

Stan Kukawka is the president of Consultants to Business, located in Vista, California. Prior to founding his own management consulting company in 1980, he gained twenty-five years of management experience with two world-renowned electronics companies. After earning a B.S. in mechanical engineering from Lawrence Technological University in Detroit, Michigan, he did graduate work in business management and human resources management at the University of California, Riverside. Kukawka has taught management courses at Lakeland College in Sheboygen, Wisconsin, and applied economics in high schools in Vista, California, and is an adjunct faculty member at the Claremont School of Theology.

As a longtime Methodist, Kukawka has served as lay leader at both the Whitefish Bay, Wisconsin United Methodist Church and The United Methodist Church of Escondido, California. While in Wisconsin he served on the board of laity for the Garrett-Evangelical Theological Seminary. He was also a consultant on long-range strategic planning for the Claremont School of Theology, and is a member of the National Advisory Board. He is a lay member of the California-Pacific Annual Conference of The United Methodist Church and a member of the Conference Council on Finance and Administration.

### Dr. Frank M. Witman

Frank Witman is a United Methodist pastor, having served most recently as the senior pastor of the United Methodist Church, Simi Valley, California for twenty-eight years. He earned both his Master of Theology and Doctor of Ministry degrees from the Claremont School of Theology. In his last two pastorates, Witman has been involved in the building of new sanctuaries and related improvements, and the raising of well in excess of $2.5 million for debt elimination. An adjunct faculty member at the Claremont School of Theology since 1992, he received the Distinguished Ministry Award from the school in 1993, and serves as a member of the National Advisory Board.

He has been involved in church camping for forty consecutive years, as co-dean of senior high camps for twenty-four years and adult camps for thirteen years, and served on the staff of senior high camps for the other three years. In addition, he has been the supervising chaplain for the Simi Valley Police Department since 1978. He served for nine years on the California-Pacific Conference Council on Finance and Administration.

Witman has served as a member of the board of the over $30 million United Methodist Federal Credit Union (UMFCU) since 1964, and as chairman of the board since 1976. In the last eight years, he has presided over the mergers of three other credit unions into the UMFCU.

# General Index

# Resource Index

*Includes checklists, forms, formats, sample letters, instructions, announcements, work sheets, brochures, policies, procedures, examples, charts, listings, reports, etc.*

# Notes

# Notes

# Notes

# Notes

# Notes

# Notes

# Notes

# Notes

# Notes

# Notes

M8082-12
13